# Women Warriors

## The Hidden Spies of World War II

By Donna Pedace

**The SOE Memorial Shown on the Book Cover**

The granite SOE Memorial Monument on Lambeth Palace Road in London displays a likeness of agent Violette Szabo, a French/British agent who was captured, tortured, and then executed in a concentration camp. The Duke of Wellington unveiled the monument on October 4, 2009.

**Photos**

The author made extensive efforts to identify the sources of the photos included in this book. Unfortunately, the photographers who took the posed headshots of the female SOE field agents remain unknown. Many of the other photos were taken privately without the photographer's credit.

Women Warriors Copyright @ 2024 by Donna Pedace

All Rights Reserved

ISBN: 979-8-9904249-0-6

Library of Congress #TXu002434917

Printed in the United States of America

Edited by Craig Haines

Formatted by RMK Publications, LLC.

# In Recognition

To my husband, **Bill Pedace**, for his infinite patience and support.

To my mother, **Dorothea Ellen Woodcock Anderson**, who taught me resilience and the importance of doing what needs to be done.

To **Craig Haines** for his great help and encouragement.

To numerous friends and colleagues who graciously read, critiqued, and encouraged me with comments and suggestions.

To **M.R.D. Foot**, the "official historian" of the SOE. After the war, he was allowed access to government archives 33 years before any of the documents became public. He wrote several books, saving the important details of this short-lived organization. Many of those original documents have since disappeared. All historians and authors owe him a great deal of thanks for his exhaustive work telling the story of the SOE agents and their actions during World War II. This book and many others would not have been possible if he had not documented the activities of the SOE and their field agents.

**Michael Richard Daniell (M.R.D.) Foot, CBE, TD**

# Foreword

I stumbled upon the idea for this book a few years ago while writing *Scandalous Women of the Old West – Women Who Dared to be Different*. In a resource book I was using, I found a penciled note someone had left about a woman named Nancy Wake. The note said she had worked in intelligence in WWII. I had never heard the name, so I tucked the note away to check on her later.

After the publication of that book, I found the note again and did a quick check on the Internet. I was intrigued as I read about her working for the Special Operations Executive (SOE). While I had seen the organization's name before, I didn't know anything about it. I then "went down the rabbit hole" when I began to do more research about Nancy, the organization, and what the women working for the SOE had done during World War II. Their patriotism, their bravery, and their sense of adventure inspired and amazed me. I was a little ashamed to admit that my previous knowledge of them was near zero.

Women have contributed so much to every culture, but they have often received little recognition from those who have written about it. Especially in military history, the vast majority of authors have included very little about women's contributions.

Unfortunately, by the time I decided to write this book, all the female SOE field agents who served in France during WWII had passed away, so no personal interviews were possible. My primary resources were England's National Archives and the many books and papers written by others who had first-hand knowledge of the SOE or the agents themselves.

The official records at the National Archives for almost all the women remained classified until the late 1960s and early 1970s, and some were declassified only at my request. Because the women were forbidden to talk about their service for so many years, many died without their families ever knowing about their brave SOE experience.

My intent in writing this book is to shed light on the lives of a remarkable group of women and their extraordinary contributions during WWII. Where possible, I have included personal details about their lives before and after the war. Their stories are presented chronologically, starting from when they began working as private citizens with the Resistance in France or when they arrived in France as the SOE field agents.

The term *Resistance* will be used for a collection of groups that fought against the Nazi occupation of France. It is used for groups in more urban areas. The term *Maquis* is used for groups of rural fighters.

# Contents

In Recognition

Foreword

Acronyms and Definitions

# Acronyms and Definitions

**ATA -** British Air Transport Auxiliary. Many women ferried planes wherever they were needed.

**ATS –** British Auxiliary Territorial Service

**BCRA –** French Central Bureau of Intelligence and Action of the Free French Movement

**CARTE –** French Carte resistance network was the brainchild of André Girard, an artist living in Antibes on the French Riviera in 1941. Girard took the code name Carte, which also became the name of his mostly imaginary resistance network. It took the SOE some time to realize that the organization barely existed and was poorly organized.

**CBE –** British Commander of The Most Excellent Order of the British Empire

**CdeG –** French Croix de Guerre 1939–1945. French military decoration was created on September 26, 1939, to honor people who fought with the Allies against the Axis forces at any time during World War II

**DSC –** USA Distinguished Service Cross. U.S. gallantry medal awarded for active operations against the enemy.

**DSO –** British Distinguished Service Order

**FANY –** British First Aid Nursing Yeomanry (Princess Royal's Volunteer Corps) an all-female registered charity formed in 1907 that was active in both nursing and intelligence work during both World Wars. Its members wore a military-style uniform, but they were not part of the Regular Army or Army Reserve. During WWII, FANY worked closely with the SOE to give the female agents a cover story.

**FFCC –** French Forces Francaise Combattantes, Free French organization

**GC –** British George Cross. The highest civil decoration of the United Kingdom. It is the highest gallantry award for civilians and military personnel in actions that are not in the face of the enemy or for which purely military honors would not normally be granted.

**GM –** British George Medal. The second highest civil decoration of the United Kingdom. It awards civilian gallantry in the face of enemy action and brave deeds more generally.

**KCBC –** British King's Commendation for Brave Conduct. British commendation to acknowledge brave acts by civilians and members of the military in non-warlike circumstances during a time of war or in peacetime where an existing award would not otherwise recognize the action.

**JEDBURGH Teams –** Joint Operations were made up of an Englishman, an American, and a Frenchman, of whom two were officers and the third a sergeant radio operator. All were trained in guerilla tactics, leadership, and demolition work. Their objectives were to provide a general staff for the local resistance wherever they landed and to coordinate the local efforts in the best interests of Allied strategy. Thirteen teams were parachuted into France in June 1944, with 80 more teams to follow. Members were in uniforms, whereas SOE agents wore typical civilian clothing. The working relationship with SOE Circuits was delicate.

**LdH** – French Ordre National de la Légion d'Honneur. Highest decoration in France.

**Maquis** – French members of Resistance groups who operated in rural areas.

**MBE** – British Member of the Most Excellent Order of the British Empire. Member of the British order of chivalry.

**MI6** – British, also known as the British Special Intelligence Service. British government agency responsible for the collection, analysis, and appropriate dissemination of foreign intelligence. MI6 is also charged with the conduct of espionage activities outside British territory.

**MiD** –British Mentioned in Dispatches Award. An official report written by a superior officer and sent to the high command which describes the person's gallant or meritorious action in the face of the enemy. British commanders-in-chief of a theatre of war or campaign were obliged to report their activities and achievements to the War Office as dispatches, which were published in The Gazette. British

**Nazi Nacht und Nebel – Night and Fog –** German. On December 12, 1941, Hitler's chief of staff, Field Marshal Wilhelm Keitel, issued Hitler's infamous "Nacht und Nebel" order. The purpose of the order was that no one would be told where certain prisoners of war had been held or what happened to them. They would "disappear" from the world. Initially, it was intended to only apply to civilian resisters, but some SS officers chose to also use the order for spies and foreign commandos. By the end of WWII, hundreds of thousands of Nacht und Nebel prisoners had disappeared. Many SOE agents fell into that category. Vera Atkins, the lead recruiter and overseer of more than 400 "F" Section SOE agents, took on the formidable task of finding the 118 missing SOE agents, and she found 117 of them.

**OBE** – British Order of the British Empire

**OSS** – USA, The Office of Strategic Services was the intelligence agency of the United States during World War II. It was formed as an agency of the Joint Chiefs of Staff (JCS) to coordinate espionage activities behind enemy lines for all branches of the United States Armed Forces. Other OSS functions included the use of propaganda, subversion, and post-war planning.

**RAF** – British Royal Air Force

**Resistance** fighters – Primarily French citizens, although they could be of any nationality, living in urban areas who were fighting against the German occupation.

**SAS** – British Special Air Service is a special forces unit of the British Army. It was founded as a regiment in 1941, and in 1950, it was reconstituted as a corps. The unit specializes in a number of roles, including counter-terrorism, hostage rescue, direct action, and special reconnaissance. Much of the information about the SAS is highly classified, and the unit is not commented on by either the British government or the Ministry of Defense due to the secrecy and sensitivity of its operations.

**SIS** –British Special Intelligence Service  - also known as MI6.

**SIS** – USA Special Intelligence Service was a covert counterintelligence branch of the United States Federal Bureau of Investigation located in South America during World War II. It was established to monitor the activities of Nazi and pro-Nazi groups in Central and South America. The organization and OSS were forerunners to the Central Intelligence Agency. USA

**SIS "D" Section** -  British precursor of the SOE. Section D of British SIS was formed in April 1938 and began its operations against the Nazis in March 1939. By September 1940, it was operating in over 20

countries across Europe, pioneering sabotage, 'black' propaganda, and political subversion. Section D was the main inspiration for the SOE and provided much of the early staffing and expertise of the latter.

**SOE** - British Special Operations Executive was established to conduct espionage, sabotage, and reconnaissance in France. SOE agents allied themselves with resistance groups and supplied them with weapons and equipment. The weapons and supplies, and usually the agents, were often parachuted in from England.

**SOE "F" (French) Section – British** "F" (French) Section was established to conduct espionage, sabotage, and reconnaissance in France. SOE agents allied themselves with Resistance groups and supplied them with weapons, supplies, and cash. The weapons and supplies, and usually the agents, were parachuted in from England.

**SOE "RF" Section** – British. Following the creation of the SOE's "F" Section in the summer of 1940, French anti-German sentiment was split into at least two camps—those who supported General. de Gaulle and those who did not. To keep these camps apart, the "RF" Section (pro-Gaullists) was established in early 1941.

**SS** - "Schutzstaffel," German for "Protective Echelon," initially served as Nazi Party leader Adolf Hitler's personal bodyguards and later became one of the most powerful and feared organizations in all of Nazi Germany

**WAAF** – British Women's Auxiliary Air Force

**WRNS** – British Women's Royal Naval Service

**Chapter 1**

# Introduction to the Special Operation Executive (SOE)

This book contains brief stories about the lives of a group of fifty-two (52) courageous women who dared to break all the accepted rules regarding women in war zones. They agreed to be field agents and go into German-occupied France during World War II (WWII) to do what they could to help bring down the Nazi Government and end the Nazi occupation of France.

"Female spies." The word conjures up images of James Bond villainesses in slinky dresses, purring double-edged one-liners through a haze of cigarette smoke as they coax information out of the enemy. Spying wasn't really perceived as glamorous until after the Bond myth took hold. Women have always been essential parts of the intelligence business, simply because women could often eavesdrop, run messages, or pass information without being noticed and suspected as men would have been. During the mid-1900s, few men believed that a woman could deceive them with spycraft.

The real lives of the women who volunteered to go behind enemy lines were much more mundane – and dangerous. The price that was often paid for such courage could be horrifying. It could, and often did, include imprisonment, torture, sexual violence, mutilation, and death. Any mix of those horrors awaited the women if they were caught.

In the dark days that followed the fall of France, a new volunteer fighting force was hastily improvised at the direction of British Prime Minister Winston Churchill to wage a secret war against Hitler's armies. This force was called the **Special Operations Executive (SOE.)**

The author acknowledges that the "F" Section (France) of the SOE played only a small part in WWII, but the stories of the female SOE field agents working in France deserve to be told. Too often, women's contributions have been ignored or pushed aside. This book is a modest attempt to share some of the stories of each of these brave women.

On June 19, 1940, Churchill wrote a memorandum proposing to create an organization "To coordinate all action by way of subversion and sabotage against the enemy overseas." The army of Nazi Germany was in the process of occupying many countries in Europe, including France which would initially be divided into the Occupied Zone and the unoccupied or "Free Zone." (Vichy France).

At Churchill's instigation, Lord Maurice Hankey, Chancellor of the Duchy of Lancaster, persuaded Section D and MI(R) that their intelligence operations should be coordinated into one organization to be known as Special Operation Executive (SOE.) On July 1, a cabinet-level meeting arranged the formation of a single sabotage organization. Hugh Dalton, the Minister of Economic Warfare, was appointed to take responsibility for the new organization. SOE was formally created on July 22, 1940.

The British government knew an irregular war required irregular warriors. The mission of the SOE was to "Set Europe Ablaze" with guerrilla sabotage and subversion tactics. On September 3, 1943, the Objectives and Methods of Irregular Warfare were listed as the following, and they would be the guidelines for all SOE operatives for the remainder of the war:

A. Politically

1. To undermine enemy's morale and that of his collaborators

2. To Raise morale of Occupied Territories

B. Economically

1. To damage enemy's material

2. To improve and augment our own material, e.g., By infiltration of weapons, explosives, sabotage equipment

C. Strategically

1. To damage enemy's manpower and communications

2. To improve our own manpower and communications. e.g., By infiltration of "organizers," radio sets and operators, etc.

Dalton used the Irish Republican Army (IRA) during the Irish War of Independence as a model for the SOE. One of the primary goals of the SOE was to form and arm saboteurs, called the Resistance in urban areas and the Maquis in rural areas of France. These groups carried on guerrilla actions against the German Army before D-Day. After the Allied Landing on June 6, 1944, they made the rear areas untenable for German soldiers.

Few civilians were aware of the SOE's existence until the end of the war. It was frequently known as "Churchill's Secret Army" or the "Ministry of Ungentlemanly Warfare." For security purposes, its various branches, and sometimes the organization as a whole, were concealed behind names such as the "Joint Technical Board" or the "Inter-Service Research Bureau."

The SOE faced opposition from within the British military itself. Established military units resented the SOE and were wary of its operation outside the usual command structure. Although the SOE worked with all existing British military intelligence groups, it did not answer to any "normal" military hierarchy or military intelligence agency.

The Secret Intelligence Service (SIS) - now known as MI6, viewed the SOE with great suspicion. The head of the SIS, Sir Stewart Menzies, repeatedly stated that the SOE agents were: *amateur, dangerous, and bogus.* He exerted considerable external pressure on the fledgling organization. SIS did not want the SOE to disrupt its agents' intelligence-gathering operations.

3

The Bomber Command also resented loaning aircraft for the SOE's 'unethical' clandestine missions. They wanted to win the war by bombing Germany to its knees. But with Churchill as the SOE's guardian, the SOE survived until the war ended.

The French "F" Section was the largest division of the SOE during WWII, running over 80 Resistance Circuits. At its head was Maurice Buckmaster, who had built up an immense knowledge of France while working there before the war.

The SOE believed conditions in France made women especially suitable for this clandestine role. From early 1942 until the end of the war, many young Frenchmen were sent to Germany as forced laborers unless they were considered "essential" workers in France. Healthy young men on the street would automatically attract German attention. Thus, women would arouse less suspicion.

After the war, French General de Gaulle was intent on convincing France and the world that only the French had liberated the country. He quickly tried to erase any traces of the SOE's contribution to the Resistance efforts.

The British government dissolved the SOE on January 15, 1946, and its operations and some agents merged with other departments. Many of the records were never seen again. Some ended up at the National Archives, but many disappeared, making it difficult to fully understand women's activities during the war. Many of its official papers are still classified based on political and military sensitivity. Several of the records of the women in this book were still classified when the author requested copies of their files. They were declassified at the author's request.

The SOE's "RF" Section acted as a liaison between the SOE's "F" Section and the supporters of General de Gaulle's Free French government-in-exile.

## Recruitment and Training of Female SOE Field Agents

The SOE directly employed or controlled more than 13,000 people, about 3,200 of whom were women, most of whom worked in administrative roles. The SOE pioneered recruiting women to go into active war zones, much to the irritation and sometimes anger of other government agencies.

The SOE was far ahead of contemporary attitudes about the value of women during wartime. Female field agents volunteered, knowing that arrest, torture, and execution were a very real possibility - a fate that awaited many of them. Some joined because they needed income during the war, some joined for adventure, but all joined because they had a burning passion to defeat the Nazis and free France from the tyranny of occupation.

Many female SOE agents joined The First Aid Nursing Yeomanry (FANY) as a cover story. It was an independent, all-female registered charity formed in Britain in 1907. FANY was active in both nursing and intelligence work during both World Wars. Members wore a military-style uniform, but the organization was not part of the Regular Army or Army Reserve. During WWII, FANY worked closely with the SOE to give the female agents a good cover story for their family and friends.

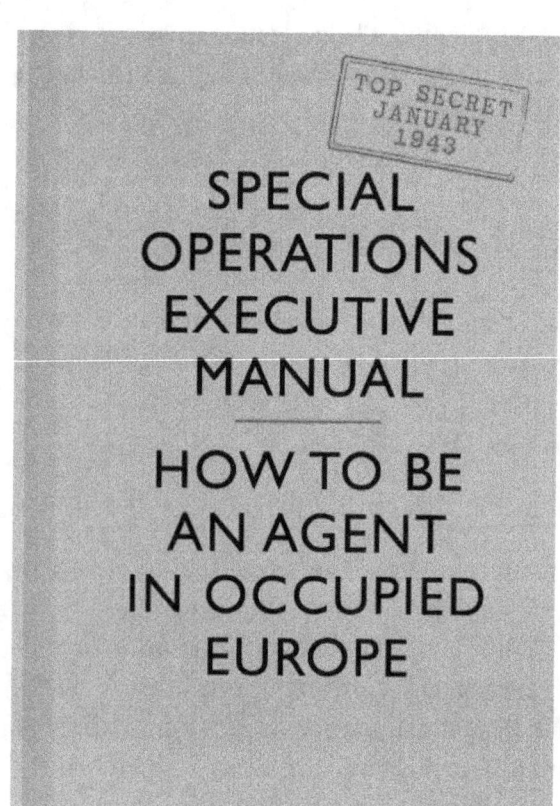

The SOE training program, which was the same for men and women, consisted of

- physical training
- the use and care of weapons
- forgery
- unarmed combat and silent killing
- Morse codes, other codes, and ciphers
- some level of wireless transmission and receiving
- elementary explosives and demolition, including planting bombs inside dead rats
- map reading
- field craft, including forgery, making false keys, burglary, how to poison guard dogs used by the Nazis
- parachute jumping for most, but not all, recruits.

The official 1943 SOE Manual, *How To Be An Agent In Occupied Europe* was a training guide given to all SOE recruits. Throughout the manual, prospective agents are reminded of the utmost secrecy required in relation to working for the SOE:

Like the men, all female SOE agents had to sign the Official Secrets Act. They were forbidden to tell their husbands, boyfriends, or other family members or friends about working for the SOE, what they were doing, or where they were stationed.

**It should be noted that despite many of the SOE women being captured, tortured, and executed, there is nothing in the German records to indicate that any of the women gave up SOE secrets to the Germans.**

The author is pleased to identify one potential "new" name to the group of female agents who worked in France for the SOE. While doing research for this book, a friend discovered a British newspaper clipping that referred to the death of a woman who had been an SOE agent. She was not listed in "the bible" about the "F" Section, written by the SOE historian M.R.D. Foot, in his book *SOE In France*. She was not listed in any other books or documents reviewed by the author. However, there is significant evidence that Nicola Trahan served with the SOE as a teenager. She would not have been the only teenager in the SOE, although she and the others may have lied about their ages. There is some contradictory evidence, so her status remains questionable. Unfortunately, she died in early 2024, before she could be interviewed. Further details are given in her chapter. It is possible that additional women may be identified as a result of her recent obituary and the media surrounding her death.

Even after the war ended, few in the public knew about the SOE or the fact that female agents worked behind German lines until the following letter from Squadron Leader William Simpson, Distinguished Flying Cross, was published in the *Sunday Express* newspaper on March 11, 1945:

*WAAF girls parachuted into France (it should be noted that most, but not all, female SOE agents were also WAAF officers.)*

*Who are the WAAF officers who parachuted into France to join the Maquis months before D-Day? This question has plagued Air Ministry officials ever since Sir Archibald Sinclair (Secretary of State for Air) praised WAAF parachutists in the House of Commons last week.*

*Officially, it remains unanswered – for reasons of security. Two only have been named in the press. One Sinia D'Artois (nee Butt) is the young daughter of a group captain. She married the French-Canadian officer who jumped with her. The other, Maureen O'Sullivan, is also young and pretty. She comes from Dublin.*

*The interesting thing about these girls is they are not hearty and horsey young women with masculine chins. They are pretty young girls who would look demure and sweet in crinolines. Most of them are English girls who speak perfect French. Some were educated in French convents; others attended Swiss finishing schools. A few are French girls who escaped from France and agitated for a chance to go back and work underground. Cool courage, intelligence, and adaptability are their most important attributes. They have to be able to pass themselves off as tough country wenches, and smart Parisiennes.*

*They were taught parachute jumping in the North of England. They trained with male agents and paratroopers of all nationalities and leapt with them from fixed balloons and moving aircraft.*

*But parachuting was a secondary part of their training. They also had to absorb complicated secret details of underground organization and train the Maquis in radio operating.*

*After months of intensive training, there often followed weeks of anxious waiting. Then, dressed in the appropriate French civilian clothes of their first role, they were flown by night bomber into moonlit France.*

*Sometimes they dropped 'free' at a pre-determined point. On landing, they fended for themselves, reported to a friendly farmer, then set off at dawn to contact the leader of their resistance group.*

*Usually, however, they landed with arms and food, floating down with the packages and containers. As courier, she went from group to group of the Maquis. It was easier for a girl to pass unnoticed in France, stripped of men by the Germans.*

*Often, she was on the spot when supplies were dropped and helped to unload and hide the containers. It sounds easy enough. In fact, it is about the most cold-blooded and creepy task that any young woman could choose.*

*Death and torture are present realities. Atrocity details are well known. There were traitors in the Maquis itself working to betray. Sometimes, they succeeded.*

*But so great was the courage and spirit of these girls that they could afford to send back humorous messages.*

*One complained that what with washing and darning, and running around with messages, she had little time for routine work!* (the author notes that the agent in question was furious at his suggestion that she was washing and darning – something she said she definitely did NOT do, except for her own clothing.)

*Another, who had walked for weeks to return to France, had to jump over Kent – due to engine trouble in the bomber which carried her. As soon as she had collected herself, she asked to be allowed to go on with the job the same night.*

*Behind the veil of secrecy, not yet raised by the Air Ministry, there are great stories of courage and endurance. For the agent has no status, no friendly uniform or consul to rely on. With her friends, she is outside the law – until it catches up with her.*

*There was one girl I met in Vichy, France, four years ago. Since then, although not in the WAAF, she has been back and forth many times. Acting as courier and wireless operator, she has also organized Maquis bands. No doubt she has fought with arms, for her first aim is to kill Germans.*

*Amongst her perilous adventures are included escapes over the Pyrenees into Spain. And she knows the filth, discomfort, and despair of Spanish prison camps. But nothing could dismay her. She went on.* (These two paragraphs are almost definitely describing Virginia Hall.)

*All these unknown young girls of the WAAF have proved one thing forever. The toughest tests of courage and endurance faced by men can be passed with honour by women.*

Maurice Buckmaster, head of the "F" French Section, wrote about the women serving during WWII: *It has been suggested that women agents should never have been sent, that they were forced to undertake missions to which both by temperament and by nature, they were unsuited and in physique and spirit inadequate. The dead cannot be revived by such accusations; they can only be dishonored. Those of us who know of the work done by women like Violette Szabo, Noor Inayat Khan, Denise Bloch, among those who died, and by Lise de Baissac, the sisters Jacqueline Nearne and Eileen Nearne, and Nancy Wake among those who survived, can only feel anger and contempt for those who try to denigrate Baker Street by questioning the ability of women to fight alongside men and who impugn the efficiency of headquarters by doubting the readiness of brave women to face perils and, if necessary, to die for their countries. These women did an invaluable job and one for which, whatever people may say, they were admirably suited. Coolness and judgment were vital qualities; none lacked them. Courage was their common badge.*

By the summer of 1944, fifteen female SOE agents were imprisoned in either France or Germany. They all suffered terrible conditions, and most had been tortured. Only two of the fifteen would survive their imprisonment. All the SOE agents working in the field had lived with the daily knowledge that they could be captured at any time and could face imprisonment, torture, or execution.

None of the women who worked in France during the war returned unchanged. They had dealt with daily stress and danger. They had seen terrible atrocities done by vengeful German soldiers, especially toward the end of the war. They knew of many fellow agents and Resistance/Maquis fighters who had been killed or captured and not heard from again. The effects of the war remained with them for the rest of their lives. Some managed to build a new life that included family and friends, but many failed to flourish after the adrenaline faded.

Three SOE "F" Section female agents received the George Cross. The three women were Noor Inayat Khan, Odette Sansom, and Violette Szabo. Two of the awards were given posthumously to Noor and

Violette. The George Cross is the highest gallantry award for civilians and military personnel in actions that are not in the face of the enemy or for which purely military honors would not normally be granted.

It would be a grave disservice to allow the sacrifices these women made to be forgotten or overlooked.

## SOE Circuits

The SOE operations in the field were organized around a system of Circuits, or networks, each covering a specific sector of France. SOE Circuits were composed of three primary agents: a Circuit leader, a Courier, and a Radio Operator. In the larger Circuits, there often was more than one courier and one radio operator.

The Leader headed and coordinated the Circuit and identified possible targets for sabotage. The Leader was responsible for helping to coordinate local Resistance/Maquis fighting groups and encourage them to work in a planned manner.

Only four female agents were entrusted to take significant Circuit leadership roles within France: Nancy Wake, Virginia Hall, Lise de Baissac, and Pearl Witherington. Each ran their own Circuits or carved out a unique position that involved giving direction to Resistance fighters and other SOE agents. All female agents did valuable work and were given occasional opportunities to prove themselves as leaders, but those four received almost immediate recognition for their essential roles.

The Circuits recruited, armed, and worked with local French Resistance fighters to sabotage German operations. Typical operations involved blowing up trains, bridges, supply depots, factories, or other infrastructure that allowed the German Army to operate in France. They also conducted hit-and-run guerrilla attacks on soldiers or military facilities, but these actions were less frequent.

Some Resistance groups were regarded as brutal, unorthodox, and highly controversial. Their actions in occupied countries often led to dreadful reprisals against the local population, and many in the military considered the civilian death toll too high a price to pay for the SOE's successes.

## Couriers

The exact duties of the couriers differed depending on the mission of the Circuit to which they were attached. Still, almost all were responsible for taking messages to and from the Circuit leaders to the radio operators and to the Resistance groups working under the coordination of the Circuit leaders. The couriers traveled through German roadblocks daily, each time risking their lives.

They might also find safe houses for SOE agents, downed pilots, and sometimes Resistance fighters. They were frequently responsible for finding safe locations for parachute drops of new agents, supplies, weapons, and ammunition for the Resistance groups. Once the drops had been completed, the courier separated the items, which could weigh hundreds of pounds, and found ways to transport them to different Resistance groups.

Many couriers participated in actual sabotage operations of the Resistance fighters. There were many instances where couriers set explosives to blow up railroad lines, factories, or power stations. There was at least one documented incident where SOE agent Nancy Wake killed a German soldier with a "karate chop" to the neck when he was about to alert other soldiers about their presence.

Couriers frequently stepped in if the Circuit leader had to be away, and they filled in as radio operators if the Gestapo captured their operators.

## Radio Operators

One of the most dangerous jobs for SOE personnel in France was that of the radio (wireless) operator. Radio operators were extremely vulnerable to detection. With aerials strung up in attics or disguised as washing lines outside, they tapped out Morse code on the keys of transmitters. They waited, usually alone, for a signal in reply saying the messages were received. If they stayed on air for more than twenty minutes, their signals were likely to be picked up by the Germans, and detection vans would then trace the source of their signals. When the operator moved location, the bulky transmitter had to be carried, sometimes hidden in a suitcase or in a bundle of firewood.

As with all countries under German occupation, the Gestapo employed considerable resources to track down wireless operators. The Gestapo regarded radio operators as a rich intelligence source because they knew every message sent to and received from London. Toward the end of the war, the life expectancy of radio operators in France was six weeks.

The radio operator was the only connection between the Circuits and London. Resistance groups could not function effectively without arms, explosives, and other support, which could only be obtained through communicating with London. The operator sent and received messages about where the supplies would be parachuted or landed.

Early SOE radio operators used a radio that weighed almost 33 pounds and was concealed in a suitcase, making it very cumbersome for the women to transport as they moved locations. The machine's aerial was 66 feet long, so the operator had to have room to spread it out. It could be powered by either a car battery or AC electricity. Toward the end of the war, the operators were issued a smaller radio that weighed only 8 pounds and was more powerful.

Radio trainees were told that if captured, they would very likely be tortured by the Gestapo for their personal codes, which a German operator could use to 'play-back' their wireless to London.

Agents volunteering for radio duties were sent to a technically challenging course at the Wireless and Security School. Apart from learning to send and receive Morse Code at a sufficient speed, they needed to understand radio wave propagation and the use of ciphers. They also learned how to repair their radios in the field. They needed to prove their competence in using various security measures intended to make it difficult for German signal direction-finders to pinpoint their location.

The Gestapo knew that radio operators were the weak link in the Circuit's operation. Signal detection vans full of listening equipment would begin to home in on the source. As the equipment became more sophisticated, other vans would join to triangulate the source within a city block. Then, men on foot would use aerials to walk up and down the street to pinpoint the signal and find the transmitter.

## German Occupation of France

After Germany invaded France on May 10, 1940, they struck a deal with the French government that the areas generally in northern France would be under complete control of Germany. The areas to the south (free zone) would be administratively controlled by the newly established Vichy government. On June 22, 1940, the headquarters were established in the town of Vichy. For a time, the French in the southern part of the country had a false sense of being relatively free of German control. Initially, many from the north fled to the south, as did many refugees from other occupied countries. That illusion evaporated when the full might of the German Army moved south on November 10, 1942. The below map shows the demarcation line between the north and south of France.

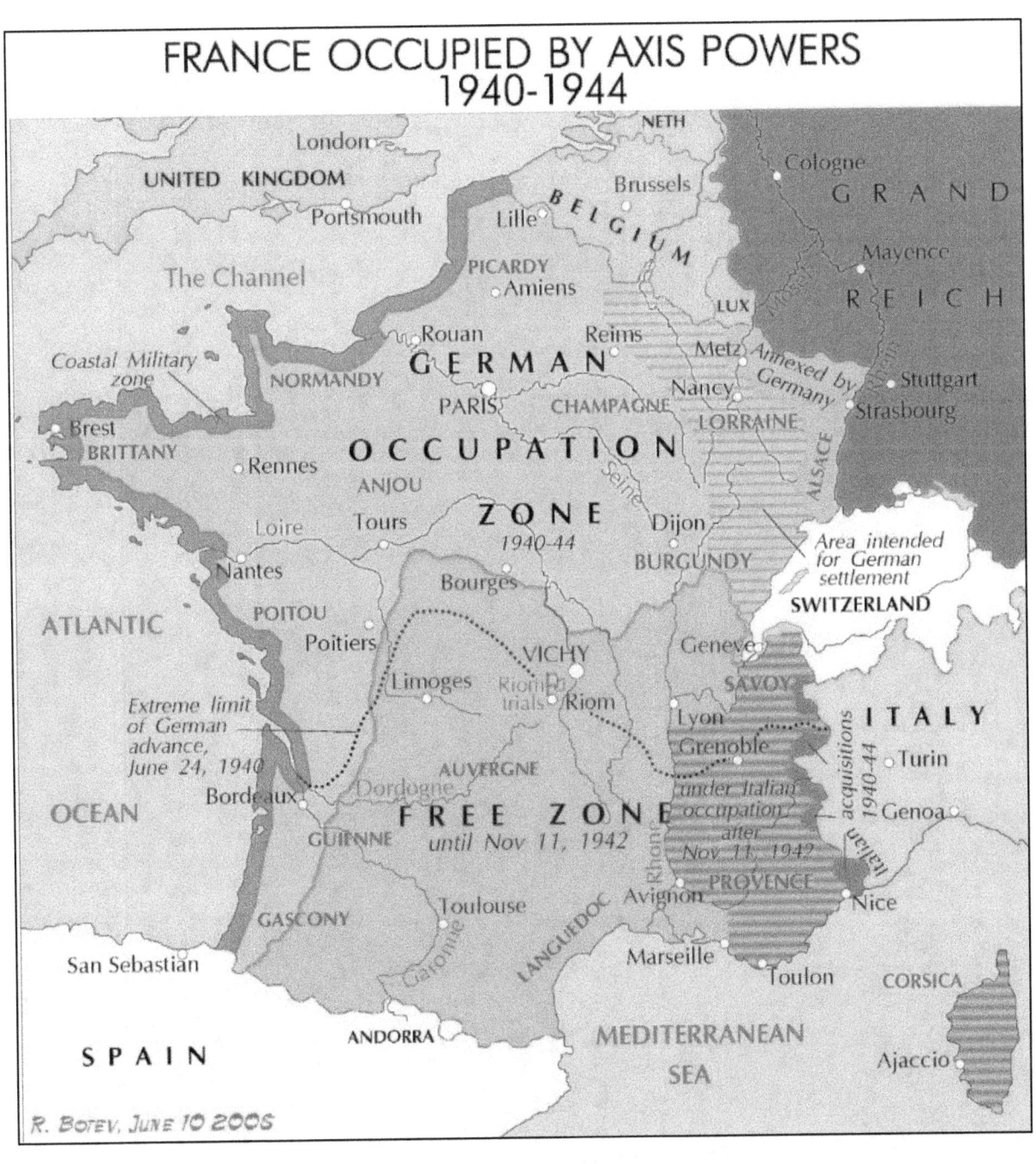

# Chapter 2

# Vera Atkins – British Spy Master

June 16, 1908 – June 24, 2000

The first line in Vera Atkins' *New York Times* obituary reads in part: *Vera Atkins, who recruited, trained, and watched over the legendary British secret agents who parachuted into France to sabotage the Nazis in World War II.*

Vera Maria (Rosenberg) Atkins was an unlikely candidate to become the acknowledged "Spy Master of Great Britain" during WWII. She coordinated the work of over 400 agents in France and was especially protective of the female agents she sent into enemy territory. Vera was said to have inspired the character of Ms. Moneypenny in the James Bond books. One of her early colleagues commented about Vera, intending it as an insult: *she had a very manly brain.*

Vera was born in Romania on June 16, 1908, to wealthy German-Jewish Max Rosenberg and British-Jewish Zeffo Hilda Atkins. She had two brothers and all the children used the mother's last name as the Nazi influence grew throughout Europe.

She was unusually tall for a woman at five feet nine inches, she was said to be popular, and lived an active social life in her affluent community. She studied at a finishing school in Lucerne, Switzerland, followed by additional education in modern languages at the Sorbonne in Paris. Vera was fluent in Romanian, French, English, and German, and she traveled to many European countries during her youth and young adulthood.

Because of the rising threat of the Nazis, Vera moved from Romania to England in 1938. After volunteering in various war efforts, she joined the SOE in early 1941. Vera was hired as a secretary in the "F" (French) Section, working under the direction of the head of the "F" Section, Maurice Buckmaster. Many who worked in the in "F" Section later said: *She was the boss.* Buckmaster was often criticized for letting Vera make so many management decisions.

There were strong objections to having female field agents working for the SOE. Vera and Buckmaster believed that women would be almost invisible because the Germans would refuse to believe that women could do such work. Most of the women worked as couriers or wireless operators.

Vera experienced considerable discrimination at the SOE because she was a woman, but it would have been much worse if her colleagues had known she was Jewish. Many of her colleagues thought she was unnecessarily secretive about her background. Some even thought she was a spy working for either Russia or Germany. Maurice Buckmaster, her direct boss and the leader of the "F" Section, knew of her Jewish heritage. His wife had Jewish ancestry, and he was strongly opposed to anti-Semitism and was determined to see that Vera was treated fairly.

**Maurice Buckmaster, the head of the "F" Section of the SOE and Vera's boss.**

Vera feared that people at the SOE would hold it against her if they knew of her Jewish heritage. Rumors persisted for years that she paid $150,000 to a Nazi intelligence agent in Belgium to help a cousin obtain a passport to leave the country in 1940. It was later proven to be true.

Due to her expertise, Vera gradually took on greater responsibility and became an essential player in the lives of her agents. She eventually coordinated the training and preparation of over four hundred agents who went to France. A leader of the training section was said to have called Vera: *Really the most powerful personality in SOE.*

In October 1942, Buckmaster recommended that Vera be promoted. He sent the following memo with his recommendation: *to bring the case of Miss Atkins to your notice. She at present receives the top secretarial salary but is serving in the capacity of an officer of the Section and is considered very able and efficient. She has very good qualifications and is a great asset to the F. Section. Her work is equivalent in responsibility to any other woman officer in the Organization.* Subsequently, Vera was promoted from her secretarial position to an Intelligence officer in the "F" Section.

Vera's application for British citizenship had not yet received approval. In a letter to the Home Office supporting her application, in February 1944, Buckmaster noted that the SOE wanted Vera to run a special station in France that would coordinate post-D-Day operations. He wrote: *If Miss Atkins goes overseas as a Romanian subject, we fear that she will be both obtrusive and much restricted in her movements.*

Subsequently, her British citizenship application was approved on March 24, 1944. She was commissioned into the Women's Auxiliary Air Force (WAAF) as a Flight Officer and appointed as an intelligence officer in the "F" Section.

Vera interviewed most of the new recruits for the position of field agent, including almost all of the women. The criteria used to select women as possible agents varied. Those who spoke fluent French or who had a French parent or had spent time living or working in France were ideal candidates. Some had previously worked with the French Resistance.

Vera was responsible for ensuring that when agents arrived in France, they had excellent false identities and foolproof cover stories. Even with such meticulous preparation, their work was very dangerous. She informed each recruit that he or she would be undertaking dangerous work and there was a 50% chance that they might be killed. Each person was told to consider the risk for a few days before deciding whether to accept the invitation to join the SOE.

**Vera, in her Women's Auxiliary Air Force (WAAF) Flight Officer Uniform.**

Vera had lived in France and knew the country well, and she was well-versed in what the agents would have to know to blend into the local community. That knowledge was critical in preparing agents to work and live in the country.

It was critical that Vera stay up to date with the changes forced upon the French by the German occupation so she could share that information with the agents during their training. She scoured magazines for information and talked to returning agents about whether ration cards in France were currently issued weekly or monthly, current curfew hours, what documents an agent would need to move around the country, and the current clothing worn by locals. She put some of the most important points she gleaned into leaflets she named "Titbits" or "Comic Cuts" that were given to each agent.

The agent training consisted of many areas of instruction. It began with classes on how to interrogate and be interrogated, along with training on how to stick to their cover identities and stories. The agents then moved to the Scottish Highlands, where they learned how to handle weapons and use explosives. A survival course followed in Hampshire, where they learned defensive and offensive fighting, how to make fake documents, and how to use Morse code. Finally, they practiced parachute jumping near Manchester.

Most SOE agents were either parachuted into France or flown there in Lysander airplanes which could land in small fields. A few agents went by boat. Just before their departures, Vera scrutinized their clothing one last time looking for English labels, laundry tags, or any sign that they came from Britain. She completed their disguises by handing them a packet of French cigarettes, a recent issue of a French newspaper, or photographs of fictitious relatives.

Vera almost always went with the agents to their departure airfield to wish them well on their missions. She usually gave the women agents a gold makeup compact. The compact could be used for its normal purpose or sold if the agents found themselves in trouble and needed cash. Buckmaster gave the men a gold cigarette lighter.

Vera interacted closely with agents over the entire time they worked for the SOE. She took on a mentorship relationship with "F" Section men and women. She: *Supervised the financial arrangements and private questions affecting officers leaving for the field and invariably inspired them with the feeling that their requests would be attended to, whatever difficulties might arise.* All agents had to make a will prior to deployment to France, and Vera was the keeper of those wills, along with information about who was to be contacted if an agent was captured or killed.

Vera maintained a relationship with many of the agents' families. Because agents could not disclose information about their work or whereabouts during the war, she often acted as an intermediary to reassure families. This was particularly true following an agent's disappearance. Most often, the SOE did not know what had happened to the agent, so she had to be very circumspect in communicating with the families.

She wrote to many of the families monthly, often telling them fictitious news about their relative. If the SOE knew that an agent had been killed, she would send a personal note expressing her condolences in addition to the official letter that was sent from the military. After the war, this became a very difficult responsibility as Vera discovered the terrible fate of so many of the missing agents.

Paris was liberated from Germany in August 1944. Vera and Buckmaster traveled to France to analyze the situation for the agents still in France. She was desperate for information about the missing agents. Unfortunately, there was little information available. After Vera returned to Britain, she began filing casualty reports and combing through the latest reports about missing agents.

When the war ended, Vera requested the assignment to go to France and Germany to investigate the fate of the missing agents. Higher-ups were reluctant to grant her request until they learned of a report made by British intelligence officer Prince Yurka Galitzine. He was a young British intelligence officer tasked with gathering evidence of German war crimes. His report stated that at least three female agents were shot at a prison camp.

With Galitzine's help, Vera received approval to find the "lost" SOE agents. Atkins was attached to the J.A.G. War Crimes division which was tasked with investigating the disappearance of missing agents. In early December 1945, she went to Germany with a list of 52 agents. That list would grow to 118 male and female agents who were unaccounted for. Over time, she interviewed many former agents, local French Resistance members, German soldiers and guards, Gestapo agents, and prison and concentration camp staff.

For the next several years, Vera crisscrossed France and Germany, visiting all the prisons and concentration camps that were believed to have held the SOE prisoners. The extent of the torture and killing of millions of people, including the SOE agents, was unknown to the world until the end of the war. As Allied soldiers began liberating the concentration camps, they finally learned of the horrors that had been inflicted on captives. The existence of gas chambers and crematoriums and the starvation of prisoners was beyond anyone's imagination until the stories and photos began to filter out.

Vera discovered that some of the missing agents had been killed, and many more were arrested and tortured by the Nazis. Many agents were executed after suffering terrible imprisonment conditions. She eventually learned the fate of 117 of the missing agents. She concluded that the final agent had absconded with SOE funds and fled France. He was never located.

Vera's investigations led to the trial and conviction of many of those responsible for the torture and executions. Vera participated in three war crimes trials. Vera, along with others who participated in these inquires, acted as the defender of the lost agents, both men and women. Her efforts to find the final answers about what happened to the missing SOE agents may have been her most significant contribution.

During the trials of the German guards and officers, Vera showed no emotion, and many reporters wrote about her "coldness." Those who knew her felt that it was her way of trying to protect herself from the full weight of the horrors that she learned had been inflicted on the SOE agents and millions of other prisoners.

**Vera with other war crimes investigators, 1946**

Vera interrogated the infamous Nazi "spy catcher," Hugo Bleicher, just after the war. He commented: *She turned out to have more aplomb than all the other officers put together. She boxed me in with astonishing ease and consummate tactics.*

Bleicher's persuasiveness influenced even those who prosecuted him. He maintained that his job was to: *arrest spies, imprison them, and then entertain them with Viennese waltzes.* He denied mistreating prisoners, and SOE agents captured by him said he was *extremely nice and polite.* His British and French counterparts respected him for his expertise. According to author Sarah Helm, Bleicher was never charged with a crime. He was, however, briefly imprisoned to obtain information about other Nazis.

Vera's interviews with the Auschwitz commandant, Rudolf Hess, were also used at the trials. Vera was horrified when he corrected her comment that 1,500,000 Jews had been killed to tell her the correct number was 2,345,000. She later commented that he seemed very proud of the number and of the wonderful records kept by the Gestapo. Hess was found guilty and sentenced to life imprisonment. Hess was found dead on August 17, 1987, aged 93, in the prison garden. He had hanged himself.

SS Officer Hans Kieffer was someone Vera had long wished to interview, but he had not yet been found by the Allies. Kieffer had run a special German headquarters at Avenue Foch in Paris. At the Avenue Foch basement prison, suspected spies were kept in relatively comfortable circumstances in the hope that they could be persuaded to cooperate. Some SOE agents had spoken fondly of Kieffer. However, Vera had no illusions about his true character. She knew that he also often directed his subordinates to convince agents to talk by using brutal methods such as being submerged in ice-cold water or viciously whipped.

Vera interrogated a fellow officer of Kieffer's who told her Kieffer was working as a caretaker in a hotel in Garmisch, a resort town in Germany. The tip turned out to be correct. Kieffer had left his wife, who was dying of cancer, and his children and went into hiding in Garmisch. Kieffer was apprehended at the hotel. Vera finally had the opportunity to interrogate him. He recognized her name since he met and personally interrogated many captured SOE agents.

Vera displayed a photograph of Noor Inayat Khan, who was the last agent that Vera was looking for. Kieffer instantly recognized her as a prisoner he knew as Madeleine. Kieffer seemed annoyed as he recalled: *She told us nothing. We could not rely on anything she said. I cannot remember her real name but I am sure in this, she also lied to us.* Vera informed Kieffer that Noor and the other women he sent to Karlsruhe had been taken to concentration camps and killed. Startled, Kieffer burst into tears. Vera later reported that she told him: *Kieffer, if one of us is going to cry, it is going to be me. You will please stop this comedy.*

Kieffer's recollections confirmed what Vera had learned from other sources of Noor's courage. Noor was imprisoned and tortured longer than any other female agent and longer than most of the male agents before being executed. But she refused to divulge any secret information to the Gestapo. Kieffer was found guilty at the end of his trial on war crimes and received a death sentence. An appeal was refused, and he was executed by hanging on June 26, 1947.

Vera wanted Noor to receive the highest award Britain offered for bravery—the George Cross. Vera continued to advocate for the award long after the war's end, and in 1949, Noor Inayat Khan received the George Cross posthumously.

Vera's longest interrogations were with the officers and guards of the Ravensbrück and Sachsenhausen concentration camps. Anton Kaindl had been Sachsenhausen's commandant, but he would tell Vera nothing about the missing agents. Ravensbrück commandant Fritz Suhren initially claimed to know nothing about gassings, hangings, or English or French prisoners, although he seemed startled when he was asked about the crematoriums. He would eventually be very forthcoming to Vera about the women agents.

**Ravensbrück Commandant
Fritz Suhren**

**Ravensbrück Second-in-Command,
Johann Schwarzhuber**

Perhaps the most detailed interviews she conducted were with Johann Schwarzhuber. He effectively commanded the entire Ravensbrück complex, acting as the second in command to commandant Fritz Suhren.

The Ravensbrück trial was held in Hamburg, Germany. SOE agents were executed or died of starvation and disease at Ravensbrück, which was one reason the British were trying the case. The prosecution team asked Vera to provide testimony.

Ravensbrück commandant Fritz Suhren was not present at that trial, as he had escaped from custody. He was later captured, tried, and hanged. The unsavory characters in the court docket included: SS camp overseer Dorothea Binz, who was known for her cruelty; "nurse" Vera Salvequart, who prepared "patients" for the gas chambers; and Carmen Mory, who had overseen the camp's "punishment block."

Another star witness for the prosecution was one of Vera's surviving agents, Odette Sansom. She personally testified that Ravensbrück prisoners had been crowded into windowless cells, put in solitary confinement with light for only 5 minutes per day, and forced to subsist on nothing but thin soup and potatoes. They labored in quarries, factories, and fields for long hours without a break. Those who weakened were often beaten or shot. Many died of starvation or ill health brought on by the brutal conditions. Others were deliberately murdered by being shot or gassed.

Vera gave testimony against Schwarzhuber at his trial, and he willingly repeated what he told her to the court and even added more detail when speaking about the execution of three of the SOE women, Violette Szabo, Lilian Rolfe, and Denise Bloch.

Present for the killing of the three women were: Schwarzhuber; the chief camp doctor, Trommer; SS Sergeant Zappe; SS Lance Corporal Schult; SS Corporal Schenk; and the camp dentist, Hellinger.

Schwarzhuber had a remarkable memory for details and was very free in talking about the agents' deaths to the court. His statement about the three women read: *I accompanied the three women to the crematorium yard. A female camp overseer was also present and sent back when we reached the crematorium. Zappe stood guard over them while they were waiting to be shot. All three were very brave, and I was deeply moved. Suhren was also impressed by the bearing of these women. He was annoyed that the Gestapo did not themselves carry out these shootings. The shooting was done by SS Lance Corporal Schult with a small-calibre gun fired through the back of the neck. They were brought forward singly by Corporal Schenk. Death was certified by Dr. Trommer. The corpses were removed singly by the internees who were employed in the crematorium and burned. The clothes were burned with the bodies.*

**Camp Commandant Johann Schwarzhuber of the Ravensbrück concentration camp, hearing his death sentence.**

Schwarzhuber was married and had three children. Before the war, he had been a printer by profession. The war changed the trajectory of his life, and he worked in some of the worst German killing camps. He had previously worked as an SS officer in Dachau, Sachsenhausen, and Auschwitz before being promoted to the second-in-command at Ravensbrück. He oversaw the mass gassing of thousands of women and children. Vera's interviews with him and her testimony at the trial were deciding factors in his sentence. Schwarzhuber was found guilty of war crimes and was sentenced to death. The execution was carried out on May 3, 1947.

Vera's determination to discover what had happened to the missing agents led to the discovery of the details of the missing agents and gave some closure to their families.

In 1947, Vera concluded her investigation of the missing SOE agents and returned to Britain. After turning in her report, Vera rented a remote cottage on the coast of Wales and remained there for several months, seeing few people. Someone close to her speculated that she took that time for herself to heal.

**After the war, Vera (left) with Hedwig Rosenberg (her sister-in-law) and Agent Odette Sansom.**

Vera sent hundreds of agents to France who were later captured and tortured, and too many were executed. One can only imagine how that might affect anyone in her position. She also had one more reason to mourn - the death of her mother, Hilda Rosenberg. They lived together until her death, and it was a significant loss for Vera.

Vera returned to London and found a job as an office manager with the Central Bureau for Educational Visits and Exchanges. She continued working for the government in various roles until 1961 when she took early retirement at 53 and moved to a home she inherited in Winchelsea, East Sussex.

Vera was honored in 1948 with the Croix de Guerre and, in 1987, was named a Knight of the French Legion of Honor. Queen Elizabeth appointed Vera as a Commander of the Order of the British Empire (CBE) in 1997.

Vera was not yet done with her involvement in the stories of SOE agents, as she served as consultant on the film *Odette,* about Odette Sansom, that was released in 1950. Maurice Buckmaster played himself. At *Odette's* opening, Vera and Maurice sat in the audience as did King George VI and his Queen consort Elizabeth Bowes-Lyon.

When author Jean Overton Fuller was researching the Noor Inayat Khan story he sought and received information from Vera. *Madeleine* was published in 1952. Vera applauded the book as "a very striking portrait." Vera was also an advisor on the 1958 movie *Carve Her Name with Pride* about Violette Szabo.

Because Vera and others campaigned for "F" Section memorials, they began to be erected at some of the former concentration camps during the 1970s. She worked on creating these memorials, including raising money and ensuring that the inscriptions were complete and correct.

**Valençay SOE Memorial in Valençay, France**

In 1991, Vera attended the dedication of the Valençay SOE Memorial in France. It was a special memorial erected to all 104 "F" Section agents who died during the war. Speaking about the agents being memorialized, she said: *I could not just abandon their memory*. For several years, Vera and other SOE agents and staff made a pilgrimage to that memorial every May.

**Vera, on the left, with Lynette Atkins of FANY at the Ravensbrück concentration camp memorial service in 1993.**

Well into her seventies and eighties, Vera attended parties and dinners, many of them at the Special Forces Club. In her later years, she also traveled widely, something she had enjoyed before joining the SOE.

In 1995, the French awarded Vera the prestigious title Commandeur de la Legion d'Honneur.

**Vera with Maurice Buckmaster at his retirement home in the late 1980s**

Vera was known to have had relationships with at least two different men in her early life, but she never married and had no children. Shortly after celebrating her 92nd birthday, an infection forced Vera into a hospital for treatment. To help her during her recovery, she was moved into a nursing home, where she fell and broke a hip. She was transferred back to the hospital, where she caught a severe staph infection. She died on June 24, 2000, at the age of 92.

**Additional notes:**

After the war, Buckmaster described Vera in his book, *They Fought Alone*, as follows: *My secretary, my personal assistant (the indispensable Vera Atkins), recruiting officer, briefing officer, escorting officer (for observing and reporting back on the training behavior of our agents), signals officer and planning officer.*

Sarah Helm, who wrote a biography of Vera, met her only once and said that even many years after the war Vera remained an intimidating figure with a precise upper-class accent. She remained a heavy smoker with a chilly, even haughty demeanor. Helm was impressed by Vera's amazing ability to summon up certain historical details about the SOE years, even while she evaded other questions. Ian Fleming, himself a spy, may have used Vera as the model for Miss Moneypenny, the secretary to his fictional James Bond. He said: *In the real world of spies, Vera Atkins was the boss.*

Following is a brief excerpt from **Vera's obituary in the *New York Times*** By Douglas Martin on June 27, 2000 (the obituary is quite lengthy):

*Ms. Atkins had no rank, but the blunt force of her personality, described by The Times of London as a "sledgehammer," pervaded the operation. She worked 18-hour days. A British television documentary in 1997 reported that she sent off each agent with the brisk shout of a French expletive.*

**Vera's obituary from the Washington Post:**

### British Spy Master Vera Atkins, 92

*Vera Atkins, the World War II British spymaster who inspired the efficient and unflappable Miss Moneypenny in the James Bond series, has died. She was 92.*

*Born Vera Maria Rosenberg in Bucharest in 1908, she moved to England in 1933, later adopting the surname of her English mother. Ms. Atkins was educated at the Sorbonne, and her knowledge of France led to her recruitment into the French section of Britain's Special Operations Executive, the organization responsible for supporting the resistance in Nazi-occupied Europe.*

*She was principal assistant to Col. Maurice Buckmaster, director of the Special Operations Executive, work said to have inspired the character of Miss Moneypenny, secretary to James Bond's boss. In her work for Buckmaster, Ms. Atkins coordinated a network of nearly 500 spies across Nazi-occupied France--briefing them on the life that awaited them, helping concoct elaborate cover stories and false identities, and communicating with the families they left behind. Once in France, they were kept informed by the British Broadcasting Corp.'s French Service through coded messages after the evening news broadcasts.*

*About 118 agents never returned. A few were killed in action, but most were reported to have been arrested by the Germans. Some disappeared into interrogation centers and concentration camps. One of the most famous, Violette Szabo, was shot.*

*Ms. Atkins felt a strong responsibility toward her charges and traveled to Germany after the war to investigate the missing agents. She managed to trace all but one of them, and the evidence she gathered helped bring their killers to court for war crimes. "I could not just abandon their memory," she said. The information she gleaned formed the basis of the roll of honor listing 91 men and 13 women of the French section on a memorial unveiled at Valençay in the Loire Valley in 1991.*

*Some accused the French section of the Special Operations Executive of amateurism, but Dwight D. Eisenhower credited it with shortening the war by six months, calling it the "equivalent of 15 [troop] divisions."*

*Ms. Atkins settled into a quiet life in an English seaside cottage, but her war work was not forgotten. The French government named her a commander of the French Legion of Honor, and she was made a commander of the British Empire by Queen Elizabeth II.*

*Ms. Atkins never married. Ms. Atkins died June 24, her family said. No cause of death was given. There are no immediate survivors.*

# Chapter 3

# Virginia Hall Goillot

April 6, 1906 – July 8, 1982

Code Names: Marie Monin, Diane, and Camille, Philomene,

Alias: Mlle. Marcelle Montagne

Klaus Barbie, a.k.a. "the Butcher of Lyon," head of the Gestapo, put out the word to find and destroy "The Limping Lady," whom the Third Reich considered the most dangerous Allied spy of WWII. They believed Virginia was responsible for more sabotage missions, jailbreaks, and leaks of Nazi troop movements than any other spy in France. Barbie was right to fear her, but he never managed to uncover her true nationality — or her real name.

Little in her early life indicated that Virginia Hall would attain that kind of notoriety. She was the youngest child of Barbara Virginia Hammel and Edwin Lee Hall. Virginia was athletic, funny, and intelligent and was voted: *the most original, different, and capricious* in high school. Raised in an affluent and sophisticated family in Baltimore, Maryland, Virginia went by the nickname "Dindy." In high school, she played baseball, hockey, and tennis. Throughout her school years, Virginia also performed in theater productions, experiences that were very useful in creating disguises and evading capture during the war.

**Page from her 1924 yearbook**

The family had a summer place in the country at Box Horn Farm in Parkton, Maryland. Virginia learned to milk cows, a skill she would later use when tending goats as a part of her cover story during the war.

Virginia attended Radcliffe and Barnard Colleges, finishing college with a year at the Ecole des Sciences Politiques in Paris and two years at the Konsularakademie in Vienna. She majored in languages. In addition to her native English, she was fluent in German, French, Italian, and spoke a little Russian. Other students later said she was always poised, self-confident, and very popular with boys and girls. In 1929, she returned to the U.S. and took additional French classes at George Washington University in Washington, DC.

Virginia loved travel and adventure and was determined to join the U.S. Foreign Service and become a diplomat. She was unfazed by the fact that only six women served in that capacity among more than 1,500 diplomats in the State Department during the 1930s. Despite those odds, Virginia began working as a clerk for the U.S. Embassy in Warsaw, Poland, in July 1931, with a salary of $2500 per year. She later worked at the U.S. Consulates in Izmir, Turkey; Vienna, Austria; and Tallinn, Estonia. She hoped the positions would be her steppingstone to a more senior position.

While on a hunting trip with friends in Turkey on December 8, 1933, Virginia tripped over a fence and accidentally shot herself in the left foot. Gangrene set in, and the leg was amputated just below the knee. She had a very difficult time with infections, probably sepsis, even after the lower leg was amputated. She had the best doctors in Turkey, and her mother sent an American doctor to Istanbul to help with Virginia's care. The doctors had serious concern about whether she would survive the many infections. The American Consul had a State Department official personally visit her mother in the U.S. to tell her of Virginia's accident and the resulting problems. The Consul visited her every day, and he was astonished at her fierce resilience. It was not until January 6, 1934, that her mother was told that Virginia was finally out of danger. Virginia had spent over a year in the hospital.

Against her doctor's advice, she returned to work at the Consulate the day after her release from the hospital. There was little available in Turkey in the way of a prosthesis, and Virginia was determined to walk again. She knew she needed the best available prosthesis technology. She was soon on a ship back to Washington, DC. After several more operations to clean up the remaining portion of her leg, she had a seven-pound wooden leg built. She named the leg "Cuthbert," and she referred to it by that name for the rest of her life.

**Virginia's accident and the resultant loss of her leg made the news.**

Virginia returned to work in November 1934, this time posted to Venice, Italy. She stepped back into a full workload, determined not to let the wooden leg slow her down. The wooden leg and foot did not do well with steps or inclines, so Venice was a constant physical challenge for her. Her mother came to stay for a few months to try to help Virginia adjust to living with the wooden leg. It was apparently a stressful time for both of them. Her mother never again visited her in Europe.

Virginia returned to the U.S. in January 1937 to once again apply to become a diplomat. She was 30 years old and had worked at three different legations. She believed she had the necessary skills and experience. However, her application was rejected based on an obscure rule barring amputees from higher levels of diplomacy. Family, friends, and several people in the State Department pushed her case all the way up to President Roosevelt, but he decided not to interfere and let the decision stand. Virginia finally had to accept that she would never reach her goal of a higher position.

Perhaps as punishment for her fighting the rejection, she was transferred to the same position in the increasingly authoritarian state of Tallinn, Estonia. The man who replaced her in Venice was granted vice-consult status and higher pay. She had not received a pay raise in seven years of service. She arrived in Tallinn at the end of June 1938. Few knew of her wooden leg, which she always concealed with heavy black stockings. Her limp only became pronounced when she was tired.

Virginia watched as surrounding countries seemed to be joining in the Nationalistic fever and restricting citizen rights and press freedom. She could see that Germany was quickly moving toward a large military buildup, and she was horrified when British Prime Minister Neville Chamberlain met Hitler in Munich in September 1938. She finally had enough and resigned from the State Department in March 1939. Only six months later, Germany attacked Poland on September 1, and two days later both Britain and France declared war on Germany. Virginia left Estonia for London. She tried to volunteer at the British Auxiliary Territorial Service (ATS), but she was again rejected because of her wooden leg.

Virginia returned to Paris as the German army continued to spread across Europe. Since the United States was still neutral in the war, she volunteered in February 1939 to join the Ambulance Service in France. They were desperate for help and didn't care about her wooden leg. Virginia also helped find safe houses for stranded or downed pilots and helped them escape over the Pyrenees over what would later become known as the PAT Line. She was still working with the ambulance service when the Nazi forces invaded France on May 10. Virginia moved to the relative safety of Valençay in the Loire Valley before traveling to Spain and moving on to England.

George Bellows, a British undercover agent, met Virginia shortly after she arrived in Spain. After learning of her experience in the diplomatic arena and as an ambulance driver, he gave her the phone number of a "friend" in London and suggested that she contact him. The number belonged to Nicolas Bodington, a recruiter for the SOE. It was almost a year before she called him. After their meeting, he sent a note to his boss the next morning, January 15, 1941, suggesting that she be hired and sent back to France to gather information. Without waiting for an answer, he asked MI5 to conduct a rigorous vetting of her, which was completed on February 17. MI5 gave her a positive recommendation, and she officially joined the SOE on March 3, 1941.

It was agreed that she would be the first female "F" Section agent and the first liaison officer of either sex to enter France. She would coordinate the work of local Resistance leaders and future SOE agents. Interestingly, there was no mention of her wooden leg in her file. It is uncertain if the SOE knew about her leg – or didn't care about it. The U.S. State Department seemed to delay her visa for the return to France. While waiting for it, the SOE sent the first two male agents to France, Pierre de Vomécourt and George Bégué in May 1941.

Being a very secretive man, it is possible that Bodington failed to mention her recruitment to either Vera Atkins or Maurice Buckmaster when they later joined the "F" Section. Vera would forever claim that Virginia was NOT a member of the SOE, but she was trained by them and worked for and with the SOE Circuits and agents throughout the war.

Beginning on April 1, 1941, Virginia took classes in weaponry, communications, and other essential spycraft. She learned how to spot someone following her, how to make secret ink using urine, how to change her voice/walk/looks to avoid detection, and how to search desks and rooms for hidden documents. A real bugler was even hired to demonstrate how to pick locks. After unsuccessfully trying other newspapers to find a cover story for Virginia, the SOE found George Backer, the publisher of the *New York Post,* who agreed to "hire" her as a correspondent.

She left England by boat on August 23, 1941, and arrived in Vichy, France, in late August. Virginia didn't write many stories but could send her reports openly because the U.S. was not yet at war, and the Gestapo did not censor them. She filed "news" stories with her editor in New York. The Nazis never realized that her news reports were all coded and being forwarded to SOE headquarters in London.

On September 4, 1941, the Post published the following real account from Virginia: *The years have rolled back here in Vichy. There are no taxis at the station, only half a dozen buses, and a few one-horse shays. I took a bus using Gazogene charcoal instead of gas to my hotel. Vichy is a tiny town used once by summer visitors to take the cure. It is an infinitesimally small place to accommodate the government of France and the French Empire, which has commandeered most of the hotels. I haven't seen any butter, and there is very little milk. I also see little clothing in the shops, and that is extremely dear. Shoes, however, are abundant and gay with their cloth or crocheted uppers and painted wooden soles. Women are no longer entitled to buy cigarettes, and men are rationed to two packages a week.*

After a month in Vichy, she moved to Lyon, where she thought she would have more success locating Resistance members who were willing to work with her. Virginia took advantage of her status as a journalist to move around France to gather information about what was happening in the country. Her travels were still risky, as the French police or German soldiers would often search the trains. She noted that the security police paid more attention to people sitting in the least expensive train cars, so she always booked first class. She memorized everything she could to minimize any incriminating paperwork.

Virginia made friends in Lyon with key police officers, other government officials, and businesspeople who were against the Nazi occupation. They often provided her with information and alerted her to potential problems with pro-German French police and the Germans.

On a personal level, she was desperate for soap, as there was little to be had in the French shops. She requested that the SOE send her some soap with the next drop of supplies, saying: *If you could ever send me a piece of soap, I should be both very happy and much cleaner.* There was a serious epidemic of scabies in humans for the first time in almost a hundred years. Without soap, those living or moving in close contact with others were at great risk of catching it. Virginia was also often desperate for medical socks for her leg stump.

The supplies sent by the SOE could include items for the agents that were difficult to come by in France during the occupation. They could be as basic as soap, shampoo, and razor blades. The SOE did its best to comply with the requests from the agents, as they knew that those small luxuries would mean a great deal to the agents working under such stressful conditions on a day-to-day basis. Space in the containers for such personal items was a challenge.

Virginia had an apartment but kept a separate escape option at a local convent. Despite the ever-increasing threat of capture by the Germans, she continued working behind the lines in France for fourteen months – a long time for any SOE agent. Virginia was remarkably skilled at obtaining information about German troop movements and the locations of their military posts and radioing that information to London. She assisted with the safe return of escaped prisoners of war and downed airmen to England, and she recruited French citizens to provide safe houses for the men. Virginia located drop locations for supplies and weapons flown in from England for the local Resistance fighters.

The SOE had great faith in Virginia's abilities and opinions. Her personnel file indicated that: *Her job was to provide intelligence about conditions, etc., in France, develop various contacts with a view to resistance possibilities, act as a channel for transmission of instructions to "F" Section agents, and look after agents generally.*

Virginia often met new agents when they arrived in France and helped them settle into their Circuits and their new clandestine life. She helped new agents with introductions to friendly French and she gave them food, tobacco, wine, and coupons for shoes and clothing. She became a "friendly aunt" to many of the agents. Other female agents would stop by her apartment when they were in the area. Several women agents later spoke about how helpful she was and how wonderful it was to talk to her about their stressful lives and duties in France. She provided valuable counseling when they were experiencing difficulties, and she sometimes interceded for them with their Circuit leaders.

The first male SOE agent sent into France, George Bégué, had been arrested on October 24, 1941. He and eleven other SOE agents and Resisters were sent to the Beleyme prison in Perigueux. Among that group was Jean Pierre-Bloch, a local Jewish Resistance member. His wife, Gabrielle Sadourny "Gaby," was arrested at the same time but was released after a couple of months. The conditions at the prison were terrible, and the men lived in filthy, rat-infested cells. Several different groups, including the SOE, tried to gain their release to no avail. Gaby was allowed to visit her husband periodically and she took food that may have helped keep the men alive, as they received only one meal a day of watery soup.

In desperation, Gaby went to Virginia and requested her help in freeing the men. Knowing that the prison was all but impenetrable, they waited until the men were moved to the Vichy-run Mauzac internment camp. Virginia produced a plan to smuggle in small tools and metal so the men could make a cell key.

They even smuggled in a radio transmitter with the help of a friendly priest. Virginia provided money to Gaby to use as a bribe to a camp guard, but his only request was for their help in his escaping France and going to England. The guard was able to convince the camp commandant to shut down one of the guard towers during nighttime, saying it was too unstable to have guards going up and down the ladder to the watch tower.

Meanwhile, Virginia was planning for safe houses for the men and for an escape route out of France once they were free. She gathered the necessary fake papers, food coupons, and train tickets to get them away quickly and safely. On July 16, 1942, the men used their homemade key to get out of the cell, shimmied under the two lines of barbed wire fencing, and escaped. They were taken to Lyon, and eventually over the Pyrenees into Spain. After some time in a Spanish jail for entering the country without valid visas, the men made their way to England by October.

The United States entered the war on December 11, 1941, giving much needed hope and military might to the fight against Nazi Germany.

In one of Virginia's last reports to the *Post* on January 22, 1942, she wrote that petty larceny, theft of food and transport, had assumed unknown proportions: *Owners don't blame the culprits; they know the poor people are hungry. The average weight loss today is 12 pounds per person, not only from lack of food but increased physical activity and mental strain…people separated from their loved ones…prisoners of the Germans.*

Virginia could freely travel in occupied countries and played a significant role in intelligence gathering. For instance, in two letters dated June 1942, she wrote of the deteriorating situation for European Jews. In the first she wrote that: *The Jewish question in Cracow has been fundamentally and drastically solved by this evolution of Cracow into a German city. A Jewish quarter built on the other side of the Vistula houses eighteen odd thousand Jews who remain in the city, but they are effectively isolated. In Poland, the Jews are separated from the rest of the population, while from Hungary comes the news that Jews will be completely excluded from military service.* While summarizing the situation in Eastern Europe, She also commented on the changing environment in Paris. She noted that: *The Jews in Paris, meantime, are wearing the badge of their race…a five-pointed yellow star.*

**Virginia, with downed American flyers**

The British National Archives personnel files on Virginia show the following comments about her working with other agents: *Practically every "F" Section agent sent to France during this period was in touch with her, and she helped them in every possible way, providing paper cover* (fake documents), *etc., and looking after them when in difficulties. This close interaction between agents resulted in Hall's loyalty to the F Section and the section's agents. Furthermore, this demonstrates Hall's authority within the field not only because agents were told to contact her, but also because of the increased level of her intelligence about the F Section due to her continual interactions.*

Klaus Barbie and the Gestapo knew of Virginia's work with the Resistance. He did not know her identity, but people talked of a woman who limped at the sites of sabotage actions, so he flooded the area with wanted posters with a good likeness seeking the "Limping Lady." The Gestapo orders were unequivocal: *The woman who limps is one of the most dangerous Allied agents in France. We must find and destroy her.*

Virginia should have been easy for the Gestapo to find, as she was tall at 5'7' and very thin; she had high cheekbones and a strong chin and profile. Plus, she walked with a limp due to her wooden leg. It was amazing that the Germans could not find her, but it became increasingly difficult for her to hide her identity.

Virginia had an issue with one SOE agent, Georges Duboudin, code name *Alain.* He was in charge of the Spruce Circuit and felt that Virginia and her Resistance fighters should be under his command. She would have none of it and found him to be incompetent, despite his exaggerated reports to London. He drank a lot, had relations with numerous women other than his wife, and failed to pull together an effective Circuit or group of Resistance fighters to work with. Virginia considered him a significant security risk. She refused to tell him anything about her operations or give him access to her many French contacts.

Well-respected SOE agent Peter Churchill arrived in Lyon and assessed Duboudin the same way Virginia did. He reported that to the SOE headquarters. He provided a glowing recommendation of Virginia's work. He also said that the SOE should make it clear to everyone that she was in charge of her own operation. He said she was: *A walking encyclopedia, knows everyone, is in with everyone, and is liked by everyone.*

Duboudin was recalled to London in October 1942. He returned to France a few weeks later to work in the Playwright Circuit but was captured within a few days. He later died in a concentration camp from pleurisy.

Virginia filled in as a radio operator for other Circuits when they were without an operator. Couriers frequently came to her with messages from various Circuit leaders. She also helped to dispense SOE funds to Circuit leaders. All these connections meant she had more communications and interactions with Circuits in the southern part of France than anyone else. Each interaction brought danger to her door, as the Gestapo could have been trailing any of the other agents.

By September 21, 1942, Virginia knew that the Gestapo was closing in around her, and she felt that she had to leave France before being captured. She asked London to arrange for her to fly out of France on the PanAm Clipper. She wrote: *I think my time has come. My address has been given to Vichy, although not my name, but it wouldn't be hard to guess.*

On November 9, 1942, the German army was about to move over the demarcation line into southern France, and she was warned that she had to leave immediately. Virginia knew it was too late to fly out, so she packed her bags and carried them almost two miles to the train station. She narrowly escaped Lyon, just ahead of the Gestapo.

Thousands of posters were distributed all over southern France offering a huge reward for the capture of *Marie Monin*, the alias that the Gestapo had for Virginia.

The train took her to Perpignan, 300 miles from Lyon and close to the Pyrenees Mountains. When she arrived, she hired a Spanish guide to lead her and others over the Pyrenees. Her companions, two Frenchmen, and a Belgian army captain said it was a brutal winter crossing for seasoned mountain men, never mind a woman trying to do it with a wooden leg in heavy snow. They walked for three days and more than 50 miles, crossing the Pyrenees Mountains in freezing cold and mountain snow to safety in Spain. In a message to the SOE in London, she commented, *Cuthbert is giving me trouble, but I can cope.*

A reply came from someone unaware of the name of her wooden leg that suggested: *If Cuthbert is giving you trouble, have him eliminated.*

Her prosthetic leg was attached with leather straps. When she walked up and down stairs or hills the leather would chafe, and the stump would blister and bleed. The ankle of the false leg would not bend like a normal ankle and would pitch her forward, meaning she had to be very careful going up and down stairs. Climbing up and down the Pyrenees had to be not only very difficult and painful but also very dangerous for her. Years later, when her niece asked her what the worst part of the war was for her, she said she still couldn't believe she had survived crossing the mountains during her escape from France.

**The Pyrenees Mountains crossed by Virginia and companions during the winter.**

Virginia had no official entry papers when she arrived in Spain and was thrown into the notorious Figueres prison for six weeks by the Spanish police. She dared not explain why she had entered the country without legal documents, as many German spies were stationed along the border. Virginia shared a cell with a prostitute, and the woman agreed to take a letter to the U.S. Consulate when she was released from prison. The Consulate quickly arranged for Virginia's freedom.

Virginia returned to London, where she improved her wireless radio skills. She had done radio work before, but she was mostly self-taught, and was very slow at it.

The SOE transferred her to Madrid on May 17, 1943, where she worked for the SOE for several months. She was using the cover story of being a foreign correspondent for the *Chicago Times*. The British refused to send her back to France since she was marked for death by the Gestapo. She sent a letter to SOE headquarters saying: *I thought I could help in Spain, but I'm not doing a job. I am living pleasantly and wasting time. It isn't worthwhile; after all, my neck is my own. If I am willing to get a crick in it, I think that's my prerogative.* Still, the Brutish felt it was too dangerous for her to return to France.

Buckmaster sent her a reply that read: *Dearest Doodles, What a wonder you are! I know you could learn radio in no time; I know the boys would love to have you in the field; I know all about all the things you could do, and it is only because I honestly believe that the Gestapo would also know it in about a fortnight that I say no, dearest Doodles, no.*

King George VI personally awarded her an MBE in July 1943, a lesser award than the OBE for which she had been turned down the previous year. Because she was still working as a field agent, the award was not publicly announced. Virginia was called back to London by Christmas, where she worked with Vera Atkins, briefing agents about to go to France or debriefing those who were returning. But she desperately wanted to return to France to continue her work there.

Since the U.S. was now involved in the war, Virginia began talking to a representative of the U.S. Office of Strategic Services (OSS), equivalent to the SOE, in January 1944. She received the transfer to OSS with the rank of second lieutenant. At her request, OSS returned her to Brittany, France, on March 21, 1944, with the code name *Diane* and the alias of *Marcelle Montagne*.

OSS had to send her back to France on a fast British torpedo boat, as she could not parachute because of her wooden leg. She was set ashore in a wooden dingy, landing on the Cotentin Peninsula, carrying the radio transmitter she would use to communicate with London. With her was SOE agent, Peter Harratt, code name *Arami.* They sometimes presented themselves to locals as a peasant couple.

She joined up with the Resistance in the Haute-Loire region in central France with a mission to use her leadership skills to help organize sabotage groups. She called in air drops of supplies, weapons, and money as needed, and she also served as her own radio operator. Her identity card listed her as *Mlle. Marcelle Montagne* and identified her as a social worker. During six months, she organized, armed, and trained three units of about 300 men.

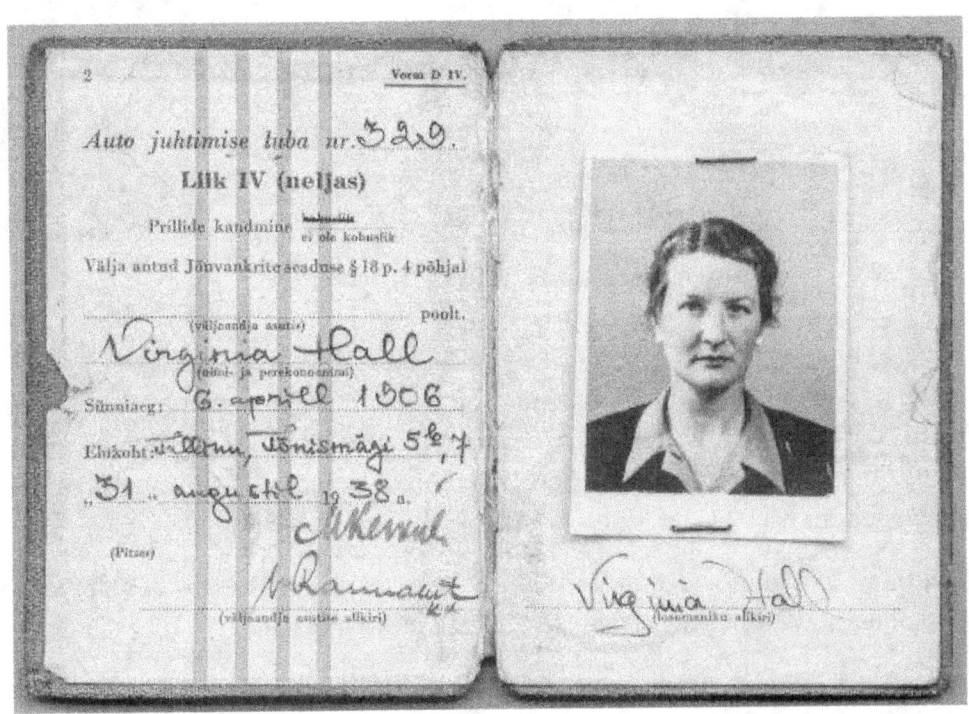

**OSS identity card, it was held at OSS headquarters for her safety.**

She sent the following report to OSS headquarters about her settlement in her new post: ...*I contacted farmer Eugene Lopinat, who found a little house for me with one room, no water or electricity, located by the side of the road at the other end of the village from his farmhouse. He arranged for me to eat and work at his own house. Here, I cooked for the farmer, his old mother, and the hired hand over an open fire as there was no stove in the house. I took his cows to pasture and, in the process, found several good fields for parachute drops...* One wonders if her wealthy family knew about her living conditions for most of the war years.

Virginia disguised herself as an old peasant woman and had the veneer of her lovely teeth ground down to fit the role. Her brown hair was dyed dingy gray-black and held in place by a hairpin. She padded her slim figure with full skirts and oversized woolen blouses with a big sweater or coat. She regularly took milk to the town market, where she could mix with the German soldiers and listen to their conversations to obtain information she could send to OSS.

Virginia made friends with a few prostitutes who spent time with the German soldiers, and they would pass on valuable information they overheard. She was said to escape detection by the Nazis because she was an expert in disguises and could rapidly change her appearance.

**Virginia pretending to be a goat herder's wife**

To evade the Gestapo looking for her radio transmission location, she moved on to the Nievre area, where she lived in the attic of the local police officer. She moved houses again and began taking care of a group of goats pastured alongside a busy road where she could watch the movement of German troops; information which she sent back to the Allies.

She moved twice more to avoid detection. In mid-July, she was sent back to the Haute-Loire area with orders to set up another new Resistance group called the Heckler Circuit.

Working alone, Virginia distributed money and supplies, located new drop zones and safe houses for downed pilots and new agents. She sent and received wireless messages and went out many nights to wait for the air drops. Between July 14 and August 14, 1944, she coded and sent 37 messages to London about

German troop movements. One of those messages was the very important first notice that the German General Staff was moving from Lyons to Le Puy.

Her French counterpart, Edmund Lebrat, had rigged a temporary generator with a bicycle to power her radio. Finally, she had security and logistical support from a group of about 30 Resistance members who assisted her in retrieving the supplies and sorting them for delivery to various fighting groups.

In addition to the usual tasks, she recruited and trained men for the Heckler Circuit and did some training for the Saint Circuit.

Virginia trained the new Resistance fighters in guerrilla warfare techniques. After Allied forces landed near Marseille and began a pincer move with the D-Day forces against the retreating Germans, she began organizing, training, and arming three battalions of fighters to harass and slow the fleeing Germans. In 1944, in an OSS report, Virginia's team was credited with blowing up four bridges, derailing several freight trains, taking down multiple telephone lines, killing 150 German soldiers, and capturing 500 more. At the peak, over 1,500 people worked in Virginia's Heckler Circuit.

The OSS ordered Virginia to relocate close to the Swiss border, and it was there that she met the man who would later become her husband, Second Lieutenant Paul Goillot. He was of French heritage and had parachuted into France on September 4, 1944, to join her unit. They formed a bond almost immediately, and when they received leave, they went to the now-liberated Paris for a holiday. It was Virginia's first fun trip since the beginning of the war. Paul saw his mother and sister in Paris, whom he had not seen in nine years; his father had recently died. After their trip, she returned to London on September 25, 1944.

A colleague in the OSS, William T. Hornaday II, met her in London and later said: *She sometimes carried her detachable brass foot in a pack or leg bag. I have always had the greatest respect for that lady. Her courage knew no bounds.*

In London, Virginia met Lt. Rene Julian Defourneaux for the first time. He had earlier replaced her at Cosne-sur-Loire after she moved to a new location. He said of their first meeting: *I was completely surprised at her appearance. She looked like an old lady with dark gray hair, dressed entirely in black, and with a black pearl choker, which relieved to a degree the severity of her appearance. However, she still looked like a queen. She exuded authority, an eighteenth-century dowager, though she was only thirty-eight at the time. She had just returned from France, and there was an alertness about her as if she were still watching for an ambush. I had the feeling that she was so iron-willed that the Germans didn't really want to tangle with her!* He noted that she carried an umbrella that doubled as a cane. He would meet her again several years later and say that she looked years younger and that her face was then bright and cheerful.

Virginia had one last wartime OSS assignment in Europe. She was sent to Italy to prepare to go undercover in Austria with the code name *Camille*. She took her future husband, Paul, with her to prepare for the infiltration into Austria. However, The German forces collapsed sooner than expected. OSS canceled the operation, and they returned to Paris.

**Virginia**

**Virginia, after the war**

After returning to the U.S. on September 26, 1945, Virginia became one of the first women to work at what would eventually become the Special Activities Division of the soon-to-be-established successor agency to the OSS, the Central Intelligence Agency (CIA). President Truman signed Executive Order 9621, dissolving the OSS in the fall of 1945. It would be another two years until the official creation of the CIA on September 18, 1947.

Virginia received recognition from the U.S. when, by the direction of President Harry Truman, she became the only woman and the only civilian to be awarded the U.S. Military Distinguished Service Cross for her activities during World War II. It was awarded for: *Extraordinary heroism in connection with military operations against the enemy.* President Truman wrote in the Citation: *Miss Hall displayed rare courage, perseverance, and ingenuity; her efforts contributed materially to the successful operations of the Resistance Forces in support of the Allied Expeditionary Forces in the liberation of France.*

The President wanted the award ceremony held at the White House, but Virginia refused and requested a quiet presentation service with only her mother in attendance. She asked her Paris commander to reject President Truman's offer of a White House presentation. On June 13, 1945, he wrote: *Miss Virginia Hall...feels very strongly that she should not receive any publicity or any announcement as to her award...She states she is still operational and most anxious to get busy. Any publicity would preclude her going on any operation.* Virginial returned to the U.S. in September 1945 and, at her request, the founder of OSS, General William Donovan, officially presented the award on September 27, 1945, in the privacy of his office three days before the OSS was disbanded.

**Virginia received the Distinguished Service Cross from the founder of OSS, General William Donovan.**

**Female version of the MBE Medal, awarded by King George VI in 1943.**

Virginia received the Croix de Guerre from France on March 16, 1946, to honor her work during the occupation. She had earlier been honored with the MBE from England.

After the war, Virginia worked in Europe on contract as a "field representative" for what would become the Central Intelligence Agency (CIA). She spent all of 1947 traveling between Italy, Switzerland, and France. As she had when she worked for the SOE, she used journalism as her cover. But her real work was to collect economic, financial, and political intelligence on postwar Europe. She also reported on the Communist movements growing in Italy and Yugoslavia.

When she returned to the U.S., she joined the National Committee for Free Europe, an intelligence front organization under the Radio Free Europe program.

After the war, Paul Goillot remained with OSS as it transitioned into the CIA. Despite her mother's strenuous objections, Virginia and Paul began living together in New York City in 1950. Her mother considered him too uneducated for her daughter. They were frequent party hosts and friends said that: *she was an elegant hostess with an enigmatic air and a voguish home in the European style, Paul poured the drinks and cracked jokes.*

Although Paul was born and spent his first few years in France, his family emigrated to the U.S. when he was only eight. When Paul was 22, his parents moved back to France in 1936, but Paul decided to remain in Manhattan. When the U.S. entered the war, he joined the Office of Strategic Services (OSS). He was sent to France where he set up Resistance units and trained fighters alongside Virginia.

Virginia officially joined the CIA in Washington, DC, on December 3, 1951, when she was 45. She and Paul left New York City and moved to the Washinton D.C. area. She was initially assigned to the Office of Policy Coordination of the French paramilitary desk, making $8,360 annually. Virginia was the first female paramilitary officer in the CIA. She handled routine desk duties but slowly worked through various departments.

In 1954, she reached a staff level due to her vast experience in the field during the war. In May 1955, she transferred back to the Balkans desk and was given the task of planning a major operation as a case officer. Her passport had stamps from France, Switzerland, Germany, and Britain before returning to CIA headquarters.

She joined the Career Staff in 1956, becoming one of the first women to achieve that position, which designated the most valued officers. Unfortunately, her supervisor was transferred, and she was sidelined to a desk job for the next several years. One can only imagine the frustration that must have caused this incredibly competent and experienced field agent.

A CIA colleague, Angus Thuermer, described Virginia as a: *gung-ho lady left over from OSS days overseas during her time at the CIA. Young women in sweater sets and pearls listened raptly to Virginia Hall gas with muscular paramilitary officers who would stop by her desk to tell war stories. She was elegant, her dark brown hair coiled on top of her head with a yellow pencil tucked into the bun. She was always jolly when she was around the old boys. She was a presence!*

On April 15, 1957, Virginia and Paul gathered a few friends and were finally married in a small ceremony. She informed her family, including her unhappy mother, a few weeks later. Virginia was 51 years old. She changed her name at work and officially moved into Paul's home in Chevy Chase, Maryland. They had lived together before but kept separate apartments and homes.

After the excitement of his work with the Resistance, Paul was dissatisfied with his work at the CIA and took early retirement. He opened a restaurant, but the business did not do well, and he became Virginia's househusband. Virginia's niece, Lorna Catling, described Paul as a funny roughneck with a great sense of humor and being very good for Virginia. He was shorter than she and eight years younger, but the niece thought they were happy and had a lot of fun together.

Another colleague at the CIA, E. Howard Hunt, said about her later years at the Agency: *I was distressed at the insensitive treatment accorded to Virginia Hall toward the end of her career. No one knew what to do with her, and she was usually at a lonely desk in war plans or the paramilitary offices. She was a sort of embarrassment to the noncombat CIA types, by which I mean bureaucrats. Her experience and abilities were never properly utilized. At the very least, she should have been lecturing to trainees at the CIA indoctrination "farm" near Williamsburg. She was out of the loop, the proverbial round peg, and through no fault of her own. I really ached over her and her low-level status.* (Hunt and G. Gordon Liddy later plotted the Watergate burglaries and other clandestine operations for the Nixon administration.)

Virginia retired from the CIA in 1966 at the mandatory retirement age of 60, taking a disability retirement due to the many health issues from her wartime service. In a declassified CIA report about her career from the Archives, the Agency admitted that her officers felt she had been sidelined -shunted into backwater accounts. They felt that she had so much experience that she overshadowed her male colleagues, who felt threatened by her, and that her experience and abilities were never properly utilized.

After retirement, Virginia and her husband moved to a farm in Barnesville, Maryland, where she enjoyed gardening and birdwatching, two avid hobbies. Her niece said she planted thousands of bulbs that she and Paul enjoyed each spring and summer. Paul was an excellent chef and did most of the cooking, a skill Virginia had never mastered and had little interest in learning. They had five pet French poodles and several cats who were farm "mice catchers."

**Virginia and Paul at their retirement home, photo courtesy of Lorna Catling**

Virginia learned to work on a handloom and often wove her own cloth. She also made goat cheese from the farm's goat milk and shared it with neighbors. Unfortunately, Paul suffered a stroke that significantly changed his personality and made their lives more difficult. She also suffered from health problems associated with her work during the war. She moved to the Shady Grove Adventist Hospital in Rockville, Maryland, where she died on July 8, 1982. Virginia was buried at Druid Ridge Cemetery in Pikesville, Maryland. Paul lived another five years.

At the time of her death, almost no one knew of her incredible service during WWII. For many years, the story of her involvement and that of practically all the other female SOE agents during the war remained classified. Unfortunately, after the war ended, the British and U.S. governments decided to classify almost all the accomplishments of the women who worked behind enemy lines during WWII.

The SOE and OSS shared what the male spies had done with the public, and those men were hailed as heroes. Many of the women died without their families knowing anything about their valuable – and dangerous -- service. Even after declassification in the late 1960s to the mid-1970s, Virginia rarely talked about the war and took most of her personal stories to her grave.

(On a side note, when the author requested data on one of the SOE women in early 2023, she was told by the British National Archives that the file was still classified. When she asked why, the response was, "Would you like us to declassify it?" to which she replied a definite "yes!" They did declassify it in late 2023. That was the first of seven files she was able to get declassified.)

In 1988, the Military Intelligence Corps added Virginia's name to its Hall of Fame wall. Today, a CIA training facility for recruits is named *The Virginia Hall Expeditionary Center*, and both The International Spy Museum in Washington, D.C., and The CIA Museum in Langley, VA, have displays honoring Virginia.

In December 2006, during the 100th anniversary year of Virginia's birth, the French and British ambassadors to the United States publicly commemorated her service. The CIA Museum had commissioned a painting of Virginia, which was unveiled that year at the French Ambassador's residence in Washington, D.C. The museum shared the following info from their exhibit, *The Art of Intelligence*. Ambassador, Jean-David Levitte read a letter from French President Jacques Chirac given to Virginia's family. He wrote: *Virginia Hall is a true hero of the French Resistance. On behalf of her comrades in the Resistance, French combatants, and all of France, I want to tell her family and friends that France will never forget this American friend who risked her life to serve our country.* The British ambassador presented Virginia's family with a certificate to accompany the Member of the British Empire (MBE) medal, which Virginia had received from King George VI in 1943.

Several books have been written about Virginia and two movies have been released covering her life: *A Woman of No Importance* in 2017 (based on the book of the same name) and *A Call to Spy* in 2020.

**Shown here is a portrait of Virginia commissioned by the CIA Museum. The painting portrays Virginia in the early morning hours, radioing London from an old barn near Le Chambon sur Lignon to request supplies and personnel. Power for her radio was provided by a discarded bicycle rigged to turn an electric generator, the clever invention of one of her captains, Edmund Lebrat. Proto of painting from the CIA Museum**

**Chapter 4**

# Madeleine Damerment

November 11, 1917 – September 13, 1944

Code Name: Solange, Alias: Martine Dussautoy

Madeleine Léonie Zoé Damerment's story is one of courage and sacrifice. Despite the brevity of her mission, her dedication to the Resistance movement and her selflessness in aiding others speak volumes about her character. The official historian of the SOE, M.R.D. Foot later described Madeleine in his book, *SOE in France* as: *brave, young, and gentle Madeleine Damerment…*

Madeleine had one of the shortest missions of any SOE agents sent to France, as the Germans captured her when her parachute set down behind German lines, She was brutally interrogated and executed only seven months later.

**Madeleine, as a young woman**

When the Germans invaded France in May 1940, Madeleine and her family supported the efforts of the Resistance movement. Madeleine was only 22 when she began working with Capt. Michael Trotobas as a civilian assistant in the SOE's Farmer Circuit. Her actions demonstrated her commitment to the cause of freedom and her willingness to put herself in harm's way.

Her work in assisting downed Allied pilots and facilitating their escape through the perilous PAT escape route to Spain highlighted her personal bravery. Despite the dangers and uncertainties, Madeleine remained resolute in her mission to defy oppression. Her actions exemplify the spirit of resistance and solidarity that defined the struggle against German tyranny during WWII.

A SOE report spoke to her efforts during the early days of WWII : *Her work was precarious as she was constantly out in the streets with British airmen and prisoners of war and had (she) been caught in this sort of thing, (the) death penalty would have been unavoidable.*

In early 1941, the Gestapo arrested her parents but later released them. It was a warning to Madeleine that she was being watched. She moved out of her family home and began staying in safe houses. The arrest of her parents and the constant threat of surveillance underscore the high stakes of resistance work during wartime. Despite the danger, Madeleine persisted in her mission to aid the Allies.

Harold Cole, an SOE agent turned traitor, betrayed those working with her in the escape network in 1942. The betrayal of her escape network by Cole must have been a devastating blow to Madeleine and all those involved. She was forced to flee her homeland to evade capture.

Madeleine's journey to freedom was fraught with adversity, The Spanish police arrested her when she crossed the border and put her in jail because she did not have legal entry documents. She became ill while in jail, and the British Consul arranged for her release and hospitalization. When her health improved, the Consul arranged for her to travel to England.

After arriving in London, she volunteered to return to France to work as an SOE agent. In her eyes, the decision to continue her work as an SOE agent was simply the natural course of action, driven by a desire to contribute to the ongoing struggle against the German occupation.

The SOE received a favorable report on her previous work within the French Resistance: *Damerment worked for us for a short time during 1940-1941 and had to be sent out of France as we feared she was being sought by the Gestapo. She did very good work for us, and we have no objection to her being employed for SOE.* An SOE agent in France presumably wrote the memo, although it was not signed.

When the SOE interviewer asked why she offered to return to the known dangers in France, the interviewer reported: *She was modest and looked upon the whole matter as something very natural. She said many French women are willing to do this sort of work every day.*

**Capt. Michael Trotobas**

Madeleine was not aware of it, but the man she had assisted as a civilian courier before she left France, the former SOE Circuit leader Trotobas, was killed on November 27, 1943. The Gestapo had captured fellow SOE agent, Francois Reeve. During torture, he gave up the address of Trotobas's safe house. The SOE's guidance to captured agents who experienced torture was to try to remain silent for at least 48 hours to allow their colleagues and associates time to relocate. Reeve broke down in less than two hours. Germans broke into the safe house at 7:00 AM the next morning, giving Trotobas no time to escape.

Trotobas killed the leader of the German troops and wounded another German before being killed himself. The Germans fatally shot his assistant and lover, Denise Gilman. Denise was an employee of the SOE but was never officially an SOE agent as she did not go through the SOE training in England. The tragic fate of Capt. Michael Trotobas and Denise underscores the relentless brutality faced by those involved in the resistance against Nazi occupation. The SOE instructed Madeleine to join FANY, as they did with most female SOE agents. They gave her the code name *Solange* and a cover story that included the alias, *Martine Dussautoy.* Initially, the SOE planned to train her to be a radio operator, but she did very poorly in those courses, so they added supplemental training to improve her previous experience as a courier.

Madeleine went through the various training modules in England and Scotland. After her weapons training, her report read: *She has improved and is now a fair shot with pistol and carbine but is lacking in aggressiveness. Very good at explosives and demolitions, both in theoretical and practical work...she is extremely keen and makes up splendid charges (explosive charges).*

The Commandant of SOE training, Captain Parson, reported the following comments about Madeleine: *I have not a great deal of faith in this student. Although she has a good brain, she is too temperamental and not sufficiently impersonal for a first-class student. She has, however, a good sense of humour and a certain amount of charm and intelligence.*

After spending Christmas of 1943 in England, Madeleine reported to the training facility at Beaulieu, Hampshire, for a warfare course on clandestine techniques. The "House on the Shore" was a finishing school for SOE agents. The house sat on 24 acres with private boat access overlooking the Solent River in an exclusive and protected corner of southern England. It was one of more than a dozen large homes scattered around the country that the SOE used for training.

Major Wedgewood, an instructor at the House on the Shore, wrote a mixed report on Madeleine: *She is quite intelligent, practical, shrewd, quick, and resourceful. She has imagination and cunning. Although she seemed keen, she did not always work very hard. Her character is strong, but she is self-centered, rather irresponsible, and sometimes impatient and turbulent. She is temperamental, and personal relationships play a considerable part in her life. She seemed deeply attached to friends. Her personality is vivacious, and she can be pleasant when she wants to be, but she is also inclined to be malicious and sullen when she does not get her own way. She has a strong sense of humour. The student should make a satisfactory subordinate under a strong leader, but she would need careful handling.* (Many women who participated in the SOE training received harsh evaluations from their instructors, who frequently criticized them for their "feminine" traits.)

Despite mixed training reports, Madeleine was approved as an agent after completing her final parachute course. After a delay of several days due to weather, Madeleine, radio operator Capt. Lionel Lee, code name *Mechanic*, and Circuit leader Major Joseph Antoine Antelme, code name *Antoine*, were dropped by parachute near Chartres on the night of February 28-29, 1944.

The presence of experienced agents like Antelme underscores the seriousness of their mission and the importance of their task. Antelme was on his third war assignment in France. They expected to be met by SOE agents from the Phono Circuit, who were to help them acclimate to the area and local Circuit operations.

The team was to establish a new Circuit named Bricklayer, which would be a sub-Circuit to the large Physician Circuit. Their mission would involve building crucial relationships with various Resistance groups, a task that required diplomacy and trust-building, identifying safe houses for agents and others in need of safety and scouting locations for airdrops of agents and supplies would be additional responsibilities.

Unfortunately, Madeleine never had the opportunity to use her training, as her world changed dramatically when her team parachuted into a welcoming committee of German soldiers. Unknown to the agents or the SOE, the Germans had captured radio operators Frank Pickersgill, Ken Macalister, and Noor Inayat Khan and obtained their radio passcodes.

Using the stolen passcodes, the Germans sent fake messages to the SOE, giving them coordinates to drop the incoming agents. Because the agents' correct radio codes were used, London was not suspicious. Unfortunately, the SOE later sent an additional ten SOE agents into German hands before the deception was discovered.

When Madeleine and her fellow agents reached the ground, the waiting German soldiers captured them. The captives were taken to Avenue Foch, the Gestapo Paris Headquarters, for interrogation. Antelme and Lee refused to talk despite being tortured and the two men were sent to a concentration camp. In accordance with Adolf Hitler's "Nacht und Nebel" directive to make irregular combatants "disappear," Antelme and Lee, along with 17 other male SOE officers were executed at the Gross-Rosen concentration camp in Germany in July or August 1944.

**Circuit leader France Antelme**

**Radio Operator Lionel Lee**

Madeleine was also tortured during her interrogation in Paris. The harrowing experiences endured by Madeleine and other captured SOE agents at the hands of the Gestapo illustrate the brutality and injustice of war. Their steadfast refusal to provide any useful information despite torture demonstrates their courage and resilience in the face of unimaginable suffering. After getting no helpful information from her, the Gestapo sent Madeleine to Fresnes Prison and then on to Karlsruhe Prison, a civilian prison for women, on May 13, 1944. Also at Karlsruhe Prison were six additional female SOE agents: Yolande Beekman, Andrée Borrel, Vera Leigh, Éliane Plewman, Diana Rowden, and Odette Sansom.

Later interviews and records attest to the fact that the women were supposed to stay in the civilian section for only two weeks, but the Gestapo continued to extend the time. The warden of the civilian women's section, Fraulein Becker, complained that the SOE women should not be in her area. Vera Atkins, head of the SOE's recruitment section for France, later commented that had the warden kept silent, the women might have remained safe in Karlsruhe until the war's end.

Madeleine remained at Karlsruhe for four months before the Gestapo transferred her and three other SOE female agents to Dachau Concentration Camp on September 12, 1944. A German guard, Christian Ott, who accompanied the women to Dachau, later wrote a report that said that he had personally seen a telegram from the Reich Security Head Office (RSHA) signed by Dr. Ernst Kaltenbrunner, head of the RSHA saying the four women were to be "executed at Dachau." As the war was turning against the Germans, they seemed intent on killing as many of their prisoners as possible. They wanted to erase all traces of their brutal treatment of the captives.

Following is one of the reports of how the four women were executed: *Early on the morning of September 13, 1944, the camp guards took four SOE agents, Éliane Plewman, Yolande Beekman, Noor Inayat Khan, and Madeleine Damerment, to a yard adjacent to the crematorium, where the camp commandant read their death sentences. They were forced to kneel, and a guard shot each of them in the head. Each woman's body was put in the crematorium, and their ashes were scattered somewhere in the camp.*

Other reports say that the women were "cruelly executed," and some statements said they were beaten before being killed. Madeleine was 26 years old.

**Éliane Plewman, Yolande Beekman, Madeleine Damerment, & Noor Inayat Khan**

In recognition of Madeleine's ultimate sacrifice, she was posthumously awarded the French Legion of Honor, Croix de Guerre, and the Médaille de la Résistance. The British awarded her the King's Commendation for Brave Conduct while enduring torture by the Germans without divulging any SOE secrets.

Madeleine's name is recorded on the Brookwood Memorial in Surrey, England, and, as one of the SOE agents who died for the liberation of France, she is listed on the "Roll of Honor" on the Valençay SOE Memorial in the town of Valençay, France. There is also a plaque on the south wall of the crematorium at the former Dachau concentration camp, where the four SOE agents are remembered.

```
COPY                           From: Sq/Officer V.M.Atkins,
                                     J.A.G's Branch,
                                     War Crimes Section,
                                     Headquarters,
                                     BRITISH ARMY OF THE RHINE.

                                     25 Jun 46

J/G D.Gorrum,
M.O.1 (S.P.)
The War Office
----------------

Subject:  Mrs. E.S.Plewman F.A.N.Y.
          Miss Madeleine Dammerment @ Dussautoy, F.A.N.Y.
          Mrs. Y.E.M.Beekman nee Unternahrer,
          S/O W.A.A.F. 9922.
------------------------------------------------------------

          It has now been established that the above-named were executed
in the camp of Dachau in the early hours of 13 Sep. 44, probably by
shooting.  The full circumstances surrounding this case are not yet
known but the fact that they were killed in the early hours of 13 Sep.
44 has been definitely established.  I assume that you will take the
usual casualty action.

          The facts, as far as they are known, are as follows:

          Eliane Plewman was captured at Marseilles on or about 23
March 44:  it is believed that she passed through the prison of Les
Beaumettes in Marseilles and was then sent to Fresnes near Paris.
Ylande Unternahrer was captured near St.Quentin on or about 15 Jan 44
and she was first taken to 84 Avenue Foch, Paris and later transferred
to Fesnes.  Madeleine Dammerment was captured on landing on 29 Feb 44
near Chartres.  I believe she was taken to Fresnes straight away.

          On 12 May 44, they left Fresnes Prison together with Odette
Sansom, who has returned safely, and Diana Rowden, Nora Inayat-Khan,
Vera Leigh and Andree Borrel, who were killed at Natzweiler on 6 Jul 44.
They went straight to Karlsruhe where they were put into the civilian
jail for women and they remained there until the early hours of 12 Sep 44.
I have seen the following witnesses apart from Mrs.Odette Sansom in
connection with their stay in Karlsruhe:-
```

The letter on the next page was sent by Vera Atkins, head of the SOE recruitment section for France, to a J/G. D. Gorrum at the War Office on June 25, 1946, after Vera determined the fate of three of the above women:

# Chapter 5

# Nancy Wake - "The White Mouse"

August 30, 1912 – August 7, 2011

Code Name: Helene Alias: Madame Andree Joubert

Everyone agreed that Nancy Wake was a force to be reckoned with during WWII, including the Gestapo. She was one of the most decorated women of the war. She was also frequently described differently than most of the female agents, one example was: *flamboyant, she was strapping, voluptuous, and she radiated sexuality.* A male SOE agent she remained friends with for life, Francis Cammaerts, said of her: *Nancy Wake, the sexiest woman it has ever been my privilege and pleasure to know.* He later asked Nancy to become the godmother to his children.

She had a unique background that allowed her to effectively assist the Resistance movement in France and later to work with the Resistance as an agent for the SOE. Since she had immersed herself in French society and culture from her early days working as a journalist in Paris, she had an extensive set of friends and associates who would later help her with her work during the German occupation.

In 1912, Nancy Grace Agusta Wake was born in Wellington, New Zealand, as the fifth child of Charles Augustus Wake and Ella Rosieur Wake. She carried Māori blood from her grandmother, who was believed to have been the first Māori woman to marry a European. When Nancy was two years old, her family moved to Sydney, Australia.

Nancy's father soon abandoned the family and returned to New Zealand, and as far as is known, she never saw him again. She and her five brothers and sisters remained in Sydney and were raised by their mother. Nancy's early life was marked by hardship and instability, with the absence of her father and the challenges she faced at home. Growing up in such circumstances, she developed a determination to forge her own path and create a different future for herself. Despite the religious fervor of her mother, Nancy sought a life beyond the confines of her upbringing, driven by a desire for independence.

When Nancy was fifteen, she and her mother took a trip back to New Zealand to see Nancy's grandmother and many other relatives who Nancy had never met. She immediately fell in love with her warm-hearted grandmother, who was so different from her mother. Her trip to New Zealand provided her with a glimpse of a different world, one filled with warmth and acceptance, particularly from her grandmother. Nancy loved the opportunity to travel and was determined to do more of it.

The rift between Nancy and her mother, served as a catalyst for Nancy's departure from home when she was only 16. Despite the challenges she faced as a young woman without formal training or experience, Nancy's determination led her to a job as a nurse's aide in the mining town of Mudgee. Here, she honed her medical skills, learning how to set broken bones, clean wounds, treat a fever, and treat minor medical problems. These skills would later serve her well during WWII.

**Nancy, at 19 years of age**

Nancy's return to Sydney when she was 18 marked a significant milestone in her journey toward independence and self-determination. Fueled by her indomitable spirit and a fierce determination to live life on her own terms, she embarked on a path that would eventually lead her to become an important figure in the resistance against Nazi occupation during WWII. This period of her life was characterized by a growing commitment to forge her own destiny.

Nancy was frequently described as being a "tough cookie." Her rough manner and colorful language were emblematic of her boldness, reflecting a determination to live life on her own terms. Nancy raucous laugh and her zest for life remained constant throughout her long life.

The unexpected gift of 200 pounds from her aunt Hinamoa provided Nancy with a newfound sense of freedom and opportunity. In 1930, such a sum was a significant amount of money, equivalent to $4,685.00 U.S. in 2023. This financial support empowered Nancy to pursue her dreams, unencumbered by financial constraints.

Nancy knew what she wanted to do – travel! When the money arrived in 1932, she booked herself a one-way, first-class ticket on an outbound ship, *Aorangi II*, for 100 pounds. When built in 1924, the ship was the world's largest and fastest motor ship. After landing in Vancouver, she took a train to New York City, where she stayed for three weeks before taking another ship to London.

When she arrived in London, her money was nearly gone. Despite her financial challenges, she enrolled at Queen's College to study journalism. Though journalism may not have been her passion, Nancy understood the necessity of finding a means to support herself and pursued her studies with determination.

Upon graduating from her journalism course, Nancy's audacity propelled her into the world of newspapers. Her willingness to bend the truth in her job interview, coupled with her adeptness at shorthand, secured her a position at Hearst newspapers. She later said she lied to the interviewer by saying she had extensive experience in Egypt and could even read and write Arabic. He asked her to write something in Arabic, so she wrote his quote in shorthand. He didn't know the difference and hired her. She said: *I wanted the job, gospel truth, I was so good at that kind of thing, I should have been a criminal.*

In 1933, at 21 years of age, she was posted to Paris as a Hearst European correspondent, receiving pay for each article that they agreed to print.

Nancy's ability to quickly adapt to her surroundings and immerse herself in the local culture speaks volumes about her resourcefulness and openness to new experiences. Despite never having taken a French lesson, she embraced the challenge of learning the language with enthusiasm, picking up the basics from colleagues and friends. Within a short time, her French improved to the point that tourists were asking her for directions and suggestions, thinking she was a local.

Nancy's willingness to learn not only extended to mastering the language but also to familiarizing herself with the local customs and expressions, including colorful curse words and phrases. Her genuine immersion in the culture enriched her experiences and endeared her to those around her.

Nancy had grown into an attractive and sensual woman, which also endeared her to the French. She soon purchased the ultimate accessory for a French woman, a dog she named "Picon." He became her constant companion, and apart from her work during the war, he remained with her until he died.

Her paper sent Nancy to Marseille, and she was on the street on October 9, 1934, when Vlado Chernozemski, a member of the pro-Bulgarian Revolutionary Organization killed King Alexander of Yugoslavia as he came ashore from his ship. The French Foreign Minister, Louis Barthou, a part of the welcoming committee, was also shot and killed. The police killed the assassin. The events of the day provided Nancy with her first big story.

The following year, she and four fellow journalists went to Vienna. She witnessed German soldiers attacking Jewish stores, whipping the store owners, setting fire to their store goods, and other terrible mistreatment of Jews. Nancy's eyewitness account provided a chilling picture of the rising tide of anti-Semitic violence and oppression in Europe.

She later said: *What I will never forget is being in the main square of Vienna, and seeing these poor unfortunate Jews tied to those massive wheels that were rolled along, with them turning over and over as the wheels turned, and even as they went these huge fat Brown Shirts were beating them with whips! I couldn't believe, just couldn't believe what I was seeing! Right there and then, I made up my mind that if ever I got the chance, I would do everything in my power to hurt them, to damage the Nazis and everything they stood for!*

During a later trip to Berlin for the newspaper, she witnessed a public speech by Hitler and the almost trance like reaction from the crowd. That experience solidified her reaction against him and the Nazis. She experienced such a loathing for the German soldiers that later she gladly worked with the Resistance during WWII.

Nancy loved the vibrant social life in Paris, characterized by her immersion in the local party scene and her integration into the expatriate community. Her dedication to perfecting her French, including mastering slang and colloquialisms, allowed her to fully embrace the Parisian lifestyle and feel a deep connection to the city and its culture.

As she mingled with local journalists, intellectuals, and friends from both American and French backgrounds, Nancy found herself at the center of a dynamic and diverse social circle. Despite the looming shadow of political tensions Nancy continued enjoying the present moment and embracing the vibrant energy of Parisian life.

The influx of primarily Jewish refugees fleeing Germany served as a stark reminder of the growing threat posed by Nazi aggression. Despite the mounting evidence of Germany's rearmament and expansionist ambitions, England and France remained largely silent, unwilling, or unable to confront the escalating crisis. Nancy's experiences in Paris during this turbulent time offer a compelling glimpse into the complexities of life in pre-war Europe, where the allure of cosmopolitan glamour coexisted with the ominous changes in German politics and the rapid rearmament of their army and air force.

In 1937, Nancy met Henri Edmond Fiocca, a wealthy French steel industrialist in Marseille. Henri was 14 years older and was known as a playboy, but once they began seeing each other the affair became serious. Years later, she said of Henri: *I was madly attracted to him; he was charming, he made me laugh all the time, and he was dead sexy.* After a long and very happy courtship, they agreed to marry.

Nancy wanted to return to England to visit a health spa before the wedding in August 1939. Although she had long expected it, she was surprised on September 3, to learn that Britain had declared war on Germany. In a testament to her resourcefulness, she swiftly arranged passage on the only available boat—a commercial car ferry. At the request of the parents, she collected the daughter of a French friend, and they embarked on the journey back to Marseille.

Fearing that Henri would soon be called up to the army to defend France, they moved up their wedding and were married in Marseille on November 30, 1939. They had a smaller-than-planned but still lavish wedding reception. Nancy wore an expensive black silk wedding gown with a pink underskirt. She loved to stand out from the crowd. She was always mischievous and later wrote that she spiked the punch served to Henri's conservative father and extended family, which made for a much happier reception. His father and sister never accepted Nancy as a part of the family, but they did have a good time on their wedding night.

Henri asked her to find and furnish an apartment, and she took one that overlooked the city and the port. Nancy's life with Henri opened up a world of luxury and extravagance that was previously beyond her reach. Embracing her newfound status as a well-to-do socialite, Nancy enjoyed the opportunity to enjoy the finer things in life. With Henri's support, she spared no expense in furnishing their apartment with exquisite furniture, luxurious rugs, and elegant chandeliers, creating a home that exuded opulence and refinement.

Nancy also embraced the culinary arts, taking cooking lessons with the renowned chef, Pepe Caillat. Her newfound passion for gourmet cooking allowed her to entertain guests in style, impressing them with her culinary skills and impeccable taste. Henri often took her to Cannes for a few days, and they both enjoyed visiting the casinos and meeting with friends. Nancy didn't like to gamble, but she loved spending time with people she met there.

They were living in Marseille when Germany invaded France. Many French had deluded themselves into believing that the Maginot Line and their 800,000-troop army would protect them from invasion by Germany. The Maginot Line was a defensive line composed of forts, blockhouses, and pillboxes, connected by trenches and tunnels. Minefields stretched for over 130 miles from the Alps in the south to the Ardennes Forest in the North. Their army was the largest military in Europe. Unfortunately, the outdated fortifications and the poorly prepared army were no match for the German invasion.

Barely a month after their marriage, Henri received word before Christmas that he was called to the military and needed to report in early 1940. Henri went to the military to get his uniforms and gear, only to discover that the equipment and clothing were outdated or in poor working order. They had no matching uniforms, so his coat was too big and his trousers too small. His gun didn't work, and they didn't have the correct ammunition for it. His division was clearly not prepared for war. Henri went to his tailor and had custom-made uniforms crafted for him.

Beginning in April 1940, all of France watched closely as the German army quickly marched through Denmark, Norway, Luxembourg, the Netherlands, and Belgium, coming ever closer to France.

To feel useful, Nancy volunteered as an ambulance driver. With Henri's support, she commandeered one of his business trucks and transformed it into an improvised ambulance. A mechanic who worked for Henri taught her to drive – in one day. Nancy set out for a location along the Rhine River. Her meager training as a nurse's aide back in Australia came in handy, although she had never seen such severe injuries before.

In the absence of military transportation, Nancy's improvised ambulance often carried civilians alongside her patients, despite her wild driving style regularly causing anxiety among her passengers. She drove many Jews out of immediate danger, as well as others fleeing into France ahead of the German advance. When they were ordered to evacuate, Nancy continued her rescue missions, defying danger to rescue wounded soldiers and civilians from the chaos of battle.

Soon after Henri reported for duty, the French government collapsed. Germany occupied Paris on June 14, 1940. On June 22, 1940, the Second Armistice at Compiègne was signed by France and Germany. The collapse of the French government and the subsequent surrender to Germany marked a dark and tumultuous period in French history. In the wake of these events, many high-ranking French officers, including Brigadier General Charles de Gaulle, left for England after the government surrendered to Germany. De Gaulle established the Free French operation, essentially a French government in exile. Henri's unit was disbanded, and he returned to Marseille.

Over 330,000 Allied troops were evacuated from the beaches of Dunkirk. The operation commenced after large numbers of Belgian, British, and French troops were cut off and surrounded by German troops during the six-week Battle of France. The aftermath of the Dunkirk evacuation left thousands of foreign troops and civilians stranded in Europe, seeking refuge from the advancing German forces.

The division of France following the armistice agreement between France and Germany resulted in the establishment of the Vichy regime, which governed the southern part of the country. Led by Marshal Philippe Pétain, the Vichy government collaborated with the occupying German forces and implemented policies favorable to the Nazi regime. Headquartered in the small city of Vichy, the government imposed its authority over local town governments, requiring them to comply with German directives.

This collaboration extended to the local police force, many of whom joined a pro-German group known as the Milice. Operating with the authority of the Vichy government, the Milice became notorious for their brutality and ruthlessness, often employing tactics reminiscent of the Gestapo.

With much of France occupied by the enemy, those fleeing the conflict gravitated towards the "Free Zone" of Southern France, where the new Vichy government retained some degree of control. Among the areas in the Free Zone, the coastal region around Marseille emerged as a particularly attractive destination for refugees.

Perceived as relatively safe compared to other parts of France, Marseille offered a strategic location that facilitated escape routes and access to international waters. The port city's proximity to the Mediterranean Sea made it a vital hub for those seeking passage to neutral or Allied territories. Marseille became a melting pot of diverse nationalities and cultures as refugees from across Europe converged in the city, sharing a common goal of finding safety and sanctuary amidst the chaos of war.

Henri tried to do business as usual, and Nancy began to use their money to buy as many essential food items as possible. She also purchased a considerable stockpile of French wine. They shared their provisions with friends and others who either didn't have money or were affected by the ever-dwindling food supplies in the markets.

Nancy's involvement with the Resistance began unexpectedly, sparked by a chance encounter with British officer, Captain Ian Garrow in a bar in late 1940. She learned that Garrow and around 200 other British officers were interned in Fort St Jean just outside Marseille. He described the conditions at the Fortress as very poor, with little food or warm clothing provided by the French military authorities.

Nancy offered to get him food and cigarettes the following day. He showed up with two fellow officers, and she "adopted" them and began giving them regular supplies. She became especially fond of Garrow, who would later become involved in smuggling people out of France. That chance encounter with Garrow was the beginning of Nancy's personal resistance to Hitler and his war.

Deeply affected by Garrow's account, Nancy soon forged a friendship with him. Nancy's decision to aid Garrow and his fellow prisoners marked the beginning of her clandestine resistance to the Nazis, as she risked her safety and freedom to aid the officers.

Nancy and her husband helped the officers as much as they could by providing food, occasional housing, and money to the officers. By Christmas 1940, Nancy was taking messages from the officers to Resistance groups in Cannes. Nancy's dual life as a supportive wife and as a busy courier for the Resistance movement epitomizes her remarkable courage. She was traveling as a respectable married French woman, but there would have been severe consequences if the Germans had caught her.

As Nancy carried more messages between different Resistance groups, she learned important lessons in how to avoid German checkpoints, how to act and what to say if she was stopped and questioned, and how to find safe places to stay. Although she didn't realize it then, it was perfect training for later when she would work in a more professional capacity for the British SOE.

Nancy and Henri's acquisition and distribution of radios to various Resistance groups represented a critical lifeline for communication and intelligence gathering during the war. Prior to obtaining reliable radios, they had to rely on fragmented information from individuals passing through their area, limiting their access to vital updates on the progress of the war.

The dangers inherent in listening to radios during the early stages of the war cannot be overstated. The German occupiers strictly controlled access to information, and individuals caught listening to forbidden broadcasts faced severe consequences. As the war progressed, the Germans caused them to "disappear" into jails or concentration camps. Later, they could face a firing squad.

Nancy was heartened by the courage and resilience of the British when the German Luftwaffe began the blitz bombing of London. From July to November of 1940, the Luftwaffe targeted naval defenses, airfields, and radar facilities. The British planes trying to defend the country were outnumbered four-to-one. During September, the German planes focused on London, beginning fifty-seven successive nights of bombing the heart of the city. Despite those horrendous attacks, the British resolve and morale held up, which inspired Nancy to do all she could to hurt the Germans occupying France.

Through most of 1940 and into 1941, Nancy worked as a courier. She and Henri spent more time and effort working to support the Resistance and help endangered locals and Allied troops escape from German-occupied areas. They sometimes allowed those hiding from the Germans to stay in their chalet in Nevache until someone could safely smuggle them out of France. Nevache is a small village set in the Alps close to the border with Italy. Italy was allied with Germany, so great care had to be taken to hide the Allied soldiers and others needing sanctuary.

The Vichy government decreed in October 1940 that all foreign-born Jews were illegals and were to be sent to concentration camps. With the collaboration of local authorities, thousands of Jewish individuals were rounded up and detained in French concentration camps. The government in Paris passed the same decree, and, in a short time, over 30,000 Jews were in French concentration camps. Those numbers grew as French-born Jews were also incarcerated. Recognizing the grave danger facing these innocent men, women, and children, Nancy helped them avoid arrests and escape over the mountains to Spain.

Count Albert-Marie Edmond Guérisse's was a Belgian Resistance member who organized French and Belgian escape routes for downed Allied pilots. His contribution to the Resistance was undeniably significant. Under the alias "Pat O'Leary," he played a pivotal role in establishing the PAT escape network, which would become one of the most vital lifelines for Allied service members seeking to evade capture by the enemy. Nancy never liked Guérisse, finding him arrogant and self-important.

Nancy's friend, Captain Garrow was arrested by Vichy police in October 1941 and later interned at the Mauzac (Dordogne) concentration camp. A former British soldier, Harold Cole, who had worked with the Resistance for a short time, betrayed Garrow. After the Resistance caught Cole stealing money intended for use by the PAT escape efforts, he went to the Germans and gave up the names of more than 50 Resistance members who were later executed. Cole's betrayal represents an egregious act of treachery. Cole's decision to collaborate with the enemy, motivated by personal gain and self-preservation, led to the arrest and execution of many loyal Resistance members. Garrow escaped the firing squad only because he was an Allied officer.

Nancy Wake with Captain Ian Garrow (centre) and husband, Henri Fiocca (right).
Christopher Long 'Secret Papers' Portrait Magazine

**Count Albert-Marie Edmond Guérisse took over leadership of the PAT escape route.**

Nancy set up a fake identity that she was Garrow's cousin, which allowed her to visit him in prison regularly. She paid a camp guard to help Garrow escape from Mauzac prison in December 1942. He crossed the Pyrenees to the British Consulate in Barcelona. Garrow returned to England at the beginning of February 1943 and was awarded the Distinguished Service Order (DSO) on May 4 of the same year.

The PAT line furnished guides and safe houses to enable downed British pilots, Jews, and others at-risk for Nazi arrest to flee to safety. It is estimated that over 7000 people escaped over the PAT Line and other similar routes set up later. MI9 in Britain provided the funding to keep the Lines operational.

Nancy had a friend who was a doctor in a small village. He was also the mayor of the town, which enabled him to forge identity papers for Nancy and many of those trying to escape France. Those papers were invaluable in helping to shield the escapees from the Germans as the individuals moved about the Free Zone. Despite being stopped and questioned numerous times, Nancy could usually talk herself out of any situation. When asked whether she was ever afraid during the war, Nancy later said, *I really don't know why, but it never really gripped me like that. I always felt that one way or another, I would be alright.*

Nancy was jubilant when the Japanese bombed Pearl Harbor on December 7, 1941, with Germany declaring war on the U.S. on December 11. Finally, she thought, the U.S. would join the fight and turn the tide. She saw hope for Europe for the first time since the Germans invaded France.

The Nazis were determined to stamp out the strong Resistance groups operating in the southern part of the country. The Gestapo was also talking about "The White Mouse," a woman they knew had been hiding and moving Jews, soldiers, and others to the escape routes. They called Nancy "The White Mouse" for her ability to remain hidden and elude capture. By the fall of 1942, the Gestapo put her at the top of their most wanted list, offering a five-million-franc bounty ($835,221 in 2023 U.S. dollars) for her capture, dead or alive.

**Nancy & Henri**

In September of 1942, the Germans demanded that 350,000 French men and women volunteer to work in German industries. Either they would volunteer, or they would be conscripted. Many men fled to the countryside or the forests to hide from the conscription. Many of those men would eventually join the rural Resistance groups known collectively as the Maquis. On November 11, 1942, the Germans marched into southern France in large numbers.

The Germans were steadily closing in on Nancy's location in Marseille, and she felt they were watching her night and day. To elude capture by the local police working with the Germans or by the Germans themselves, she and Henri put together a scheme for her to leave France. She secretly packed her clothes and shipped them to Madrid, Spain, which was still a free country. Nancy walked out of the house in November 1942, pretending to be going shopping, and never returned. She lived with friends or in safe houses until she could safely leave the country. She didn't know it, but she would never see Henri again.

Nancy's first three attempts to escape France by hiking over the Pyrenees Mountains were cut short by bad winter weather. During another attempt, the Germans arrested her after she tried to flee a train being searched by the Germans. They didn't realize who she was, and after some rough interrogation, they accused her of being a prostitute from Lourdes, who was working with the Maquis. They accused her of being involved in blowing up a cinema the night before, although she had nothing to do with it.

The Germans kept her jailed in Toulouse for four days with no food and little water and subjected her to frequent questioning. On the fourth day, Guérisse, (under the pseudonym of Patrick O'Leary) convinced the police that Nancy was his mistress. He showed fake papers saying he was a member of Malice, the political paramilitary organization made up of mostly ex-police and military forces created with German help by the Vichy regime to help fight against the French Resistance. They released Nancy with apologies.

The head of the Malice was a Frenchman named Joseph Darnand, a man who had sworn personal allegiance to Hitler. He recruited what Nancy called the "scum of the earth, but the scum of that scum." Darnand recruited 30,000 members, and their daily brutality was often more feared than that of the Gestapo.

A few days later, Guérisse helped ten prisoners escape from the same jail. The group hid in an apartment rented by a friend of the Maquis until they could be safely smuggled out of France. The men stayed in the apartment with Nancy and her friend, Francoise. Nancy later remembered that the days were filled with laughter, despite the danger of being discovered. She always managed to find fun and laughter, no matter how difficult the situation.

The group split up, and Nancy traveled by train toward the mountains, preparing to try to escape again. With her were an English military officer, a French Resistance radio operator, a New Zealand airman, and a former French policeman. The train began to slow, and they heard that German soldiers were boarding to check for Maquis fighters.

As her small group jumped from the train and headed toward the top of the hill through the nearby vineyards the soldiers began shooting at them with machine guns. After reaching the hilltop, Nancy discovered she had dropped her purse during her escape. It contained numerous pieces of valuable jewelry she planned to take out of the country, including her 3-carat diamond engagement ring. Other jewelry also had sentimental and financial value.

The group was afraid to get back on a train, so they began the long cold walk to the safety of Toulouse and Francoise's apartment. To avoid detection, they hid during the day and walked at night. They had no food with them, and Nancy once raided a farmer's field and found some lettuce buried in the dirt. She offered to share it with the others, but they refused, so she ate it herself, dirt and all.

It took them eight days to reach the town of Canet-Plage. When they arrived at a safe house, they were hungry and filthy and had scabies from sleeping in sheep barns along the way. They couldn't risk going to a doctor, so they were all scrubbed with a stiff brush and disinfectant. Nancy said it was an agonizing but effective treatment. They got themselves cleaned up and took the train back to Toulouse.

As Nancy was again trying to plan her escape across the Pyrenees Mountains to Spain., Guérisse agreed to meet with a recruit to the Maquis movement. The man turned out to be a Gestapo agent, Roger le Neveu - German Spy Agent 47, and he arrested Guérisse, who was sent to the Dachau Concentration Camp. Fortunately, he survived the internment.

Nancy finally escaped France, but the trip over the mountains involved travel covered by loose coal in the back of a coal truck, followed by over 48 hours of mountain walking. She and her companions had to make it out and through a danger zone of about 30 kilometers (18.6 miles) within Spain, patrolled by the Germans, before finally reaching free Spanish soil. Unfortunately, they were captured by the Spanish police at their last safe house and jailed for three days. The British Consul paid 1000 pounds to the court and a gold bracelet to the judge to get her and the others with her released.

Nancy finally reached Barcelona, where she remained for a few days before getting Spanish papers that allowed her to travel. She and others who had escaped from France traveled by train to Madrid, then by ship to Gibraltar. After two weeks, they were put on a small boat that traveled in a 70-ship convoy to Scotland, then by train to London. On June 17, 1943, many months after kissing Henri goodbye and leaving Marseille, she reached her destination.

Henri had stayed behind in Marseille to arrange for someone to run his family business and protect his father and sister. He thought his position would protect him. Unfortunately, that was not the case. The Gestapo arrested, tortured, and executed him on October 16, 1943. Nancy knew nothing of his capture and would not learn of his death until the end of the war.

She expected Henri would soon join her in London, so she rented a flat and furnished it as best she could. Months went by with no word from him. To keep herself busy, she volunteered at the canteen of the Combined Operations Headquarters. Finding that the organization consisted of mainly society women who didn't understand the idea of work, she soon dropped out of the group.

She tried to sign up to work for the Free French Movement headed by Charles De Gaulle, but they turned her down, thinking she was a spy for the British. The British and the Free French group had different ideas about how to fight the Germans, and the relations between the two groups continued to worsen.

The SOE approached her, and it was apparent they knew of her past work with the Resistance. Vera Atkins, the senior female recruiter in the SOE, described Nancy as "An Australian Bombshell." Like almost all the female agents who would work for the SOE, Nancy joined the benignly named organization, the First Aid Nursing Yeomanly (FANY). This arrangement was to hide the real reason the women would be out of touch from their family or friends as they worked in their assigned areas around Europe or northern Africa. Nancy began the intense 16-week spy training program.

During her SOE training, she met Maurice Buckmaster, the man in charge of the "F" Section. He previously lived in France as a tutor and, like her, loved all things French. He also worked as a journalist for the French newspaper *Le Matin* in Paris, so the two had much in common. The training courses were split into several segments taught in different regions of England and Scotland, and the trainees moved every few weeks to new training facilities.

Nancy loved the training in Scotland because she felt it was much more practical. She thought the new knowledge and experience would make her more effective when she returned to France. This training was followed by parachuting, a necessary skill for most of the SOE agents being sent to German-occupied areas in Europe.

Nancy described the best part of the training: *"The students weren't just taught how to blow up a train, for example, they were taught how to do so to cause maximum damage to the enemy. The best thing, they were told, was to derail a goods train in a cutting – meaning that it would then be blocking the line for a long time, as it couldn't be easily moved aside. If it were a German troop train though, better do it on high ground as more Germans would be killed as it tumbled down the slopes. If there were possibly French on board though, they were to be more careful. Steer by the star of causing as much damage to the Germans as possible, and as little to the natives. Victory lay partly in having the local population fully behind them, not in killing them."*

She had lessons in Morse code for radio work; how to disable a car with sugar, sand, or honey in the gas tank; and where best to place explosives to blow up a bridge. She felt that the explosive training was the most valuable for her, as that was something she had never done in her prior work with the Maquis.

During her training, she met Violette Szabo, another woman who would be remembered for her work with the SOE. Nancy said Violette was "very beautiful and great fun" and they became friends. Unfortunately, Violette would later be captured by the Germans and executed at the Ravensbrück concentration camp.

Nancy's ratings were high throughout the grueling schedule of classes, with excellent marks for her shooting skills and fieldcraft. A note on her record said: *She put the men to shame by her cheerful spirit and strength of character.* She was also said to be able to outdrink any man in the training group. Nancy's code name was *Helene* in London and *Andree* for the French people she would meet. All agents were required to choose a verse or slogan to identify themselves when communicating directly with London. Many chose a line from a poem, song, or biblical phase – but not Nancy. In keeping with her always playing for a laugh, she picked a ribald poem:

> *She stood right there,*
>
> *In the moonlight fair,*
>
> *And the moon shone*
>
> *Through her nightie,*
>
> *It lit right on,*
>
> *The nipple of her tit,*
>
> *Oh, Jesus Christ Almighty!*

After finishing her training, Nancy was flown from England in a Liberator B-24 and parachuted back into France on April 30, 1944, five weeks before D-Day. The SOE assigned Nancy to be a courier working with Major John Farmer, code name *Hubert,* who would be the team leader, and radio operator Denis Rake, better known as "Denden." Rake refused to parachute, so he traveled by boat and was to meet them in France.

A funny incident happened just as Denden was preparing to leave for France. The SOE office had secured a large amount of money to send with him for the Maquis fighters. It was brought to the office and when they dumped it out to put it in his large case, they discovered it was brand new bills, not the used bills normally sent with agents. It was believed that new bills would arouse the suspicions of the Germans.

Buckmaster gathered the office staff, and they spent several hours "dirtying" the bills with oil and grease. They rumpled them up, put rubber bands around large stacks of bills, walked on them, and scribbled on them to muck them up. When they were thought to be dirty enough, Denden put them in his bag and headed out for the boat that would take him to France.

Nancy in her wartime uniform. Nancy was one of the few SOE female agents who received her "parachute wings" (seen here on her uniform) while still working for the SOE. Others had to wait many years and often had to push the government to get the "wings."

Nancy and Farmer landed in rugged country near the town of Montlucon. They would be working as a freelance team living with the Maquis as they moved from mission to mission. The team's purpose was to be a liaison between London and the Maquis (rural French) Resistance groups. They worked in an area close to the large Stationer Circuit, led by Maurice Southgate. Southgate was not happy about the arrangement and thought they would siphon off some of his Maquis fighters.

Unbeknownst by them, their contact had been arrested. They hid for a week in a safe house and then finally went to deliver messages they had from SOE headquarters to Southgate.

Southgate's description of meeting Nancy for the first time: *I was exhausted, tired – and I didn't have time! It was six weeks before D-Day...Anyway, I went out to see these two bodies, Nancy Fiocca and John Farmer, who'd been put up for the night in a farm. And who did I see but Nancy Fiocca – that I didn't know before – she was the most beautiful girl that I think I've ever seen. With a dozen men around her. She was washing her feet in a small little white, enameled basin, with a blue border round it. She could only wash about two toes at a time, the basin was so small! There she was with this little basin and water on a half-cut tree; she was bare from her head to the waist. Titties all over the place – but by God, they were beautiful; they held! – but what was amazing was that by the side of her, she had a Sten gun, ready to shoot.* That incident says so much about Nancy, a woman who was direct, brave, who loved life and wanted others to enjoy it too.

Without access to the arrested contact, Nancy and Farmer went in search of the Maquis themselves. After two days of searching, they finally located a group high up in the hills and began the process of earning their trust. Initially, the Maquis leadership failed to understand what help a single man or woman could provide.

Nancy and Farmer had a rocky relationship throughout their time together. After the war, he said of her: *She was a woman of very high energy. Incredibly high energy, but she also had very clear ideas of how she wanted everything to be done, and how she wanted everything done was HER way. She was a great agent, there was no doubt about that, but not always the easiest to get on with...*

Unfortunately, Denden was still missing, and since he was their radio operator, they had no way to contact London to find out where he was. After being moved from one Maquis group to another, Denden finally showed up. He was an openly gay man and had been with a new lover for the past few weeks, much to Nancy's and Farmer's irritation. They soon learned that Rake thought all men were gay; they just didn't know it yet. His belief caused a few misunderstandings with some of the Maquis fighters and with some families who would hide them periodically.

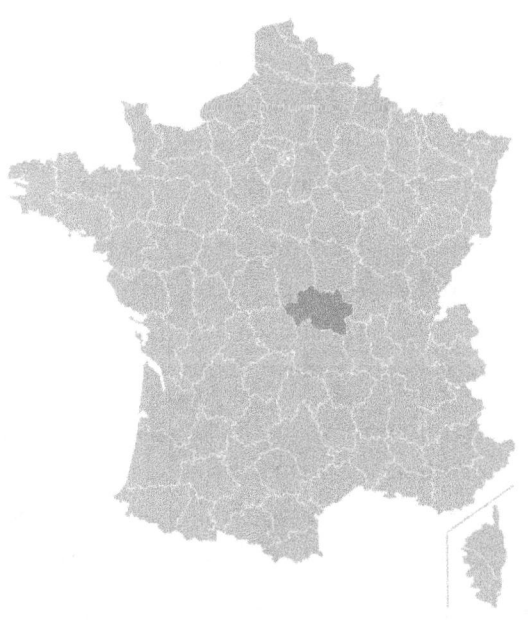

**Area where Nancy worked for the SOE**

Nancy's initial duties were to select the locations where material (mostly guns and explosives) and money would be dropped by parachute from Allied planes. After Nancy retrieved the items from the drop, she would allocate them among the Maquis, including pay to individual fighters. She also kept a list of physical targets the Maquis was to destroy before the Allies invasion, including communication lines, railroad lines and engines, and gun factories.

Once they had radio communication, the weapons and other supplies from London began arriving regularly at assigned parachute drop areas. Those supplies finally brought the Maquis around and they slowly began to work with the Circuit, eventually taking orders about which train to hit, which supply depot to bomb, etc. They would eventually even take orders from Nancy. During WWII, the SOE would drop over 650 tons of explosives, 723,000 hand grenades, and 500,000 small arms to be used by Resistance groups.

**A sample of items in a weapons case dropped to the SOE Circuits**

Since most of the men had never used the newly received types of guns before, Nancy and her two fellow SOE agents trained the fighters to clean, assemble, and fire the new weapons. Since she carried the cash that London sent to the groups, she began paying for food and other necessities that the fighters had previously been stealing from the local population. The cash infusion encouraged the locals to support the Maquis instead of turning against them.

Unlike most Circuit members, Nancy, Farmer, and Denden lived with the Maquis in whatever field or forest camp they set up. For security reasons, the group moved every 3-4 days, being ever fearful of being found by the Germans. Approximately 22,000 Germans were garrisoned in the region, with some 7,000 Maquis working every night to undermine them.

The Maquis in their area were loosely scattered between 17 groups, each with a different leader. Nancy worked with all of them to provide communications, support, and supplies, and she sometimes participated in operations to destroy bridges and railroad tracks. Nancy later wrote that she loved being actively involved, as she found it exciting and gave her a sense of satisfaction to do direct damage to the Germans.

Nancy felt that the secret to her being accepted and respected by the men was that she could outdrink almost all of them. Farmer later wrote: *She had a remarkably high tolerance for alcohol, and the men respected that. It was absolutely incredible, I had never seen anyone drink like that ever, and I don't think the Maquis had either. We just couldn't work out where it all went, and how she could stay conscious! In my long life, it remains one of the most extraordinary things I have seen.*

Nancy was unorthodox in many ways. After the war, she said that she had often flirted her way out of difficult situations with German troops. She said: *A little powder and a little drink on the way, and I'd pass their (German) posts and wink and say, Do you want to search me? God, what a flirtatious little bastard I was.*

Nancy and her SOE group tried to convince the Maquis to avoid direct conflict with the Germans in hopes that the fighters could remain strong as they worked toward what came to be known as the D-Day invasion. They wanted a maximum Resistance effort behind the German lines, as the Allies would come ashore and begin attacking the Germans from the sea.

The Maquis did not always listen to the advice from the SOE agents, and in May 1944, one leader of the local Maquis, a man known as Gaspard, gathered 3000 fighters to stage a major attack against the Germans. The Germans learned of the plan, and on June 20, they beat him to the punch and did a counterattack with 5,000 soldiers, forcing the Maquis to flee after taking heavy casualties. Nancy and her team retreated with the Maquis on a three-day walk to the village of Saint-Santin.

Nancy had a group of 40-80 Maquis who helped with her responsibilities, and they moved from camp to camp together. The men set out the torches each night a plane was scheduled to drop weapons and supplies, then they helped unpack and sort all the items. The guns had to be cleaned and assembled before they could be given out to fighters. Her men would also help transport the supplies to the various Maquis groups scattered around her area. With the Maquis, Nancy fought against repeated German assaults, and she went on sabotage sorties with the men and took part in lightening quick attacks on German troops.

Her relationship with Farmer, the leader she had entered France with, was never warm and friendly, but it slowly improved. After the war, he told the *Daily Telegraph* newspaper: *She was magnificent and incredibly popular with the Maquis. The partisans, many of them pretty tough boys, worshipped her and were all a little scared of her. They could never really get used to calling a spade a spade. After one night in August, she became almost a legend in Maquis country. The Germans found our camp and attacked.*

*There were only eighty of us. With a small Colt automatic, which she always carried, and a bazooka, Nancy led a section of ten men against a German machine-gun post, knocked it out, and led the section safely back.*

During one engagement, approximately 22,000 German troops attacked an area where over 5,000 Maquis fighters were encamped on a plateau at Chaudes-Aigues. Nancy and her SOE team were stationed nearby. Nancy exhibited extraordinary courage, reportedly driving back and forth across the battlefield in a van to deliver ammunition and weapons to the Maquis fighters.

The Maquis displayed remarkable strategic skill in their efforts to repel the Germans. Their successful maneuvers allowed the team to evade capture and eventually regroup at a farmhouse. Exhausted from the intense combat and continuous operations over the preceding 36 hours, Nancy and her group finally managed to get some rest.

The Maquis had prepared an escape route by placing flat stones just below the surface of a rapidly flowing river, hiding the rocks with dead tree trunks. When they had to flee the area, they released the tree trunks and just walked across the river on top of the stones. The Germans thought the river current was too strong for anyone to cross, so they didn't bother searching along the riverbank.

The SOE agents and different segments of the Maquis headed south, crossed mountains, and then gradually proceeded north. It took them four days to reach the village of Saint-Santin. They had easily evaded the German infantry, but German planes constantly circled the countryside looking for them. Nancy later reported that on their escape route, they came across an earlier battlefield, where many dead German soldiers were left behind. She was horrified at the number of dead Mongols (who had been recruited by the Germans as mercenaries) who had been allowed to slaughter and plunder the dead. She said that the pockets of the dead Mongols were filled with money, gold, and cut-off fingers with rings still on them.

Nancy wrote in her memoir that during the retreat, the group's radio operator, Denden, was afraid German patrols would capture them, and he buried his radio and destroyed his radio codes. After they escaped and regrouped, they desperately needed a radio to be in touch with London. Nancy took on one of her most dangerous missions. She borrowed a bicycle, rode it to Chateauroux, and located an SOE radio operator, but he refused to send a message to SOE Headquarters for fear that she was working with the Germans.

Nancy finally found a Free France operator who agreed to send a message to Algiers, where an operator could send it on to the SOE headquarters in London. Her message updated London on their situation and requested an airdrop of a new radio/codes for her group. She bicycled back to Saint-Santin, traveling almost 250 miles in 72 hours. Nancy reported no interference by the Germans during that ride, although she had passed through many checkpoints. Her excuse for being out was the huge cache of fruits and vegetables she had in her bike basket The Germans allowed her to pass, thinking she was a housewife out shopping.

When Nancy arrived back at the safe house, her feet and legs were in painful spasm, and her thighs were rubbed raw and bleeding. A local doctor treated her, and she slept for three days. It took another couple of days before she could sit, stand, or walk without pain. After the war when asked what she was most proud of doing during the war, she said, "The bike ride."

A new radio operator affiliated with the Free French parachuted to their drop zone 48 hours later, ensuring their communication with London for the remainder of the war. It was one of the few times Nancy knew of the Free French working willingly with the SOE.

Nancy's group seldom spent more than two nights in any location. One morning they awakened from sleep to the sound of gunfire not far away. They quickly abandoned the farmhouse they were sleeping in and soon learned that 6000 Germans were approaching their location. They had 200 experienced Maquis with the three SOE agents, plus 30 new recruits.

Several bazookas had been airdropped to them the night before, but no one had training on how to use them. Two American arms experts had parachuted in with the bazookas, but they didn't speak French. Some of the recruits volunteered to try to use the bazookas, so Nancy ran from gun to gun, translating from the American soldiers to the raw recruits. Somehow, they managed to knock out several German gun positions with the bazookas and slow the approach of the German soldiers. Fortunately, some Free French troops began harassing the Germans from the rear, allowing Nancy's group to escape and move to a safe location.

Nancy later wrote about the type of sabotage they often did after D-Day: *We mostly did these ambushes when we could find the time. We used to pick a nice high point so we could see, and then we'd place these bombs covered with plants by the side of the road, and we'd run a long piece of string from the trigger up to our hiding place and then wait for the convoy.... At the precise moment when the first bombs exploded, the Maquis would themselves explode into action. Often from both sides of the road, they would pour sustained fire on the stunned Germans who, superbly trained, would be rallying to return fire as quickly as they could.*

Even as she was firing her own Sten gun or hurling grenades for good measure, she would shake her head in wonder at the ferocity of the partisans fighting for their homeland. The action never lasted too long, as the Maquis fighters knew that the Germans could quickly call up reinforcements and surround their small group. The fighting would stop as quickly as it had started.

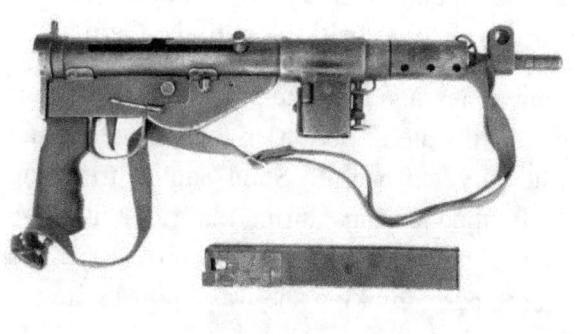

Sten Gun

One day, Nancy and the Maquis she was traveling with freed three women being held by another Maquis group. The Maquis thought the women were spies and had been sexually abusing them. Nancy interrogated the three and agreed that one was a German spy. The other two French women were released, but she demanded that the third woman be executed, as they were always on the move and they had no way to hold her. Before being shot, the woman admitted her allegiance to Hitler and that she had been supplying information to the Germans. At first, the men were hesitant to shoot a woman, but Nancy said if they were afraid, she would do it herself. The men finally agreed and the woman was shot by a firing squad so no one would know who had fired the fatal bullet. Nancy later said she had no remorse about the woman's death.

As D-Day approached, hundreds of new French recruits streamed into their area. Many had been waiting to see how the war would play out between the Nazis and the Allied forces – as they wanted to be on the winning side.

D-Day finally arrived on June 6, 1944, and over 7000 ships participated in the deadly landings on the shores of Normandy. More than 800 planes dropped paratroopers just behind the German lines at 2:00 AM. Following the paratroop planes, bombers dropped over 15,000 tons at selected German targets. At 6:30 AM, more than 155,000 troops began leaving the ships and heading to the shore, suffering terrible losses before pushing the Germans back from the headlands.

As planned, the Maquis and many other Resistance groups stepped up their operations by blowing up designated targets. They hit telephone and telegraph lines, bridges, railroad lines, and factories.

After the invasion, the Allied planes began dropping more supplies and guns each night in Nancy's area. They were preparing for the secondary Allied landing on the southern coast, called Operation Dragoon, which occurred on August 15, 1944. Nancy was frantic, trying to keep up with outfitting everyone and staying connected with the many Maquis groups that had sprung up as the French began to see the tide turning against the Nazis.

The German troops began departing France quickly following the Allies' Operation Dragoon, carried out by the Seventh U.S. Army. This invasion force was significantly bolstered by three U.S. divisions, an airborne strike force, and a contingent of French commandos. They landed on the coast between Toulon and Cannes. This operation brought over 85,000 Allied soldiers and 12,000 vehicles into southern France. The overwhelming Allied presence prompted a swift German retreat from the region.

Nancy's group played a big part in helping to corral the German soldiers remaining in southern France. One operation was close to the small village of Cosne-d'Allier, beside the Allier River. The German soldiers fleeing from the approaching Allied army could use two essential bridges in the town. One was for vehicle and pedestrian traffic, and the other was a railroad bridge. Her SOE team knew they had to destroy both bridges to keep the Germans from escaping and regrouping back in Germany. She went with Henri Tardivat, John Alsop, and a small group of Spanish fighters and drove right into town.

Nancy's group unloaded their explosives and began attaching them to the first bridge. They warned the townspeople to stay away and then pushed the plunger to blow it up. Next, they targeted the railroad bridge to prevent the Germans from escaping by train. After successfully destroying both bridges, they quickly left the town, accompanied by the cheers and gratitude of the local people.

One of Nancy's favorite men in the OSS was John deKoven Alsop. Alsop served in the U.S. Army and with the Office of Strategic Services in England and France. Alsop was one of the early Americans who parachuted behind enemy lines in France and worked with Resistance fighters to spot enemy airfields, garrisons, factories, and other vital targets.

Another favorite man that Nancy loved working with was Capt. Henri Tardivat, who she felt was one of the most competent Maquis leaders in southern France. She traveled and worked with him for the last several months of the war, and they would remain friends for life.

**French Resistance leader Henri Tardivat**

There was an important munitions warehouse in the Mont Mouchet area, and her Maquis group decided it had to be destroyed because it was a vital resupply depot for the Germans. Despite it being heavily guarded, they hatched a plan to attack it one evening. Fourteen of them participated in the raid, including Nancy. They overpowered the guards, broke in the doors, and set explosive charges inside the building. She reported that she killed one of the guards with her bare hands to prevent him from raising the alarm.

The guard had cut Nancy's arm before she hit him, but a local doctor stitched her up after the operation and may have saved her life. After the war, during a T.V. interview, when the interviewer asked her about the incident, Nancy said: *They'd taught this judo-chop stuff with the flat of the hand at SOE, and I practiced away at it. But this was the only time I used it – whack – and it killed him all right. I was really surprised.*

Nancy's experience contradicted the prevailing military theory that insisted women were incapable of such violent acts. Nancy later said: *I hate wars and violence, but if they come, then I don't see why we women should just wave our men a proud goodbye and then knit them balaclavas.*

After the secondary Allied landing, the Maquis group that Nancy worked with felt more confident about staying in one place, and her group used the abandoned 54-room Chateau de Loyere (Fraqnes) in the Loire Valley as their headquarters. She felt it was a luxury to stay in one place and to sleep in a bed again.

Chateau de Loyere

Nancy, Denis Rake (Denden - the wireless operator), and John Alsop "liberating" a wine cellar.

SOE and Resistance fighters help Nancy celebrate her 32nd birthday, August 30, 1944, at the Chateau

The Allies liberated Paris on August 25, 1944, and the whole country was celebrating, even though thousands of Germans soldiers were still in the area, trying to flee the country before they were killed or captured. In September 1944, the liberation of the city of Vichy was being celebrated and Nancy and her SOE and Maquis friends hurried to participate in the festivities.

At that event, a woman who had worked at the Hotel du Louvre et Paix in Marseille that Nancy and Henri had frequented pushed through the crowd and told Nancy that Henri had been captured and executed after Nancy fled from Marseille two years before. Henri was arrested in May 1943 and died by firing squad five months later, on October 16. Since fleeing France, Nancy had received no word from or about Henri and feared for the worst, but it was especially difficult to hear the news on this day of celebration.

Nancy immediately left for Marseille, and Farmer, Denden, and John Alsop went with her. There she learned the awful truth of how Henri had been betrayed by someone the Resistance thought was a fellow fighter. His torture had been long and terrible once the Germans learned he was the husband of "The White Mouse." They tortured him trying to get him to tell them where she was. In truth, Henri never knew where she was after she left their home.

After Henri was arrested, three female Gestapo agents lived in their apartment, and they took or destroyed all their valuable furniture and art. The bank vault where Henri had left money and valuables for her had been emptied by the Germans before they left the city. Nancy had nothing left of her marriage, and she knew she would have to start over and make a new life now that the war was over.

Nancy said her goodbyes to a few of the Maquis fighters and their leaders, many with whom she had bonded during their difficult days. She drove to Paris with her SOE team, Farmer, and Denden. They and the other SOE teams in France were reunited with Colonel Buckmaster. He was very generous in his praise of their work and promised that England would always be grateful for their sacrifices.

Over the next year, they learned of the many SOE agents who did not survive the war and of others who had survived but been captured by the Germans. They knew those agents would live with the memory of their torture for the rest of their lives. Almost 100 of the 469 men and women SOE agents had been killed, and many more were wounded and or tortured during the war.

Nancy flew back to London on October 16, 1944, but the war dragged on until May 8, 1945, when Germany finally surrendered. On June 8, 1946, London put on a victory parade that was a thrilling finale to the war for Nancy. She and a few SOE female agents participated in the parade, riding four to a jeep.

The crowds were excited and surprised to see a group of women, a few wearing parachute wings. Very few people knew that women had worked as spies during the war, so they didn't know what to make of women who had learned parachuting skills. After working in secret behind enemy lines for so long, the women enjoyed all the attention, especially the cheering from the crowds along the parade route. Nancy later wrote of her thrill at saluting King George VI and the Royal Family opposite Marlborough Gate.

Later, she and a group of SOE officers returned to France with Colonel Buckmaster to meet with the Maquis fighters they could find. It allowed her to say goodbye to many she had worked with during the trying days of the occupation.

Her good friend, Capt. Tardivat, joined the revitalized French army and continued to push the remaining German soldiers out of France. He was seriously injured in a battle, and a leg was amputated. After the final surrender of the Germans, he moved to Paris and began a successful life in business. He married his childhood sweetheart, and they named their daughter after Nancy, who stood as godmother to the baby.

After the war, Colonel Maurice Buckmaster wrote the following job reference letter for Nancy:

*March 1st, 1946*

*To Whom It May Concern*

*Mrs. Nancy Fiocca was employed by my department for about a year, during which time she volunteered for a special and most dangerous mission in enemy occupied territory. She accomplished this task with outstanding success and displayed great qualities of personal bravery, endurance, and determination. Her strong personality gave her the undisputed leadership of a large number of French patriots, whom she organized, with great tact and savoir-faire, to attack the enemy. Under continuous fire from superior forces, she showed exemplary courage.*

*She has much shrewdness and common sense and has accomplished an outstanding important task with unqualified success.*

*Maurice Buckmaster*
*Colonel G.S.*
*(Demobilized July 1945)*

One of her friends from her SOE days helped her get a job at the British Passport Office in Paris. She was grateful for any job, as millions were without work in England. She was especially pleased that the post was back in Paris, a city she loved. After a year in that posting, she was transferred to a similar position in Prague in 1947 for a temporary assignment. She didn't like Prague and was pleased to soon return to Paris.

The British newspaper *The Star* reported the following letter from Nancy the day after she received the George Medal, the highest award Britain gave to non-military personnel:

*Over the phone from Paris today a musically girlish voice asked me: Can you get me an exciting job? I'm so bored...*

*Owner of the voice was Mrs. Nancy Fiocca, wartime heroine who has just been presented with the Geoge Medal for exploits in France in 1944. You would think she had seen her full quota of thrills...But Mrs. Fiocca assured me today she is ready for more. (I'll do anything and go anywhere – to the North Pole if possible._*

*At the moment, grey-eyed, dark-haired Mrs. Fiocca works in the Visa section of the British Embassy. She has a furnished flat, gives dinner parties, and goes to occasional cinemas and theatres. But all the time, she hankers after life with the partisans...*

Nancy left the Passport office in late 1948 and returned to Sydney. To pay for the passage, she worked as a nurse on the Svalbard ocean liner, which carried 899 displaced refugees from Germany to a new life in Australia. Nancy was about to begin a new life, too. The ship arrived in Sydney on January 16, 1949, She arrived to find that Australia knew who she was and what she had done during the war. She was greeted as something of a celebrity, and even her mother, from whom she had been estranged for almost 17 years, welcomed her home.

Nancy was delighted to spend time with her favorite family member, her brother Stanley. He had been captured during the war and held as a prisoner by the Japanese in the infamous Changi Prison Camp. He was still recovering from his mistreatment at the camp, but they spent weeks talking about their past, the war years, and what they would do in the future.

She ran unsuccessfully for the Federal legislative seat of Barton against the Deputy Prime Minister, Dr. Herbert Vere Evatt. The Liberal Party officers had convinced her that her wartime notoriety would allow her to win the contest, even though she was a total political newcomer and had not lived in Australia for almost 17 years.

Nancy took to campaigning with her usual vigor and enthusiasm and worked the district, knocking on doors and going to every available event to let people get to know her. Unfortunately for Nancy, the Liberal Party was made up of very conservative voters. Many did not appreciate her carefree attitude and very liberated female behavior.

When questioned about her behavior by the local media, she responded: *What did I care about trying to be a lady? After what I had been through, the thought that I would worry about whether or not I wore stockings or a hat was completely ludicrous. If any of them ever wanted to chip me about it, I told them off in the strongest possible language.*

Nancy lost the election but did far better than anyone had expected, especially after the Prime Minister himself came to the district to speak in favor of her opponent. She ran again in the election of 1951 but again was beaten at the polls – but she lost by only 127 votes! After her second defeat, she returned to London in late 1951 in search of a decent job, which was hard to come by for women in Australia at that time.

She was hired to the staff of the Air Ministry in Whitehall, in the department of the Assistant Chief of Air Staff (Intelligence), where she remained for five years. She was delighted that one of her responsibilities was lecturing to the Reserve Units on evasion and how to escape capture by an enemy, and to specialist aircrews who might need those skills in some future military event.

In 1953, she completed the interrogation reports of the POWs held during the Korean War. She was horrified by the Nazi treatment of prisoners during WWII and was disgusted with the atrocities inflicted on prisoners by the Chinese communists and the Koreans during the Korean War.

Nancy was appointed to write the classified Manual of Combat Survival for the Air Ministry. While researching that project in the War Office Archives, she discovered that the War Office had given others credit for dangerous actions that she had undertaken in Marseille. That discovery disillusioned her.

As a "thank you" for her work on the Manual, she was allowed to take a complimentary roundtrip military flight for a visit to Australia. On the return flight home, the aircraft needed some maintenance, and they landed in Libya. They had a few days' layover while waiting for replacement parts to arrive. Also on the plane was a British Army Brigadier. He acquired transport and allowed a few people to go with him to visit WWII military cemeteries in the country. Nancy was impressed by the British cemetery's care but felt the French cemetery's care was a disaster.

Nancy received recognition for her wartime exploits during the publication of a series on wartime heroes written by the London *Daily Express* in 1956. She had earlier agreed to be interviewed by Russell Braddon, who was writing a book about her life. She loved working with him and enjoyed telling him about her many adventures. Braddon published his book: *Nancy Wake: World War Two's Most Rebellious Spy* in 1956. She wrote the following on the front page of the book: *I dedicate this book to everyone in France who helped us, even if it was only by refraining from helping the enemy, for that in itself required courage, but especially I dedicate it to my comrades in the Maquis d'Auvergne.*

The book brought her immediate media attention, and there was great interest in making a movie about her life during the war. Various production companies paid for Nancy to travel to England, France, and even to Los Angeles to look at locations and discuss the possibility of the movie. She was disappointed when all the trips came to naught, and the movie was never made. But she had enjoyed the travels and the opportunity to see a few old friends in France and England.

Nancy re-married in December 1957 to John Forward, a former Flight Lieutenant and bomber pilot. John had been shot down in 1942 and spent the remainder of the war as a POW in Stalag Luft III in Germany. Despite being four years younger than Nancy, he loved to laugh, enjoyed a drink, and proved to be an excellent companion and lover.

Nancy and John moved to Malta, where he had a new station assignment, and they remained there until 1959. They then relocated to Australia, where Nancy settled into a quiet homemaker life while John worked at a textile company. However, Nancy's restless spirit soon found it difficult to remain at home for long.

Nancy again tried her hand at politics by running as a Liberal candidate in the 1966 Federal legislative election. She was again unsuccessful in her campaign, and she and her husband finally retired to Port Macquarie, a small town on the east coast.

The Sydney Morning Herald interviewed Nancy on October 2, 1968, and when asked about why she had worked with the Resistance and the SOE during the war, she said, *"Freedom is the only thing worth living for. While I was doing that work, I used to think that it didn't matter if I died, because without freedom there was no point in living."*

In 1984, a TV production company wanted to do a mini-series about her war years, and she returned to France with two of the writers, where they had a wonderful time as she retraced her steps during the war. She introduced them to many of her local friends and people she had known before and during WWII. It was a memorable visit for her, as she was 72 years old and many of her friends were already gone. She didn't think she would make the trip again.

Nancy published her autobiography, *The White Mouse,* in 1985. She used the name the Nazis called her because of her ability to elude capture during the war. She received considerable media coverage after the book's publication and was frequently interviewed on radio and TV.

**Nancy on the campaign trail in Australia**

**Nancy and her newly published memoir**

The TV mini-series, *Nancy Wake*, was released in Australia in 1987, and later released as *True Colors* in the U.S. To her delight, Nancy made a cameo appearance in the movie. Later, Nancy commented about the series: *The mini-series was well-acted, but in parts it was extremely stupid. At one stage they had me cooking eggs and bacon to feed the men. For goodness's sake, did the Allies parachute me into France to fry eggs and bacon for the men? There wasn't an egg to be had for love nor money, and even if there had been, why would I be frying it when I had men to do that sort of thing?* Unfortunately, Nancy received almost no money for sharing her life story.

After the series, she was interviewed by many domestic and foreign news agencies. Some of her comments during those interviews included: *I have only one thing to say: I killed a lot of Germans, and I am only sorry that I didn't kill more.*

On life after the war: *It's dreadful because you've been so busy and then it all just fizzles out.* Speaking of her time during the war, *I was never afraid. I was too busy to be afraid.*

Her second husband died in 1997, leaving her with few financial resources. Nancy had no children or other family members able to help her, so she sold her medals to support herself. She said: *There was no point in keeping them, I'll probably go to hell, and they'd melt anyway.* Her health was not great, and she had two minor strokes.

Another biography was written about Nancy by Peter Fitzsimons, and it was launched in June 2001 with the title of *Nancy Wake, A Biography of Our Greatest War Heroine*. It was uncertain if Nancy's health would allow her to attend the publication festivities. However, when she heard 300 people would be there, including the Commander of the Australian Defense Forces, Lt. General Peter Cosgrove, she rallied and was in full form for the event.

The new book gave Nancy the financial means to return to England, and she left Australia for the final time in 2001, moving to the Stafford Hotel in St. James' Place in London. It had been a British and American Forces Dining Club during WWII, and she had great memories of the hotel. Nancy always enjoyed a good drink, and she spent most mornings having a gin and tonic while she entertained everyone at the bar with her war stories. The hotel manager had a special chair made for Nancy at the end of the bar, and that area had a plaque saying, "Nancy's Corner."

**Nancy in "her" seat at the bar**

After hearing about Nancy from a hotel patron, Charles, Prince of Wales was reported to have invited her to Buckingham Palace for afternoon tea. She later accompanied the Prince to the London premiere of the film *Charlotte Gray* in 2002, and her appearance was widely covered in the British media. Nancy loved the attention.

During the early days of WWII, Nancy had become friends with an Englishman in Marseille, Bob Hodges. Forty years later, she discovered that Hodges had become the Air Chief Marshall Sir Lewis Hodges, and he personally introduced Nancy to Queen Elizabeth at a garden party at Buckingham Palace, where she and other women who served the country during WWII had their photo taken with the Queen.

**Nancy with Prince Charles**

**Nancy (second from right) and other women heroes from WWII with Queen Elizabeth**

**Nancy and her medals**

After the war, she received the following awards for her service to the Resistance movement in France:

*Ensign Wake's organizing ability, endurance, courage, and complete disregard for her own safety earned her the respect and admiration of all with whom she came in contact. The Maquis troop, most of them rough and difficult to handle, accepted orders from her, and treated her as one of their own male officers. Ensign Wake contributed in a large degree to the success of the groups with which she worked, and it is strongly recommended that she be awarded the George Medal*

**The George Medal from the United Kingdom on July 17, 1945**

The prestigious George Medal was awarded by the British Ambassador, Sir Oliver Harvey, at a cocktail reception at the British Embassy. One of the many incidents he told of her bravery *"During a German attack, due to the arrival by parachute of two American officers to help win the Maquis, Ensign Wake personally took command of a section of ten men whose leader was demoralized. She led them to within point-blank range of the enemy, directed their fire, rescued the two American officers, and withdrew in good order. She showed exceptional courage and coolness in the face of enemy fire.*

In 1966, M.R.D. Foot, the official SOE historian wrote of Nancy: *Her irrepressible, infectious high spirits were a joy to everyone who worked with her.*

The Medal of Freedom with Bronze Palm from the United States, 1947, with a citation concluding:

*Her inspiring leadership, bravery, and exemplary devotion to duty contributed materially to the success of the war effort and merit the praise and recognition of the United States.*

**Left to right, France's Croix de Guerre with two Palms and a Star, The Medaille de la Resistance in 1970.**

**France also honored her with a Chevalier (Knight) of the Legion of Honor from France in 1988**

Nancy moved to the Star and Garter Home for Disabled Ex-Service Men and Women in 2003. She lived out her remaining years there and enjoyed receiving visitors and letters, as she loved it that so many still remembered her. She brightened up in 2006 when she learned that the Duke of Edinburgh would personally be presenting her with the Returned Services Association (RSA) Award from New Zealand. She was taken in a wheelchair to the ceremony and entertained everyone with her war stories.

**AFTER THE PRESENTATION: RNZRSA National President John Campbell (second from left), RNZRSA representative in the UK, Patrick Nolan, and His Royal Highness the Duke of Edinburgh with Nancy Wake surrounded by close friends and surviving colleagues from her World War II SOE days**

*"Wednesday 15 November 2006. This was the morning when HRH Prince Philip, the Duke of Edinburgh, himself an RNZRSA Badge in Gold Holder and Life Member, would make the presentation, on our behalf, of the Badge in Gold to Nancy Wake the "White Mouse." A great occasion. We assembled in a magnificent room at the Palace and waited for the Duke. Nancy was in good form, and she had some of her closest surviving friends from her World War Two days and her Special Operation Executive (SOE) times surrounding her, for what she clearly saw as a special event in her life."*

Nancy died at London's Kingston Hospital from a chest infection on August 7, 2011, just shy of her 99th birthday. Her death was headline news around the world. She requested that her ashes be scattered in central France, and that was done near Montlucon, where she served during much of the war. Most of her medals have been retrieved and are now on display in the Second World War Gallery at the Australian War Memorial in Canberra.

Several books have been written about Nancy's war contributions, and portions of her story are included in many more about the war years. TVNZ (New Zealand) released a docu-drama, *Nancy Wake: The White Mouse*, in 2014.

**Returned Services Association (RSA)**

**The Badge in Gold from New Zealand, 2006**

**A Companion of the Order of Australia, 2004**

When remembering Nancy, nothing encapsulates her spirit quite as much as the words of her fellow Resistance officer and close friend, Henri Tardivat: *She is the most feminine woman I know, until the fighting starts, then she is like five men."* Another Resistance fighter, Martin, was quoted as saying about Nancy, *"One of the hardest fighters the partisans had ever had, a leader, a great organizer, fearless, fantastic, and also Tres Belle.*

# Chapter 6

# Christine Granville

Also known as: Krystyna Skarbek, Maria Skarbek, Krystyna Gettlich, and Karystyna Gizycka

May 1, 1908 – June 15, 1952

Code Name: Madame Marchand    Alias:  Madame Pauline, Jacqueline Armand

Krystyna Skarbek was the first and the longest-serving female agent in SOE, first in Poland and later in France.  She was the most prominent Polish female spy in WWII. She used many names but was generally known within intelligence circles as Christine Granville, although she did not legally take that name until she was midway through her career with the SOE. (The name Christine will be used throughout this chapter)

A former model and beauty queen, Christine used her intellect, looks, and charm to become one of Europe's most successful intelligence agents working behind Nazi lines. Christine's methods were more controversial than those of most female agents, employing a combination of seduction, daring, and cunning to achieve her missions. Her remarkable contributions to the Allied war effort made her a legendary figure in the annals of espionage.

**Christine, as a young woman**

Christine was often celebrated for her irregular warfare missions and daring exploits in Nazi-occupied Poland and France. British spymaster Vera Atkins of the SOE described her as *"very brave, very attractive, but a loner and a law unto herself."* Exaggerated stories of her legion of lovers were passed around inside and outside government circles. She was never embarrassed about enjoying the company of men.

Christine (Maria Krystyna Janina Skarbek) was born on May 1, 1908, in Warsaw, Poland, the daughter of Count Jerzy Skarbek and Stefania Goldfeder Skarbek. Her father was Roman Catholic, but her mother belonged to an assimilated and very wealthy Jewish family. Her mother's substantial dowry paid off her father's debts and allowed them to live comfortably for several years.

Christine and her father were avid outdoors enthusiasts. She began riding horses at an early age. Unlike most women of her time who rode side-saddle, Christine sat astride the saddle. Christine was a serious hiker and became an expert skier who often skied in the Tatra mountains of southern Poland. Christine was said to be a very happy young woman, and photos from throughout her life almost always showed her smiling.

By the late 1920s, the family had exhausted her mother's dowry, and they had to give up the family estate and move to Warsaw. Krystyna's father died in 1930 when she was 22 years old. That same year, she was the runner-up in the *Miss Poland* beauty contest. On April 21, 1930, Christine married a businessman, Gustaw Gettlich, in Warsaw. However, they soon realized they were not compatible and had an amicable divorce.

Christine enjoyed the company of several men before marrying again on November 2, 1938, to Jerzy Gizycki. He was described as brilliant, eccentric, and moody. He had run away from his wealthy family at fourteen and spent years traveling and working around the world, including as a cowboy and gold prospector in the United States. He served briefly as the secretary at the Polish legation in Washington, DC, and worked on the Polish Olympics Committee.

Later in life, Gizycki was a mostly unsuccessful author who spent much time searching for material for his books in Africa and other locations. He loved Africa and returned to various countries on the continent several times. Shortly after their marriage, they moved to Kenya and then to Addis Ababa, the capital of Abyssinia (later Ethiopia). When WWII started, they were determined to help free their country from Nazi occupation. They left Africa and went to London to find a way to be involved in the fight.

Christine and Gizycki had a troubled marriage and separated after arriving in England, but they did not divorce until many years later. She later said about Gizycki, *"He was my Svengali for so many years that he would never believe that I could ever leave him for good."* After their separation, Christine began her work for what would soon become the SOE.

After Germany invaded Poland on September 1, 1939, Christine arranged a meeting with the British Secret Intelligence Service (SIS). She presented a bold plan: she would travel to Budapest, Hungary, which was still a neutral area at the time. From Hungary, Christine proposed to ski over the Tatra Mountains to enter Poland. Once there, she could serve as Britain's eyes on the ground and establish a communication chain to relay intelligence back to London. Her audacious plan demonstrated her determination and resourcefulness, qualities that would make her an invaluable asset to the British intelligence efforts during the war.

Christine had many friends in Poland who she thought would help her gather information about the Nazis and to get the information back to London.

The SIS was desperate for information about Nazi operations in Poland and were impressed with Christine's plan. They hired her as the first female agent to serve in the field, marking the beginning of her long and distinguished career. By the end of World War II, she had become the longest-serving SOE female agent. Her effectiveness in the field was said to be a significant factor in Britain's decision to recruit more female agents, recognizing the unique strengths and contributions women could bring to intelligence operations.

Christine set off for Hungary in December 1939 under the auspices of Section "D", the precursor of the SOE. The SOE was established in July 1940, and Christine later transitioned over to the "F" section of the SOE. Her cover story for being in Hungary was that she was a journalist. When Christine arrived in Hungary, she met a fellow agent, Andrej Kowerski, a Polish man who was already a war hero. He previously lost a portion of a leg in a pre-war hunting accident, making him the first disabled man to complete SOE's parachute training. Christine had known Kowerski as a child, and they quickly established a close personal relationship, which continued intermittently until her death.

**Christine and longtime lover Andrej Kowerski**

Christine was very concerned about the safety of her mother, who remained in Poland. Kowerski located her mother who was teaching at a secret Jewish school. As a Jewish aristocrat, she was in great danger of being arrested by the Nazis. Despite the risk, she refused to leave the school and was later picked up by the Nazis in January 1942 and sent to Warsaw's Pawiak Prison. She was never heard from again. Christine assumed her mother had died or been executed in the prison. The irony is that Pawiak prison had been designed by Christine's great-great-uncle, Fryderyk Skarbek, in the mid-19th century.

Christine made several crossings of the mountains on skis that first winter, providing the SOE with valuable intelligence, including microfilm plans of new German U-boats and gases.

Christine led people at risk of being arrested by the Germans back to Hungary. She and Kowerski organized surveillance of all roads, rail, and river traffic on the borders with Romania and Germany. Christine was credited with providing intelligence on oil transports to Germany from Romania's Ploiesti oil fields. Her efforts significantly disrupted the flow of resources crucial to the German war effort, highlighting her commitment to the defeat of the Nazi's war machine.

One important piece of intelligence she sent back was photographs of German troops massed along the border of Russia when Russia and Germany were still supposedly allies. She predicted that Germany was planning to invade Russia, but the SOE ignored her report, which later proved to be correct. Her information reached the ears of Prime Minister Winston Churchill, but he was not convinced until Germany invaded Russia in June 1941.

In January 1941, both Christine and Kowerski were captured by the Gestapo in Hungary. After two days of intense interrogation, Christine deliberately bit her tongue to produce blood from her mouth. She convinced the guards that she had tuberculosis, a contagious disease. Having witnessed her father's death from TB, Christine knew how to mimic the symptoms convincingly. Fearing they might catch TB themselves; the guards released both Christine and Kowerski. This resourceful act demonstrated Christine's quick thinking.

**Christine with French Resistance Fighters, photo courtesy of the Imperial War Museum**

Upon their release, The British felt that she should be removed from Hungary as quickly as possible. She was smuggled out in the trunk of a British Embassy car into Yugoslavia. The British gave her a new passport and the name of *Christine Granville*. She used that name for the rest of her life and later took that name legally when she became a naturalized British citizen in December 1949. When getting the new passport, Christine knocked seven years off her age.

**Christine's SOE ID**

Kowerski was also given a new passport and the fake name of *Andrew Kennedy*. The SOE provided them with an Opel vehicle, which they drove from Yugoslavia through Turkey, Palestine, Syria, and Lebanon, to the SOE headquarters in Egypt, arriving in May 1941. The British were astonished that Christine used her well-known charm to obtain travel approval as they moved through each country. Those who knew her frequently credited her as being incredibly persuasive, highlighting her exceptional ability to navigate complex situations and secure cooperation from various authorities.

When Christine and Kowerski arrived in Cairo, the British worried that they might be double agents. Both were dismissed from the SOE while they were under investigation. Kowerski was reinstated six months later, long before Christine was allowed back into the SOE. She remained under suspicion for two main reasons: her previous contact with the "Musketeers," a Polish intelligence organization, and the ease with which she obtained a transit visa from the pro-Vichy French consul to travel through Syria and Lebanon. This visa, typically granted only to Germans, allowed her to travel freely through Nazi-sympathizing countries, raising concerns about her loyalties.

After the SOE reinstated Christine, they initially tried to give her menial office jobs. She refused to do office work because she wanted to return to the field. She was eventually cleared of suspicion. While in Cairo, the SOE tried to train her as a radio operator, but Christine failed to pass the test – perhaps because she wanted a more active job. Her French was good, and she studied to improve her English to be more effective in helping the French Resistance work with American soldiers, as they were beginning to be seen in France.

Major SOE Networks in France, June 1943

**Note Jockey Circuit in lower right**

The SOE finally agreed to return her to as a field agent. She parachuted into southern France on the night of July 6/7, 1944. Christine replaced Cecile Lefort as the courier for Francis Cammaerts, the man in charge of the Jockey Circuit and all clandestine affairs in the region. Cecile had been captured and tortured by the Germans and was executed toward the end of the war.

One of the horrors of WWII that Christine and Cammaerts witnessed but could do nothing to stop was the massacre of the village of Vercours in mid-July 1944. Christine had seen horrors in Poland and Hungary, but it was hard to see this carnage so soon after arriving in France. There had been a battle between the Germans and the Maquis, with the Maquis finally slipping away. In their anger and frustration, the Germans turned on the residents of Vercours and killed many, including 90 babies, children, and seniors. The Germans also took their revenge on another nearby village, Oradour, killing almost everyone.

*Churchill's 'favorite spy,' Christine, sits by a water duct near the bridge she helped the Resistance blow up in France in 1944.*

Christine had two main responsibilities, one was to assist Cammaerts and the Maquis by providing coordination and support. The second was to attempt to subvert any Polish units fighting for the Germans, encouraging them to defect and join the Allies. These tasks were crucial in undermining German efforts.

Christine quickly proved her reputation for composure, keeping a cool head and exhibiting bravery when faced with imminent danger. What may have been Christine's most famous exploit during the war occurred on August 17, 1944. She obtained the release of two SOE agents, Francis Cammaerts and Xan Fielding, and a French Officer, Christian Sorensen, from a Gestapo jail three hours before their scheduled execution. After the men were captured and sentenced to death, she met with Captain Albert Schenck, an Alsatian who acted as liaison officer between the local French prefecture and the Gestapo in Digne-les-Bains, France.

Christine told Schenck that she was a British agent and the niece of British General Bernard Montgomery. Christine claimed to have the authority to secure their release, saying he would be turned over to the angry villagers if he allowed her agents to be executed. They both knew the American forces were about to enter their area, and she assured him that the war would soon end. She convinced him to release the men through a combination of lies, threats, and a two-million-franc bribe, which Christine obtained from a special airdrop from London. This event was fictionalized in the last episode of the British TV show *Wish Me Luck.*

M.R.D Foot wrote of the incident: *the Polish Christine Granville (Pauline) by a combination of steady nerve, feminine cunning, and sheer brass persuaded their captors that the Americans' arrival was imminent and bought the party's release three hours before they were to have been shot.*

The American Army liberated the village two days later. Christine and Cammaerts met with the commander, Brigadier General Frederic B. Butler, but he tried to ignore them and called them "bandits." After his rude behavior, the two went to the town of Gap, where the Maquis had captured the German garrison. Butler and his forces arrived soon after them. Using a megaphone, Christine spoke to hundreds of Polish and Italian soldiers who had been conscripted to fight in the German army and convinced them to take off their German uniforms and join the Allied forces.

Most soldiers agreed and removed their uniforms, but General Butler refused to allow them to join his troops. He threatened Cammaerts and Christine with arrest and court martial if they didn't leave the area. Fortunately, Butler's superior officer, General Alexander Patch, had a greater appreciation for their experience and asked them to be the liaison between the American army and the Maquis.

**Christine with other SOE agents and Allied officers**

The war in France ended for Christine in August 1945. The SOE recalled her to London and later sent her to the Polish mission in Bari, Italy. With the war ending, she returned to Cairo, where she was demobilized. After being separated from her husband for eight years, another chapter of her life closed when her marriage to Jerzy Gizycki finally ended on August 1, 1946, with the divorce becoming official at the Polish consulate in Berlin.

Christine's fellow agent, Francis Cammaerts, said of her: *She was independent, humorous, and fiercely anti-pompous...To use the word brave or courage about her would be a wrong use of the word.*

Her bravery and daring exploits during the war were officially recognized. Christine was awarded the prestigious George Medal in 1947, the OBE from the British, and the Croix de Guerre from the French.

Christine's exciting life of wartime adventure began to unravel after the war. She applied to become a British citizen, but her application was not approved until the end of 1949. By then, Christine's family and their wealth were long gone, leaving her with no relatives or funds. Her one-month severance from the SOE was quickly exhausted, and she needed to find work to support herself.

Christine dreamed of working in the diplomatic service at the British United Nations office in Geneva, but she was turned down because she was not yet an English citizen. She took work as a housekeeper, shop girl, and switchboard operator.

Christine finally found work as a stewardess on a cruise ship, and her beauty and charm found her many male friends. During that time, she met a man who would eventually end her life, Dennis Muldowney. They may have had a brief affair, but she soon broke off the friendship. He remained obsessed with her, although Christine continued to reject his attention.

**Collection of her military honors**

Christine life began to improve and she even reconnected with her previous wartime lover, Andrej Kowerski. She returned from a working cruise out of Durban, South Africa, on the *Winchester Castle* in June 1952. A few days later, as Christine was leaving her room in London's Shelbourne Hotel, Muldowney approached her in the hallway and tried to convince her to go away with him. When Christine again rejected him, he stabbed her repeatedly, killing her instantly. Christine died on June 15, 1952, at the age of 44. Muldowney pleaded guilty to killing her and was hanged ten weeks later.

# THE EGO OF A MURDERER
## Everyone knew of woman he killed—none knew him

### HE 'PURSUED' A HEROINE—
### —A HERO ONLY TO HIMSELF

#### Express Staff Reporter ARNOLD LATCHAM

WITH hands in pockets and a casual smirk on his face, Dennis George Muldowney got what he wanted at the Old Bailey yesterday. He wished to be the centre of attention. He wanted to be sentenced to death. He got both wishes.

He was accused of murdering Christine Granville, 37-year-old Polish countess who, as Jacqueline Armand, was a wartime British agent and a heroine.

Mr. Justice Donovan looked at the cocky little exhibitionist called Muldowney in the dock and said to him: "Do you intend to adhere to your plea of guilty? Because if you do, there is only one thing left—and that is to pass sentence."

In a firm voice with a hint of brogue—for in spite of his name there is no Irish in him—Muldowney replied: "I

#### GRAND PRIX RECORDS GO
## Derek rode faster and faster

##### Express Staff Reporter

DEREK FARRANT, going faster the further he rode, smashed the Manx Senior Grand Prix lap record four times yesterday and beat 83 rivals in the 226-mile record.

From the start, Farrant, a 23-year-old fruiterer from St. Leonards, Sussex, shot into the lead on his A.J.S. motor-cycle fitted with a Matchless engine.

In lap two he smashed the lap record with a speed of 88.76 miles an hour. In lap four he did it again, with 89.57 miles an hour. In lap five he pushed it up to 89.63 miles an hour.

In the sixth and final lap of the twisting course the crowd roared as Farrant, with the race "in his pocket," went even faster.

Crouched flat, with only his white crash helmet showing over the handlebars he flashed across the finish with a final lap speed of 89.64 miles an hour.

#### 'A perfect race'
His average speed was 88.65

**CHRISTINE GRANVILLE**
*"Her memory untarnished"*

former Countess Skarbeck should fall in love with him.

At least he said she had.

But Christine Granville felt differently. To her it was just a passing friendship. She served in other ships, but Muldowney pursued her with letters. And when she stayed in London, he persisted with his attentions even more.

Muldowney could not forget her. His ego would not let him. On June 15 he was waiting for her again at her hotel and there he killed her with a cheap knife at the foot of the stairs.

#### A gallant lady

To the police he told a romantically untrue story. "We became friendly," he said. "It developed into a love affair. She led me to believe that she was in love with me and could not live without me." He told this story with the same self-satisfaction that he displayed in the dock yesterday.

The last word was with Mr. Roger Frisby, who, when it was all over, rose and said to the judge:—

"I am instructed to say on behalf of her family and her friends that there is not one particle of truth in the allega...

**MULDOWNEY—**
*—The unknown who thought a countess loved him; who killed her when she repulsed him; and who was eager for the world to see him sentenced to die for her.*

## So witness gets a cell

A witness who continually inter...

## TWO-GUN DIES IN

##### Express Staff Reporter

GEORGE "DEADPAN" KING, gunman and gang strong-arm man, died yesterday because he ignored

Over two hundred mourners attended Christine's funeral, and they recounted her brave service during the war. Attendees included Kowerski, Francis Cammaerts, and former SOE head, Colin Gubbins.

Her longtime lover, Kowerski, died from cancer in Munich, Germany, in December 1988. His ashes were flown to London and interred at the foot of Christine's grave in St Mary's Roman Catholic Cemetery, Kensal Green, London.

The Shelbourne Hotel was sold in 1971, and the new owners found Christine's trunk in a storage room. It contained her clothes, papers, and the SOE-issued dagger. Most of that material is now in the Polish Institute and Sikorski Museum in London.

**Christine's grave marker**

**A bronze bust of Christine was unveiled at the Polish Hearth Club in London in May 2017.**

In 2020, the English Heritage unveiled a Blue Plaque (seen below) honoring Christine at the site of the former Shelbourne Hotel. London's famous Blue Plaques are a permanent sign installed in a public place in the United Kingdom and elsewhere to commemorate a link between that location and a famous person, event, or former building on the site, serving as a historical marker .

# Chapter 7

# Danielle Reddé "RF" Section

Code Name: Marocain or Morroccin, Camille Fournier

Alias: Maria Kermarec, Eddy Daniel

Very little about Danielle can be verified. The information below is gleaned from bits and pieces mentioned about her in several reports and documents, few of which could be verified by the National Archives.

Danielle, alias *Eddy*, was a Frenchwoman who began working directly for the Resistance in Lyon, France, in 1941. In October 1942, she worked as a civilian courier alongside the SOE radio operator Australian Lt. Tom Groome, code name Georges de Milleville.

They both worked with the PAT escape line, which sheltered downed pilots and others until they could safely escape France by hiking over the Pyrenees Mountains into Spain. The radio operator was continually at risk of being detected by the German's roving signal detection vans. By 1943, Groome was the last radio operator sending or receiving messages for the PAT escape line. The authorities had previously captured five other radio operators. On January 11, 1943, the Gestapo arrested Groome and Danielle in Montauban.

Groome and Danielle were taken to a Gestapo facility in Toulouse for questioning. Groome was laid out on a table in a second-floor room for interrogation/torture by the Gestapo. Suddenly, to everyone's surprise, Groome made an audacious escape by jumping through the closed second-floor window and attempting to escape. *L'Agent de Liaison,* a post-war "liberation newspaper," published a sketch of the scene.

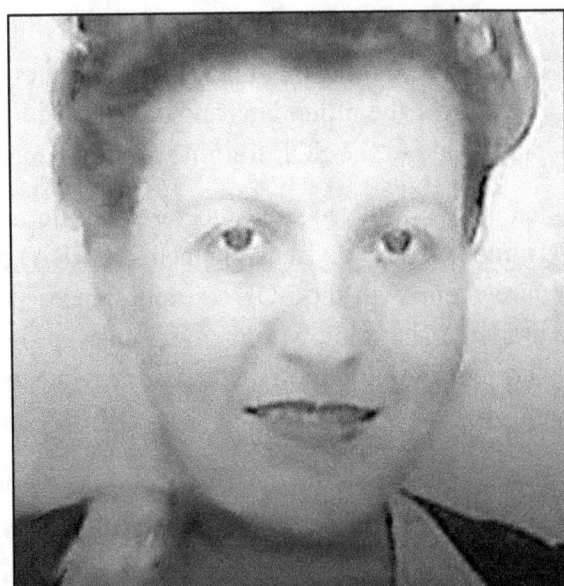

**Danielle**

Tentative sans parachute

**Newspaper sketch of Tom Groome breaking through a second-floor window in Gestapo headquarters in a daring escape plan.**

Groome was injured during the jump, and the Gestapo were able to recapture him quickly. However, his dashing escape attempt was not entirely in vain. In the confusion after he jumped, the Gestapo ran out after him and left the doors open and unguarded. That open door allowed Danielle to escape.

Danielle reported what had happened to the head of the PAT line. There was nothing that the group could do to help Groome, as he was firmly in the hands of the Gestapo. He was later sent to Natzweiler-Struthof, Mauthausen, and the Dachau concentration camps. It is unknown if he survived the war.

Since the Gestapo knew what Danielle looked like, she had to be much more discreet in her movements, and eventually, she decided that it was too dangerous in France. She, too, took advantage of the escape route and hiked over the Pyrenees in March 1943. It is believed that she traveled with Nancy Wake over the mountains and on to London, reaching there in June 1943. Both women would eventually participate in the SOE training program and return to France to work with the Resistance.

Danielle's route to the SOE took a little longer than Nancy's, as Danielle first joined the Free French Bureau Central de Rensignements (BCRA) on June 14, 1943, after arriving in London. The BCRA had an agreement with the SOE to train some of their people and to provide them with transportation back to France. It is unknown when she entered the SOE training, but it is probable that she would have had a shorter training period due to her previous work with the Resistance.

Danielle parachuted back into France on January 1, 1944, <u>OR</u> February 9, 1944 (the reports differ) and landed near Montlucon. She worked as both a radio operator and a courier for the Lyon Circuit and possibly also for the Free French group in the city of Lyon. The Allied Army liberated the area in August 1944, and she was released from service.

**The author believes the following information to be about the same Danielle Reddé, but so many aliases were used that it is difficult to verify the reports.**

Reports indicate that Danielle returned to London by ship from Calcutta, India, on May 3, 1945. It is unknown what mission took her there, but the SOE had some agents in East Asia. There is some evidence Danielle, using the name, Sous-lieutenant Simone Fournier, accepted a mission to help liberate Allied prisoners of war from Japanese camps in Indochina. On August 22, 1945, she may have been working under the name of Edith Fournier (a name she had used in France) when she and a Lt. Klotz parachuted into Thachik, Laos. She would have been working as a radio operator - if it were her on that mission.

During that same period, General de Gaulle awarded Danielle the Medaille de Combattant Volontaire de la Resistance, the Medaille Commemorative des Services Volontaire dans la France Libre, the Croix de Combattant, the Croix de Guerre Avec Palme, and the Chevalier de la Legion d'Honneur.

A Colonel Roos and a Captain Goudry wrote in their December 14, 1945, recommendation for her to receive the Croix de Guerre award: *Danielle parachuted with her radio into what was a very dangerous part of Laos with no reception committee. Despite being wounded on landing and surrounded by hostile forces, she showed calm and composure thanks to her constant efforts and devotion; she saved numerous human lives and participated in the evacuation of all the French from the province where she was working and transmitted vital military and political messages.*

Unfortunately, the wound required her to be hospitalized in Bangkok. Once she recovered, she accepted another mission to Saigon on March 29, 1946. That mission involved helping the women and children who had been imprisoned in Shanghai during the war. The British awarded her the Medal of the British Empire and an Honorary Colonial Medal for that work. She received additional medals from the French Government in 1953.

It is uncertain if the above missions involved the same Danielle Reddé trained by the SOE, OR if the missions were undertaken for the SOE or some other agency in England, OR if they were done at the behest of a French Government agency.

No information has been found concerning her later life or when and where she may have died.

# Chapter 8

# Giliana (Gillian, Gigliana) Balmaceda Gerson
## "DF" Section

Sept. 29, 1910 - ?

Giliana was the first woman that the SOE sent into France in late May 1941. Prior to her mission, a few other women were already in France, working with the Resistance and later for the SOE, or they were initially sent to another country and subsequently moved to France. The only male SOE agent sent to France before her was radio operator Georges Bégué, who arrived on May 5, 1941. Giliana's mission was exploratory, aimed at establishing safe houses and securing local support for future SOE agents.

Giliana was born Giliana Balmaceda Provasoli in Chile on September 29, 1910. She moved to Paris while still young, where she worked as an actress. In Paris, she met and married an Englishman, Haim Victor Gerson. Victor worked in Paris as a wealthy dealer in fine rugs and carpets. He grew up in Southport, Lancashire, and was the son of a prosperous fabric merchant. Previously married, Victor experienced significant personal tragedy when his first wife passed away and their son was killed in a traffic accident before he met Giliana.

**Giliana as a young woman**

After Germany invaded France, Giliana and her husband took the first opportunity to leave for England on June 18, 1940. Victor, demonstrating foresight, had sent most of his rug stock to England before the invasion. In England, Victor and Giliana resided in his home in Grove End Gardens, London. Shortly after their arrival, they were both recruited by the newly established SOE. Victor persuaded the SOE that he could establish a network in France to accept and support the SOE agents and create an escape route over the Pyrenees Mountains into Spain.

To make the plan successful, the SOE needed information about supporters in France, the identification of potential safe houses, and information about documents that would be necessary for agents to work within the country. Giliana offered to obtain that information. Since she and Victor had married only shortly before moving to England, she still had a valid passport from Chile, listing her name as Gigliana Balmaceda Provasoli Gerson, along with a visa valid for Vichy France.

She traveled legally from Spain into France on her Chile passport, pretending to be on vacation. By May 23, 1941, Giliana was in southern France which the Germans had not yet occupied. She met and interviewed many people she thought might be willing to provide support for the SOE agents. Giliana exercised great caution in her approach, carefully choosing who to engage and how to initiate conversations. She spent considerable time in cafes, gauging local sentiments about the German occupation. Giliana avoided those she suspected might betray agents to the Germans, relying on her keen instincts to identify trustworthy individuals. Her list of contacts she compiled proved invaluable, serving as a crucial resource for incoming agents over the first few months of SOE agent engagement.

Giliana preferred older couples as potential hosts because they had a plausible reason to be home most days. These families often needed the financial support that London would provide in exchange for helping agents. She learned what documents locals needed to carry daily and collected actual documents such as bus and train schedules, resident permits, and ration cards. The SOE could use these documents as templates to create fake documents for their agents. She also connected with some Spanish ex-Republicans who were willing to help establish the escape route over the Pyrenees.

Giliana remained in France for six weeks, traveling easily from one town to another. With her sharp eyes and the retentive memory of an actress, she wandered unrebuked into forbidden areas. Giliana noted the legal and illegal ways to cross between the German-occupied zones in the north and the unoccupied regions in the south of France.

She learned the rules for hotel stays and discovered that the police or Gestapo frequently checked the register books to find out who was staying overnight. She noted the curfew times and the penalties if you broke the curfew, as agents might well do in the future. These details could mean freedom or capture for the SOE agents. Giliana left France in late June 1941 going back to Spain, then to Gibraltar, and finally home to London on August 25.

Giliana's known history ends at this point. She may have continued to work in some capacity at the SOE or some other government agency, but her records at the SOE end after her return from France.

Victor underwent some training with the SOE, despite the full program not yet being established. He made his first of six wartime trips to France in September 1941. Leveraging information provided by his wife, he successfully established the escape route he had proposed prior to her journey to France. This escape route facilitated the safe passage of hundreds of individuals to Spain. In recognition of his efforts, Victor was awarded the Member of the Order of the British Empire (MBE) on November 11, 1943, and later the Officer of the Order of the British Empire (OBE) on June 6, 1946, with the rank of Major.

After the war, Victor returned to managing his rug and carpet business, and it is assumed Giliana remained with him. The dates and locations of their deaths are unknown.

AUSTRALIAN WAR MEMORIAL    AWM2016.961.2.34

**Photo of Victor and Giliana in later life, photo courtesy of the Australian War Memorial**

**Chapter 9**

# Vera Leigh

March 17, 1903 – July 6, 1944

Code Names: Simone and Almoner   Alias: Suzanne Chavanne

Named Vera Glass at birth in Leeds, England, on March 17, 1903, her mother abandoned her almost immediately. An American, Hiram Eugene Leigh, and his English wife adopted her soon after and renamed her Vera Eugenie Leigh. Her adopted father was a highly successful Thoroughbred racehorse trainer/owner and breeder in the United States and Europe.

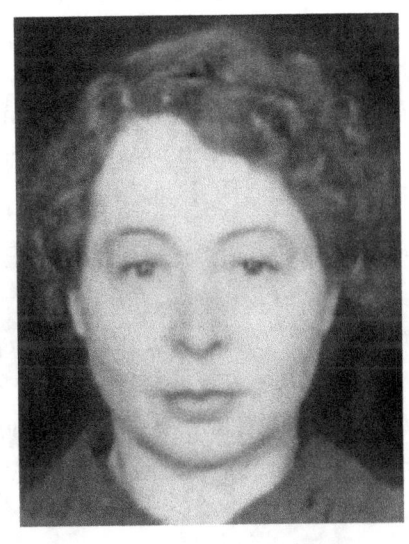

In 1894, a horse, Chant, trained by her father, won the Kentucky Derby. The New York Times reported on December 4, 1898, that going into the 1899 racing season, Eugene Leigh had the largest horse racing stable in the United States.

Due to conservative politicians trying to outlaw racing in the U.S., Leigh moved his breeding and horse training operation to Europe in 1901. Two years later, he and his wife adopted Vera, providing her with an affluent lifestyle. The Leighs also had three other daughters.

**Vera, when she joined SOE**

Leigh and his family moved to France when Vera was still a baby, so she grew up speaking French and English. Leigh spent countless hours at her father's stables, where she became an accomplished rider. As World War I raged across Europe, the family sought refuge in the United States in early 1917. After the war ended, they returned to a recovering France. Leigh's father took on a new role as manager and trainer for the prestigious racing stable of Pierre Wertheimer, a prominent figure in horse racing and the owner of the Washington Post Newspaper.

After Vera's college years, she went to work at the fashion house of Caroline Reboux in Paris. Following her apprenticeship, she and two other women formed their own millinery house in 1927, *Rose Valois*. It was considered one of the leading milliners of Paris in the 1930s, 40s, and 50s. Although Vera would leave the shop in 1940, it remained open until 1970. The shop allowed Vera to socialize in the sophisticated fashion world of Paris.

When the Nazis first occupied Paris, Vera thought her father's U.S. citizenship gave her a claim of neutrality and would keep her safe. However, she soon realized that the Germans were arresting many foreign nationals, regardless of their nationality, and that she could be arrested at the whim of the Gestapo.

In 1940, seeking to escape the tightening grip of the German army, Vera left Paris for Lyon, hoping her long-time fiancé, M. Charles Sussaix, the managing director of a Portuguese-owned film company, could help her flee to England. In Lyon, Vera encountered Virginia Hall, an American spy renowned for her cleverness, government contacts, and bravery. Virginia's suggestion that she work with the Resistance resonated with Vera, who hated the German occupation and what it had done to France. Vera decided to remain and join the fight, dedicating herself to aiding stranded English soldiers escape over the Pyrenees Mountains. This decision marked the beginning of a new chapter in her life.

Vera assisted the Resistance until the Germans began to arrest even U.S. citizens. Concerned for her safety, she took the same escape route in early 1942. The Spanish police arrested her and put her into an internment camp at Miranda de Ebro, just south of Bilbao. She remained there until Virginia Hall was able to convince the British embassy to arrange her release. She traveled to Gibraltar and then on to London by late 1942.

She volunteered to work at the SOE. The recruiter who interviewed her wrote: *(she) is a smart businesswoman. It is clear that commerce is her first allegiance.* The SOE staff had no reason to question her desire to be of help, and they thought her perfect French would be a great asset for field work back in France. Like most SOE women who did field work, she joined FANY. Her newfound dedication to fighting against the Nazis led her to break off the seven-year engagement to Sussaix. Vera committed herself to the SOE and the work ahead.

Once she began her official SOE training, instructors wrote the following comments about Vera: *Supple, active, and keen, confident, and capable, a very satisfactory person to teach, a very pleasant personality, full of guts, had the ability to keep up with the men and was about the best shot in the company. She had a hard time dealing with maps and diagrams but was extremely good with her fingers; she could do fiddling jobs with charges and wires and all that remarkably quickly and neatly.* There were also several notes about her interest in fashion and her concern about her appearance – she hated her hideous khaki uniform.

After completing her training, she, Julienne Aisner, Sidney Charles Jones, and Marcel Clech, a radio operator, were flown back to France on the night of May 13/14, 1943. They landed in a field near Tours. Henri Déricourt was part of the welcoming group.

Vera had chosen her own code name, *Simone*, and the SOE gave her the alias of *Suzanne Chavanne*. Her cover story was that she was a milliner's assistant, a natural story for her. She worked as a courier for Sidney Jones, who headed the Inventor Circuit, a sub-Circuit of Prosper. Her primary responsibility was the usual carrying of messages, a crucial link in the complex network of her Circuit. She also worked for Henri Frager, who headed the Donkeyman sub-Circuit of Prosper, ensuring that critical information flowed smoothly between all the Resistance groups and the Circuit leaders.

Vera and agent Julienne Aisner became good friends and visited whenever they could. In their world of secrecy, it helped to have another woman to talk to who understood the stress, uncertainty, and danger of their work.

Many downed airmen spoke no French, and Vera would sometimes accompany them through the streets of Paris to help them get to their safe houses. During one of those trips, she accidentally ran into her sister's husband and discovered that he was also hiding downed airmen. Since none of her family knew of her involvement with the SOE, it remained a secret between them.

On July 2, 1943, a month after the Prosper Circuit had been betrayed, Nicolas Bodington, deputy to Buckmaster, the head of the SOE "F" Section, flew to France to determine what had happened to cause such massive damage to Prosper. A few days after his arrival, Vera requested an interview and told him that Henri Frager of the Donkeyman Circuit had accused Henri Déricourt of being a traitor.

Bodington met with Frager and left the meeting wondering if Frager himself might be the traitor. Earlier, others had also accused Déricourt of being the traitor. Despite these accusations, Déricourt was highly regarded at SOE headquarters, leading many agents to believe that headquarters was protecting him. After the war, Déricourt faced trial for treason but was acquitted by the British court.

Vera was lax in adhering to SOE security guidelines, often visiting the same shops and cafes she frequented before the war. This behavior made her noticeable to both the local police and the Gestapo. She lived in an apartment in the upscale Sixteenth Arrondissement, which was near the Gestapo headquarters on Avenue Foch. Unbeknownst to her, her apartment was also close to the residence of the German spymaster Hugo Bleicher.

After the war, Bleicher remarked that he frequently saw Vera. He described her as: *parading around and playing spy*, which made him very aware of her actions within the Circuit. Despite the war and her involvement with the SOE, Vera continued to visit and dine out with old friends as if she were still a carefree shop owner.

One concerning issue for Vera was a doctor's appointment that suggested she might have tuberculosis. Despite this worrying diagnosis, there is no evidence that she followed up with the appointment for an x-ray to verify the diagnosis.

Unfortunately, her life took a very different turn on October 30, 1943. Double agent Roger Bardet betrayed the Inventor Circuit, leading to the Gestapo, accompanied by Hugo Bleicher, arresting her, her Circuit leader Sidney Jones, and his bodyguard at the Chez Mas café. Jones endured almost a year of imprisonment and torture before being executed at the Mauthausen concentration camp on September 16, 1944.

Vera was sent first to the Gestapo headquarters on Avenue Foch for interrogation. However, they seemed to know all about her activities, as she had made too many mistakes. Getting no helpful information from her, she was sent on to the Fresnes Prison, the same prison where most captured female SOE agents stayed for at least some time while the Gestapo determined their fate.

On May 13, 1944, exactly one year after her arrival in France, Vera, along with Andrée Borrel, Sonia Olschanezky, and Diana Rowden were all moved back to the Gestapo headquarters on Avenue Foch for one night. Also present at the German headquarters were Yolande Beekman, Madeleine Damerment, Éliane Plewman, and Odette Sansom, all fellow SOE agents. Odette Sansom asked for English tea for the group, and, to their surprise, the guards served them a lovely tea using real china. This small act of kindness was the last they would experience. Of the eight women, all would receive further torture. Only Odette Sansom would escape execution.

**Fresnes Prison**

The next morning, the women were taken to a railroad station, shackled to a guard, and put on a train to Karlsruhe Prison. Karlsruhe Prison became infamous after the war when it was revealed that many prisoners sent there were designated as part of Hitler's Nacht und Nebel (Night and Fog) program. *Nacht and Nebel* was a directive issued by Hitler on December 7, 1941, targeting any resisters in Nazi-occupied areas. The directive stated that those who resisted the Germans should be "imprisoned, murdered, or made to disappear" so that their families would never know what had happened to them.

Odette spoke about the experience after the war, saying: *We were starting on this journey together in fear, but all of us hoping for something, above all that we would remain together. We had all had a taste already of what things could be like, none of us did expect for anything very much, we all knew that they could put us to death. I was the only one officially condemned to death. The others were not. But there is always a fugitive ray of hope that some miracle will take place.*

When they arrived at Karlsruhe, the women were put in separate cells. The SOE women were treated like the other women there, which was better than the conditions in most of the concentration camps. From their cells, they could hear the Allied bombers flying over and hitting targets around the prison. That gave them hope that the war might soon be over.

Less than two months later, very early on the morning of July 6, 1944, Vera, Diana Rowden, Andrée Borrel, and Sonia Olschanezky were put in a closed truck and taken to the remote Natzweiler-Struthof concentration camp situated high on a hill deep in the Vosges Mountains in France. Natzweiler-Struthof was a German concentration and extermination camp for men and was the only such German camp located in France. It held over 6000 men who had been captured from all over Europe.

**Karlsruhe Prison, front and overview.**

The camp was not expecting the four women, which caused issues in finding them appropriate cells separated from the male prisoners. A male SOE agent, Brian Stonehouse, described a woman he saw in the camp that day who Vera Atkins later identified as being Vera, upon her arrival at the camp: *(she) was wearing a brownish tweed coat and skirt. She was more petite than the blonde in grey and older, having shortish brown hair. None of the four women were wearing make-up, and all were looking pale and tired.*

Roger Linet, a French prisoner, would testify after the war: *One could see from their appearance that they hadn't come from a camp. They seemed young, they were fairly well groomed, their clothes were not rubbish, their hair was brushed, and each had a case in their hand.* Another prisoner, Dutch Major Van Lanschot, noted the women's bearing and the fact that they barely looked around the camp, and he said there was no doubt the women were "first class."

A Gestapo officer from the Karlsruhe Prison accompanied the women to Natzweiler-Struthof. He told the SS political officer, Magnus Wochner, that there were orders from Berlin that the women were to be executed immediately. This was highly unusual, and Wochner disputed the unorthodox procedure. The Gestapo officer told him not to enter the women's names into the records.

A German medical orderly, Emil Truttel, was told by the camp doctor, Dr. Plaza, to prepare 80cc's of Phenol and a 10cc syringe and to get Eugen Forster to be ready for duty with him that night. The male prisoners were all told to be in their barracks by 7:00 PM instead of the usual 8:30 PM. They were told to close their curtains or shutters and that they would be shot if they looked out.

Between 9 and 10 PM on July 6, 1944, the executions began. A prisoner, Dr. Albert Guerisse, who had run the PAT escape network in France, recognized Andrée, and he was able to inform war crime investigators about the women's last few hours in the camp. From his vantage point, he could see the courtyard and witnessed the guards taking the women into the crematorium. He later observed four distinct bursts of smoke from the furnace, indicating that the women had been executed and cremated. Later interviews with the guards indicated that Vera, known for her love of fashion, was stripped of any clothing before being placed in the oven.

In the crematorium, there were two doctors present: Dr. Plaza and Dr. Werner Rohde. The testimony about who administered the lethal injections varies. One guard later testified that Dr. Plaza gave each woman a shot of Phenol intended to kill her; another guard testified that Dr. Rohde gave the shots. The two doctors themselves gave differing statements, but they each acknowledged giving at least one woman the injection. The women were told that the injection was to help them avoid Typhus. Very soon after the injections, each woman was put into the furnace. Tragically, one of the women – it is not known which one – regained consciousness and could be heard by the male prisoners fighting the guards as they put her into the furnace.

After the war, the camp doctor, Dr. Werner Rohde, who administered at least some of the killing injections to the four women, was found guilty of war crimes and executed. The camp commandant, Fritz Hartjenstein, received a life sentence for war crimes.

Vera posthumously received the King's Commendation for Brave Conduct, and her name is listed on many war memorials, including the SOE Agents Memorial in Lambeth Palace Road, Westminster, London. Her superiors at the SOE had recommended her for the George Cross, but approval of that award was not pursued.

# Chapter 10

# Madeleine Lavigne

February 6, 1912 – February 24, 1945

Code Name: Leveller and Isabelle

Alias: Marianne Latour, Marianne Henriette Delormes

Madeleine was unique to the SOE. When she joined the organization, she was one of the few divorced women. Additionally, she was one of the few mothers, as she had two children. Madeleine was also among a handful of agents who spoke only French.

The daughter of a fabric designer, Madeleine was described as buxom, serious, and conscientious. She married Marcel Lavigne in 1931 when she was only 19. The couple had two sons: Guy, who was born when she was 20, and Noel, who was born when she was 24.

When Germany invaded France, Madeleine's husband joined the Army but was soon captured and imprisoned by the Germans. Faced with the need to support herself and her two sons, Madeleine sent the boys to live with her parents. She then took a job as a clerk in the mayor's office at the town hall in Lyon.

Madeleine was approached by the SOE agent Robert Boiteux, who had taken over the Spruce Circuit. Boiteux had parachuted into France in May 1942. Within six months, he built up a Circuit that successfully received and acclimated twenty new SOE agents, in addition to carrying out sabotage operations.

Boiteux needed assistance in obtaining fake documents for Allied pilots shot down over France and for others needing documents to flee the country. Madeleine's job in the town office provided the perfect opportunity to assist the Resistance. Hating the German occupation, she agreed to work for him.

Madeleine sometimes traveled around the area with Robert Boiteux to provide him with the cover of being a couple visiting relatives. Boiteux gave her the code name *Leveller.*

She later became acquainted with SOE agent Henri Borosh, who parachuted in to work as a radio operator for Boiteux in January 1943. As Madeleine became increasingly involved in the Resistance effort, she allowed Borosh to keep his radio in her house. This was a highly dangerous act, as the discovery of the radio by the Gestapo would have led to her arrest and imprisonment in a concentration camp.

Boiteux returned to England on August 19, 1943, frustrated by the lack of sufficient weapons for the Resistance fighters and concerned for their safety due to the increasing success of German collaborators in uncovering SOE locations and safe houses.

In November 1943, after Madeleine's husband was released from prison, they agreed to divorce. There were rumors that Madeleine and Borosh had become very close friends during this period.

Borosh asked Madeleine to become even more involved with his Circuit when he asked her to act as a courier, helping to take messages back and forth between him and various Resistance groups. She navigated German roadblocks daily without arousing suspicion. However, by January 1944, German patrols had intensified their searches for Resistance members, making life increasingly dangerous.

The risk of discovery became so great that both Borosh and Madeleine were evacuated from France by a British military plane on February 4, 1944. Their departure was timely, as the French police were about to arrest her. After she left, Madeleine was tried as a terrorist, convicted in absentia, and sentenced to life in prison.

The SOE knew of her previous assistance in France, and they invited her to join the organization and begin their training program. She accepted the invitation and joined FANY in February 1944, shortly after which she began her SOE training.

Madeleine went through a shortened program including Morse code and radio operation, Her reports said that she didn't like handling weapons and seemed afraid of parachuting. There was even a suggestion that someone on the plane might have to "assist" her in jumping out.

Due to the SOE's desperate need for radio operators in France, they asked Madeleine to return before completing her training. She and Borosh parachuted into France on the night of May 23-24, 1944. The SOE thought that since Borosh was a trained radio operator, he could complete Madeleine's training "on the job." Madeleine used her alias, *Marianne Latour*, during her training, a name that would cause confusion about her real identity years later.

Borosh set up the new Silversmith Circuit, and Madeleine was initially assigned as a radio operator. The Circuit worked with Resistance groups in Reims and Epernay. Madeleine found two houses to rent. One was used as a base for Borosh in Epernay, and she lived in the other house in Reims. For several months, the Circuit operated from her home.

Madeleine ended up serving as both a courier and radio operator. Her radio skills were minimal but sufficient to send messages requesting weapons and supply airdrops for the Resistance. The Circuit carried out a large number of sabotage operations.

With a strong German presence in the area, Madeleine used shorter messages to minimize the risk of being found by the Gestapo. Her SOE reports later indicated the area was swarming with German soldiers: *And (she) often had to pass through areas under fire, showing great courage and common sense.*

Another document, believed to have been written by Borosh, stated: *A most courageous and tactful woman who rendered great service to the cause…She did her job unquestionably well…a great-hearted lady for whom I have much respect and liking.*

The Allies liberated Reims on August 29, 1944, and the SOE released Madeleine from the organization in September. Due to her lifetime prison sentence, she could not return to Lyon. Her two sons had been living with her parents while she worked for the SOE, so she set up a new home in Paris, and her sons joined her there.

Unfortunately, only five months later, she succumbed to an embolism (blood clot) and died on February 25, 1945. She was only 33 years old. Buckmaster wrote: *We deeply grieve the untimely death of this French woman, who deserved so much from her country.*

In November 1946, Madeleine was awarded the King's Medal for Brave Conduct. Her SOE Commendation read: *She rendered very great service by her courage under enemy fire and by her tact. She was Silversmith's right arm and deserves the highest praise for the work she carried out with him.*

There are no verified photos of Madeleine.

# Chapter 11

# Yvonne Rudellat

January 11, 1897 – April 23 or 24, 1945

Code Names: Soaptree, Jacqueline, Suzanne, Christiane

Alias: Jacqueline Viallet, Jacqueline Gautier, Jacqueline Leclaire

Yvonne was the only grandmother who served as an SOE field agent in France. She was also the first woman specially trained by the SOE and sent to live and work in German occupied France. Giliana Gerson had been sent to do an earlier evaluation, but there was never an intent for her to remain and work with Resistance forces. A few women in earlier chapters had worked in France, but they began as civilians working unofficially with the Resistance. They were only later trained by the SOE and returned to France to work as agents.

Yvonne Clair Cerneau was born on January 11, 1897, in Maisons-Lafitte, a town near Paris. Her father worked as a horse dealer for the French Army, while her mother was known for her domineering nature towards her husband and children. Tragically, all eight of Yvonne's older siblings died during infancy, which undoubtedly caused profound trauma to her parents. Yvonne also had a younger brother, but he sadly passed away at the age of 18.

Yvonne had a good relationship with her father, and whenever her mother would allow it, she traveled with him on horse buying/selling trips. After her father's early death, Yvonne's relationship with her mother became strained. While still in her teens, she moved to England and found a job working in London at a retail shop on Regent Street. Unfortunately, her mother soon moved to London and settled into Yvonne's apartment.

Friends described Yvonne as a vivacious, dainty charmer with dark hair and hazel eyes. She had a very deceptive air of fragility because she possessed a strong will.

On October 16, 1920, at the age of 23, Yvonne married Alex Rudellat, a 41-year-old Italian. The marriage may have been Yvonne's way of finally escaping her mother's control. Following their wedding, her mother returned to France. However, Alex's mother soon moved in with them, a custom in Italian households. Yvonne now found herself caring for her husband's mother.

In 1922, Yvonne gave birth to her only child, Constance Jacqueline. The family's life was marked by frequent relocations, driven by Alex's ventures in buying and selling homes. Their transient lifestyle meant that they often inhabited a small part of a house while renting out the rest. They remained at 146 Warwick Way, London, for the longest period, where they lived in the basement and leased the brighter, more spacious upstairs rooms.

**Yvonne Rudellat,**
**photo believed to be taken in 1942**

Yvonne asked for a divorce in 1929, but Alex refused. They continued living together, but in separate bedrooms for another 12 years. There were rumors that Yvonne may have had affairs with one or two different men during those years, but the rumors were never confirmed.

Ten days after England and Germany went to war in 1939, Yvonne's 17-year-old daughter, Constance, joined the Auxiliary Territorial Service (ATS). She soon met Ronald Pepper, a Royal Army Pay Corps sergeant, and they married on December 12, 1939. Yvonne's son-in-law also moved into the basement with the rest of the family.

At 43, Yvonne became a grandmother when her daughter gave birth to her first child. Despite the passage of time, a friend noted that Yvonne: *Was still attractive and physically tough, with greying, tousled hair.* However, life took a devastating turn on the night of April 16, 1941. The German blitz bombed London mercilessly, and Yvonne and Alex's home was reduced to rubble. Alex's financial foresight proved invaluable. He had earlier buried money in the basement floor. As they sifted through the debris, Alex unearthed their hidden savings. This small fortune enabled them to purchase a new home, ensuring that their large clan could stay together.

After losing their home in the blitz, Yvonne sank into a deep depression and she tried to take her own life. However, she decided she would not let the war or her circumstances defeat her. Determined to forge a new path, she enrolled in a local training school to improve her clerical skills.

After finishing the courses, she secured a job at Ebury Court, a hotel and drinking club on Ebury Street frequented by SOE personnel. The continuing German occupation of France weighed heavily on Yvonne. Each new report of the atrocities committed by the occupiers deepened her sense of despair and frustration. She was vocal at her job about wishing she could help in some way with the war effort.

The SOE recruitment agent, Captain Selwyn Jepson, heard her comments and learned she was a French native, fluent in the language, and knowledgeable about the culture. The SOE was always desperate for such people who could go to France to obtain information about German military actions and movements. Jepson contacted Yvonne, and she expressed interest. He sent her to Wanborough Manor for more in-depth interviews. She passed the interviews and agreed to join the SOE on May 15, 1942. Later reports would say: *She was cool and efficient, someone well able to organize and keep her nerve.*

The SOE had earlier decided that women agents must pass the same training courses as the men. Yvonne was the first woman sent to the paramilitary training course at Wanborough. Instructors modeled how they dealt with future female agents based on her behavior and reactions. She went through the training in borrowed battle dress or khaki denim overalls. Her first training officer was not impressed with having a woman in the course and called her: *A little old lady.*

Yvonne was commissioned as an ensign in FANY on June 1, 1942. Theoretically, this commission would give her protection under the Geneva Convention. However, since FANY was a civilian organization rather than a military one, such protection was proven to be a myth when the Gestapo captured FANY officers.

Yvonne's next training courses were held at Boarmans, one of ten houses on the Beaulieu Estate in Hampshire. Three new female agents joined her: 22-year-old Andrée Borrel, 45-year-old Valentine "Blanche" Charlet, and 52-year-old Marie-Thérèse Le Chêne. The courses covered the skills she needed in her future role as a courier.

One instructor wrote of her: *The first impression of fluffiness is entirely misleading. Her air of innocence and anxiety to please should prove a most valuable cover asset. She is extremely thorough and sincere in anything she does, and together with her preserving and tenacious qualities, she will see any job through to its conclusion.*

The SOE judged Yvonne to be too old to take the parachute training, fearing that she would be injured and unable to go to France. Yvonne had long dreamed of parachuting, so that was a great disappointment for her. She passed her final courses on June 21, 1942.

Yvonne had a gun strapped to her leg when she parachuted into France. When asked if she thought she could use it to kill an enemy, she responded: *If a German or anyone stops me and tries to search me, there is only one thing to do. I will have to shoot him. I don't want to do that. It would be difficult to bury him. The ground is so hard... If it happens, I hope it is near an asparagus bed where the earth is soft and sandy.*

Few men in the government wanted to be the one to officially send the first women to live and work behind enemy lines, so the question of sending Yvonne was kicked upstairs. In 1942, the First Sea Lord, the Chief of the Imperial General Staff, and the Chief of the Air Staff discussed whether they would send Yvonne to France. They weighed the question of her being a woman and, perhaps more importantly, that she was old enough to be a grandmother. Would the rough Maquis fighters take her seriously? Could she do the physically demanding work of a courier? She would be the test case for all female SOE agents. Eventually, they agreed to send her. If she succeeded, other women agents would be sent.

She and three male SOE agents flew to Gibraltar on July 18, 1942. She traveled under the code name *Soaptree* and the alias, *Jacqueline Viallet*. Two German fighters attacked the plane and destroyed one of its engines, but the pilot managed to reach the Gibraltar airport, flying 50 feet above the water. From Gibraltar, the agents took a specially outfitted felucca on July 20 and, after very rough seas, landed at Antibes, near Nice, on July 30, 1942.

Her landing made her the first officially trained female SOE agent to live in France. Five other women who would later become official SOE agents were already working with the Resistance in France, but they were working as civilians.

Once inside France, Yvonne began using the alias, *Jacqueline Gautier.* They assigned her as the courier for one of the Sub-Circuits of leader Francis Suttill, code name *Prosper*. He was in charge of what would become the largest Circuit in France, the Physician/Prosper group.

After landing, Yvonne took the train from Cannes to Lyon, where she picked up fake identity papers from American Virginia Hall, before traveling to Paris. Although Yvonne's mother was again living in France, there is no indication that she visited her.

Yvonne needed to cross the German demarcation line between southern and northern France. Because some prisoners had recently escaped from the Germans, there were increased patrols and checkpoints all along the line. Maquis members hid her in a locomotive tender to get her through the checkpoints.

She traveled to Tours, where she joined the Monkeypuzzle Sub-Circuit, run by Raymond Flower, code name *Gaspard.* She acquired a bicycle and installed herself in an inconspicuous cottage in Touraine.

Another agent who met her in France said: *she had an old-maidish look, her age and hard life brought lines in her forehead and a rather weary stoop to her shoulders.*

Yvonne was immediately responsible for taking messages between Flower and various Maquis groups. In addition, she was responsible for managing the parachute drop zones to prepare for the arrival of new agents, weapons, and supplies for the Maquis. Between April and June 1943, she set up the reception parties for twenty different parachute drops, including thirteen that brought in new agents. She helped them acclimate to the area and the dangers of working behind enemy lines before sending them to their assigned Circuits.

Several names would eventually be used by Yvonne, creating problems for her identification at the war's end. She chose the official alias of *Jacqueline Gautier*. Jacqueline was for her daughter and Gautier because it was a common name in France. She thought it would avoid attracting attention. Her cover story was that she was from the town of Brest but had been bombed out of her home. Since she had experienced that in London, she could easily talk about the experience of losing everything.

Yvonne later worked with Pierre Culioli. Culioli was the son and grandson of French military officers, and he was a French Infantry Lieutenant. Culioli was a small, wiry man with a nervous manner, horn-rimmed glass, and a toothbrush mustache. His wife had been killed by a German Bomb in June 1943, and he was committed to defeating the Nazis.

Neither Yvonne nor Culioli had a good relationship with Flower. Flower seemed to see traitors everywhere, as he reported both Yvonne and Culioli as spies. Flower believed that Culioli was a double agent for the Germans, and he requested a poison pill to kill him. Based on his report, radio operator Gilbert Norman parachuted into France on October 31, 1943. Norman carried with him a poison pill to kill Culioli. None of the SOE agents was willing to administer the pill. Flower also attempted to get rid of Yvonne by leaving incriminating items in her room.

Fortunately, the pill was not used as both agents were vindicated by the SOE agents later sent in to verify Flower's claims about them. Culioli was furious that his loyalty had been questioned. After that incident, he and Yvonne broke off relations with Flower, who was later recalled to Great Britain.

With the approval of the leader of the Prosper Circuit, Culioli and Yvonne created a sub-section of the vast Proper Circuit. The new Adolphe Sub-Circuit reached from the Belgian border to the Atlantic coast. The new group settled in the Solange area. Culioli posed as a forestry official and he and Yvonne settled down in a woodland cottage near Romorantin in the Loire Valley. They both used the last name of *Leclaire*, and Yvonne posed as Culioli's wife to make them less conspicuous. She continued to work as his courier, and they ran an efficient small Sub-Circuit, preparing for the expected Allied invasion.

The neighborhood liked the "couple," who were known as refugees from a bombed area. Culioli said of their living arrangement: *It was much easier traveling about with a lady. As a couple living like husband and wife, nobody paid any attention to us.*

By March 1943, Yvonne had not only bicycled hundreds of miles across the Loire region delivering messages, but she had also taken part in several missions. She would often fill her covered bicycle basket with explosives and take them to different facilities scheduled to be blown up. She would pedal right past German guard stations and through roadblocks, managing each time to avoid being stopped and searched.

Yvonne helped set up the charges to blow up the 300,000-volt cables of the Chaigny power station south of Orleans and two train locomotives at Le Mans station. She also helped blow up or damage trains, a railway bridge, and a German military food depot. Culioli wrote of her in a report: *(She is) an extremely valuable colleague and is fast becoming a demolition expert.*

They continued to recruit new Maquis fighters and to organize, receive, and disperse parachute drops of agents and supplies. They also helped organize other sub-circuits and trained the new agents.

Two Canadian SOE officers, John Kenneth Macalister and Frank Pickersgill, arrived in their area in mid-June 1943. Since the Canadians were new to France, Yvonne and Culioli thought it safer to help them reach their Paris destination. They agreed to take the two men to the Beaugency train station by car and then escort them the rest of the way to Paris on the train.

The Canadians had a parcel containing wireless telegraphy equipment and unencrypted messages addressed to leaders in the Prosper Circuit addressed to them by their code names. Having those names written down broke all SOE security rules. The parcel was labeled as a Red Cross package, but they all knew that it could be very incriminating if the Gestapo stopped the group.

They began their drive on June 21, 1943 (there are differing reports about the exact date), but the Germans stopped them at a roadblock in Dhuizon. The guards told the Canadians to get out of the car and took them for questioning. Two guards got into the car with Yvonne and Culioli and told them to drive to the town hall. The two of them passed inspection at the town hall, and they returned to the roadblock in hopes that the Canadians had also been cleared and released.

When they arrived back at the checkpoint, the guards told them to return to the town hall. They knew that was a bad sign and sped off as fast as they could. Three German patrol cars followed them with sirens blaring. Some six miles down the road, they saw another roadblock ahead. They knew they would be arrested if they stopped, so they drove toward it at full speed.

As the guards at the roadblock realized that the incoming car was not going to stop, they began firing at it. The guards in the car behind also started shooting. Yvonne turned to check on the vehicles following them and two bullets hit her. One of the bullets struck her in the back of her head, penetrating her skull. Culioli, who was with her, thought she had been killed. In a state of panic and lacking his cyanide pill to avoid capture, he drove the car straight into a tree (or a ditch, as reports vary), hoping the crash would kill him. However, he survived the crash with only minor injuries. When he got out of the car and attempted to escape, the Germans shot him in the leg.

The Germans arrested Culioli, and, finding that Yvonne was still alive, they took her to the Blois hospital. The surgeon who examined her determined that the bullet had stopped just short of entering her brain. He felt it was too dangerous to try to remove the bullet, so he left it in place. Reports say that he thought the wound would cause some loss of brain activity.

As Yvonne was recovering, the Gestapo tried to interrogate her but could learn nothing. She appeared not to understand the questions and became very confused. Whether the confusion was real or whether she was pretending is not known.

Meanwhile, the Gestapo examined their car and found the Canadian radio and all the messages – with names - for Prosper leaders. Their discovery resulted in mass arrests of the vast Prosper Circuit agents. That action would come back to haunt Culioli after the war because he was accused of being a double agent and giving vital information to the Gestapo. The first trial found him guilty, but he was given a second trial and acquitted of those charges.

Culioli's capture resulted in him being sent to Avenue Foch for interrogation, then to Fresnes Prison, and finally to Buchenwald. He managed to survive Buchenwald, where so many political prisoners were killed. He eventually escaped from captivity while being transferred from one camp to another toward the end of the war.

The Gestapo gave up on their efforts to interrogate Yvonne, and despite her still being very ill and unable to walk, they transferred her to Fresnes Prison in late September 1943. The Gestapo labeled her as NN (Nacht und Nebel – Night and Fog), meaning she would "disappear without a trace" so that her family and friends would never know what had happened to her. She was using the name of *Jacqueline Gautier,* the name she had first used when entering France.

Yvonne remained at Fresnes until the end of July 1944, when she was transferred to Fort de Romainville. The Fort was a Nazi prison and transit camp on the outskirts of Paris. The Germans had transformed the Fort into a prison with the intention of using it as a staging area before resistors and other prisoners were sent to Nazi concentration camps. During the war, 3900 women and 3100 men went through the prison. One hundred fifty-two others were executed by firing squad and never left the Fort.

Sometime late that summer, Yvonne was sent to Ravensbrück concentration camp. Her left sleeve had a red triangle, identifying her as a political prisoner. A few female SOE agents who were also imprisoned there had worked with Yvonne in the Prosper Circuit, and they tried to communicate with her. She seemed not to know them and said that she was someone else. Perhaps the damage caused by the bullet did affect her memory.

Yvonne was later sent with a group of women to the Bergen-Belsen concentration camp. How she was transported is unknown, although some reports said the guards marched the group there on foot, meaning they walked 200 miles. She reached the camp on March 2, 1945. There was a typhus epidemic raging in the camp when she arrived. 20,000 prisoners had already died. Yvonne contracted the disease.

The Allies liberated the camp on April 15, 1945, but Yvonne and at least 14,000 more prisoners would die within a few days of the liberation. Records show that she died on either April 23 or 24. The Allies had no idea who she was, and she was quickly buried in a mass grave with thousands of others. Reports put the number of bodies in the mass grave at between 5,000 and 20,000. The rapid burial was done to stop the disease from spreading further.

Yvonne was recommended for the Military Cross, perhaps at the instigation of Suttill. She is the only female officially recorded as being recommended for it during World War II. She was ineligible as the Military Cross could not be awarded to a woman. Before anyone knew where her final incarceration was, a citation dated March 15, 1945, recommended her for an OBE or the George Medal "when she is liberated." She did receive the lower level MBE honorary because she was not a British citizen. Because the award cannot be given posthumously, it was backdated to April 23, 1945, the last day she was known to be alive. The French government later awarded her the Croix de Guerre.

Because she used so many names in France, no one at the SOE knew what had happened to Yvonne after the war ended. Vera Atkins, the overseer of the female agents in the 'F' Section of SOE, finally traced her movements and learned of her death in July 1946. The last injustice done to Yvonne is that her death certificate has a misspelling of her last name; it is listed as Ruddelat. Her daughter finally got the name corrected on the certificate and on at least two memorials that also listed it incorrectly.

She is commemorated by an obelisk at Romorantin-Lanthenay in France, where she is one of four members of the SOE to be listed. She is also commemorated on a plaque at the Valençay SOE Memorial, along with 91 men and 13 female SOE agents who were killed or died while working for the SOE in France. In the UK, she is commemorated on a marble plaque on the wall of St Paul's Church, Knightsbridge, London, as one of 52 members of FANY who gave their lives in the war.

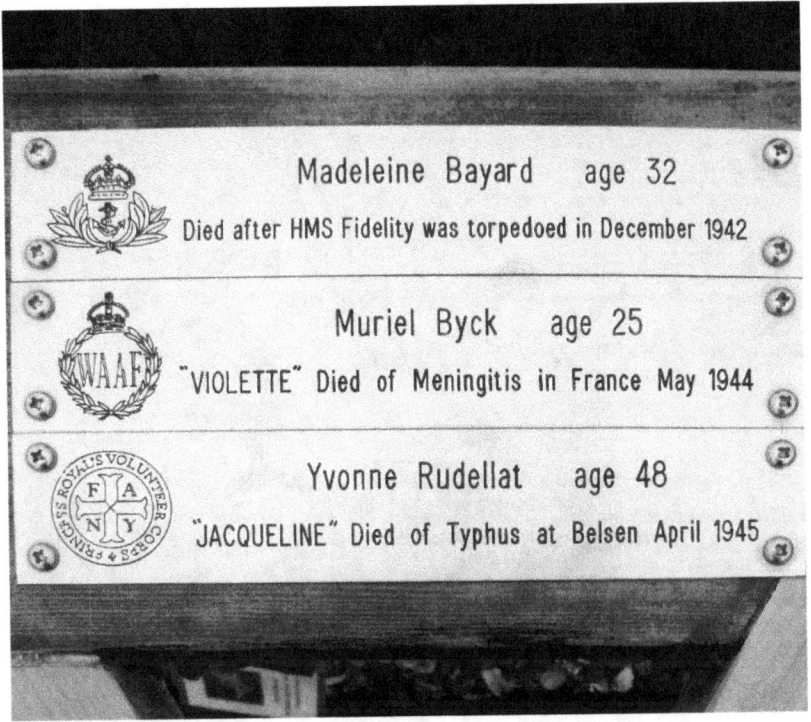

# Chapter 12

# Blanche Charlet

May 23, 1898 – October 11, 1985

Code Name: Christiane  Alias: Madame Sabine Lecomte

Blanche was one of the first four women recruited and trained to work as SOE agents in France. The other women in her training class were Andrée Borrel, Yvonne Rudellat, and Marie-Thérèse Le Chêne. When she reported for training, she was forty-four years old, making Blanche one of the oldest agents sent behind enemy lines in France by SOE.

Valentine Blanche Charlet was born to Belgian parents. She lived much of her life in Belgium and spoke fluent French, but only passable English. She managed a successful art gallery in Brussels before immigrating to England in May 1940, after the Germans invaded Belgium.

Her French language skills brought her to the attention of SOE, and Blanche was recruited to join the organization in 1942. As with most female SOE agents, she joined FANY.

Blanche went through the standard SOE training program except for the parachute training, as SOE thought it would be too risky because of her age. Her training report described her as being: *small, dark-haired, attractive, and lively.*

After successfully completing her courses, she was sent to France on a small boat converted for military use. She was put ashore on September 1, 1942, along the French Riviera, which at that time had relatively few German soldiers. The mass German invasion of southern France did not occur for another two months, beginning on November 11.

Blanche traveled to Cannes, only to discover that her contact had been arrested. The only other contact she had was American Virginia Hall in Lyon, so she moved on and located her. Virginia told her to report to the Ventriloquist Circuit, led by Philippe Albert de Crevoisier, Baron de Vomécourt, with support from radio operator Brian Stonehouse. Blanche joined them as a courier.

Unfortunately, Stonehouse sent a too-long message to London on October 24, 1942, and a German radio detection group located him just as Blanche was arriving at his location. Both were arrested. Stonehouse sent the only message he could, "Danger," before he shut down the radio and was arrested.

**Blanche with Brian Stonehouse, courtesy of Justin Davis Collection**

For the first few days of their imprisonment, they were both held at the same jail. They were able to communicate with each other and they concocted a story they would stick to throughout their interrogations.

Stonehouse was moved to three different concentration camps, Mauthausen, Natzweiler-Struthof and Dachau, but he managed to survive until the end of the war. He was tortured repeatedly but refused to give up any helpful information. After the war ended, he moved to the United States and had a very successful career photographing and painting socialites and celebrities. His paintings were used by magazines including *Vogue, Harper's Bazaar*, and *Elizabeth Arden*. In 1979, he returned to Britain and became a portrait painter. His clients included members of the Royal family. One of his last portraits was of Mary, The Queen Mother.

After three weeks at the local jail, Blanche was sent to Castres prison in southern France on November 13, 1942. While many captured agents were tortured, Blanche did not receive such treatment. She successfully portrayed herself as a poor, ignorant woman who knew nothing of the war, politics, Resistance groups, or much of anything else. She also used the tactic of appearing to faint whenever the Germans put pressure on her during interrogations.

According to fellow SOE agents, there was a belief that Blanche and Brian Stonehouse had developed a romantic relationship. This relationship may have added to Blanche's guilt over their capture, as she had noticed a roving radio-detection vehicle in the area where Stonehouse was working but failed to alert him or others in the Circuit about the car. This oversight could have contributed to their arrest. Reports indicate that while in prison, Blanche tried to kill herself, further suggesting the depth of her despair and guilt.

Between 1941 and 1943, the Vichy regime operated Castres as a "secret" prison, and the Germans and the French police used it for the imprisonment of political opponents, such as communists, resistance fighters, or Spanish republicans. The prison housed the most recalcitrant prisoners. Many of the detainees were later sent to concentration camps.

German writer Rudolf Leonhard was a prisoner, and he described the conditions of detention: *Detained without having been tried, we nevertheless had to endure two heavy penalties: hunger and cold. Not only was the food terrible, but the prison director was shamelessly prospering at our expense.* According to Jonny Granzow, in his book *September 16, 1943, the Escape from Castres Prison*, the daily ration was only one slice of bread, and everyone was held in total isolation.

The Castres prison had poor security, which allowed Blanche and 40-50 other prisoners to manage to get pistols and keys to their cells, enabling them to escape on September 16, 1943 (topic of the book above). This escape, a notable event described in the book above, was coordinated by the German Resistance fighter Werner Schwarze from his residence in Toulouse. Schwarze successfully raised 20,000 francs for the escape operation from a businessman in Lyon, who was later captured and executed by the Nazis. (The author wonders if the businessman might have been the husband of SOE agent Nancy Wake but has found no records to verify that belief. Nancy's husband frequently provided financial support for Resistance operations. and he was executed by the Nazis.)

The prison was in the middle of town, so the escapees left in small groups to avoid attention. It was one of the more successful group escapes during WWII. Only two of the escapees, two officers of the Free French forces, were re-captured.

One of the escapees was Suzanne Warenghem, the wife of British soldier and SOE agent, Harold Cole, who had become a double agent and was working with the Germans. Suzanne was not an SOE agent, but she had been working with the SOE as a local hire. She later claimed she had no knowledge of her husband's traitorous actions. After the war's end, the Allies charged Suzanne with being a collaborator, along with her husband, but she was acquitted. It was only during that trial that she finally accepted that her husband had worked as a double agent for the Germans. Suzanne divorced her husband, changed her name to Suzanne Warren, and never saw Cole again.

After their escape, Blanche and Suzanne found shelter with a local farmer, who then took them to a Benedictine monastery. The monks hid them for two months in a guest house. The two women attempted to cross the Pyrenees mountains into Spain but had to turn back due to the harsh winter weather. With the assistance of other SOE agents, they made it safely to Paris and then to Lyon.

In Lyon, Blanche feared being recognized, so the two women moved closer to the Swiss border, near the Jura Mountains. There, Blanche resumed her work as a courier, facilitating communication between different Resistance groups. It remains unclear what Suzanne did during this time.

There is some discrepancy between the reports of how the two women finally returned to England. M.R.D Foot, the SOE historian, wrote that they escaped over the Pyrenees Mountains into Spain and then on to England. Other reports indicate that Blanche and Suzanne traveled to the Brittany coast, where they were taken by a rowboat to a torpedo boat that transported them to England.

Regardless of which account is correct, they arrived in England on April 20, 1944. Blanche resigned from the SOE soon after. Her continuous time serving in France was among the longest of any of the female agents in SOE.

On February 16, 1946, King George VI awarded her an MBE for "services in France during the enemy occupation."

Blanche never married and died in Greater London on October 11, 1985, at the age of 87.

# Chapter 13

# Andrée Borrel

November 18, 1919 – July 6, 1944

Code Names: Denice and Monique   Alias: Denise Urbain

From her earliest years, those who knew Andrée described her as a tomboy who was strong and athletic. She loved to play sports and roughhouse with the boys, matching them in games and activities. She spent hours at a time hiking or riding a bike, a skill that would prove very valuable when she joined the SOE.

Andrée may have had the least formal education of any of the female SOE agents. Born into a low-income family on the outskirts of Paris, she needed to leave school at 14 to work in a dress factory to help support her family.

Soon after the German invasion of France, Andrée enrolled in a crash course to become a nurse's aide and began working for the Red Cross on January 20, 1940. She trained with the Association des Dames de France and was soon assigned to the quasi-military Beaucaire Hospital in Nimes. When the hospital was about to be closed, she was allowed to resign.

She had been working with Lieutenant Maurice Dufour, a member of SOE's "RF" Section, at the hospital. They formed a romantic relationship, but there were complications because Dufour was married with a 10-year-old son. Although she was not an SOE agent at the time, she began her first direct work for the SOE by helping Dufour smuggle people out of France.

By August 1941, Dufour and Andrée had already set up several safe houses where they could hide British pilots who had been shot down and others needing to escape from France. The individuals would stay at the safe houses until they could be safely guided to Spain.

Dufour and Andrée were betrayed in December 1941. The Germans knew of the location of the safe houses, and they arrested over fifty locals who were helping with the escape route. The police stopped and tried to question Dufour, but he escaped. Fearing arrest, both of them went into hiding. Knowing the Germans were close to capturing them, they hiked over the Pyrenees in mid-February. Once in Spain, they moved on to Portugal and, from there, flew to England. Dufour flew out on March 29, 1942. Andrée stayed behind working at the Free French Propaganda Office at the British Embassy, but she flew out on April 24 of the same year.

**Andrée on her bike**

When he arrived in London, Dufour was held captive by the Free French government working in London. After the war, he filed a lawsuit against the French government claiming that they (Free French personnel) kept him captive and tortured him in the basement of their headquarters. They may have even shot him in an effort to force him to give up SOE secrets. In that lawsuit, he said that the Free French had threatened to capture and gang rape Andrée if he did not tell them everything he knew about SOE.

After being released, he went to the SOE and reported his treatment. He later claimed that the SOE gave him money, a house in the country, and a promise that he could remain in Britain if he kept quiet about the incident until after the war's end. The British government already had problems dealing with Gen.de Gaulle's operation and didn't want further conflict with the Free French. Dufour and Andrée never saw each other again.

Not knowing of Dufour's treatment, Andrée also tried to join General de Gaulle's Free French group in London. They again insisted that she tell them everything she knew about SOE's operation in France, including all the details about the PAT line. She refused to disclose that information, and they rejected her application.

Soon after, Andrée was recruited to join the SOE and became the first—but not the last—French woman recruited who had already worked for the Resistance in France. The SOE knew of the help she had given Dufour on the escape line and thought she would be an excellent addition to the SOE. She accepted on May 15, 1942, and began her training.

Captain Jepson, Andrée's SOE interviewer, commented: *Since arriving in London, she attempted to join the Corps Féminin of the Free French movement, but they have made it a condition that she should give them all the intelligence concerning the organization for which she was working in France. This she refuses to do and apparently, they refuse to employ her unless she does. I think that she would make an excellent addition to our own Corps Féminin, and it should not be difficult to get her... She said that she was perfectly willing to let us have the information she refused to give to the Free French.*

Andrée joined FANY as an ensign, and she went through the SOE training program to become a field agent within their "F" Section. She was promoted to lieutenant upon the successful completion of her training.

The training commandant's report contained the following appraisal of Andrée: *Of sound intelligence if lacking somewhat in imagination. She has little organizing ability and will do her best work under definite instructions. She is thoroughly tough and self-reliant, with no nerves. Has plenty of common sense and is well able to look after herself in any circumstances, and she is absolutely reliable. Has lost her attitude of over-confidence and has benefited enormously from the course and developed a thoroughly level-headed approach towards problems. A very pleasant personality, and she should eventually develop into a first-class agent.*

The men Andrée trained with found her: *informal by habit, lower-class, and scrappy.* She was said to be: *accessible, playful, easy to like, easy to share a smoke and a laugh with, but innocent too, neither hardened nor hurt by the rough wear of war.*

*Andrée in her FANY uniform*

Her fellow female trainees were often shocked by her comments. Yvonne Rudellat was horrified when Andrée told her that the best way to deal with a sleeping German was to stab his brain with a pencil through the ear. It is not known if she knew that trick from experience or if it was something she had been told. Marie-Thérèse Le Chêne saw through her assumed toughness to the innocence beneath and tended to mother her.

Andrée and Lise de Baissac became the first female SOE agents to parachute into France on September 24, 1942. Two other SOE female agents, Yvonne Rudellat and Virginia Hall, were already in France, but they had arrived by boat. Andrée and Lise learned to jump with a parachute at RAF Ringway Parachute

Training School, near Manchester. They were part of Operation Whitebeam, which was to set up Resistance Circuits and Sub-Circuits in Paris and Northern France.

Andrée dropped to the ground first, and they both landed in a field near the village of Mer, about 100 miles southeast of Paris. Resistance team members picked them up and provided them with lodging that night.

The two women had not trained together and didn't yet know each other well. Lise would later say about Andrée that: *She was a girl of the people. She was formidable. Very courageous, very prepared.* The two female agents spent the night in a safe house and then went their separate ways to different Circuits.

Years later, Lise recalled the experience of the flight and parachute jump: *As it happens, we went twice. The pilot wouldn't drop us the first time because the lights of the landing field were not quite accurate, so we had to come all the way back, which was very trying. You were squashed in that little place with a parachute on your back and your legs drawn up, and, of course, there was the danger, too. Back in England, they told us the reception committee had a man missing so they couldn't place the lights for the signal the way they were supposed to.*

*We went back again the next night. We sat on the floor of the airplane, much too tense for conversation, which in any case was not possible because of the noise. I don't remember how long it was until the dispatcher opened the hole, which meant we were arriving. We crept nearer, getting our legs into position. We had drawn straws and luck gave Andrée the first jump. I went immediately after her. You had to jump very quickly, one right after the other, because the plane is going on and you might be dropped very far from each other.*

In November 1942, radio operator Gilbert Norman arrived in France to work for the Prosper Circuit. Associates described Gilbert as handsome, gray-eyed, with a mustache. He was twenty-seven, and Andrée was twenty-three when they met. He came from an upper-class background and used a cover story that he had contracted syphilis seven years before and was too sick to be in the military. He and Andrée took to one another very quickly. Others in the Circuit believed that Andrée and Gilbert may have developed a close relationship during their few months of working together.

The SOE assigned Andrée to work as a courier to the Physician/Prosper Circuit, the largest in France. (The Physician Circuit was usually called the Prosper Circuit, but they were the same Circuit.) It was under the leadership of Francis Suttill, and he was very unhappy about the SOE sending a woman to work with him. He was married and thought having a woman in his immediate group would be a risky distraction.

Radio operator Gilbert Norman, he was executed at the Mauthausen Concentration Camp in Austria.

But Andrée's performance changed his mind. She was quickly considered a valued member of his team. Suttill had a very strong accent when speaking, which everyone thought would bring him to the attention of the French police. Andrée was assigned to travel around the Circuit with him and do most of the talking.

Suttill and Andrée took a month-long trip around central France, exploring the potential for setting up resistance networks. He posed as an agricultural salesman. As they traveled, they looked for possible safe houses and good landing sites for supplies.

Within six months, Suthill, with Andrée's help, connected with almost 10,000 local Frenchmen who wanted to fight against the Germans and were willing to work with SOE. Suthill promised to provide supplies and weapons. The Circuit spread to more than seven different towns and villages, all working together to inflict damage on the German army. Over a few months, the SOE sent in more than 240 large containers of weapons and ammunition for the fighters.

Suthill wrote a report of Andrée's performance in March 1943: *Everyone who has come into contact with her in her work agrees with myself that she is the best of us all. In J...'s absence, she acted as my Lieutenant. Shared every danger. Took part in a December reception committee with myself and some others. Has a perfect understanding of security and an imperturbable calmness. Thank you very much for having sent her to me.* He made her second-in-charge of the Circuit that same month, a position usually given to the radio operator – assuming that position was held by a man.

Francis Suthill, leader of Prosper Circuit. He was executed at the Sachsenhausen concentration camp near Berlin

Andrée helped Suthill train Resistance fighters in the care and use of the British weapons and explosives. A later citation reads: *she took part in several coups de mains, notably an operation at Chevilly power station in March 1943. She distinguished herself by her coolness and efficiency and always volunteered for the most dangerous tasks.* Another SOE agent described Andrée as: *not of great education, but she was entirely wonderful, cool, calm, brave always, a good comrade for men, and an excellent friend, not nothing more, you understand.*

The Prosper Circuit decided to blow up the electric plant that serviced the railroad line bisecting France from east to west. The railroad was critical to the far-flung German army squadrons stationed throughout France. Andrée carried most of the explosives to the site in her backpack, and she transported them by bicycling past German roadblocks.

She and a male agent, Jean Eugene Worms, placed the explosives at the base of three electric pylons. Seven other teams did the same thing to twenty-four other pylons carrying 300,000 volts each. Other groups were putting explosives along the railroad track itself. After setting her charges with a time delay, she left the area and was about two miles away when the explosions went off successfully, one after another.

The Prosper network grew rapidly, and soon, 30 SOE agents were working in the group making it the largest Circuit in France. Things were going so well that they became complacent, resulting in loose security. Radio operator Jack Agazarian claimed to have transmitted messages for 24 different agents, which was against SOE regulations about multiple agents using a common radio operator. Agents also ate together in restaurants, violating SOE rules regarding agents meeting and socializing together. A possible double agent, Henri Déricourt, may have been feeding information to the Germans about Prosper.

The Gestapo prepared to mount a major operation against the Prosper Circuit. On the night of June 15/16, 1943, two SOE agents, Canadians John Kenneth Macalister and Frank Pickersgill, parachuted into France near one of Prosper's groups led by Pierre Culioli. On the morning of June 21, Culioli and Yvonne set off with the two Canadians to catch a train to Paris, unaware that the Germans had set up extensive roadblocks. The Germans captured them and found letters, radio crystals, and instructions in the car, clearly labeled "For Archambaud."

The documents led the Germans to Archambaud (Gilbert Norman, Suttill's wireless operator) because, as Culioli admitted after the war, he had Archambaud's address in his briefcase. Shortly after midnight of June 23, 1943, a German officer pretending to be one of the recently parachuted Canadian agents came to the apartment where Gilbert and Andrée were staying and arrested both of them. The apartment was full of fake identification cards and other documents. The Germans learned from the papers where Suttill was, and they arrested him the next day.

By the end of August 1943, the Germans had captured many of the 30 SOE agents associated with the Prosper Circuit and hundreds of local French who worked with SOE. The Germans killed many outright, and many others died later in concentration camps.

The Gestapo took Gilbert to their Paris headquarters at 84 Avenue Foch. The Germans used Gilbert's captured radio and codes to transmit false messages to SOE Headquarters in London. Gilbert did not give the Germans the second part of his security check. Omitting the security check from a message was explicitly designed to warn London that the SOE radio operator had been captured. However, London failed to heed their own warning system and sent a response telling him to correct the omission. Gilbert was executed on September 6, 1944, at the Mauthausen Concentration Camp in Austria.

After Suttill's capture, he was also interrogated and probably tortured at Gestapo headquarters at Avenue Foch. He was later sent to Sachsenhausen concentration camp near Berlin. They placed him in solitary confinement in the prison block until he was hanged or shot on or about March 23, 1945.

Andrée was also interrogated and tortured at Gestapo headquarters at Avenue Foch, but she refused to provide any information about her activities or fellow agents. After the war ended, German officers said that she showed such fearless contempt for the Germans that they stopped questioning her.

She was transferred to Fresnes Prison. Andrée's family reported after the war, that she had managed to smuggle a few messages out to them. The notes were written on cigarette paper and folded into her lingerie. Somehow, she convinced the prison matron to allow her to send the lingerie to her sister to be laundered. How she convinced the prison matron remains a puzzling issue, as it was so uncharacteristic of prison protocol.

On May 14, 1944, she and seven other female SOE agents were sent to Karlsruhe Prison. The other women were Vera Leigh, Diana Rowden, Sonia Olschanezky, Yolande Beekman, Madeleine Damerment, Odette Sansom and Éliane Plewman.

Less than two months later, very early on the morning of July 6, 1944, Andrée, Diana Rowden, Vera Leigh, and Sonia Olschanezky were put in a closed truck and taken to the remote Natzweiler-Struthof concentration camp.

A male prisoner, Brian Stonehouse, described Andrée when she arrived at the camp: *There was one tall girl with very fair hair. I could see that it was not its natural colour as the roots of her hair were dark. She was wearing a black coat, French wooden-soled shoes, and was carrying a fur coat on her arm...* Assuming his description was correct, how she managed to still have a fur coat remains a mystery.

It is unknown why the Gestapo sent them to the camp so quickly and demanded their immediate death. Andrée Borrel was 25 years old when she was killed. A description of the short time the women were at the camp and of their execution is given in Chapter 2, Vera Atkins (pages 15-17), and Chapter 9, Vera Leigh (pages 94-96).

After the war, the camp doctor, Dr. Werner Rohde, who administered at least some of the killing injections to the four women, was found guilty of war crimes and executed. The camp commandant, Fritz Hartjenstein, received a life sentence for war crimes.

**The crematorium at the Natzweiler-Struthof concentration camp in Germany**

Andrée was awarded the Croix de Guerre and the Medaille de la Resistance by France and the King's Commendation for Brave Conduct (KCBC) by Britain.

The Natzweiler-Struthof concentration camp is now a French government historical site, and a plaque is posted honoring Andrée Borrel and all the other SOE agents killed in the camp.

# Chapter 14

# Denise Bloch

January 21, 1916 – c February 5, 1945

Code Name: Ambroise

Denise was one of the fearless Jewish women who decided to fight German tyranny in any way she could. Denise first worked directly with the Resistance in France as a civilian and later as an SOE agent. The acknowledgment of the contributions of Jewish men and women in the Resistance efforts is a testament to their courage and dedication to freedom and justice.

Although she had difficulty fitting into the SOE rules and regulations, Denise brought extensive wartime experience and contacts to the SOE network. After years of harassing the German occupation forces in France, her actions led to her capture and execution shortly before the end of WWII. Her tragic end underscores the severe risks faced by the agents.

Denise Madeleine Bloch was born in Paris on January 21, 1916, to French Jews Jacques Henri Bloch and Suzanne Levi-Strauss. She was one of four children and the only girl. She was a tall, sturdy woman with broad shoulders that seemed to suggest she could take on the world.

When the Germans invaded France, her father and two of her brothers joined the French Army, and all were taken prisoner by the Germans in 1940. Her father, Jean Louis Jules Barrault (he changed his name after the war), survived their internment, but her brother, Jean-Claude Léon Bloch, died in a German concentration camp.

Denise's younger brother, Jean-Pierre Bloch, and his wife, Gaby Bloch, also became Resistance fighters. Both were captured and imprisoned in the early days of the war. Gaby was released after three months to care for their three children. Jean-Pierre later escaped from prison and made it to England, where he became a key official in de Gaulle's Free French movement, working in the intelligence area. He became the Undersecretary of the Interior in exile, serving in the Free French headquarters after it moved to Algiers in the summer of 1943. He served with distinction with Pres. Charles de Gaulle's government after the war.

When the Germans advanced into Paris, Denise, her mother and younger brother recognized the imminent danger. To evade the widespread arrests and deportations targeting Jews, they fled the city in July 1942, finding refuge in Lyon. There, Denise secured a position as a secretary at the Citroën manufacturing facility. Her boss, Jean-Maxime Aron, a Jewish engineer became actively involved with the Resistance.

The critical situation spurred Denise to join the effort, and she began relaying messages among various Resistance groups. While doing that work, she met several SOE agents.

Denise began working with the SOE radio operator Brian Stonehouse and courier Blanche Charlet, and she witnessed their capture by the Germans on October 14, 1942. Realizing Denise was in danger, SOE agent Capt. Paul Sarrette, code name *Louis*, agreed to escort her and her Citroen boss, Aron, to Marseilles. Denise sent a note to her mother telling her the plan, but the Germans intercepted the letter and arrested Aron. She and Sarrette escaped, and Denise went into hiding for several months. She bleached her black hair to blonde to help evade notice, but her 5ft 10in height made her stand out.

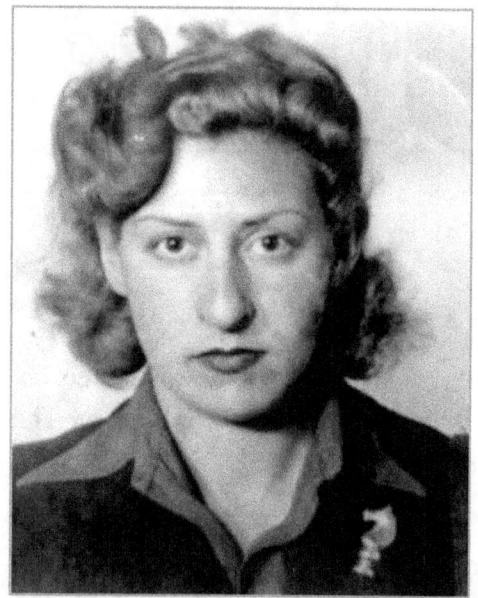
Denise

In January 1943, Sarrette took her to Toulouse, where she was introduced to the Circuit run by the SOE leader, George Starr. Despite not having met her, Starr was initially resistant to having Denise join his Circuit. He openly talked about having her "liquidated." However, he did not act on those threats, highlighting the tense and often distrustful environment within the Resistance networks.

Because the Germans were still searching for her, the SOE made plans to evacuate Denise to England via the escape route over the Pyrenees into Spain. However, the particularly harsh winter that year, with deep snow, made it impossible for her to cross the mountains. Her escape group returned to Toulouse, where she finally met Starr in person.

Despite his earlier reluctance to have Denise join his Circuit, Starr was impressed by Denise's manner and work history. He asked her to work as his courier. They stayed in the isolated village of Castelnau-sur-l'Auvignon, where there was considerable speculation by other SOE agents that the two became lovers. With no radio operator in the Circuit, Denise made weekly trips to Toulouse to send Starr's messages to the SOE in London, relying on the radio operator Marcus Bloom. However, Bloom's arrest in April 1943 severed their only line of communication with London, further complicating their operations.

Starr's decision to send Denise over the Pyrenees with a written report was a significant breach of SOE protocol. She was instructed to demand a radio operator for Starr's Circuit. Remarkably, Denise and her guide completed the arduous trip in a record-breaking 17 hours. Although the Spanish police briefly detained her, she was released and managed to traverse Spain in just 21 days, arriving in Gibraltar. From there, she was flown to London on May 21, 1943. This rapid journey was particularly impressive, as it typically took agents two to three months to complete the same route.

On July 29, 1943, a French court convicted Denise in absentia and sentenced her to ten years of hard labor for her collaboration with the Resistance.

After delivering Starr's written report to SOE, Denise was thoroughly debriefed. She strongly advocated for the SOE to only send agents with excellent French language skills and knowledge of French customs into France. The SOE heeded her advice and began to emphasize these requirements when recruiting new agents, reflecting her significant impact on their operational strategies.

Denise also provided critical advice for male agents, noting that many young men were frequently conscripted by the French police or the Gestapo for labor work in Germany. She cautioned that future agents should avoid appearing too young or should pretend to be sick to avoid being arrested without cause and sent to a work camp in Germany. This information was vital in safeguarding male agents and their effectiveness in occupied France.

London's response to Starr's request for a radio operator was to send an airplane to hover over the area where Starr was staying so they could communicate by short-range S-phone to verify that he was still alive and his Circuit was in operation. Eventually, Starr's tactic of sending Denise to London was effective. The SOE soon sent two additional female agents to Starr's Circuit, radio operator Yvonne Cormeau and courier Anne-Marie Walters.

Denise told the SOE that she wanted to return to France, but they thought the risk was too high. However, they encouraged her to join FANY and the SOE and go through their training program. Despite her contemptuous attitude toward the SOE training, they convinced her that they would train her to work as a radio operator and that she could return to France - but to a different part of the country where she would not be known.

The job of radio operators working behind German lines was very stressful. They worked mostly alone, often for long hours, seven days a week, always trying to evade the Nazis and their radio frequency detection equipment.

The SOE personnel file held by the National Archives in Kew, England, contains this report written during her training period: *An experienced woman with knowledge of the world. She has courage and determination and a thorough understanding and hatred of the Boche (Germans.) Has complete self-assurance and is capable of handling most situations.* Denise successfully completed her 10-month training program.

All SOE agents were issued suicide pills when they left England, often concealed in coat buttons or women's makeup compacts. While some agents refused the pills, it is not known if Denise carried hers. While the horrors of the concentration camps were not yet generally known, everyone understood that being Jewish significantly increased her risk if captured.

Denise and former Grand Prix racing car driver Robert Benoist were flown into the area around Nantes, France, on March 2, 1944. Benoist's orders read: *You will be accompanied to the field by AMBROISE (Denise), who is to act as your W/T operator. She will be under your command, but it must be understood that she is the ultimate judge in all questions regarding the technicalities of W/T and W/T security. She will encode the messages herself. They should be as short and clear as possible since it is of the utmost importance that her time on the air should be reduced to the minimum.*

They joined up with another former racing car driver, Jean-Pierre Wimille, to revive the Clergyman Circuit. Their first mission was to work with the local Resistance to destroy communications by blowing up the power line towers and cutting or disabling the railroad line along the Brittany coast in preparation for the Allied invasion.

Denise's versatility was evident as she worked for several months both as a radio operator and a courier. She also took part in numerous missions with Resistance fighters. One report to the SOE detailed how she successfully evaded a German checkpoint, an incident that could have had disastrous consequences for her: *On one occasion, she was carrying her radio in the usual suitcase pack when she was about to travel on a bus. She saw a Gestapo inspection in progress at the bus stop. So, she engaged one of the Gestapo agents using very poor German, causing him some amusement, and asked him to hold her case whilst she bought a newspaper. She then showed her papers to a civilian inspector, returned for her case, and got cooly on the bus with no trouble.*

On June 17, 1944, only eleven days after D-Day, Benoist called a meeting at his villa of the critical members of his Circuit – in direct conflict with SOE policy to never get all the key people together in one location. The rule noted in Benoist's orders read as follows: *It is never our policy to get together large groups of men since, in our opinion, the only effective basis for effective action is the small self-contained group. This applies in your particular case since all targets given to you can be dealt with by small groups.*

Benoist told the group he was leaving to visit his dying mother and instructed the group to disperse if he did not return by noon the next day. Unfortunately, Benoist and his sister, Charlotte Perdrigé, were captured by Germans lying in wait outside his mother's apartment. Under interrogation, one of them may have revealed the large Circuit meeting, believing the group had dispersed. However, the group had not followed Benoist's instructions, and on June 18 at 8 PM, the Germans raided his villa, capturing the entire leadership team, including Denise.

**Robert Benoist, former Grand Prix Racecar Driver, SOE Agent in WWII**

Denise was taken to the infamous fifth floor of the Nazi's headquarters at 84 Avenue Foch in Paris, where she was interrogated and beaten, then taken to the Fresnes Prison. She remained there until August 8, 1944. The Allies had landed on the coast in June and were moving toward Paris. To move them away from the Allies, Denise, and other imprisoned female SOE agents were transferred to Ravensbrück concentration camp, the dreaded women's prison in Germany.

Meanwhile, on September 9, 1944, the camp commandant at Buchenwald concentration camp received an order to give 16 of the male prisoners "special treatment." At Buchenwald, that meant execution by being choked to death while suspended above the floor with piano wire hung from a meat hook. Denise's former Circuit leader, Benoist, was among the 16 executed on September 11, 1944.

Denise was moved to the prison with fellow SOE agents Violet Szabo and Lilian Rolfe. The three of them volunteered for a work party outside the prison at Torgau because they thought the conditions would be better. They tried to escape but were caught and sent back to Ravensbrück. They were severely beaten and put in an underground bunker until October 19, 1944, when they were sent to Konigsberg, Germany (the Soviet Union annexed that town after the war, and it is now Kaliningrad, Russia).

The women endured harsh conditions, forced to do heavy labor building a new airport during winter with no warm clothing and subsisting on thin soup made from water and potato peels and a small bite of bread each day. By mid to late January 1945, they were sent back to Ravensbrück in such poor physical condition that they could no longer work. Other prisoners later reported that Denise was suffering from gangrene. They were once again placed in solitary confinement.

After having endured so much torture and mistreatment, the three SOE women, Denise, Violet, and Lilian, were executed at Ravensbrück. The details of their execution and the trial of those responsible for killing them are described in detail in the Vera Atkins Chapter 2 (pages 16 & 17).

The three women had no grave, but Denise is memorialized in the Bloch Family's gravesite at the Montmartre Cemetery in Paris, and she has a plaque in several war memorials for the female SOE members who lost their lives during the war.

After the war, Denise received the following awards: Britain awarded her the 1939-45 Star, the France and Germany Star, and the War Medal with King's Commendation for Brave Conduct; France awarded the Chevalier of the Legion d'honneur, the Croix de Guerre with Palm, and the Medaille de la Resistance. She is also listed on the "Roll of Honor" for the 13 women and 91 men members of the SOE who gave their lives for France's freedom at the Valençay, France, SOE Memorial.

# Chapter 15

# Lise de Boucherville Baissac

May 11, 1905 – March 29, 2004

Code Name: Odile, Irene, Marguerite, & Adele.

Alias: Madame Irene Brisse, Madame Janette Bouville

Lise was one of the first two SOE women who parachuted into France. Her instructors recognized her abilities very early in the SOE training program, and she was among the very small group of SOE women thought to be competent enough to run their own Circuit.

Lise was born Lise de Boucherville Baissac on May 11, 1905, as the only daughter in the affluent family of Marie Louis Marc de Boucherville Baissac and his wife, Louise Marie Jeanette Dupont. The family were large landholders in Mauritius. Mauritius is an island about 1,100 nautical miles off the southeastern coast of East Africa, east of Madagascar.

In addition to their large plantation, her father represented the Sun Insurance Company of London. Her mother was the sister to Vice Consul Britannique Tamatave Anatole Jules Paul Henri Marcelin Sauzier. The entire family was bi-lingual, with French as their preferred language.

When Lise was fourteen in 1919, the family moved to Paris, and she attended The Lycée Henri-IV, a public secondary school. Along with the Lycée Louis-le-Grand, it was widely regarded as one of France's most prestigious and demanding sixth-form colleges.

Three years later, Lise fell in love with a man who would become her husband many years later, Gustave Villameur. He was a poor artist, and her parents forbade the relationship. Lise would remain single for the next 30 years, but she was a determined woman. She knew who she wanted to be with and never wavered in that decision.

After finishing school, Lise worked as a secretary in Paris, which was very unusual for young women from a wealthy family. Lise was described as a slender woman with striking eyes and short fair hair (although some reports said she had black hair). She was 5 ft., 5 in. tall.

When the Germans invaded France in May 1940, her older brother, Jean, immigrated to England and enlisted in the British army. Lise and her younger brother, Claude, wanted to move to England, too, but the German occupation made it increasingly difficult. They individually hiked over the Pyrenees to Spain and then traveled from Barcelona to Lisbon, Portugal. They met up again in Gibraltar but had to wait five months before finally traveling on to London, arriving in late 1941.

Lise later noted her shock at the way so many French reacted to the German occupation: *I was very, very unhappy to see the retreat, the flight of large parts of the population - all the people from the north who fled before the Germans. I thought it was wrong to have done that, that one had to fight. It was painful, terrible to see the fall of France.*

Claude joined SOE, and Lise was later recruited when the SOE began accepting women. When Captain Jepson interviewed and invited Lise to join, she immediately accepted. She was commissioned into FANY and became a member of the second SOE training class that included women. Lise was the oldest in the class. With her in the class were Odette Sansom, Andrée Borrel, and Jacqueline Nearne.

Lise received some of the most positive instructor comments of any of the women. Her training reports were overwhelmingly favorable and indicated that she was: *intelligent, extremely conscientious, reliable, and sound in every way...capacity to sum up a situation, make a decision and stick to it without becoming flustered...a very high degree of self-confidence.* Another instructor wrote: *She was very much ahead of her fellow students and, had she been with others as mentally mature as herself, she would have shown herself even more capable.*

*Lise de Baissac, Mauricienne, du S.O.E.*

**Lise de Boucherville Baissac in her FANY uniform**

Lise was approved as a full-fledged SOE agent and was given the code name *Odile*. On the night of September 25, 1942, she and fellow agent Andrée Borrel were the first two SOE women to fly out of the Tempsford airfield and parachute into France. Andrée jumped first, with Lise close behind. They jumped from a Whitley bomber and landed in the Loire Valley. Lise was thirty-seven when she made that jump.

After landing, Andrée moved north to work in the Prosper Circuit in Paris, but Lise moved south to Poitiers. She was given the very unusual task for a woman of setting up a brand-new Circuit to be known as Artist. She was one of only four female SOE agents given the responsibility of running their own operations during the war. She lived alone in a two-room apartment. Lise presented herself as *Madame Irene Brisse*, a widow seeking safety and calm during the war.

The responsibilities of her Artist Circuit were different from those of most other Circuits. She was to receive new SOE agents arriving in France, get them acclimated to work in occupied territory, and then move them to other Circuits. She was also expected to collect information about German activities in the area, locate drop zones for supplies for the Maquis fighters, and act as the liaison between the large Prosper Circuit and the sub-Circuits Scientist and Bricklayer.

She had no radio operator, so she had to travel back and forth to Paris or to other Circuits in the area to update London on her activities and to receive instructions from the SOE. During her 11 months in Poitiers, she received and briefed 13 new agents and organized the departure of SOE agents and others leaving for England.

She also collected air-dropped supplies and built a support network to transport these supplies to the Maquis. Her stationary Circuit made her an easier target for inquisitive police or Gestapo agents who might find her suspicious. The SOE instructed her not to participate in any direct operations against the Germans.

Due to her frequent travel between different Circuits, she occasionally saw other SOE women like Yvonne Rudellat, Andrée Borrel, and Mary Herbert. She usually worked and lived alone, except for periodic visits from new agents or those staying with her before departing for London. Reflecting on her experiences, she later said: *I was very lonely. Very, very lonely. You grew to know very well what solitude was. Because you are alone; you have false papers; you never have a telephone call; you never get a letter.*

Lise took private Spanish lessons with a local professor to help fill her downtime, and she became friends with another instructor. But both teachers knew her by her false name and cover story, so she could never be open and honest with them.

In the course of her work receiving new agents and arranging for agents to leave France, she worked with Henri Déricourt and thought highly of him. She had no reason to suspect him, but many SOE agents thought him to be a double agent. He was tried for treason after the war but acquitted by the court.

Lise later reported how important it was for all SOE agents to look like locals. Store-bought clothing was in short supply and rationed; people often wore old clothing. Lise, who had always dressed in an expensive and elegant fashion in her private life, had to wear discarded clothing. She later commented about how drab she felt during her SOE service.

She was so effective in her work that the Gestapo soon learned about her and assigned extra Gestapo agents to find her base of operation. In June 1943, a double agent betrayed the large Prosper Circuit. Many agents were arrested, some never to be seen again. The SOE recalled her to London for her safety, along with her brother Claude and Major Nicholas Bodington, and sent a plane to pick them up on August 17, 1943.

The SOE recognized Claude's leadership qualities, but they also regarded him as "volatile" and "stubborn". "F" Section leader Maurice Buckmaster would later call him: *the most difficult of my officers without any exception.* Buckmaster thought both Claude and Lise shared the family characteristic of being "difficult but determined." In the words of M.R.D. Foot, Claude was of: *exceptional character but suffered no fool gladly. He was an imposing man with the air of someone who expected to be obeyed.*

Lise's usual method of passing information to Claude was for her to travel to Bordeaux and sit in the corner of a friendly café that Claude passed almost daily. Sometimes, she would sit for long hours, even into the night, before he would pass by. He would join her for coffee or a meal, and she would share her information. They could also reminisce and talk about family and friends. They would part, and she would return to her lonely apartment.

**Lise's brother, Claude Marie Marc Boucherville de Baissac**

During Claude's first mission to lead his own Circuit, he formed an intimate relationship with fellow SOE agent Mary Herbert, something that was strongly discouraged. Mary became pregnant with their child. Lise and Mary became good friends and Mary was one of the few people Lise could laugh and talk with without security concerns.

When Claude returned to England because his Circuit had been betrayed, he took Lise with him but left Mary behind in France. It is not known what Lise thought about his abandonment of Mary. Most SOE agents faulted Claude for leaving the pregnant Mary behind.

Mary went into hiding, but she had no radio and no way to tell SOE, Claude, or Lise where she was. She stayed with a friendly local family until the baby was born. She gave birth to a daughter, Claudine, in December 1943. Mary and the baby then moved into Lise's former apartment in Poitiers.

After Lise returned to London, the SOE gave her a promotion within FANY to the rank of captain. She was debriefed about her activities in France and asked about ways to improve the program. After her evaluation, the following was a part of the notes written in her file: *One of our most successful girls. A good organizer and administrator. Was popular with her contacts and much loved in the region. She perhaps suffered from the family faults (excess of personal ambition and touchiness), but she is always ready to see reason and invariably puts her work first. Is "difficult" but devoted and has made a very large contribution to the success of "F" Section.*

For several months, Lise worked in Britain with new agents in training, including Yvonne Baseden and Violette Szabo. While doing a parachute jump with the new agents, Lise broke her leg and had to wait for it to heal before returning to France.

**Lise with a FANY ambulance**

On April 9, 1944, she was ready to return to France, but due to her leg injury, she could no longer parachute. The SOE flew her and Philippe de Vomécourt to France. As they left the plane, agent Jaqueline Nearne climbed in to return to England. The welcoming agents provided a bicycle for Lise to ride to her safe house.

Due to her injured leg, she couldn't keep up with the group. She later wrote: *I was a right long way back, and I had to follow them...they had turned right or left. I couldn't see. Luckily, I turned right, and it was there that I found them. Had I turned left, I don't know what would have happened to me...But that was really frightening. I still remember that...Perhaps it's the most difficult moment of all my missions. Should I turn right or left?*

On this second trip, the SOE gave her two new code names, *Marguerite and Adele*, and another alias, *Madame Janette Bouville*. She became another widow seeking a quiet environment. Lise's orders were to join Tony Brook's Pimento Circuit in Lyon. His code name *Alphonse*. She thought she was to be a co-leader, but he wanted her only as a courier.

While the courier's role was important in each Circuit, she was accustomed to leading her own Circuit and was unhappy in the courier role. The Maquis fighters that Pimento Circuit was working with had strong communist or socialist leanings. They were also very chauvinistic and made it very clear that they had no room for a woman within their circle. The leader, Tony Brook, joined in with snide comments about her being a woman.

When she returned to London after the war's end, she made the following comment about that Circuit: *If I had known all this (the group's politics) before going out, I should have realized at once that I was not the person they needed. I'm not at all surprised that they didn't want me, but what does revolt me whenever I think of it is the disloyal manner in which Tony behaved towards me, who arrived in his organization with the best intentions. I think his behavior has been unworthy of his intelligence, which I know to be great.*

Lise asked to be transferred to the reformed Scientist Circuit in Normandy under the leadership of her brother, Claude. London agreed, and she moved to that group. Claude also had a new code name, *David*. He returned to France on February 11, 1944. When Claude arrived back in Normandy, he commented about the Maquis that: *the secret army is so secret, I can't find it.*

Over the next three months, she concentrated on organizing Maquis groups and directing them regarding targets to be hit, supplying them with arms, and identifying landing sites for the arrival of supplies. After D-Day, those same sites would be used to bring in commandos. Claude and Lise had to train the local fighters to use the new weapons. Lise arranged for the transport of the supplies to the Maquis groups by using farm wagons, jeeps, and delivery vans. Both Lise and Claude tried to keep to their orders to plan operations but not to participate in them.

Lise cycled between the Maquis groups they worked with and other Circuits, often covering 40-60 miles daily. She took small arms and explosives to the fighters and relayed instructions about new targets. Groups organized by her used tire-busters that caused heavy losses to the enemy, and contrary to her orders, she took part in a few attacks on enemy columns.

When a radio set broke down, Lise and her radio operator, Pippa Latour, cycled to another village to use a replacement radio. She carried crystals for the set and codes in a belt around her waist. They were both stopped and searched by a German soldier doing a spot check, but the guard did not find the radio parts or codes, and they continued on their way.

There were German soldiers everywhere, and they could stop and search anyone at any time. The risk rose daily as Lise moved about the area on her bicycle taking directions to the Maquis fighters.

An incident, which could easily have proved fatal, occurred when a group of retreating Germans moved into the house in which Lise was living. When she returned to her room that afternoon, she discovered that the soldiers had opened her sleeping bag, which was made of her parachute silk. One of the soldiers was sitting on it, but they fortunately didn't know what it was. She calmly gathered her belongings and left the house. She returned two days later after the soldiers had moved on.

A note in Lise's file said: *She was the inspiration of groups on the Orne and by her initiative caused heavy losses to the Germans with tyre bursters on the roads near St Aubin-le-Desert, St Mars, and as far as Laval, Le Mans, and Rennes. She also took part in several armed attacks on enemy columns.*

While everyone in SOE knew an Allied landing was coming somewhere along the coast, no one knew the location or when it would occur. Unknown to Claude and Lise, Normandy would be the landing site of Allied forces in the D-Day invasion on June 6.

After D-Day, the primary tasks of the Scientist Circuit were to disrupt communications between the German military groups, mine roads, cut rail and telephone lines - anything to delay and harass the German army. They also armed new Maquis groups that would later take vengeance on the Germans. Sharing information with and between the Circuits and the Maquis groups in all the chaos after D-Day was challenging for Lise as it required her to travel many miles every day.

Once the D-Day landing happened, the Scientist Maquis fighters gathered intelligence on German troop movements. The SOE operations were carried out in an environment in which large numbers of German soldiers were present as they attempted to repel the invading Allied forces. Claude, Lise, and other SOE agents stayed on the move and slept in a different location nearly every night, often in farmer's barns or sheds. The area was crawling with German soldiers, with some moving forward to engage the Allies advance forces, while others were being pulled back toward Germany.

Once the Allied forces landed and began to move away from the coast, Frenchmen who had not previously been involved in the Resistance effort suddenly came forward and wanted to enlist. They wanted to be seen as working on the winning side. As the tide turned on the Germans, Charles de Gaulle's Free French forces quickly moved into the Scientist area of operations. Claude resisted leaving the area as de Gaulle began spreading the word that the Free French had been solely responsible for fighting the Germans.

While working with the Scientist Circuit, Lise followed orders and kept her cover story of being a poor widow in a Normandy village. On July 25, 1944, the American army launched a second landing called "Operation Cobra," which pushed the German army out of the Scientist Circuit area of operation.

On August 13, Claude and Lise greeted the lead unit of U.S. soldiers. They met the American soldiers dressed in their long-unworn British military uniforms. The villagers were shocked. They thought Lise was just a lonely widow living among them, and here she was with other SOE agents, turning the area over to the US Army.

Lise remained in place until a black car pulled up in front of her lodgings, and Vera Atkins, head of the recruitment and oversight of all SOE agents in France, stepped out to personally bring Lisa in from the cold. Rather than getting into a fight with de Gaulle, SOE removed both Claude and Lise by flying them to England.

Lise and Claude returned to France in September 1944 to help look for missing SOE agents. They were especially keen to find Mary Herbert, the mother of Claude's child. They finally traced her to Poitiers and found her, along with her baby daughter, living in Lise's old lodgings. They all returned to England together. Claude married Mary, but the couple did not live together, and it was apparently a marriage of convenience to give the daughter a legal name.

England awarded Lise the prestigious MBE, a civilian award, but she refused to accept it. She and Pearl Witherington were upset that they did not qualify for military awards since SOE men in the same positions did qualify. Lise wrote to Vera Atkins: *The work which I volunteered to do in 1942 was of a military nature, and later, when open warfare became necessary, we organized and carried out open attacks on the enemy. I was sent to the field on two missions, and had I been arrested, I would most probably have been shot. I understood when I undertook this work that it was to be kept secret and did not, therefore, expect any recognition. I should have been honoured, however, to count myself amongst those it has now been decided to decorate, but I feel the award of the MBE is one I cannot qualify for, as I have not rendered long and devoted service in a civilian capacity.* Witherington reflected a similar sentiment, specifically highlighting the fact that: *Our training, which we did with the men, was purely military, and as women, we were expected to replace them in the field...*

Lise was previously recommended for the George Cross medal by Buckmaster, head of "F" Section of the SOE, who wrote: *a very courageous woman, very diplomatic. She did everything.* Captain Blackman, the leader of a Special Air Service (SAS) group that had received support from Lise on several occasions, recommended her for an OBE, writing: *She risked her life daily... The part she played in aiding the Maquis and the British underground movement in France cannot be too highly stressed.* His recommendation was rejected because she was a woman.

Lise did accept the Croix de Guerre Avec Palme from the French in 1946, which had a citation from General de Gaulle himself. She was later made a Chevalier of the Legion d'Honneur.

After the war, Lise returned to England, eager to continue working. While most of the SOE women were released immediately to make room for the returning men, the SOE agreed to keep her on for a while and assist in finding her other employment. Eventually, she found work that aligned with her pre-war interests, becoming an announcer and translator for the BBC and the French Service in London.

Lise spoke about fear during an interview: *You know you are in danger all the time, but you always think that you will go through. I have never been afraid really that I would be caught. It never occurred to me. I think that we're all like that. If you're frightened, you can't do anything.* But she did say she was sometimes nervous. She also said: *The loneliness of a secret life required cold-blooded efficiency for long weary months was needed more than heroism.*

Lise learned that her long-ago love, Gustave Villameur, who had been married, was now divorced and a successful artist and interior designer. It is not known who made the contact, but they married on October 17, 1950. They moved into an apartment over his studio, which was set high above the port in Marseilles. Lise was 45 years old. They also owned a home in St. Tropez, where they entertained their friends, art critics and buyers, as well as people she had known during the war.

After waiting for so many years for the man she loved, they had a happy life together for 28 years until he died in 1978. At that time, she moved into a luxurious apartment in Marseilles, where she would live the rest of her life.

Sixty years after her initial parachute jump into France in 1942, Lise watched as six young FANY women and paratroopers from the Ecole des Troupes Aeroportees (ETAP) parachuted onto the same spot she and Andrée Borrell had landed. Then, ETAP's commanding officer finally presented her with her parachute wings, which had been initially denied to most of the SOE women who made the jump during WWII.

In 1988, when Lise was 83 years old, author Liane Jones met and interviewed her in Marseille. The following is her description of Lise: *I was taken aback by her appearance when she opened the door – she was so small and fragile, with white hair and a pretty face. I had been expecting someone more formidable. But within a few minutes, it was obvious why "F" Section had chosen her for this job. She is vital but self-contained, generous but cool.* Lise said to her: *I tell you frankly that I have no more interest in the war, I am quite happy to tell you whatever you want to know. I enjoy living alone, I was very happy while I was married to my husband, but now I am alone again I don't mind. I have always been very well able to occupy myself and I like being independent.*

Lise told her of an unexpected letter she received from a man named Remy Clement that brought back a light-hearted memory. He wrote that: *They had spent a night in the hay together. His name then had been Marc. And it was quite true! She said, smiling. This man had been arranging the pick-up for Claude and I to go back to England and we had to stay overnight with him in a barn waiting for the aeroplane. I thought that was so funny. I wrote back, saying, You are quite right, we did!*

Lise was the vice-president of the France-Bretagne Association of Marseille and was very active in social events. A friend commented on the parties that Lise hosted in Marseille: *They were very smart affairs, where you were expected to perform, The conversation wasn't idle chatter and gossip; oh no, you had to be right up to the mark. Lise has always liked to be challenged intellectually. She and Vera (Atkins) made a formidable pair.*

In 2004, she fell and broke her hip. Like so many elderly patients with a broken hip, she developed a respiratory complication in the Marseilles hospital and died on March 28, 2004, at 98 years of age.

**Lise shortly before her death**

Her obituary in the London Guardian described Lise as: *A Grande Dame of the old school: fiercely independent, courageous, elegant, and modest.* After reading her obituary, Jean-Paul Salome, a French film director, decided to make *Female Agents*, a movie loosely based on Lise's experiences, and it was released in June 2008.

# Chapter 16

# Mary Herbert

October 1, 1903 - January 23, 1983

Code Name: Claudine, Maureen    Alias: Marie Louise Vernier

Mary had the unusual distinction of being the only woman working for the SOE in France who had a baby during her war service. The father, Claude de Baissac, was the leader of the Scientist Circuit, where she was assigned as a courier. It was quite scandalous and required her to stop her SOE work late in the pregnancy.

Mary Katherine Herbert (also called Maureen) was born in Ireland on October 1, 1903, the younger daughter of a military family. Her father was Brigadier General Edmund Herbert. Mary was an intelligent woman who graduated from London University with an art degree. She also had a gift for languages and spoke not only English but also Italian, French, Spanish, and German.

After receiving her original degree, she obtained an Arabic diploma from the University of Cairo, Egypt. Later, Mary added Russian to her repertoire of languages. Mary worked in Australia before moving back to Europe where she worked for the British government at their embassy in Warsaw, Poland. When WWII broke out, she moved back to London and worked as a civilian translator for the Air Ministry.

A relative, Claudine Pappe, described her: *Mary was a tall, slender, fair-haired woman, who was naturally courteous and considerate of other people, generous and trusting, and in some ways naïve. She was attractive with an engaging smile, made and kept friends easily and her knowledge of art, literature and languages made her an interesting companion.*

**Mary Herbert**

Mary enlisted in the WAAF on September 19, 1941, but requested a transfer to the SOE in March 1942. She participated in the second SOE group of trainees. She was the first WAAF officer to volunteer for the SOE and was given a retroactive commission with the rank of section officer. It was backdated to January 15, 1942.

Fellow female trainees included Lise de Baissac, Jacqueline Nearne, and Odette Sansom . Mary was 39, making her one of the older SOE recruits. She was tall at 5'7" and thin, and some agents thought her too fragile to survive in the harsh world of the Resistance environment in France.

Most SOE trainees had some courses in Scotland, but her group had almost all their training at the Special Training School 31 at Beaulieu in Hampshire, England. There were eventually eleven different SOE training schools on the Beaulieu estate. Approximately 3,000 SOE agents passed through the training program.

When Mary completed her training, she expected to be flown to France. However, she was transferred to a small submarine and crossed to Gibraltar with fellow agents Marie-Thérèse Le Chêne, Odette Sansom, Marcus Bloom, and George Starr. From Gibraltar, they went by a small felucca to the south coast of France. The boat smelled so strongly of sardines that they feared they would be sick before arriving in France. The group went ashore on October 31, 1942.

After coming ashore, Mary took a train to Cannes and then another to Bordeaux but, fortunately, had no problems from the German soldiers on the train. The SOE assigned Mary to work as a courier to the Scientist Circuit. The Circuit leader was Claude de Baissac, code name *David.* Claude was a strong-willed man from Mauritius who was considered one of the more effective SOE Circuit leaders.

She and Lise de Baissac, a fellow SOE agent and Claude's sister, liked and trusted each other, and they became friends as they were the only two SOE women in the area.

Claude was not an easy person to work with. Buckmaster said of him: *the most difficult of all my officers without any exception.* But he was also very effective. He recruited tens of thousands of people to work with the Scientist Circuit on sabotage operations and information gathering. They were excellent at obtaining valuable intelligence about German troop movements in and around Bordeaux and the naval operations around the docks.

Mary and Claude soon developed a personal relationship, and she became pregnant. In June 1943, before the couple could make any decisions about the future, the Circuit was impacted by a betrayal. Germans penetrated the largest Circuit in France, the Prosper Circuit. The Gestapo moved in to arrest the SOE agents and many of their supporters. Over 300 Resistance fighters were arrested and killed because of the betrayal. Because Mary's Circuit worked with Prosper, there was a significant risk to their own agents. Consequently, London ordered Claude to return to England to avoid arrest. He flew out of France on August 16, 1943, taking his sister Lise with him, but leaving Mary in France.

Claude left Andre Grandelement as his replacement as the leader of the Scientist Circuit. Grandelement did not do well as a leader, and he was replaced by radio operator Roger Landes, code name *Aristide.* Landes was furious that Claude left Mary behind. She continued to work, bicycling between Resistance groups that were still functioning,

**Claude de Baissac, Scientist Circuit leader and the father of Mary's child**

**Roger Landes**

until her pregnancy became evident. Landes did all he could to help her and insisted that she step back from her duties as her pregnancy progressed.

Landes and Mary escaped the arrest squads, and he helped get her into a nursing home in LaValence where she could stay until the birth of her child. He and a few fellow agents had to flee over the Pyrenees Mountains for their safety on November 20, 1943. Mary was the last member of the Circuit remaining in France. Mary's daughter, Claudine, was born by caesarian section in early December 1943. Mary was 40 years old, and Claudine was the only child she would ever have. Mary used her SOE code name as the name for her daughter.

Mary and her daughter moved into Lise's old apartment in Poitiers. On February 18, 1944, only two months after her daughter was born, the Gestapo raided the apartment looking for Lise but instead found Mary. The Germans knew that Lise had rented the apartment and suspected that she worked for the British. They mistook Mary for Lise and arrested her, placing her in solitary confinement. Mary insisted that she had sub-let the apartment and didn't know anything about Lise or any spy network.

Mary's knowledge of Arabic was helpful as she told the Gestapo that she had lived in Cairo and had only come to France for safety when the war began. They put her daughter in the care of a local convent orphanage through the office of the French Social Service.

Mary was held and interrogated for two months but apparently not tortured. She stuck to her story, and the Germans finally accepted that a new mother still nursing a baby was probably not a spy. They released her during Easter week in 1944. It took her some time to trace her daughter's whereabouts, but she finally found her, and they were reunited. They returned to the apartment in Poitiers, where they remained until the Allies moved into the area.

In September 1944, Claude and Lise returned to France to search for Mary and the child. Once they found them, they took them back to England. It is unknown if Lise or Claude initiated that trip as Claude's behavior suggested he had little interest in being either Mary's husband or a father to Claudine.

Once safely back in England, Claude and Mary were married on November 11, 1944, at Corpus Christi Church in London. They may have married only to give their child legitimacy, as the couple never lived together. After the marriage, Mary moved back to her father's home in Monmouthshire.

After her father died, Mary purchased a small house where she and her daughter lived. It is unknown if Claude helped with the purchase or financially supported Mary or Claudine. Mary gave private French lessons to local children for many years. When she came of age, Claudine immigrated to the U.S. and married an airline pilot.

After the war, Claude worked for the Allied Control Commission in Germany and then moved to West Africa where he worked for a mining company. He finally divorced Mary in 1959 after almost 15 years of separation. In 1964, Claude married Colette Avril, a woman from Cameroon. They moved to France, where he went into the banking business. Claude died in 1974. It is unknown if he ever saw his daughter after 1944.

Mary died of pneumonia at her cottage in Frant, Sussex, on January 23, 1983. Her daughter, Claudine, had returned from the U.S. to be with her during her illness. Mary was cremated and there is no grave site.

Mary received the Croix de Guerre from France but no acknowledgment from England, perhaps because she became pregnant while unmarried and still an agent of the SOE.

# Chapter 17

# Odette Sansom

April 28, 1912 – March 13, 1995

Code Name: Celine, Lise   Alias: Madame Odette Metayer

Very few women populated the spy ranks on either side of the conflict during WWII. Few of those were married, and almost none had children. One exception was Odette Sansom of the SOE, the mother of three daughters.

Odette's harrowing experiences during the war seem more appropriate for a movie than for real life. She endured terrible deprivation after being captured by the Gestapo, yet she never broke or gave up any important information about the SOE or the Resistance fighters she knew. Her courage and fortitude are the stuff of legends. She was the first woman to receive Britain's prestigious George Cross.

During her lifetime, she probably received more public recognition than any other female SOE agent, much to the irritation of many fellow agents and the anger of others who saw her self-promotion as undeserved. Her reports on her brutal interrogation and imprisonment were retold in books and a motion picture. She was one of the few SOE women to survive the Nazi concentration camp experience.

Odette Marie Leonie Celine Brailly was born in Amiens, France, on April 28, 1912, the daughter of French parents Emma Rose Marie Yvonne Brailly (Quennehen) and Florentin Desire Eugene 'Gaston' Brailly. Her father was killed in WWI at Verdun in 1918 and was posthumously awarded the Croix de Guerre for heroism.

As a child, Odette suffered from polio, which kept her bedridden for months. She later had a mysterious illness that blinded her for three and a half years. When she was finally able to leave home, she was educated in convent schools where she was considered a difficult student. Perhaps surviving those early illnesses built a strength and resolve in her that no one suspected when she agreed to join the SOE.

**Odette in her FANY uniform**

**Odette and her daughters**

At 19, Odette married Englishman Roy Patrick Sansom on October 27, 1931. After the birth of their first daughter in France, they moved to England. Over five years, they had three daughters: Francoise Edith, born in 1932; Lily Marie, born in 1934; and Marianne Odette, born in 1936. When England entered the war, Odette's husband joined the British Army, and she and the children moved from London to Somerset for their safety.

In 1942, the SOE invited Odette to join the "F" Section. Odette's invitation came because of a mistake. The English government had requested citizens to send photos of the French coastal areas in hopes they could be used in war planning, along with information about how they obtained the images. In error, she sent her photos and a brief explanation of living close to the beaches in France to the wrong government department. The photos and her explanation of her background arrived at the War Office and came to the attention of Colonel Maurice Buckmaster.

Buckmaster thought Odette, a Frenchwoman married to an Englishman, was a perfect recruit for the SOE work. Odette initially rejected the invitation. She had three daughters to consider, and their father was already serving in the military. The SOE finally convinced Odette to leave her family to work in France when she learned of the suffering of those in her birth country.

She later said: *I thought, Oh, I don't know…I was torturing myself about what's right, what's wrong, and I think – perhaps if I do the training, they will see that I'm not right, and at least I will come back then feeling it's been done and I'm no good, and I will be satisfied. By that time, I knew about the work, of course, because they had told me more or less what would be expected. I was so sure that I could not do the training anyway, and I would be back, able to pass on to something more practical, and that's how it happened.*

Odette left her daughters in a convent school and entered the SOE training. The courses were designed to prepare her and other SOE agents to avoid discovery and capture in a country crawling with French police working with German soldiers and the Gestapo.

Many women in SOE, including Odette, officially joined FANY. Like most of the women who joined the SOE, she received poor ratings during the training. Her reports are riddled with comments like: *Celine (her training code name) has enthusiasm and seems to have absorbed the teaching given on the course. She is, however, impulsive, and hasty in her judgements and has not quite the clarity of mind which is desirable in subversive activity. She seems to have little experience of the outside world. She is excitable and temperamental, although she has a certain determination. A likable character and gets on well with most people. Her main asset is her patriotism and keenness to do something for France; her main weakness is a complete unwillingness to admit that she could ever be wrong.*

Looking at similar comments shown in the reports of the female trainees, it suggests that many of the male trainers may have harbored prejudice against having women in war zones, and also their unhappiness at being assigned to train such strong-willed women.

Despite the training reports, Odette was approved to become an agent. The SOE gave Odette the code name *Lise*. The SOE decided to use her personality and determination, and they assigned her to set up her own Circuit near Auxerre. To assuage the expected reluctance of the French male egos among the Resistance fighters she would recruit, the Circuit was to have a Frenchman as a figurehead leader.

She flew to Gibraltar and then departed for the French coast on October 31, 1942, on a small felucca and landed on November 2. Fellow SOE agents Mary Herbert, Marie-Thérèse Le Chêne, George Starr, and Marcus Bloom traveled with her. The other four agents would travel to different Circuits around France.

Captain Peter Churchill, leader of the Spindle Circuit, contacted "F" Section leader Buckmaster to request that Odette be reassigned as his new courier. Buckmaster agreed. We can imagine Odette's disappointment at not being able to set up her own planned Circuit.

**Peter Churchill**

**Adolphe Rabinovitch**

The radio operator for Spindle Circuit was Adolphe Rabinovich, code name *Arnaud*. He was born in Russia of Jewish extraction and raised in Egypt. He studied in Paris and lived in the United States before the outbreak of the war. Rabinovich had been a junior wrestling and boxing champion in his youth, and everyone agreed that he was a "giant of a man." He had a quick and fiery temper and Churchill and Odette frequently needed to calm him down to avoid attention. Odette respected both men, and they quickly formed a tight team.

Churchill met several of the women agents when they arrived in France. After the war, he authored several books and he wrote of his first impression of three of the female agents. He described Marie-Thérèse Le Chêne: *as a grey-haired woman, full of common sense and good humor*. Mary Herbert: *seemed frail and so very English*. He wondered about her stamina and how she would survive the difficulties of a clandestine life. He and Odette would be married when he wrote about her, and he commented on her: *determination, self-reliance, and force of character.*

Within ten days of Odette landing on the beach, the German Army crossed the demarcation line and began to swarm into the south of France. The Italian Army, aligned with Hitler, also started to move in from the east, although in much smaller numbers.

Odette's first mission in France was fraught with unexpected challenges. Tasked with delivering a suitcase full of money to a contact in Marseille, she found herself waiting for hours as her contact was delayed. Aware of the risks of carrying such a significant amount while potentially being stopped and searched by the French police or the Gestapo, she sought refuge first in a cinema, then a café, and wandered the streets to pass the time. When she finally returned to the designated meeting spot, she was directed to yet another location. After successfully completing the handover to fund Resistance activities, she realized it was too late; she had missed the last train back to Cannes.

The contact told her that a local brothel would be the safest place to stay. When she spoke of the incident much later, she said: *It was a house mostly for the Germans. There was a woman there when I arrived. I said, "Have you got a bed?" She looked at me, she said "Huh! A bed for the night. Do you know what we are?" I said, "Yes, it's obvious – Heure du Paradis!" And I said, "Yes, I do realize that's why I'm here. Can you put me away somewhere quietly?" Then, she realized who I was and said, "Yes, all right." You know, funnily enough, those women, that type, were nearly always on our side. They were very good, very very good. Anyway, there I was. I spent the night there, came down in the morning, there was a gendarme at the desk! I thought, "Ohh!" because you were supposed to see each name in the book who'd been there. But I laughed my way out of it, and it was all right.* Female SOE agents proved time after time that they could think on their feet and deal with almost any situation that came their way.

The Spindle Circuit covered a large area, and her primary job of being a messenger required her to ride her bicycle many miles, which was a great way to stay in shape. Odette possibly assumed a leadership role within her circuit in March 1943 when Churchill was in England for meetings. During this period, she coordinated multiple parachute drops of supplies. Female SOE agents, including Odette, were often recognized for their ability to adapt and fulfill various roles within their circuits as needed.

Odette's task of frequently relocating Rabinovitch and his radio equipment was often perilous. She used her bicycle to transport the bulky gear, constantly risking detection at German checkpoints. The stakes were incredibly high, as getting caught with the equipment would have almost certainly led to her arrest and imprisonment. This task underscores the high-risk nature of SOE operations and the bravery required to carry them out.

The new Circuit, under Churchill's leadership, faced several challenges. Local Resistance fighters, previously aligned with the French CARTE Network, were hesitant to collaborate with Churchill's team. CARTE was a French operation that claimed to have thousands of Resistance fighters, but it turned out to be primarily a dream on paper. This reluctance compromised the identification of viable parachute landing sites, a critical component since these sites were necessary for receiving supplies from England.

The poor sites chosen by the CARTE Resistance members led to a dire shortage of supplies, severely limiting the Resistance's capacity to execute meaningful sabotage operations against the Germans. Consequently, the Spindle Circuit struggled to demonstrate effectiveness, drawing criticism from other Circuits for its lack of success. The overall poor performance was largely attributed to Churchill's inadequate leadership in dealing with the Resistance groups.

In January 1943, the Circuit members had a very close call when the SOE members went to a site recommended by the local Resistance. A British plane was supposed to land and pick up Churchill to fly him to London for a meeting. The Gestapo had been alerted by a traitor and was waiting to arrest the agents and any locals who were with them. The landing was successfully aborted without anyone being injured or arrested. The Circuit members were fortunate to escape, but they knew their operation had been compromised and there was a traitor in their midst.

After that experience, the Spindle team of Churchill, Rabinovich, and Odette moved away from the French Riviera to the Annecy area in the French Alps. Churchill and Odette had formed a romantic relationship and took up residence together in the Hotel de la Poste in the village of Saint-Jorioz.

A man named Roger Bardet arrived in town and made it known that he would like to work with the Circuit. Bardet was a member of CARTE, based in Cannes. He said he had been betrayed by a fellow agent and captured but had escaped from prison. Churchill trusted him, but Odette and Rabinovich did not. It turned out that their distrust was correct, as Bardet had become a double agent for the Germans.

Churchill's departure back to London on March 24, 1943, coincided with the arrival of SOE agent Francis Cammaerts, who was sent to evaluate the Circuit operations. Cammaerts found the Circuit's security measures lacking, deeming them insufficient to prevent penetration by German forces. He later said he was shocked by their casual attitude regarding security.

The Germans had obtained a list of 200 Resistance members involved in the CARTE network in November 1942, before Odette arrived in France but held it awaiting the right time to use it. A CARTE member, Andre Marsac, who frequently worked with Churchill, had fallen asleep on a train, and a Gestapo agent following him took his briefcase with the names and contact information.

The Germans were poised to act against the list of 200 CARTE Resistance fighters. Sergeant Hugo Bleicher, an agent for the Abwehr - a German military counterintelligence organization active from 1920 to 1945 - successfully manipulated an SOE agent into giving him an introductory letter to Odette. Known for his exceptional skills in espionage, Bleicher was credited with the arrest of over 100 Allied agents during the war, earning him a reputation as one of the most effective spycatchers of the era.

Churchill was in England when Bleicher introduced himself to Odette as "Colonel Henri" and spun a tale to her of them traveling together to London to "discuss means of ending the war." The double-agent Bardet spoke up for Colonel Henri and told Odette they could trust him.

**Hugo Bleicher ('Colonel Henri')**

1899–

## Hugo Bleicher ('Col. Henri')

*German champion spycatcher*

Sergeant Hugo Bleicher, the Germans' champion spy-catcher in Western Europe, succeeded in bringing down several French, Belgian and Special Operations Executive networks, and in trapping and arresting numerous agents. The career of Bleicher, a member of the German *Abwehr*, was the dream come true of the seven stone weaklings of this world. He never rose above the rank of sergeant, his eyesight was too poor for combat, his appearance was plain and unprepossessing. Yet this archetypal runt succeeded in assuming many aliases, several somewhat romantic, such as 'Henri Castell', a Belgian businessman, or 'Colonel Henri' of the Luftwaffe. Bleicher managed to acquire, what was more, an attractive mistress in Mathilde Carré (the 'Cat'). Bleicher began his clandestine career in October 1941, when he assisted in the arrest of a woman working for a British agent. The agent was connected with the French *Interallié* circuit. The result of this arrest led Bleicher to Mathilde Carré's bed, and his starring role in the destruction of *Interallié*. In 1942, Bleicher pulled off a series of arrests

which scuttled the *Autogiro* circuit, and the following year, posing as an anti-Nazi German Intelligence colonel, succeeded in duping André Marsac (formerly of the *Carte* cell). This break in security eventually led to the arrest of Peter Churchill and Odette Sansom, among others. Churchill's suspicions had, ironically, helped alert SOE in London to the danger Bleicher presented in his disguise as 'Colonel Henri'. Bleicher's work went on unchecked, however, and included setting up his own resistance cell, *Lisiana*. By this means, Bleicher infiltrated the *Donkeyman* circuit.

The invasion of Normany in June 1944 heralded the end of Bleicher's spy-catching activities, and the end of the war in Europe found him in hiding in Amsterdam. After his arrest by Canadian troops in June 1945, Bleicher spent a year in detention being questioned by the British and French authorities. They eventually decided that Bleicher was not guilty of war crimes. In 1946, he returned to Germany and his home town of Tettnang, where he became the manager of a tobacco shop.

Illustration: *Hugo Bleicher in retirement, as a tobacconist*

© 1977 Edito-Service S.A. Geneva
Printed in Italy    13-036-55-23
Keystone, London

Odette was suspicious and asked Rabinovich to send a message to London asking about "Colonel Henri." The SOE responded that: *Henri highly dangerous…you are to hide across the lake and cut contacts with all save Rabinovich.* Unfortunately, Odette thought she could delay moving for a few days, so she did not change locations.

Before Churchill's return to France, the SOE staff in London specifically instructed him to steer clear of "Henri." Upon his return, parachuting into France on the night of April 14/15, 1943, Odette picked him up and took him back to their hotel. Tragically, at 2:00 AM the following day, only seven months after Odette's arrival in France, she and Churchill were captured by Hugo Bleicher, backed by a group of Italian soldiers. Mass arrests of surrounding Resistance fighters began. Rabinovich was one of the few who escaped capture and he moved on to work with other Circuits.

Bleicher knew exactly where Odette and Churchill stayed, so it remains a mystery why she did not hide across the lake as the SOE instructed her to do. It was one of the worst mistakes any female SOE agent in France made during the war. After the war, she said that she had received a later message from the SOE telling her to stay in the hotel. SOE headquarters said that no such message was sent. It is not known which story to believe.

After their capture, Churchill and Odette claimed they were a married couple and were related to Prime Minister Winston Churchill in hopes that would save them from the death penalty. After a failed escape attempt, the guards badly beat Churchill. When they were waiting for a transfer vehicle, he told Odette that he would rather be dead than kept in prison and subjected to future beatings. She later said that she worried throughout her two years of imprisonment that he would either take his own life or do something to get himself killed.

Rabinovich escaped capture and made it back to England. The SOE reassigned him to return to France on the night of March 2/3, 1944, where he was to set up and command the new Bargee Circuit. Unfortunately, the landing site was under German control. They shot and captured him as he landed. Because he was Jewish, The Gestapo transferred him to the Gross-Rosen concentration camp in Poland, where he was sent into the gas chamber.

While Odette was at Gestapo headquarters at Avenue Foch in Paris, several other SOE women were also there. After the war, she related an incident when she demanded the staff provide afternoon tea for all the women. To everyone's surprise, the tea was served, and it was served with real China cups and plates.

When the Gestapo was unable to get any secret information from the female agents at Avenue Foch, they sent them to Fresnes prison on May 8, 1943. Churchill was also a prisoner at Fresnes, although the men and women were in separate areas. The Gestapo interrogated Odette 14 times under torture, but she continued to respond with "I have nothing to say" or some fabricated story. Odette sometimes said that she was the Circuit leader to divert their attention away from Churchill.

It was forbidden to talk to other prisoners, but Odette encountered Churchill one day. Another captive SOE agent, Diana Rowden, saw them and understood the situation. She shielded them from the guards so they could speak to each other for a few minutes. It was the last time they saw each other until they returned to England at the war's end. Odette remained at Fresnes for almost a year in a solitary 8' x 12' cell. She was later sent to Karlsruhe prison.

Under two interrogations, Churchill followed the SOE training and admitted he was an agent but said little else. He remained a prisoner until the end of the war. He was moved between several different concentration camps, along with other captured officers and diplomatic prisoners. While he spent months in solitary confinement, his treatment was considered less harsh than what was inflicted upon Odette.

A fellow countryman frequently tortured Odette at Karlsruhe. She later said he was a "very good-looking young Frenchman" who she believed was mentally ill. The Nazis used this tactic often at Ravensbrück. That meant that the prisoners could not say that the Germans had tortured them.

Odette reported that whenever she refused to answer a question, the young Frenchman would burn her back with a hot iron. If she fainted from the pain, they revived her with buckets of cold water so the torture could continue. When the burning failed to break her, the same young man methodically pulled out all her toenails, one by one, using ordinary pliers. With no medical care, infections set in repeatedly. Odette still refused to break and give up the location and identity of her wireless operator, Rabinovich. She actually didn't know what happened to him after she was arrested.

Odette's health continued to deteriorate, and she was finally moved from her dark, solitary cell. She briefly had cellmates of a mother and daughter, but then a prostitute moved in. After being in solitary for such a long time, adjusting to the constant presence and conversation of others was challenging for her after such a prolonged period of isolation. There were at least two more trips back to Avenue Foch for interrogation, but they did not involve torture. The Germans were uncertain about her possible connections to Prime Minister Churchill and perhaps they thought she was so sick that more torture would kill her.

After receiving no helpful information from her during her last interrogation, the Nazis told her she had been condemned to death. She was sent to a women's prison, Ravensbrück, in August 1944 located approximately 50 miles north of Berlin. Up to 45,000 women and children were held there at any given time. Her health further deteriorated there, suffering from pleurisy and a severely swollen gland in her neck.

During the war, Ravensbrück saw over 132,000 women pass through its gates or die within its confines, according to German records. The majority were from Poland (48,500), Russia (28,000), Germany and Austria (24,000), France (8000), many Roma (Gypsy) women and children, with only a few from the United Kingdom and the United States. More than 85% were considered political prisoners, with many being Jewish. More than 50,000 died of disease, starvation, torture, or execution at the camp.

As the war began to turn against the Germans, all prisoners had significantly reduced rations and suffered from hunger and frequent mistreatment or torture. Odette said she remained in solitary confinement in a punishment block. For three months and 11 days, she was kept in a dark cell, with the light turned on for only five minutes a day. Her body was covered in scabs, and she suffered from dysentery and scurvy. Her hair was falling out, and her teeth became loose. She lapsed into a semi-coma. When finally taken to a doctor at the camp, he gave her an injection and returned her to her cell.

Odette reported that, finally, she was allowed to move to a cell with a window, but she remained in solitary confinement for several more months until the Nazis accepted that the advance of the Allied forces could not be stopped. By that time, she had been in solitary for almost two years, with only a few brief breaks for interrogation or change of location.

The Germans knew the Russian and American forces were advancing rapidly. As the war was ending, the Germans tried to empty Ravensbrück as quickly as they could to avoid having witnesses to report what went on in the infamous camp. Thousands of prisoners were sent on a forced march to another camp, and some were released into the countryside. Other SOE women had been killed or sent to different camps. Odette was the only remaining SOE agent. They held her as a bargaining chip in case she really was related to British Prime Minister Churchill.

In a desperate attempt to save himself as the US Army approached, Fritz Suhren, the commandant of Ravensbrück, believed Odette's fabricated story that she was related to the British Prime Minister by marriage. On May 3, 1945, he forced Odette into his car and drove to surrender to the advancing American forces, hoping that her purported connections would earn him leniency. However, Odette ensured that he received no such treatment and later volunteered to testify against him at the war crimes trials for Ravensbrück guards and officers in Hamburg. Suhren was found guilty and executed by hanging in 1950.

Odette credited her ability to survive her treatment in captivity to her early years of dealing with illness and blindness. She said she kept telling herself that if she could: *survive the next minute without breaking up, that is another minute of life. And if I can think that way instead of thinking what will happen in a half-hour's time, I could accept this and survive it.*

When Odette returned to England in the spring of 1945, Vera Atkins and Buckmaster, the head of the "F" Section of SOE, met her. Buckmaster's wife, Anna, remembered the emptiness in Odette's eyes: *They were like the eyes of an animal that's died.*

Odette entered Queen Alexandra's Military Hospital for examination and treatment. Her entire body had medical issues. X-rays revealed that the fifth vertebra had been shattered, but now – two years later – had deteriorated to nothing. The starvation and scurvy, as well as the long periods without sunlight, had left her with severe anemia. She also suffered from nervous tension and articular rheumatism, which left her with a weakened heart muscle.

Odette was still missing several toenails, and one of her toes had become badly infected, causing sepsis, a life-threatening issue. After several operations, the surgeon probably saved her from dying from sepsis. She continued to receive medical treatment for over a year. Odette was awarded a total disability pension because of the long-term effects of the torture and terrible conditions she had endured.

On August 20, 1946, Britain awarded Odette the George Cross, making her the first woman ever to receive the award. The George Cross is the highest civilian award bestowed by the British government for non-operational gallantry. She received the award for her bravery under torture. She accepted the award on behalf of herself and all the SOE women who had not returned safely from the war. She also received the Order of the British Empire (OBE) and the Legend d'Honneur (Chevalier) from France.

MRS ODETTE SANSOM, imprisoned and tortured by the Gestapo when serving with the French Resistance Movement, was decorated with the George Cross by the King at Buckingham Palace. Mrs Sansom and Capt. Peter Churchill (her commanding officer in the movement, who received the D.S.O.) show their awards to Mrs Sansom's daughter Francoise.

Odette said of the other captured female SOE agents she met while in prisons in France and Germany: *We were all young, we were all different, but we all had the feeling in the beginning that we were going to be -helpful. That was why we went into it. And to have impressed the people around them as they did is almost enough. They impressed everyone – the Germans, their guards. They behaved extremely well, those women.*

One of the many newspaper articles about Odette after the war.

In her final report to SOE, she said that she had been with seven other women on the transport to Karlsruhe prison, but she didn't know their names, as they were seldom allowed to speak to each other.

Vera Atkins showed Odette pictures of the women, and Odette was able to give firsthand information about six of the seven women. She could not identify the seventh. The women were: Yolanda Beekman, Andrée Borrel, Madeleine Damerment, Vera Leigh, Éliane Plewman, and Diana Rowden.

She also gave Vera the name of a prison matron who she thought would know what happened to other women captives - a Fraulein Berger, who she said was "a Quaker and very correct." This information allowed Vera to finally track down what happened to the seven women.

After the war, Odette resigned from FANY with the rank of Lieutenant.

Odette divorced her first husband in 1946 and married her former SOE boss, Peter Churchill, in London in 1947. They spent considerable time promoting their service during the war to the media and public audiences. Several books were written about Odette, including a 1949 biography by Jerrard Tickell. Tickell was allowed access to the SOE files - a privilege given to no one else but M.R.D. Foot, the official "F" Section historian.

In 1950, Hollywood released a movie titled *Odette*. Odette became famous for enduring her torture, while other SOE female agents may have done far more to help the war effort. The notoriety that both Odette and Churchill received because of the movie irritated many former SOE agents. Their chief criticism was that neither Odette nor Churchill had directed or done any major sabotage work. Some officials and agents believed that much of Odette's story was fabricated, and they cast doubt on her integrity.

A manifesto signed by about 20 former associates accused Churchill of being in France only to collect material for a book about his experiences and asked what acts of sabotage he and Odette, or the Resistance groups they were supposed to work with had carried out during their time in France. Documents disclosed long after the war indicate that her superiors had to fight for Odette's George Cross because she was unable to prove that the Nazis had tortured her. Medical records supported her claim of being tortured but could not determine the severity of the mistreatment.

**Peter Churchill and Odette at a dinner party after the war.**

An interesting side note about her medals is that someone broke into her home in 1951 and stole the medals. Her mother was staying in the house at the time, and she made a public appeal in the newspaper to have the medals returned. To everyone's surprise, the medals were returned with the following note: *Madame, you appear to be a dear old lady. God bless you and your children. Thank you for having faith in me. I'm not really all that bad – it's just circumstances, etc., and I can't help it. Your little dog really loved me. I gave him a nice pat and left him a piece of meat – out of the fridge. Sincerely yours, A Bad Egg. PS I promise I'll not give you a second call.*

Odette and Churchill divorced in 1955. She remarried again the following year, this time to Geoffrey Hallowes, another former SOE agent. Hallowes was raised in an affluent family and had a remarkable military career. During the early days of WWII, he served and traveled extensively in the Pacific and in Asian countries, ending up in India, where he became a staff captain in Bombay (Mumbai.) From that post, Hallowes volunteered to work for "Force 133" in Cairo, an SOE operation in Egypt.

The SOE initially assigned Hallowes to work in Yugoslavia, but he was reassigned to Peterborough, England, on the "Jedburg" team 94. These were three-man teams with one British or American officer, one French officer and a radio operator. After D-Day, his team parachuted into France on August 24, 1944, to assist with sabotage, with Hallowes as the Jedburg team leader. SOE agent Virginia Hall met them when they arrived and updated them on the local situation.

His team traveled to Le Puy, where they assisted the Free French by arranging for airdrops of badly needed weapons and ammunition. Hallowes later joined the SOE Special Planning Unit 22, where he took charge of German prisoners of war and obtained useful information from them in the final months of the war. It is unknown when he and Odette met, as she was already in a concentration camp when he arrived in France.

After the war, Hallowes joined the family wine-importing company, and he was the co-founder and the first chairman of the newly created International Distillers and Vintners (IDV) in 1962. He retired from the board of IDV in 1983. He and Odette remained together until her death.

**Odette and husband, Geoffrey Hallowes**

**Odette, with several of her medals**

Odette died on March 13, 1995, in Walton-on-Thames, Surrey, England. She was 82 years old. Her medals are displayed at the Imperial War Museum in England.

**On February 23, 2012, the Royal Mail released a postage stamp featuring Odette as part of its "Britons of Distinction" series.**

# Chapter 18

# Marie-Thérèse Le Chêne 'RF' Section

April 20, 1887, OR 1890 – ?

Code Name: Adele   Alias: Madame Marie-Thérèse Ragot

Marie-Thérèse had the distinction of being the oldest woman recruited by the SOE to serve in German occupied France. She also had a unique job of distributing anti-German leaflets. While other agents sometimes posted anti-German notes around a village or town, it seems to have been Marie-Thérèse's primary responsibility.

She traveled by boat, deemed too old for parachute training. Uniquely, she joined her husband and brother-in-law in France, where they were already active as SOE agents. In a departure from standard SOE protocol, she served in the Plane Circuit under her husband's leadership.

Marie-Thérèse's maiden name is not known. There is even a question about her birth date, as different records list it as 1887 and 1890. She and her husband, Henri Le Chêne, lived in France and were managing a hotel when the Germans invaded the country. Along with her brother-in-law, Pierre Le Chêne, they moved to England, taking the last boat departing from Bayonne.

Marie-Thérèse's husband and her brother-in-law had British citizenship because their father, Achille Henry Le Chêne, was a British civil servant who had worked in His Majesty's Customs Service. Their mother, Melanie Ragot, was French.

When they moved to London, Marie-Thérèse worked as a cook, and her husband managed a hotel in the city. Her brother-in-law, Pierre, went to work as a city fireman. The SOE first recruited her husband, She was recruited shortly after, on May 16, 1942, making her either 52 or 55 years old, depending on discrepancies in her birthdate records. Pierre also joined the SOE shortly after her, further entwining the family's involvement in wartime efforts.

Marie-Thérèse participated in one of the first SOE training sessions for women. Other women in her class were Yvonne Rudellat, Andrée Borrel, and Blanche Charlet. Both Yvonne and Andrée would be captured and executed by the Germans.

Her husband, Henri, was chosen to be a Circuit leader. He and Pierre landed in France on April 22, 1942, near Lyon. After meeting with Virginia Hall and hearing that Germans had overrun the Lyon area, he decided to set up the Plane Circuit in two different villages, Clermont-Ferrand and Perigueux. He and Pierre moved to that area and began to contact locals known by the SOE to be fighting the Germans.

They soon began supplying them with weapons and supplies. A major focus of the Plane Circuit was the production of propaganda, and the distribution of the information was assigned primarily to Marie-Thérèse after she arrived.

Because of her age, Marie-Thérèse never took parachute training, but she did complete the other courses. After she completed her training, she was sent to Gibraltar by submarine and then on to the French coast on a small boat, landing on October 31, 1942. With her were fellow SOE agents: George Starr (organizer of the Wheelwright Circuit), Mary Herbert (courier for Scientist Circuit), and Odette Sansom (courier for Spindle Circuit.) Once Marie-Thérèse arrived, she had to make her way alone to join her husband. Peter Churchill, an SOE agent who greeted the group and arranged their first night's lodging, said of Marie-Thérèse: *She was a grey-haired woman, full of common sense and humour.*

When Marie-Thérèse reported to Henri's Circuit, he commented: *That he had joined SOE to get away from his wife, only to find that she had followed him.* It may have been a joke, or perhaps not.

In SOE records, Marie-Thérèse's assignment was to work as a courier in the Plane Circuit. Her brother-in-law, Pierre, was the radio operator for the nearby Spruce Circuit. Most reports of Marie-Thérèse's work in France refer to her distributing anti-German political leaflets or pamphlets. She successfully avoided suspicion as she distributed the leaflets from village to village. The Germans just saw an inconspicuous old woman in country dress moving about to shop for food or visit family members.

She successfully traveled as far as Marseille to distribute the flyers without encountering any problems with German roadblocks or patrols. In 2024, the trip to Marseille took five hours by train and seven hours by car, which would have been a long distance for a woman traveling alone in the 1940s. She used all available modes of transportation, including the train, a bicycle, and walking. She usually carried the leaflets in a basket she carried over her arm. With a kitchen towel on top, it looked like a shopping basket.

While distributing leaflets, she discovered that the workers at the Michelin factory in Clermont-Ferrand were deliberately sabotaging the quality of tires they were producing, and they deliberately caused long delays in the delivery of the faulty tires. She reported that information to SOE. The SOE then suggested that all Circuits adopt and share this sabotage technique within their operational areas. It was one of the small but very important bits of intelligence that Marie-Thérèse contributed to the war effort.

She recruited many locals willing to take her pamphlets and distribute them in factories, on the train, or in other venues. She and her recruits successfully distributed many thousands of anti-German flyers.

During October and November 1942, the Germans increased the number of radio signal detection vans in their area, and they arrested several SOE radio operators. While working as the Spruce Circuit's radio operator, Pierre was one of the few remaining operators available to send and receive messages to SOE. However, the Germans captured him on November 9. After two weeks of interrogation, which usually meant torture, he was transferred to the Gestapo headquarters in Avenue Foch in Paris. Tortured again without giving up information, he was sent to Fresnes prison, where he was the first British officer to be interrogated by the cruel SS Captain, Klaus Barbie.

After the capture of Pierre and several other Resistance fighters, Henri, Marie-Thérèse's husband, recognized the increased threat of German patrols potentially leading to his and other SOE and Resistance members' capture. Deciding to leave France, he opted for one of the few available escape routes: a perilous trek over the Pyrenees Mountains to Spain. He accomplished this journey in December 1942. When Henri reached Spain, the police put him in prison for entering the country without the appropriate paperwork.

Marie-Thérèse did not believe she could physically make it over the mountains, so she stopped her activity for a time and went into hiding in the homes of friendly locals. She did some courier work for Robert Boiteux, who took over the Circuit when her husband left France.

On August 19, 1943, the evening radio news had a secret code that told them that a plane was coming. Ten agents, including Marie-Thérèse, assembled on a field outside Angers. The Hudson plane arrived safely, and they flew back to London in time for the SOE to welcome them with a breakfast of bacon and eggs. Her husband had been released from the Spanish prison, and they were reunited when she arrived in London.

Marie-Thérèse's brother-in-law, Pierre, had been kept in solitary confinement for ten months. One of the many means of torture that he endured was being forced to climb the hated "stairs of death," where he had to climb 186 stairs carrying a 100-pound block of granite. Many prisoners died during that particular torture. He survived, but when the Allies finally freed him on May 6, 1945, he weighed only 83 pounds and was suffering from typhoid.

The three family members were reunited in 1946, and after Pierre's long recovery period, they returned to France and opened and operated a hotel in Saint-Menehould. Marie-Thérèse then disappeared from public notice. Pierre died in 1979, but it is unknown when Marie-Thérèse or her husband died or where they were buried.

There are no known photos of Marie-Thérèse.

# Chapter 19

# Julienne Aisner

December 30, 1899 – February 15, 1947

Code Name: Claire

**Julienne Aisner as a young woman**

Julienne was best known at the end of the war for having been recruited into the SOE by the alleged double agent Henri Déricourt, a friend of her second husband.

Few details are known about her early life. Julienne Marie-Louise Simar was born in the village of Anglure, France, one of three children to her French parents. Her father was a policeman who would later work in Lebanon and Vietnam. She was an attractive woman, small and full of energy.

Julienne met US Marine Corporal M. Lauler, and they married in 1924. They moved to his hometown, Miami, Florida, where she gave birth to a son. Tragically, her husband was killed in an auto accident in 1927, and she and her son moved to live with her parents in Lebanon. Eventually, following her father's retirement, the family relocated to Hanoi, Vietnam, to join her married sister. During her time in Vietnam, Julienne took up teaching English.

The hot and humid climate did not agree with her health, and she and her son returned to France in 1931, where she found a job working on movie scripts for a film company in Paris. She met a Frenchman, Robert Aisner, who also worked in the film industry, and they married in 1935. They became partners in a small film company and worked in that industry until the Nazis invaded France Through her husband's connections, she also became friends with Henri Déricourt, a significant figure who would later play a complex role during the war.

When Germany invaded France in May 1940, she saw daily evidence of the Nazi's oppression and mistreatment of French citizens. The details are unknown, but her husband was arrested and sent to a German concentration camp. He later escaped and immigrated to the United States, where friends in the film industry helped him find work as a technical advisor on the movie *Casablanca.* He incorporated the very escape route he had taken after leaving the concentration camp into that movie. He would go on to have a very successful life working in the movie business in the U.S. Apparently, he made no effort to bring Julienne and her son to live with him.

With the German invasion of France, Julienne wanted to safeguard her son, so she sent him to live with his father's relatives in the U.S. She divorced Aisner in 1941. That same year, her feisty nature showed when she was imprisoned for two months for slapping a German soldier for "inappropriate" comments.

In 1942, she met and became romantically involved with a French lawyer, Jean Besnard, who supported the work of the Resistance. Henri Déricourt reappeared in her life. He was working for the SOE, and he asked Julienne to help him find an apartment for him and his wife. He then asked her to help him find safe housing for some incoming SOE agents on the night of March 17/18, 1943.

Déricourt was impressed with how she handled both requests, and he convinced her to accept training to act as his full-time courier within the Farrier Circuit. She agreed and he arranged for a flight to take her to England on April 15, 1943, for the official SOE training. Julienne joined FANY and participated in a shortened training program of only one month. Along with another new agent, Vera Leigh, Julienne returned to France on May 14 and took up courier duties.

Déricourt's primary job in the Farrier Circuit was to arrange for the flights into and out of France for agents, downed pilots, and other at-risk individuals needing to leave France. Julienne's main responsibility was to find safe housing for the new agents. She also used her knowledge of the French political system to obtain false identity documents and ration cards for new agents.

Another challenge for her was to find an excuse for a new agent, Jack Agazarian, to avoid being picked up by the Germans to do forced labor. It was common practice for the Germans to conscript any healthy-looking man who they found without an acceptable job. She managed to get a fake X-ray made for him that showed that he had an ulcer. Then she obtained false medical papers saying he was awaiting surgery for the ulcer.

Julienne and agent Vera Leigh became good friends and visited whenever they could. In their world of secrecy, it was nice to have another woman to talk to who understood their work's stress and uncertainty.

During the late spring/early summer of 1943, the Germans arrested hundreds of people associated with the large Prosper Circuit, including the SOE leader, Francis Suttill. Déricourt and Julienne's Farrier Circuit was not directly affected, and they continued their operations. Julienne and Jean Besnard were engaged and living together in Paris when the Prosper Circuit began to fall apart.

Shortly after the Prosper agents were captured, Vera Leigh arrived at Julienne's apartment and requested an interview with Nickolas Bodington, deputy to Maurice Buckmaster, head of the "F" Section. Bodington was in France to determine why the Prosper Circuit had been betrayed and most of the leadership captured.

When Vera met with Bodington, she told him that she and her lead agent, Frager, thought Déricourt was a double agent and that he had betrayed the Circuit. Bodington was a strong supporter of Déricourt and reported back to SOE that Frager might be the traitor. The Gestapo arrested Vera soon after her meeting with Bodington.

Julienne was shocked at the idea that Déricourt might be the traitor, as she thought she knew him well and that he was loyal to the Resistance effort. Later, there would be accusations that both Déricourt and Bodington might be working for the Germans. Déricourt was recalled to London by the SOE in February 1944 and was not allowed to return to France.

The SOE provided money for the purchase of a small café and bar in Paris called Café Mas, which Julienne ran. The cafe served as a message center for the Farrier Circuit and a point of contact for any SOE agents who thought they were in danger and needed to leave France on the transports, which were always arranged by Déricourt.

In early 1944, two men with German accents approached the café bartender and asked for help escaping France. They were mispronouncing the French code phrase, although they knew what the code phrase was. The bartender was suspicious and called Julienne. She told him to send the men away, telling them they had the wrong place.

A few days later, another man came to the café and again mispronounced the new code phrase, so he was also sent away. Julienne was convinced that the Germans were closing in on their circle of agents, so she and Besnard closed the café and left their apartment in Paris. They moved to the country for safety. They married within a few days.

The SOE felt it had become too dangerous for Julienne and Besnard to remain in France. After thirteen months of working for the SOE, she, Besnard, and radio operator Andre Watt were flown back to England on April 6, 1944.

Over time, many agents reported that they felt that the Prosper Circuit had been exposed to the Germans by Déricourt, which also put Julienne under suspicion of being a double agent since he had been her original mentor and brought her into the SOE. She was questioned and put on suspension while they tried to ascertain her loyalty. Eventually, she was cleared, and she resigned from the SOE in good standing.

In 1948, Déricourt was tried for treason in a British court but was acquitted for lack of evidence. Many agents went to their graves believing that he was the traitor that caused the arrest, torture, and often execution of so many SOE agents. Stories about him being planted as a double agent by M16 have never been proven.

After the war, Besnard went to work for the BBC, and Julienne worked in the cinema section of the Ministry of Information.

Julienne developed breast cancer and died in Paris on February 15, 1947. She was 47 years old. Her husband died two years later.

**Henri Déricourt during his trial for treason. He was acquitted.**

**Chapter 20**

# Sisters Jacqueline and Eileen "Didi" Nearne

Jacqueline Nearne May 27, 1916 – August 15, 1982

Code name: Jacqueline   Alias: Josette Norville

Eileen "Didi" Nearne – March 16, 1921 – September 2, 2010

Code name: Rose   Alias: Mademoiselle du Tort or Jacqueline de Tertre

Jacqueline Francoise Mary Josephine Josette Nearne and Eileen "Didi" Mary Nearne were the only two sisters who worked as field agents for the SOE in France. They experienced very different lives during and after WWII. Both were awarded an MBE from the British government.

**Jacqueline (left) and Eileen "Didi" Nearne (right) in their wartime uniforms**

They were born in Brighton, England, to Mariquita Carmen de Plazaola, a French/Spanish mother, and John Francis Nearne, an English father. Both girls were still young when the family moved to France in 1923. The girls were educated in Catholic convents and became fluent in French, which was critical when they joined the SOE.

During the war, Jacqueline, Eileen (who preferred to be called Didi), and their brother, Francis, would all work for the SOE. Their other brother, Frederick, would serve in the British Air Force. Both parents were arrested and interred in German concentration camps during most of WWII.

## Jacqueline Nearne

At the age of 18, Jacqueline went to work as a representative for an office equipment company. When the Germans invaded France in 1939, their brother, Frederick, returned to England and joined the British Air Force. Jacqueline and her sister, Eileen, obtained British passports from the Consulate and, in 1942, tried to follow him but were stopped in Marseilles by the Germans and returned to their home. The two girls then hiked over the Pyrenees Mountains into Spain and on to Portugal and Gibraltar, where they contacted the British Embassy and obtained passage to England. Jacqueline applied to join the SOE. She was accepted and sent to Scotland for training.

Women working for the SOE often joined FANY, a group of women who drove trucks and cars for the military or manned mobile canteens for troops. During SOE training, they usually did 4-5 parachute jumps, as that is how most of the SOE women would be dropped into France to begin their work. Few of the women were given enough time by the instructors to complete the required number of jumps, and some dropped into France after only one or two practice jumps.

Jacqueline's training reports were often negative, saying she was: *mentally slow and not very intelligent, and could not be recommended.* The "F" Section Leader, Maurice Buckmaster, overruled the trainers and told them to pass her on as an agent, perhaps because the SOE was desperate to get more agents in the field. She was in the same training class as Lise de Baissac, Mary Herbert, and Odette Sansom. Lise described Jacqueline as: *movie-star gorgeous but uncertain of herself in the mostly all-male, military atmosphere.*

For some reason, the SOE gave Jacqueline the code name *Jacqueline*, which was highly unusual, as most spies were given code names that had nothing to do with their real names. The SOE gave her the alias of *Josette Norville* with a cover story that she was a chemical company representative. She was often referred to in government documents as *The Designer*.

Jacqueline parachuted into France on the night of January 25/26, 1943, along with Maurice Southgate, code name *Hector*. They landed near Brioude, and Southgate set up a new Stationer Circuit. This Circuit would become very large, covering much of central France. Jacqueline served as his courier and was helpful in connecting with the local Resistance networks. Pearl Witherington arrived by parachute in September 1943 and became Southgate's second courier.

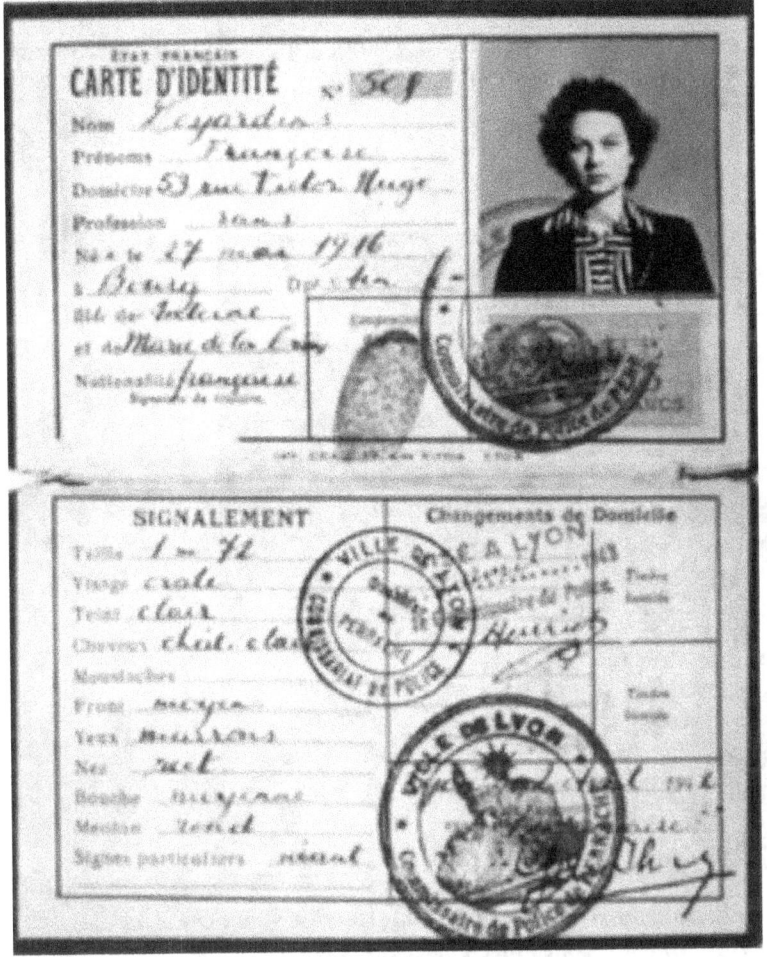

**Jacqueline's fake ID card**

Staying in contact with the ever-growing and widespread Resistance groups required Jacqueline to travel hundreds of miles to deliver and pick up messages for Southgate on a weekly, or sometimes daily basis. Jacqueline's chemical company cover story gave her the excuse to take many long train trips.

She also took messages to/from the Circuit's radio operator, Louis Pierre Rene "Amédée" Maingard de la Ville-ès-Offrans, who had to stay apart from other Circuit members for everyone's safety.

Jacqueline transported both money and messages, and she passed through police or German army roadblocks daily without ever being arrested. She was questioned several times, but the guards accepted her explanations and released her.

As she traveled around their area, she was always looking for possible landing sites for supplies to be dropped. The fields had to be large enough to allow the parachutes to drift a bit after being tossed out of the plane, close enough to a roadway that they could easily move the supplies, but also remote enough not to attract the attention of German forces or collaborators.

Jacqueline quickly learned that the French police and the Germans checked the records of hotel guests, so she often slept on overnight trains to try to avoid being stopped and questioned. She occasionally participated in sabotage work, such as helping to blow up railway lines, factories, and bridge pylons.

Jacqueline worked in France for 14 months without a break, which was much longer than usual for an agent to remain in one area without being captured. Against her will, the SOE ordered her back to England when her sister was ready to be assigned to France. Her sister arrived in early March 1944, and Jacqueline was picked up and flown out on April 9, 1944.

Jacqueline and her sister, Eileen, never met during their SOE work in France. Three weeks after her departure, Jaqueline's boss, Maurice Southgate, was arrested by the Germans, and the Gestapo posted a photograph of Jacqueline offering a reward: *For the capture, dead or alive, of an individual known as Jacqueline or Josette.* She had been called back to London just in time.

Jacqueline left the SOE with the rank of Lieutenant. After the end of the war, she helped care for her sister, who came home with both psychological and physical problems from her time in a German concentration camp. In 1946, Jacqueline acted the part of "Cat," a character based on herself, in the RAF's Film Unit's production of *Now It Can be Told*, a drama/documentary about the training program for SOE agents. A shorter version of the film was released to theaters in 1948 as *School for Danger*. Fellow SOE agent Harry Ree also starred in the movie. *Now It Can be Told* was long considered "required viewing" by those with a serious interest in SOE operations.

**Jacqueline Nearne, a former courier with the SOE, was featured in the public information film *School for Danger: Now the Truth Can Be Told*, which was produced after the war.**

Jacqueline never married but had a very successful business life. She moved to New York City and worked in the Protocol Office of the United Nations, rising to Deputy Protocol Officer. Jacqueline retired and returned to England in 1978

Jacqueline died of cancer on August 15, 1982, only four years after returning to England. For her work during the war, she received an MBE from the British government and the Croix de Guerre from the French government. A Blue Plaque was placed on the house in West Hill Street, Brighton, her birthplace.

**Blue Plaque**

**Jacqueline in NYC**

## Eileen "Didi" Nearne

Jacqueline opposed the idea of her younger sister, Eileen (who preferred being called Didi), being recruited by the SOE, thinking she was too young and immature. Didi initially failed her recruitment tests for the SOE, which were the same tests her sister had experienced not long before.

Didi was considered more happy-go-lucky than her sister, and the instructors questioned whether she had the ability and maturity to be a successful spy. Some thought she used her humor to help her get along in the male-dominated training program. Maurice Buckmaster, the "F" Section Leader, allowed her to pass through the training – just as he had done earlier for her sister, Jacqueline.

After completing her radio training at Thames Park, Didi was selected by William Savy, a French lawyer, to serve as the radio operator for the new Judex Circuit in France. Savy, who had a withered arm and was unable to parachute, opted for a different mode of transportation into France. He and Didi flew into the country on the night of March 2/3, 1944, landing near Chateauroux. Upon arrival, they settled into separate lodgings in Paris to begin their clandestine operations.

The SOE assigned Didi the alias *Mademoiselle du Tort* and the code name *Rose*. Didi and agents Lise de Baissac and Yvonne Cormeau were assigned to the new Judex Circuit. Judex's purpose was to meet all SOE agents and the Resistance groups they worked with, and to assess the effectiveness of the SOE operations.

Savy soon returned to England with information so vital that he carried it himself. He had learned of a large German ammunition cache in the stone quarries near Creil. Savy had details of the location and that over 2,000 V1 rockets were in the quarry, and they were ready to launch. By an odd twist of fate, the same plane that picked up Savy on April 9, 1944, also took Didi's sister, Jacqueline, back to England. British bombers hit the quarry location in July 1944 and destroyed the rockets.

Didi remained in the same safe house for over four months, which was unique, as the Germans typically located radio signals within a few days. She did move to a new house shortly before receiving an urgent message on July 25, 1944, that she had to transmit to London. Didi knew the Nazis had a new radio signal-detecting machine that allowed them to pinpoint radio transmissions much faster. She took the risk and began transmitting, only to be located midway through the transmission. Fortunately, she had time to burn her codes before they broke into the house. She was arrested and taken to Gestapo headquarters at Avenue Foch in Paris. She was only 23 years old when captured.

As she related in postwar debriefings, during her first interrogations in Paris, Didi was subjected to beatings and "bathtub" torture called "baignoire." She was stripped naked and put into a bath of ice-cold water, where her head was held under until she thought she would die. They would raise her to allow her to take a breath and do it all over again. She made up a story that she was just a clueless clerk sending messages to a businessman, and she had no idea he was British.

She must have been a good actress because she convinced them and escaped immediate death. Fortunately, they never discovered that she was half-British. However, they sent her to Fresnes prison. When they could not get any useful information from her, the Gestapo sent her to Ravensbrück concentration camp on August 15, 1944.

Didi joined fellow agent Denise Bloch and two other English women at Ravensbrück. All three were sent to Torgau in October 1944 for a two-month stint working in the fields digging potatoes. She and the other women were then sent to the Abterode labor camp and told to work at an airplane factory, which Didi refused to do. Told she would be shot if she didn't go to work, she endeavored to make deliberate mistakes in hopes that the planes would never work correctly.

The Germans shaved Didi's head and those of the other women to reduce the chance of lice, and they were put on an almost-starvation diet of acorn coffee, turnip soup, and a little bread. The female guards beat her with rubber truncheons, and they set dogs on her and other female prisoners. Didi never divulged her name or the names of others working in the SOE or the Resistance movement.

**Prisoners with shaved heads**

In December 1944, Didi was moved to the Markleber concentration camp near Leipzig, Germany, where she worked on a road repair gang for 12 hours each day. After surviving a few months of hard labor, the Germans began to move her and the other women prisoners to another camp. As Didi was marched through the woods at night in early April 1945, she and two French women prisoners escaped into the forest.

With no warm clothing, the three women walked through snow and ice in freezing weather for two days until they reached a small village where they found people willing to help them with food and clothing. After resting and gaining strength, they began traveling in hopes of crossing the German border to safety. The SS stopped them, but they kept their wits about them and convinced the Germans they were just off to visit family members, and they were allowed to continue the journey.

They located a Catholic priest in Leipzig who gave them sanctuary. The priest hid them in the church and got them food and a doctor to help with their open cuts and frozen feet. The advancing US Army liberated them in late April 1945. By the time of their rescue, Didi could barely walk and was in terrible physical and emotional condition. She was held and interrogated by American intelligence officers on suspicion of being a German collaborator. She had no papers, and because she worked for the SOE, she had no military personnel number, so they were unsure what to do with her.

A U.S. officer wrote a memorandum on May 2, 1945, stating: *Subject: Nearne, Eileen, alias Duterte, Jacqueline, alias Wood, Alice, Alias Rose. Subject claims to work for an intelligence organization run by a Colonel "Max Baxter." Subject stated she was flown to a field near Orleans. Subject encoded messages and signed them ROSE but claims she has forgotten her agent's number. In July 1944, Subject's transmitter was detected, and Subject was arrested by the Gestapo. She claims that despite being tortured, she did not reveal any information detriment to the British intelligence service or its agents.*

*Subject creates a very unbalanced impression. She is often unable to answer the simplest questions, as though she were impersonating someone else. Her account of what happened to her after her landing near Orleans is held to be invented. It is recommended that Subject be put at the disposal of the British Authorities for further investigation and disposition.*

The U.S. Army contacted the British authorities, and a British Major came to fetch her. She was flown to Brussels, where the British interrogated her again. Eventually, she was released after her status with the SOE was confirmed, and she was given passage back to London. After returning to England, it took some time for Didi's body to heal from the torture and deprivation, but her psychological problems were much more serious and long-lasting. She carried the psychological scars of her treatment for the rest of her life.

The SOE was concerned about her ability to adjust back into civilian life. One report stated: *We are anxious to see her reestablished in a suitable peacetime occupation. She is extremely keen to train in beauty culture, and I have no doubt she will work very hard on making a success of it if she is given an opening.*

Today, we would say Didi had post-traumatic stress disorder (PTSD), but the disorder was unknown at that time. For most of her life, Didi shunned social contact with anyone but her immediate family.

Didi had trouble finding work, and when she did, she seldom could hold down a job for long periods. She spent time in a mental hospital, where they performed electroshock therapy on her. Didi worked as a nurse's aide for a time. Because she was often unable to work, she had a limited income and lived out of a suitcase in small rooms for many years. In 1993, she visited the Ravensbrück concentration camp that had been the scene of her torture during the war.

The British government kept most of the work done by the women in the SOE classified until the late 1960s and early 1970s, so almost no one who knew her was aware of her wartime service or what she had endured. It was not until late in her life that Didi would tell anyone of her past service.

In 1997, she agreed to be interviewed for a TV show about her time in the SOE. She would only appear in a wig and speak in French to disguise her voice. During the interview, when asked about her life in the SOE, she said: *It was a life in the shadows, but I was suited for it. I could be hard and secret. I could be lonely. I could be independent. But I wasn't bored. I liked the work. After the war, I missed it. We went out fully realizing the dangers and that our lives would be in our hands. We certainly suffered – but it was worth it.*

**Jacqueline and Eileen "Didi" after the war**

When she was asked how she survived working as a spy in a country filled with German soldiers and collaborators, she said: *I wasn't nervous. In my mind, I was never going to be arrested. But of course, I was careful. There were Gestapo agents in plain clothes everywhere. I always looked at my reflection in the shop windows to see if I was being followed.* A week after that interview, a woman in her town asked her if she had been in the TV program, and she vehemently denied it.

Didi, five years younger than her sister Jacqueline, outlived her by 28 years. She passed away on September 2, 2010, at the age of 89 in a small room in Torquay, England. Tragically, her body was not discovered for several days.

After her death, her MBE from the British Government and her Croix de Guerre from the French government were discovered in her room, along with documents and letters attesting to her courage during her SOE service and later incarceration.

Stripping away the secret life she had led for so many years, the British Legion, the country's leading veterans' organization, and anonymous donors paid for a funeral service in Torquay. The funeral featured

a military bugler, a piper, and an array of uniformed mourners. During the solemn service, a red cushion was placed atop her coffin with her wartime medals. Eulogies celebrated her as one of the women who parachuted into France as secret agents by the SOE. She was provided with a military funeral fitting for someone who had endured so much for her country.

Didi's ashes were scattered at sea, per her wishes. A Blue Plaque has been erected outside the building where she spent her last years.

# Chapter 21

# Elizabeth Devereux-Rochester

December 20, 1917 – March 19, 1983

Code Name: Typist, Elizabeth   Alias: Elizabeth Le Grande.

Elizabeth was the only female SOE agent recalled from fieldwork in France because she was just "too English." Her French was very good, and her Circuit leader thought she did good work. But he was afraid that her very "English" look and bearing would bring attention to her, and she might be arrested. He thought she might give up information about their Circuit and the Maquis groups they worked with.

Elizabeth was born on December 20, 1917, into a wealthy but troubled family with several scandals attached to their names. Elizabeth had many advantages as a child and young woman. Her parents were American Richmond Rochester, Jr., and Englishwoman Aimee (Babe) Margaret Lathrop (Gunning) Rochester.

Her parents divorced when her father returned from WWI. Later, her mother married Myron Reynolds, a wealthy American businessman, in 1921. Elizabeth was four years old. He tacked his name onto that of his new stepchildren, making Elizabeth's last name Devereux-Rochester Reynolds. She primarily used the name Rochester but sometimes used Reynolds depending on where she was and what was going on in her life.

She and her sister, Aimee Christine Gunning Rochester, had an English governess and went to private schools in Europe until Elizabeth was eleven. She was then sent to an English public school (private school), Roedean School for Girls, where she spent much of her time playing various sports. Elizabeth enjoyed tennis, golf, sailing, horseback riding, and hunting. Later, she went to finishing schools in Austria and France. Elizabeth was fluent in English, French, and German.

Her stepfather was sympathetic to the Germans, and she once accompanied him on a business trip to Berlin. She was horrified to see how the Nazis were treating Jews and others who the Nazis felt were inferior to the German ideal of the white race.

She was living in France when the Germans invaded in May 1940. She wanted to do something to help the country, so she joined the American Hospital Ambulance Corp as a Red Cross driver. Initially, because her stepfather was friendly to the Germans, she could move about easily. But that soon changed, and her stepfather left France just before her mother was interned at the Vittel camp in late 1942.

Vittel was a prison camp used by the Nazis to house British and American citizens living in France. It was also used to house prominent Jewish prisoners from outside France who could be used in exchange for Germans held captive in other countries. Eventually, most of the Jews at the camp were deported to Auschwitz and killed in 1944.

Elizabeth was living in Paris, which the Nazis controlled, so she began to look for a way to leave the city. She hid her American passport but kept her French identity card and used it to move to a village near the Jura Mountains. Elizabeth was soon helping Jews and downed military pilots to hike to safety over the Jura Mountains and into Switzerland. She quickly became one of the group's leaders, helping those less physically strong than she was.

In early 1943, she moved across France to lead downed pilots and others to the edge of the eastern mountains so they could cross the Pyrenees to safety in Spain.

She realized the imminent danger of Gestapo arrest and decided to escape by the same route she had previously facilitated for others, trekking over the Pyrenees to Spain. Reflecting on the ordeal, she later said that the hike was: *the most awful experience of her life.*

**Elizabeth in uniform**

After Elizabeth reached England, she joined the Women's Transport Service (ATS). Someone identified her to SOE in the summer of 1943 and they invited her to join the organization. She agreed to work for them and began training at Wanborough, Arisaig, Ringway, and Beaulieu. After completing all her courses, she was flown back into France in a Hudson plane on October 18, 1943, landing in a field near Lons-le-Saunier. The SOE gave her the code name *Typist*.

She later wrote about the plane crew in her book, *Full Moon to France: The pilots who flew these missions, whether in big planes or tiny Lysanders, were the crack airmen of the RAF. They had to be because setting down their machines in fields lit only by flare paths cast by flashlights or bonfires required the most extraordinary skill. This time, perhaps because the other plane had already landed ahead of us and was taking off as we approached, our pilot missed his landing. Instead, we hit the church belfry. The shock was tremendous, sending cases falling all over the place. What it did to the belfry, I don't know.*

Her assignment was to work as a courier for Richard Heslop, code name *Xavier*, head of the Marksman Circuit in the foothills of the Jura Mountains. The Circuit was to be an Anglo-French mission called Cantinier. Also on the team was J.P. Rosenthal of the de Gaulle organization and Dennis Johnson, an American radio operator.

Their area bordered the Jura Mountains and Switzerland and was bitter cold in the winter. Her courier work was grueling, as she had to walk/hike over the high hills and low mountains to reach the various Maquis groups. The terrain seldom allowed for bicycles. She arrived in October, so she had a hard winter ahead of her, often with heavy snow.

She frequently took small supplies and equipment when visiting the Maquis. In all official records, she was reported to be conscientious and efficient. She had an excellent memory, and she memorized the many messages verbatim, so there was no need for her to have paperwork on her person.

There were many industrial sites in their area providing materials for the German army, making them great targets for the Maquis to attack. Unfortunately, it also meant that there were sizable groups of German soldiers in the area to protect those sites. When the Maquis hit a supply depot or manufacturing facility, the Germans would take their revenge on the local population. In one instance, they burned 500 farmsteads in the Haute Savoie area and killed every resident they could find, men, women, and children. During the winter of 1943-44, the Marksman region was the most violent in France.

In 1944, to stop the sabotage by the Maquis, the Germans sent 4,500 Milice French police into the area. The Milice were often more brutal than the Germans, and they were feared by both the local population and the Maquis fighters. In only two months, the Malice arrested more than 1000 people, many of whom were beaten or killed. Eventually, the Maquis were successful in driving them out of the area.

Heslop reported that Elizabeth: *carried out her courier work with guts and imagination.* Elizabeth was tall and carried herself with the posture and poise of an upper-class English woman. She looked so English that it concerned everyone in the group, as they feared she would attract the attention of the Malice or the Gestapo. Everyone in the Circuit became concerned that she was simply too English in looks and manners.

George Millar, a young man escaping from France, was waiting for her to take him on the next leg of his escape route when she entered the door. He later wrote: *She was genially commanding. They called her "La Grande." She demanded a drink and the location of les waters. Her appearance was intriguing. Mannishly impeccable. A superb tweed costume with a divided skirt, perfect shoes and stockings, expensive luggage including a dressing-case with gold-topped bottles and jars. Her hair was reddish, and her skin pale but healthy.* She wasn't the sort of person who lent herself physically or temperamentally to camouflage.

Her clothing was well-made and quite unlike the clothing worn by the local country women. Heslop, her Circuit leader wrote a book after the war, where he described her in the following way: *(she) looked as English as her name – but was American. She was tall, with a prominent nose, and she didn't walk, she "strode" across a room. When you saw her coming towards you in the mountains, you automatically expected to see a couple Labradors at her heels, and that her first words would be "Had a bloody good walk, you know, nothing like it for keeping fit."* (Although her father and stepfather were both American, she grew up in Europe and was schooled there.)

Her team feared that she would be arrested or followed and get the entire Circuit arrested. She had significant knowledge about the group that would endanger them if the Gestapo were able to get it from her.

Heslop finally decided to have the SOE recall Elizabeth to England. Probably hurt by being removed as a field agent, she first asked to stay, but Heslop refused. She left the Circuit but decided to go to Paris to stay with a friend and try to see her mother, who was still in the German camp.

On the night of March 20, 1944, two Germans and a member of the Milice police went to the house where she was staying and arrested Elizabeth and her friend. Someone from the old Ambulance Service she worked for at the beginning of the war had betrayed her.

The Gestapo took both women to Fresnes Prison and put them in a cell together. They concocted a story that she was American but had grown homesick for her Paris friends and had returned to see them. She was interrogated further but never suspected of being connected to the SOE. The French police put her on trial for having a fake French identity card and found her guilty, and they transferred her to the Vittel camp. She remained there until the American Army freed her when they liberated Paris.

After the war, Heslop said that: *she had done a fine job, for she had guts and determination.* Elizabeth received the Chevalier de la Legion d'Honneur, and the Croix de Guerre from France.

Despite having two living parents, Elizabeth and her sister had been adopted when young by Mrs. Amy Hansen, their great-aunt, in 1924, when Elizabeth was seven years old. The great-aunt had no living children, and the adoption was to form a line of inheritance so the girls would inherit when she died. Mrs. Hansen was a relative of Jane Stanford, the source of Mrs. Hansen's money.

Jane's husband, Leland Stanford, had been the primary owner/investor in Southern Pacific Railroad and Wells Fargo Bank, among many other businesses. He and his wife were also the founders of Stanford University in honor of their deceased son. The University tried to void the adoption of the two girls and the subsequent inheritance to have the money go to the University. There were millions of dollars at stake in the case. The court case dragged on for years, but the sisters eventually won in 1957.

Elizabeth wrote a novel in 1977, *Full Moon to France*, based on her wartime experiences. Much of the book reads like an autobiography, but we cannot know how much of it is true. In her book, she wrote about helping to set the charges to blow up a locomotive the second day after her arrival in France.

One passage in the book goes back to the aftermath of a battle in which the dreaded French Milice police and the Germans had "punished" a village because of Maquis sabotage. She wrote: *On the hills, farms were burning...our ears picked up the sound of crying coming from the house nearest us. When we entered it, we learned of the tragedy that had struck this peaceful farm as well as the surrounding houses. Hardly more than an hour earlier, the Milice and Gestapo had attacked the hamlet and not only killed all the men but forced their families to witness their execution.*

Elizabeth developed multiple sclerosis shortly before the inheritance case was settled. She lived out the remainder of her life in the seaside resort of Dinard, France. Elizabeth never married, and she died on March 19, 1983, at 65 years of age.

# Chapter 22

# Françoise Agazarian

May 8,1913 – June 24, 1998

Code Name: Marguerite Alias: Francine Fabre

Françoise Isabella Agazarian, or Francine, as she preferred to be called, was born in France on May 8, 1913, with the name Françoise Isabella Andre. Little is known about her early years, and she was already married when she worked for the SOE. She and her husband, Jack Charles Stanmore Agazarian, were one of the few married couples who both served the Allies within the SOE organization.

**Francine, around the time she signed up with the SOE**

After the completion of their SOE training, she and her husband flew into France together on a Lysander aircraft on March 17, 1943. The Lysander was the preferred mode of transport for the SOE agents, either for landings or dropping the agents by parachute over their designated areas. The same type of plane was also used to drop supplies.

Francine, code name *Marguerite*, and Jack, code name *Marcel*, both served in the Prosper Circuit in France, she as a courier, and he as a radio operator. Jack had already served one tour of duty in France for the SOE, beginning in 1942. Radio operators lived apart from the rest of the Circuit personnel and Resistance fighters for security reasons, so they seldom saw each other.

The Prosper Circuit was based in and around Paris and was the largest and most important Resistance network in France. Francine moved about not only in Paris but also out to smaller towns and villages, wherever the Resistance groups might be located.

In addition to messages, Francine carried money for the groups and occasionally small supplies and weapons. Being a native Frenchwoman was of great help to her, as she could easily move about with little suspicion from the Germans.

Francine reported that when she first arrived in France, she took a train from Poitiers to Paris. She was carrying a large cache of money, blank identity cards, and fake ration cards. She had also sewn radio crystals into the sleeves of her dress. Francine was sitting on her suitcase, which contained the money and her .32 revolver and ammunition. Sitting nearby were German soldiers, never suspecting that the shy little woman next to them was a British spy. In a later report to the SOE, she wrote about transporting hand grenades in a shopping bag with a German officer sitting next to her on a train.

It was also her job to periodically take fake ration cards - created by the SOE - into the city hall to have them swapped out for legitimate cards to obtain food rations for Resistance members and SOE agents.

Through mistakes and a betrayal, the Prosper Circuit was betrayed to the Germans. Most of the leadership and many of the Resistance leaders were captured and imprisoned. Francine and her husband were able to escape and flew out of France on June 16, 1943, only three months after their arrival. The plane that flew them back to England had dropped off three other SOE women: Cecile Lefort, Noor Inayat Khan, and Diana Rowden. All three of the women were later captured, tortured, and executed by the Gestapo.

A week after Francine and Jack flew out of France, on June 23, fellow courier Andrée Borrel, Prosper leader Francis Suttill, and wireless operator Gilbert Norman were captured and imprisoned by the Germans.

Francine remained in England. Her husband, Jack, returned to France on July 22, 1943, to determine the status of the Prosper network. Shortly after his arrival, he fell into a trap set by the Gestapo and was captured on July 30, 1943. The Gestapo knew who he was and that he knew a great deal about the Prosper network, so his arrest was a massive coup for the Germans. He was sent to Fresnes Prison, where he endured brutal torture without divulging any information about the Circuit.

Giving up hope of obtaining any useful intel from him, the Germans moved Jack to Flossenbürg concentration camp. After being kept there in solitary confinement, he was executed by firing squad on March 29, 1945.

Jack's family also contributed to the Allied war effort. His younger brother, Noel Agazarian, joined the Royal Air Force early in the war as a Spitfire pilot. He went on to be a flying ace in the Battle of Britain before being killed in action on May 16, 1941. Jack's sister, Monique Agazarian, flew for the Air Transport Auxiliary (ATA.)

Francine settled in London and lived quietly for several years. She later remarried, becoming Mrs. Francine Cais. It is believed that she died on June 24, 1998, somewhere in France, but her burial site is unknown.

**Francine's husband,
Jack Charles Stanmore Agazarian**

# Chapter 23

# Sonia Olschanezky

December 25, 1923 – July 6, 1944

Code Name: Tania   Alias: Suzanne Ouvrard

Sonia was another of the brave Jewish women who risked their lives to defeat the Nazi occupation of France. Unfortunately, she paid the ultimate price and was executed at the Natzweiler-Struthof concentration camp at the age of 20.

Sonia was not an official SOE agent because she did not participate in SOE training in England. The author decided to include her in this book because she worked for and with female SOE agents in France and was captured with them. She was treated as an SOE agent by the Gestapo and endured the same torture as the agents, and she was executed alongside them. After the war, Vera Atkins, the SOE recruiter and overseer of all agents, tried but failed to get Sonia recognition as an agent. Sonia is one of two such women included in this book; the other is Nicola Trahan.

**Sonia as a young woman**

Sonia was born on December 25, 1923, in Chemnitz, Germany, to secular Jews, Eli Olschanezky from Russia and his German wife, Helene Olschanezky. Eli had moved to Germany to study to become a chemical engineer. He met and married his wife, and they settled in Leipzig. When Germany declared war on Russia, Sonia's father was arrested and interred in a concentration camp. Sonia's maternal grandfather had good connections in Germany and was able to have her father released.

The Germans considered her father a resident alien and refused to allow him to work as an engineer, so he began working as a sales representative for a lingerie manufacturing company. The family had a good life in a nice apartment with servants. They kept their religion under the radar because they knew they could be arrested at any time.

Sonia had two older brothers, Enoch, and Tobias. Tobias later changed his first name to Serge. The family moved to Bucharest in 1926 so that the father could get a better job. Unfortunately, the job did not work out and her father invested all his money to partner with another man in opening a new business. Sonia loved to dance and was invited to join the children's dance theater, Le Theatre du Petit Monde, at the age of ten. She soon earned money for the family by dancing at parties and school events using the stage name of *Donia Olys*. Sonia appeared on television demonstrating dance in 1937 at the International Exposition in Paris. She was reported to be intelligent, energetic, capable, resourceful, and to have a steady nerve.

Her father's enterprise failed, perhaps due to partner fraud, and the family moved to Paris in 1940. Again, another of her father's business plans failed, and he lost most of their money. The family's lifestyle changed dramatically, and her father became ill and depressed. Both brothers had to leave school in their teens to earn money to support the family. Sonia began working as an au pair to earn income for the family. The family was now stateless, as her father could not return to Russia, and her mother's German citizenship was considered void by the Nazis. Both brothers joined the French army to obtain citizenship.

The Nazis invaded France in May 1940, and within two years, all those with Jewish heritage in France were ordered to wear a six-pointed yellow star on their clothing. The star was used to identify them as Jews, and they were terrorized by both the army and the local German population. Sonia was arrested in the spring of 1942 and sent to the Drancy deportation camp to await transfer to an extermination camp in Germany.

Her mother contacted a friend in Germany, who provided an official document saying that Sonia had "economically valuable skills" needed for the war effort. Her grandfather paid bribe money, which, along with the document, was enough to get her released by the fall of 1942. After her release and against her mother's warning, Sonia made the dangerous decision that she had to do something to impact the Nazis' terrorism of Jews, and their occupation of France.

Sonia's brother, Tobias (Serge), was captured and sent to a POW camp in Poland, but he later escaped. Her other brother, Enoch, worked with the Resistance within the Robin Circuit. He, too, was captured and executed on April 18, 1944, at Auschwitz. Prisoners who survived the war thought that he had been sent to the gas chambers. His family did not learn of his death until the war's end.

Sonia was introduced to Jacques Weil, a fellow Jew who worked with the Resistance groups in the area. Sonia began working with Weil as his courier, and she began receiving pay from the SOE in November 1942. The SOE gave her the code name *Tania* and told her to use the alias *Suzanne Ouvrad* when interacting with unknown local people.

Weil had been working with the SOE as the leader of the Juggler Circuit, which was also called the Robin Circuit. In January 1943, Juggler became a small sub-circuit of the huge Prosper/Physician Circuit. Most of the Resistance fighters working within Juggler were Jewish.

Initially, Sonia took messages between Weil, Suttill, Norman, and the various Resistance groups with which they were working. In addition to her regular courier duties, Sonia collected intelligence about German army movements and installations as she traveled around the area. She also participated in blowing up a German munitions train just south of Paris.

Although Sonia felt they made an impact by destroying German armaments, they all knew that other weapons would soon be shipped in from Germany. The efforts of the Resistance and Maquis groups had to be constantly repeated, with changes in place and type of action. Sonia also supported the sabotage efforts of blowing up electric transmission lines, train sheds, and locomotives.

Due to a chain of events resulting in the Prosper Circuit being betrayed and infiltrated by German agents, the Germans were zeroing in on Prosper and the smaller Juggler Circuit. Weill left France for the safety of Switzerland in July 1943 to avoid capture. For unknown reasons, perhaps to remain with the family, Sonia remained in France and continued to facilitate communications between Resistance groups.

Sonia discovered that the Gestapo was using captured SOE radio codes to send fake messages to the SOE headquarters. She sent a message alerting the SOE of that danger, but because she was not a known SOE agent, headquarters did not recognize her name and ignored the warning.

In response to the fake messages requesting them, more SOE agents were parachuted into France, and the Germans captured them immediately. Because of the collapse of Prosper, SOE agents and hundreds of Resistance fighters were captured, including Suttill, Norman, and Andrée, on June 24, 1943.

Several SOE agents were captured in early January 1944. The Gestapo captured Sonia later the same month, on January 22, when she arrived at a pre-arranged meeting with an SOE agent. She was interrogated and then sent to Fresnes prison. She remained at Fresnes prison until May 13, 1944, when she and SOE agents Diana Rowden, Vera Leigh, and Andrée Borrel were all moved to the Paris headquarters of the Gestapo on Avenue Foch. They found four other female SOE agents there: Yolande Beekman, Odette Sansom, Éliane Plewman, and Madeleine Damerment. The seven female SOE women - and Sonia - were sent by train to Karlsruhe prison and put in separate cells. The Germans thought that Sonia was also an SOE agent.

Less than two months later, on July 6, 1944, Sonia, Diana, Vera, and Andrée were taken from Karlsruhe to the Natzweiler-Struthof concentration camp in France. Germany operated almost 1000 prisoner-of-war camps in Germany and other occupied countries during WWII. Little is known about the reasoning as to why some prisoners were moved from camp to camp and sometimes from country to country during their internment.

A Gestapo officer from the Karlsruhe Prison accompanied the women to Natzweiler-Struthof, a camp for men. The Gestapo officer told the SS political officer, Magnus Wochner, that there were orders from Berlin that the women were to be executed immediately. This verbal request was highly unusual, and Wochner disputed the unorthodox procedure. The Gestapo officer told him not to enter the women's names into the records.

It is unknown why the women were moved to a camp for men, or why their executions had such urgency and had to be done on the same night as their arrival. There were male SOE agents at the same concentration camp who were not subject to that order.

The women were not expected, so their arrival created a lot of confusion and attention. The guards put them in separate cells but some of the women were able to communicate with a few male prisoners to identify themselves. SOE agent Brian Stonehouse later described Sonia as: *Another girl had very black oily hair, and wore stockings, aged about twenty to twenty-five years, was short and was wearing a tweed coat and skirt.*

From Stonehouse's description, Vera Atkins, searching for missing SOE agents after the war, mistakenly assumed he was describing Noor Inayat Khan. The two women looked similar, and this mistake would cause a considerable delay in finding out what really happened to Noor and in identifying Sonia. Because Sonia was not an official SOE agent, Vera was not looking for her.

Between 9 and 10 PM of the night they arrived at the camp, the women were executed. A description of their execution is given in Chapter 2, Vera Atkins (pages 94-96).

Despite Vera Atkins' efforts to have Sonia officially recognized for her war efforts, she was not listed on the Valençay SOE Memorial that is dedicated to the 13 women and 91 men of the "F" Section who were killed in action in France. Nor was she officially recognized for her service by either England or France.

However, she is recognized on the stone plaque, along with the other three women executed with her in the furnace room of the Natzweiler-Struthof crematorium. Her name is also included on the Vera Atkins Memorial Seat in the Allied Special Forces Memorial Grove at the National Memorial Arboretum in Staffordshire, England.

# Chapter 24

# Yvonne Fontaine

August 8, 1913 – May 6, 1996

Code Name: Nenette and Mimi

Yvonne was one of the few women who married before joining the SOE. She was married twice and divorced once. She was also the only SOE woman sent to France to have the government reject recommendations for medals and awards to be given to her after the war.

She was born as Yvonne Yvette Fontaine in Longuyon, France on August 8, 1913. Little is known about her early life. By the time the Germans invaded France in May 1940, when she was 26, she had been married twice. She had divorced her first husband, a man with the surname Fauge. It is not known what happened to the second husband, an Italian, but he was missing from her life by the time Germany invaded France. Yvonne was managing a dry-cleaning business in the industrial town of Troyes.

Knowing that Yvonne disliked the German occupation and General de Gaul's Free French movement, a local friend, Pierre Mulsant, code name *Andre*, introduced her to SOE agent Benjamin Cowburn, code name *Germain*, and his radio operator, Denis John Barrett, code name *Honore*. Mulsant was Cowburn's lieutenant at the time.

Cowburn and Barret had arrived in the area from England on April 1, 1943, to revive the Tinker Circuit and work with local Maquis groups to sabotage the German Army operating in the region. The Germans used the railway lines in and around Troyes, and Allied bombers regularly targeted the area.

Yvonne began working for Cowburn as a paid courier, earning about 10 pounds monthly. Her job, like most couriers, was to take messages between Cowburn and the various Maquis groups and locate drop zones for supplies. She worked primarily in the northwestern part of France, and she was particularly efficient in helping downed Allied pilots and their crews hide in safe houses and then escape France. While in the Tinker Circuit, she helped at least 18 airmen reach Switzerland.

The Germans discovered her group, and Cowburn had to leave France in September 1943. With the Germans hot on their trail, Yvonne, Barrett, and Mulsant escaped to England the following month, on November 15, 1943. An interesting note is that a future president of France, Francois Mitterrand, arrived from England on the same plane they used to depart.

Once she made it to England, the SOE recruited Yvonne and Mulsant based on their prior experience working with Cowburn. The SOE recruited Yvonne by her first married name, Yvonne Fauge. Even though she had previous experience in France, she had to undergo the standard SOE training. Yvonne was the only person in her class who did not speak English. All the others spoke both English and French, so it was no problem for her to communicate with them.

**Yvonne before leaving for France**

Her training reports were mixed, with one instructor writing: S*he was the most interesting person here and probably the most intelligent. A lively and indefatigable talker.* But another instructor wrote: *She was egocentric, spoilt, stubborn, impatient, conceited.* Many women who underwent SOE training received similar negative reports, and we may surmise that some male instructors had difficulty dealing with strong, independent women who "did not know their place."

Yvonne passed the training requirements and returned to France by boat on March 25, 1944. She landed in Brittany and then made her way to Paris. Yvonne met her old friends, Mulsant, and radio operator Barrett. Mulsant had set up a new Circuit called Minister in Melun, and she went to work for him again. Yvonne was responsible for finding drop zones for supplies, and people to help her receive, sort, and transport air drop packages.

She also assisted in minor ways on some of the sabotage operations. One such operation was damaging the lock gates in a canal used by the Germans to bring supplies and ammunition into the area by boat. Once the lock gates were damaged, the water level dropped, making it impossible for large barges to travel and causing delays for even small boats on the canal. Of course, this also disrupted the lives of local merchants and farmers who used the canal to bring in goods and ship their products out of the area.

The war was affecting every facet of French life, and the Free French had a campaign underway to assassinate as many German officers as they could. This brought fierce reprisals from the German Army.

In mid-June 1944, the Special Air Service (SAS), a special forces unit of the British Army, moved into the area and launched Operation Gain to fight the Germans. Operation Gain involved 58 men attached to SAS parachuting into the area around Orleans. The men were in uniform, which made them immediately recognizable to both locals and the Germans.

Their role was to sabotage the rail links running through the area and prevent German supplies from passing through. They were effective in tying down German forces, but there were several direct encounters with the Germans, and ten men were killed.

**Captain Pierre Mulsant**

**Dennis John Barrett, radio operator**

Unfortunately, SAS had not communicated with the local SOE Circuit. The SAS operation caused the downfall of the Minister Circuit and the capture and eventual torture and execution of both Mulsant and Barrett. Hearing that there had been an unscheduled parachute landing, Mulsant and Barrett went out searching for the SAS men, thinking they were pilots who had been shot down. The Germans captured both men, and they were sent to the Buchenwald concentration camp in Germany. Both men experienced extreme torture, and as the war continued to turn against Germany, they were shot by firing squad on October 5, 1944. Only 5 of the 37 SOE agents held in Buchenwald would survive the war.

Once Mulsant and Barret were captured, Yvonne had to carry on as best she could with the Maquis, but she had no radio for contact with London. She knew the Allies were advancing but had to rely on very unsure reports.

After D-Day, the ranks of the Maquis snowballed, as many Frenchmen wanted to be seen on the "right" side of the war. Yvonne had the job of trying to outfit them with weapons, ammunition, supplies, and money from London. As the Allied army approached the area, many German soldiers were pulling back toward Germany, leaving behind a less trained and disciplined group of soldiers.

When the Allied Army arrived in her area, Yvonne gathered what information she could to wrap up the SOE operations in the region, and she took that information with her when she returned to England on September 16, 1944.

When she arrived in London, Yvonne was a changed woman. She blamed SAS and the SOE for the poor communications that resulted in the capture and death of Mulsant and Barrett. She thought it was a stupid mistake and put those thoughts into writing, which she sent to the SOE leadership. She also shared her bitterness with others.

The SOE put Yvonne in lodgings with Odette Wilen and Anne-Marie Walters, two other women who were also unhappy with the SOE. The three women repeatedly rehashed their complaints with each other in the hearing of other agents. One agent reported the conversations to the SOE, writing: *Her present nervous condition is largely due to the fact that she blames the organization (SOE) for the arrests of her two friends. I was seriously shocked by the attitude of these three ladies.*

The SOE was unhappy with Yvonne's vocal criticism. Vera Atkins, head of the SOE "F" recruitment and oversight of agents, went as far as to say that Yvonne had been recruited in the field and was never an official agent. That seems a harsh criticism since Yvonne completed the SOE training in England and worked in a Circuit with other agents in France. She was even housed with them when she returned to England.

Across the Channel, France was reluctant to recognize her work with the Maquis because she trained in England and returned to France as an SOE agent. There were no known adverse reports of her work in France, but the recommendations for Yvonne to receive the Croix de Guerre from France and the Order of the British Empire (OBE) from England were rejected, presumedly because of her complaints. She received the lower level of acknowledgment of the Medal of the Resistance from France for her work with the Maquis before joining the SOE.

After the war, Yvonne married a Frenchman named Dumont, and she faded into history. It is believed that she died on May 6, 1996, at the age of 83.

# Chapter 25

# Diana Rowden

January 31, 1915 – July 6, 1944

Code Name: Chaplain, Marcelle, Paulette     Alias: Juliette Therese Rondeau

One of the SOE women destined to die by execution at the hands of the Nazis, Diana was raised in a family with a long military history, and she proved herself to be a strong and defiant woman.

Diana Hope Rowden was born on January 31, 1915, as the eldest child of Army Major Aldred Clement Rowden and Muriel Christian Maitland-Makgill-Crighton. She had two younger brothers, Maurice Edward Alfred Rowden and Cecil William Aldred Rowden.

Her parents' marriage ended in divorce when Diana and her brothers were still young. The children moved to southern France with their mother and lived near the coast. Diana and her brothers loved the beach and spent most of their free time playing in and around the water. Cousins remember her as a tomboy with reddish hair and freckles.

Diana's mother was said to be "the mad Englishwoman" by the locals, and Diana had a rather haphazard early schooling in France. Diana may have needed to help raise her brothers, and she spent a great deal of time with them. Her mother finally realized, or the father demanded, that Diana and the boys needed a more structured education, and the family returned to England.

Diana's mother enrolled her in a boarding school, Manor House, in Limpsfield, Surrey. After her carefree early childhood, Diana was said to chafe at the restrictions at the school and became reserved and quiet. Her roommate later said: *(she) was too mature for us. We were still schoolgirls in grubby white blouses concerned with games and feuds and ha-ha jokes. She was already an adult and withdrawn from our diversions; none of us, I think, ever knew her.*

In 1933, when she was 18, Diana and her mother returned to live in France. Her brothers remained in England, perhaps with their father or in boarding school. Diana enrolled at the Sorbonne, determined to become a journalist.

When Germany invaded France in 1940, Diana volunteered to work with the French Red Cross. She worked with the Anglo-American Ambulance Unit. Almost everyone with foreign nationality wanted to leave France after the Germans invaded because their passport subjected them to possible arrest. Unable to find a way out of France, she remained until the summer of 1941, often sleeping in friend's homes to confuse any Germans or French police who might be looking for her. Later that year, Diana took the same route as so many fleeing France, by hiking up and over the Pyrenees Mountains to Spain until she could make her way to England.

Soon after she arrived in London, she enlisted in the WAAF. She became an Assistant Section Officer for Intelligence and was assigned to work in the office of the Chief of Air Staff. By July 1942, she was promoted to Section Officer and moved to the Royal Air Force Station in Moreton-in-Marsh, located on the northern extremity of the Cotswold Hills.

**Diana and her brothers shortly before she began SOE training**

**Diana in uniform**

Diana needed a minor operation, and while in the hospital she met a fellow patient who happened to be a pilot working with the SOE. He was impressed with her and passed her name on to the attention of the SOE. A SOE staff member received her file and brought her in for a preliminary interview in March 1943. She passed the interview and was invited to join the SOE. Diana's WAAF assignment was transferred officially to Air Intelligence 10 to give her a cover story for family and friends, but she actually began the SOE training program.

Some comments in her training reports read: *Not very agile, but with plenty of courage, physically quite fit.* Her instructors found her to be very good at fieldcraft: (She) *did excellent stalks, very conscientious, a pleasant student to instruct. She was a very good shot, not at all gun-shy. Grenade throwing, very good.* The commandant's report read: *A strange mixture. Very intelligent in many ways but very slow in learning any new subject.* Diana passed all her courses and was given the code name *Chaplain* and her alias of *Juliette Therese Rondeau* for use with non-SOE people she would encounter in France.

Unlike many female agents, she did not parachute into France, or go by boat. Instead, her plane landed in a field in the Loire Valley on the night of June 16-17, 1943. A few minutes later, another Lysander plane landed with Noor Inayat Khan and Cecile Lefort, two fellow SOE agents. They would all meet the same tragic fate.

Her welcoming committee quickly moved her to her new assignment as a courier with the Acrobat Circuit in the Jura Mountain area, southeast of Dijon and close to the Swiss border. Her Circuit leader was John Renshaw Starr, one of the better-known SOE Circuit leaders in France. Their radio operator was John Young, who spoke very little French. One of her responsibilities was escorting him around town so he could avoid speaking in public.

**John Renshaw Starr**

Diana traveled constantly, delivering and picking up messages from Maquis groups in Marseille, Montbéliard, Lyon, and Besancon. Her usual mode of transportation was by bicycle, but Diana sometimes went by train to the more distant locations. On one occasion, she was on a train going to Paris when the Gestapo boarded the train and began checking documents. Although Diana had forged French documents, none of the SOE agents ever wanted to test them. She locked herself in the train's restroom for most of the trip and didn't come out until the train arrived in Paris.

Whenever the SOE sent a plane to drop supplies by parachute, Diana would go to the field with local Maquis to set lamps or use flashlights to guide the plane to the right area. She and her Maquis would break up the parcels and transport the items to different groups.

On July 18, 1943, her Circuit leader, Starr, was captured by the Germans. A double agent had infiltrated one of the local Maquis groups and betrayed Starr's location. Diana and Young immediately went into hiding for fear of their own capture. Thinking that the Gestapo may know her description, she cut and dyed her hair and threw away all the clothes she had been wearing.

After moving several times, Diana and Young eventually moved in with the Janier-Dubry family, which consisted of an elderly widow and her daughters, sons-in-law, and grandchildren. She bonded with the family, especially the children. Needing to remain quiet and out of sight, Diana had plenty of time to play with the children and cook with the grandmother. The grandmother, Madame Juif, later said Diana was: *as tough as a man and as tireless as a child.*

Young was still using his radio to receive messages from the SOE and to send what he could, considering the danger of being captured by the Nazis. He received a message in November 1943 that a new agent named Benoit would be arriving. After Benoit arrived, he, Young, and Diana all went out for a drink. When they returned to the Janier-Dubry home, they were relaxing when the German military police broke in and arrested all three agents.

The Gestapo had intercepted information about the new agent, and they sent in a Gestapo agent who pretended to be Benoit. After Diana and Young were taken to the police station, Benoit and the police returned to the home and searched for Young's radio. They could not find it, as Young had hidden it earlier as a precaution. Madame Juif hid a radio crystal from Young's jacket under a baby mattress, so the police didn't find that either. Benoit and the police ransacked the house and took any valuables they could find.

As with so many captured SOE agents, Diana was taken to Gestapo Headquarters on Avenue Foch in Paris for interrogation and torture. She remained there for about two weeks and then was transferred to Fresnes, the women's prison, on December 5, 1943. She remained there until May 13, when the Gestapo sent her and fellow female SOE agents Andrée Borrel, Vera Leigh, Yolande Beekman, Madeleine Damerment, Diane Plewman, Odette Sansom, and employee (but non-agent) Sonia Olschanezky, to Karlsruhe Prison in Germany. Karlsruhe had many women prisoners, primarily criminals, Romani (Gypies), and Jews. But it was a better prison than most controlled by the Germans, and the women were treated like the other prisoners, with few reports of brutality.

Very early on the morning of July 6, Diana, Andrée Borrel, Vera Leigh, and Sonia Olschanezky were put in a closed truck and taken to the remote Natzweiler-Struthof concentration camp situated high on a hill deep in the Vosges Mountains in France. Natzweiler-Struthof was a German concentration and extermination camp for men, and the only such camp located in France. The camp held about 6000 prisoners from all over Europe.

**Entrance to Natzweiler-Struthof Concentration Camp**

The camp was not expecting the four women, and there was some difficulty in arranging for their accommodation, as the camp was designed for male prisoners.

A male SOE prisoner, Brian Stonehouse, described a woman whom Vera Atkins later identified as Diana upon her arrival at the camp: *A third girl was middle-height, rather stocky, with shortish fair hair tied with a multi-colored ribbon, aged about twenty-eight. She was wearing a grey flannel short 'fingertip' length swagger coat with a grey skirt which I remember thinking looked very English.*

A description of the short time the women were at the camp and of their execution is given in Chapter 2, Vera Atkins (Pages 94-96).

Knowing only that Diane had been arrested, the SOE followed their standard procedure for handling the families of agents reported as missing or captured. When they lacked information or were unable to disclose details about an agent's status, they sent false "update" letters to the agent's parents or next of kin. These letters contained fabricated details designed to reassure the family, creating the impression that the agent was still safe and active in the field. This practice aimed to prevent panic and protect the secrecy of the agent's true situation.

Months after Diana and the other women were executed, an SOE official who had no idea that Diana had been killed, sent a standard letter to her mother on September 29, 1944. He wrote: *Dear Mrs. Rowden, I am glad to be able to tell you that we have again had good news of your daughter, Miss D. Rowden.*

Diana's mother responded on October 3, writing: *Thank you for your letter of September 29, which I was so glad to receive yesterday. It always seems such a long time between letters and when they are a week or two late, it seems like a lifetime. Actually, it is 16 months only since I saw my daughter and it seems much longer owing to being unable to send letters to and from her.*

In early October, the SOE learned that Diana had been moved from Avenue Foch. They sent another letter on October 15 to Diana's mother, telling her that the Germans had captured Diana but expressing their hope she would soon be released. Diana had been dead for over three months at that point.

Diana's mother responded: *Thank you for your letter of October 15 with its very bad news. It certainly is, as Diana would have put it, a very bad show. I do hope she may have gone into hiding and will turn up again soon. In fact, I have been expecting her home daily lately. However, you believe she is a prisoner of war and will eventually be all right. I hope this will prove true.*

Unfortunately, Diana would never return to her mother, or have a burial site that her mother could visit. It wasn't until the following year, on April 29, 1945, that Diana's mother learned of her daughter's death the previous July.

Christian Rowden (perhaps Diana's nephew) wrote the following note for her mother: *Mrs. Rowden thanks the Junior Commander Prudence Gwynne for her letter of April 29 telling her the grim details of her daughter's fate. She thanks her and her staff for the sympathy expressed and is trying to find consolation in what she has learned.*

Diana was posthumously awarded an MBE. However, the MBE was later withdrawn due to the order's policy on posthumous awards. The British government awarded her the Mentioned her in Dispatches (MiD) medal, and the French government awarded her the Croix de Guerre in 1945.

Diana's name is registered with the Scottish National War Memorial in Edinburgh Castle; at the Runnymede Memorial in Surrey, England; on the "Roll of Honour" on the Valençay SOE Memorial in the Indre Département of France; and the "Roll of Honour" in Limpsfield, Surrey. She is also commemorated on the Tempsford Memorial in the county of Bedfordshire in the east of England, and on the town war memorial in Moreton-in-Marsh. A later memorial, the SOE Agents Memorial in Lambeth Palace Road, Westminster, London, is dedicated to all SOE agents.

The Natzweiler-Struthof Concentration Camp, where Diana and the other three SOE women died, is now a French government historic site. A plaque honoring Diana and the three women who died with her is part of the Deportation Memorial on the site.

# Chapter 26

# Cecile Lefort

April 30, 1900 – February ?, 1944

Code Names:  Alice and Teacher   Alias: Cecile Marguerite Legrand

Cecile was another of the married women recruited by the SOE. She was born in London as Cecile Margot Gordon on April 30, 1900, and had American and Scottish heritage. She had come from perhaps the most privileged background of any of the female SOE agents, but her childhood was marred by a scandalous court and custody case.

The scandal involved her mother, Margaret Humble Close Gordon, who later became Lady Granville. Cicile's mother was American and her first marriage was to a wealthy American man, James Close. He was killed in a polo match in 1889. Her mother moved to England and soon married Christian Frederic Gordon, cousin of Lord Granville Armyne Gordon.

She gave birth to Cecile on April 30, 1900, but claimed that Cecile was the child of her husband's cousin, Lord Granville. Lord Granville had children from an earlier marriage, and he was a widower. Her mother's claim led to a drawn-out and very nasty divorce. Her mother's second husband, Christian Gordon, claimed Cecile was his child, and he wanted custody of her. Her mother married Lord Granville in 1902, but the custody case regarding Cecile was still going through the English court system.

The court judge, Sir Francis Jeune, ruled that Lord Granville was not a suitable person to raise Cecile, and custody would need to be shared with the second husband, Christian Gordon. After the judge's ruling, her mother fled to France on March 8, 1903, taking Cecile with her. Cecile and her mother remained in France as the British court had a warrant charging her mother with kidnapping. Her mother and Lord Granville remained married and saw each other frequently on the Continent.

Lord Granville died in 1907 while on a cruise to Yokohama, Japan, with Cecile and her mother. Following his death, his eldest son inherited the title, granting his wife the right to be known as Lady Granville. Consequently, Cecile's mother was thereafter known as Lady Harlech.

Cicile's mother, Lady Granville, called Lady Harlech after the death of her husband, Lord Granville. Photo courtesy of the National Portrait Gallery, England.

Cecile was educated in France and considered it her home. She worked as a nurse's aide in the French nursing corps as a young woman. That was where she met her future husband, a patient at the hospital where she worked. He was a doctor himself, Dr. Ernest Marie Alix Lefort. They became close when she was his nurse and, after he regained his health, they married on July 17, 1924.

Cecile lived a very comfortable life as the wife of a successful doctor. She and her husband resided in a luxurious apartment in Paris and owned a vacation villa in the village of St. Cast along the Brittany coast. Friends later said: *She had a lot of class, was very smart and cultivated, with friends in high society.* She was considered quite a sportswoman and loved to ride horses. She was also a skilled yachtswoman.

Life under German control became more dangerous for Cecile, as she was at risk of being arrested as a British national. Her husband encouraged her to move back to England. It was a country she had not lived in since she was a young child, but she had maintained her British citizenship, so she left France. Her husband stayed behind, thinking his French heritage and his position as a successful doctor would protect him from the Nazis.

In June 1941, Cecile joined the WAAF in London and worked as a military police officer. SOE recruiters learned about Cecile and contacted her. She agreed to join the organization in January 1943. Her WAAF service was transferred to FANY.

Cecile and her husband offered their vacation home on the Brittany coast to be used by the SOE as a safe house for downed pilots, traveling SOE agents, and others needing a safe house near the coast. Within a short time, the SOE set up what would become known as the Var escape line, which was based at their seaside home. Many downed pilots and SOE agents escaped France by boat from the small, sheltered bay below the house.

Cecile began her training to become a field agent in February 1943. As with many female trainees, her training reports were mixed.

One instructor, Lt. Tongue, wrote: *This student looks vague; mixed quite well; is interested in the course and could be relied on to be loyal but doubt if she has enough initiative to achieve much.* Another instructor noted her upbringing and status: *Very ladylike, very English in spite of French background, has a wide circle of friends amongst quite well known and influential people, politicians, gens du monde, artists of the Salon School, all very respectable. Inclined to blurt out things in a rather embarrassing way, which she probably would not have said if she thought first.*

Cecile, in her WAAF uniform

Cecile passed her final training sessions, although many SOE instructors and agents were very concerned about her bad accent when speaking French. She was promoted to Assistant Section Officer in the WAAF. The SOE provided her with the code name *Alice* and the alias *Cecile Marguerite Legrand*, which she would use with non-SOE people in France. She was flown to the Loire Valley on the night of June 16, 1943, along with fellow agents Diana Rowden and Noor Inayat Khan. None of the three women would survive the war.

After spending a night with the others in a safe house, Cecile rode a bike to Angers, where she boarded a train to Paris. From there, she again used a bike to meet up with the Jockey Circuit in Montelimar, where she would work as a courier. The Circuit leader was Francis Cammaerts, considered one of the best Circuit leaders in the SOE, but also one of the most troublesome.

As Cecile traveled around the area delivering messages, she located fields suitable for future supply drops. She was also responsible for separating the supplies when they arrived and getting them distributed to the various Maquis groups. She and Cammaerts didn't have a good relationship, as he did not think she was suitable for the work.

As the Circuit and the Maquis fighters conducted more successful sabotage operations against German facilities, the Germans stepped up their patrol of the area. Cammaerts told his agents to stop using their former headquarters in Montelimar. On September 15, 1943, just three months after she arrived in France, Cecile and agent Pierre Reynaud ignored his warnings and went to spend the night at the home of Raymond Dujat, a Maquis leader in Montelimar. The Germans surprised them by raiding the house that night. Reynaud and Dujat escaped, but the soldiers found Cecile hiding in the basement and arrested her.

Cammaerts was furious that the two agents had ignored his direction, as her arrest put others at risk. He was forced to scatter his agents and tell the Maquis to go into hiding for fear that Cecile would be tortured and reveal information about the Circuit. Despite her torture, Cecile never revealed anything about the Circuit to the Gestapo. After the war, Cammaerts was quoted as saying Cecile: *Should never have been sent to France as she was ill-prepared for the work there.* But he also said after talking about her privileged life: *She would have needed more courage than most to screw herself up to go (back) to France.*

Cecile was first imprisoned in Lyon and then was sent further north to the Fresnes prison, the second largest prison in France. It had 1200 cells for men and a smaller section for women. Most SOE female agents who were arrested were sent there before being sent on to prisons in Germany.

She remained at Fresnes prison for almost six months before the Gestapo sent her to Ravensbrück concentration camp, about 50 miles outside of Berlin, on February 3, 1944. Cecile traveled with several hundred other women to the camp, which already held some 30,000 women and children.

Normally, the prisoners had almost no way to communicate with family, friends, or the SOE when incarcerated. However, in Cecile's early days at the camp, Cecile was able to smuggle a couple of notes out to her husband through a friendly guard, writing: *Left for Germany, in the convoy of women. Good health, good morale. Warn the Red Cross to send shoes, warm clothes, and food.* A second message gave Ravensbrück as her address. Her husband passed both messages on to the SOE.

Ravensbrück was one of the sites where SS doctors performed horrific experiments on women. Most of the women subjected to those treatments died as a result, and those who survived were left with lifelong medical issues. Fortunately, none of the SOE women were treated in that experimental medical ward.

Sickness was endemic in Ravensbrück, and the doctors had little in the way of medications. There were reports from other prisoners that Cecile was diagnosed with either ulcers or stomach cancer and that the camp doctor, Percival Treite, operated on her. Soon after the surgery, Cecile was put to work at hard labor.

Dr. Treite was a half-British, half-German medical doctor at Ravensbrück who was tried for war crimes at the end of the war. He was defended by a dozen former female prisoners including SOE agent Yvonne Baseden, who wrote letters to the court favorable to him.

Former prisoner Mary Lindell testified in favor of Treite at the trial, saying that Treite: *Was the only man who was human, the only man who looked after the sick people as a doctor should look after them.* Another former prisoner testified that he saved the lives of many English and American women by passing them off as French and smuggling them onto International Red Cross transports toward the end of the war. However, the court found him guilty and sentenced him to death. He took his own life by poison in his prison cell.

**Ravensbrück concentration work crew of female prisoners**

By the end of 1944, Germany knew that their defeat was almost inevitable, and many of their prisons and camps became killing centers as they tried to erase knowledge of their treatment of prisoners and take revenge on the Allies and those supporting them. The conditions for the prisoners became even more draconian than they had been before.

Reports in January 1945 said that Cecile was suffering from diarrhea, malnutrition, and general exhaustion. Hearing that a nearby sub-camp, Uekermark, treated sick prisoners better, she volunteered to go there. Unfortunately, the stories Cecile heard were untrue, as that camp had been turned into an extermination center. She was warned not to go but thought that nothing could be worse than where she was. She took the transfer, along with two other English prisoners, Mary Young and Mary O'Shaughnessy.

Conditions at the camp were horrendous; the rations were even worse, the lavatories were open trenches, and prisoners were often forced to stand for five to six hours per day for roll call. Between 100 - 150 women were taken from the roll call every day, never to return to the barracks.

In February 1945 only a couple of weeks after being transferred, Cecile's name was called on the morning roll call, and she was taken from the group to the gas chamber and gassed along with several other sick women. After the war ended, the SOE could not definitively establish the date of her death, but Lloyd's of London set the date as May 1, 1945, to settle her will.

Vera Atkins reported that just weeks before Cecile was killed, she received a note from Cicile's husband pleading for the SOE to help him get a divorce. Thankfully, Cecile was spared the knowledge of his request. It seems like the ultimate cruelty in the tragic end of her life. Vera said he later asked for her understanding of his request, but she told him it was not her place to forgive him.

In September 1945, Cecile was awarded an MBE on the recommendation of Major General Colin Gubbins, the head of the SOE. At that time, the SOE only knew that she had been taken prisoner and moved to Ravensbrück concentration camp. She was also Mentioned in Dispatches (MiD) for her service on June 13, 1946, and received France's award of the Croix de Guerre on January 14, 1948.

Cecile's name appears on several memorials, including a plaque at Ravensbrück concentration camp dedicated to the four SOE women executed there: Cecile, Denise Bloch, Lilian Rolfe, and Violette Szabo.

Cecile may not have been the most suitable candidate for SOE fieldwork. She was a society woman with considerable wealth and privilege, but she courageously volunteered to try to help rid France of the German occupation. Despite torture, starvation, and terrible illness, she never betrayed the SOE secrets or the Maquis fighters. She paid the ultimate price for her bravery.

# Chapter 27

# Noor Inayat Khan

January 1, 1914 – September 13, 1944

Code name:  Madeleine   Alias: Jeanne-Marie Renier

Noor Inayat Khan was arrested and imprisoned by the Gestapo. She was held longer and perhaps tortured more brutally than any other female SOE agent. Held under the "Nacht und Nebel" policy intended to make people "disappear." There were 118 missing SOE agents from the "F" Section after the war ended, and her fate was the last to be discovered by Vera Atkins.

Noor had a unique and very privileged family background. Her father, Hazrat Inayat Khan, was a well-known poet, musician, and Sufi teacher of royal heritage. He was born into a noble Mughal family, making Noor a princess in the Indian culture. He was also the head of a Sufi sect, an ascetic Islamic religious movement that emphasized a direct, personal experience of God.

After spending almost a decade in the United States, her father established an order of Sufism (the Sufi Order) in London in 1914. By the time of his death in 1927, centers had been established throughout Europe and North America. Multiple volumes of his teachings have been published, which are still used today. His teaching emphasized the oneness of God and the underlying harmony of the revelations communicated by the prophets of all the world's great religions. His followers were pacifists in terms of any military conflict or disputes.

Noor's paternal ancestors, comprising Mughal lords and shamans, were Turkmen from the Chagatai Khanate who settled in Sialkot, Punjab. She was a direct descendant of Sultan Fateh Ali Sahab Tipu, the last Muslim leader of southern India. He was known as the Tiger of Mysore. Noor's maternal grandfather, Sangitratna Maulabakhsh Sho'le Khan, was a pioneering Hindustani classical musician and educator known as the "Beethoven of India." Her maternal grandmother, Qasim Bibi, was from the royal house of Mysore's 18th-century Muslim ruler.

Noor as a baby with her father

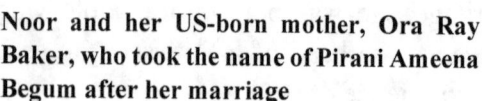

Noor and her US-born mother, Ora Ray Baker, who took the name of Pirani Ameena Begum after her marriage

Noor's mother, Ora Ray Baker, was born on May 8, 1892, in Albuquerque, New Mexico, to Erastus Warren Baker and Aletta "Etta" Margaret Hiatt. As a child, Noor and her family lived in Chelan, Washington in the U.S. Noor's mother was the niece of Mary Baker Eddy, the founder of the Christian Science religion.

Ora first met Khan in New York in 1911 when her guardian, Pierre Bernard, engaged the master musician and mystic to teach his ward Indian music. After they fell in love, Bernard forbade their marriage, and Khan sailed for London. Ora sent him a letter professing her love. After he wrote back, she snuck away from her guardian and sailed alone to England. They married in London on March 20, 1913, when Ora took the name Pirani Ameena Begum.

Noor, too, was a Sufi. She was born in Russia in the Vasoko Petrovsky Monastery in Moscow, a short distance from the Kremlin. Her father was teaching at the Moscow Music Conservatory when she was born on January 1, 1914. Her parents had two sons and two daughters, with Noor being the eldest.

Noor's family moved to England when Noor was still a baby. In 1920, when Noor was six, the family moved to Suresnes, France. Her parents kept an open house full of music and meditation, with Sufis from around the world visiting throughout the year. Noor received her formal education in Paris.

In 1926, her father decided to return alone to India. He was unwell and wanted to see his homeland again. He died there on February 5, 1927. Noor's mother went into seclusion after her husband's death. At the tender age of thirteen, Noor took responsibility for the family and became a surrogate mother to her younger siblings.

From an early age, Noor wrote poems and short stories. She had musical talent and played several instruments, as did her sister and brothers. Following in her father's footsteps, Noor studied music at the Paris Conservatory under the famous Nadia Boulanger, who also taught Aaron Copland and Quincy Jones.

Noor later studied child psychology at the Sorbonne and graduated in 1938. She joined the École Normale to continue her music studies. In her spare time, she wrote children's stories in English and French. Her stories were published in the Sunday section of Le Figaro, and her first book, *Twenty Jataka Tales*, was published in England in 1939.

Noor and her sister and two brothers

She and her family thought music and literature would be the theme of her life. But WWII intruded, and Noor stepped up for the challenge. She was 25 and still living in France with her family when Germany invaded Poland, after which England and France declared war on Germany on September 3, 1939. German armies invaded Belgium, Luxembourg, the Netherlands, and then moved into France on May 10, 1940. Noor and her family returned to England immediately after the invasion.

After one of her brothers joined the Royal Air Force in November 1940, Noor felt she had to do what she could to liberate France. She put aside her pacifist Sufi beliefs and joined the WAAF. The military was desperate for radio operators, so she began learning Morse Code and how to operate a radio. Because Noor was fluent in French, she was recruited to join the "F" Section of the SOE.

Selwyn Jepson, who recruited Noor into the SOE in February 1943, described her in his documents as having: *small, still features, dark, quiet eyes, a soft voice, with a fine spirit glowing in her*. Noor joined FANY to provide a cover story for her family.

**Noor with one of her musical instruments**

Fellow female trainees were Cecile Lefort and Yolande Beekman. Noor worked hard to overcome her dislike and fear of weapons during combat training. Some instructors had doubts about her capability to take on the dangerous work required of those going into occupied territory. Some wondered if Noor was too young and inexperienced. They also worried that she was careless and sometimes failed to safeguard the all-important codes that allowed her to receive and send messages.

As a part of her training, Noor was sent on a grueling 96-hour exercise in Wales. Her assignment was to set up live and dead letter boxes where messages could be left, and to locate three different safe locations where she could send and receive wireless messages. Those tasks were to be completed without anyone in the surrounding area becoming suspicious. Noor succeeded, but her report of that exercise was mixed and stated: *This student has obviously worked very hard and [shown] interest in exercise, but, however, she must learn to be more discreet.*

Records in the National Archives of Britain note that Noor was both praised and reprimanded throughout her training program. Many of the instructor reports were contradictory. She impressed some of her instructors with the security precautions she took during wartime simulation, following protocol by: *Taking precautions against search and surveillance. She carried no incriminating papers as she memorized her orders before leaving here.* However, during a mock police interrogation, another instructor reported: *She made several stupid mistakes during this interrogation which a little forethought could have easily avoided. She always volunteers far too much information when being questioned.*

Noor was excused from parachute training due to an earlier operation (details unknown) that made it dangerous for her to jump. She passed her other courses despite the concerns of her instructors. One report states: She is not *overburdened with brains but has worked hard and shown keenness, apart from some dislike of the security side of the course. She has an unstable and temperamental personality, and it is very doubtful whether she is really suited to work in the field.*

All the attention on her inclination to say too much during interrogation practices may have been critical in building her resolve to say nothing incriminating or revealing during her time as a prisoner while enduring repeated torture.

Noor received high marks as a radio operator. Her official title was Assistant Section Officer. Acting as a wireless operator was the most dangerous role in the SOE. By 1943, the life expectancy of a wireless operator in France was only six weeks. Many operators had already been captured, with their fates unknown until after the war.

The SOE gave each agent time off after their training and before they were sent to France to write letters that were given to Vera Atkins to periodically send to the agent's family. This pretense of communication was done to prevent the family from asking too many questions or worrying about their daughter's well-being. Some agents never gave any letters to Vera, so she often wrote them herself, under the pretense of being the agent.

Noor's cover was for her to assume the name of *Jeanne-Marie Renier*, posing as a children's nurse. She was sent with only a false passport, a few French francs, a pistol, and a lethal cyanide pill to be taken in case of capture. It was reported that she later threw away the pill.

On a moonlit night on June 16, 1943, she, Cecile Lefort, Diana Rowden, and a male agent were flown across the English Channel to France and landed behind German lines. Noor made her way alone to Paris and joined the Cinema (later to be called Phono) Circuit, with the codename *Madeleine*. The Cinema Circuit was a sub-Circuit of the huge Prosper Circuit. Like most in France, Noor's Circuit consisted of a team leader, Emile Henri Garry, a courier, and Noor as the radio operator.

Female SOE agents had a lot of authority, belying their titles of "courier" and "radio operator." The National Archives copy of Noor's service record states that: *Although you are under (Cinema's) command and will take your instructions from him, you are the ultimate judge as regards the technicalities of W/T and W/T (cryptography) security.*

In late June, disaster struck the huge Prosper/Physician Circuit within a few days of her arrival. The Gestapo captured the top operatives of that group, and their wireless sets were seized. Prosper had been the largest SOE Circuit in Europe.

On June 25, 1944, Noor sent an urgent message to the SOE reporting that the Prosper leadership, including several radio operators, had been captured. Vera Atkins, the head of SOE agent oversight, strongly advised Noor to return to England, considering it too perilous for her to remain in Paris. Noor refused, recognizing that she was the last radio link between London and Paris.

Acknowledging her determination, the SOE instructed her to go into hiding but continue supporting the remaining Resistance fighters of Prosper. Noor became an indispensable communication link in the war effort. From July to September, Noor survived a dangerous cat-and-mouse game with the Gestapo.

Noor continued to transmit and receive messages for the remnants of the Prosper Circuit. She also gathered information from friends of the Resistance about the arrests of many Resistance fighters. The secret police continued to encircle her area. By mid-August, Noor was the only SOE radio operator still working in Paris. Single-handedly, she was doing the work of six radio operators and funneling the intelligence back to London. She could only transmit for 20 minutes at a time for fear of having her location detected.

She changed her location almost daily, transmitting from churches, basements, attics - anywhere she could find temporary refuge. By September 1943, the Gestapo was aware of her activities and even had a description of her. Despite their efforts, they couldn't pinpoint her exact location, often arriving just after she had moved. To avoid capture, she frequently altered her appearance, dyeing her black hair several times.

Noor's communications were crucial in helping London pinpoint locations for supplying the Resistance. She also transmitted messages regarding the safe passage home for injured airmen. Her efforts facilitated the escape of more than thirty Allied pilots who had been shot down over France.

After only six months in the country, Noor was betrayed, and her address was sold to the Nazis. The Gestapo arrested her on October 13 as she returned to the apartment she was using. After her capture, she attempted to escape but was quickly recaptured.

Two likely suspects gave her location to the Nazis. The first suspect in Noor's betrayal was Frenchman Henri Déricourt. He was an SOE operative who arranged the air flights to bring SOE agents into France and he is written about earlier in this book.

The second suspect was Renee Garry, the sister of Noor's supervising agent, Emile Garry. Renee was accused of receiving cash to give up Noor. After the war, Renee was tried for treason but escaped conviction by one vote.

Noor's Cinema Circuit leader, Garry, and his wife were both captured and imprisoned on October 18, 1943. Garry was later executed at the Buchenwald concentration camp almost one year later, on September 10, 1944. His wife survived and was released after the war.

After her capture, Noor was tortured before being sent to the infamous Gestapo Headquarters at 84 Avenue Foch in Paris. Major Hans Josef Kieffer was a member of the feared intelligence branch of the Schutzstaffel (SS). He oversaw the interrogations in Paris. Kieffer interrogated almost all captured SOE agents, male or female, and his methods were often very effective. He tried to convince SOE agents to become double agents and work for Germany, and he sometimes succeeded. Kieffer excelled in sending false and misleading wireless messages supposedly from SOE agents to England, a tactic known by the Germans as "the radio game."

A significant reason for Kieffer's success in obtaining information from prisoners was his habit of lulling them into a feeling of safety. He would greet them with real and code names and treat them well. He would demoralize them with his knowledge of the workings of the SOE network and tell them their own agents or Resistance fighters had betrayed them. Noor was also interrogated by the civilian interpreter for the Germans, Ernest Vogt. Vogt wrote of his fruitless interrogation of Noor: *She is impossible. I never met a woman like her.*

Noor had unwisely kept copies of all her secret codes, and the Germans used her radio and her codes to trick London into sending new agents - straight into the hands of the waiting Gestapo. This deception resulted in the capture and deaths of three more female SOE agents.

Sonya Olschanezky, *Tania,* a French civilian working for the SOE, learned of Noor's arrest, and sent a message to London that Noor had been captured. She warned the SOE to suspect any transmissions from *Madeleine*. The SOE did not recognize Sonya's name, and a decision was made to disregard her warning. Sonya was later captured and executed with other female SOE agents in 1944.

Buckmaster, perhaps for political reasons, refused to acknowledge the many warnings from his staff or Sonya that Noor's transmissions were fake. Many in the British military establishment thought the SOE was frivolous and unnecessary, and military officers from other branches were lobbying to have the group disbanded. Buckmaster was fearful of any negative stories coming out of the program.

In November 1943, while still at the Gestapo Headquarters, Noor attempted another daring escape with two other prisoners, John Renshaw Starr, the former leader of the Acrobat Circuit, and Resistance leader Leon Faye. They loosened the skylight window and climbed onto the roof of the Nazi headquarters building. They escaped onto the sharply gabled roof of an adjoining building in near-pitch darkness. They broke into what they thought was an empty apartment but awakened an elderly woman who screamed. Her screams alerted the guards who ran toward the screaming and recaptured the three prisoners.

Labeled a "highly dangerous" prisoner, Noor became the first SOE female agent sent to a German prison. In November 1943, they moved her to Pforzheim prison on the edge of the Black Forest, where she stayed for ten horrendous months.

Noor was kept in isolation most of the time, shackled in chains and foot irons. She could not feed or clean herself. She was regularly tortured and interrogated but revealed nothing about her Circuit or Resistance names. Other prisoners could hear her crying at night. She was occasionally allowed to go to the food line, and by scratching messages on the base of her mess cup, Noor informed another inmate of her identity. She gave the name of Nora Baker and the London address of her mother's house.

Noor endured prison and torture longer than any other female SOE agent and longer than most SOE men.

After almost a year of torture and deprivation, Noor was taken from her cell on the night of September 11, 1944. She was driven handcuffed to Karlsruhe prison, where she met three of her SOE colleagues who were also prisoners: Yolande Beekman, Madeleine Damerment, and Éliane Plewman. Together, the women were driven to the railway station and made to board a train to Dachau concentration camp.

They reached Dachau at midnight. It was to be a long night. All night long, Noor was kicked and beaten in retribution for her continued refusal to cooperate with the Gestapo. When her frail body finally slumped on the floor, she and the three other SOE agents were taken outside and forced to kneel on the ground beside the camp crematorium. An SS guard, possibly Wilhelm Ruppert, shot her and the three other SOE women in the back of the head. The four women were killed on September 13, 1944. Additional details regarding their execution are in Chapter 4 (pages 42 & 43).

Dachau Camp

**Main Dachau Concentration Camp and separate work camp at the time of Allied liberation by the US Seventh Army**

Noor, who had initially been judged by her SOE instructors to be emotionally frail, turned out to be fierce and courageous when captured. She refused to cooperate with the Germans, showed them nothing but contempt, and in the instant before her death, after she had been tortured and beaten, a guard said she spoke but a single French word, "liberté."

After the war, Vera Atkins worked for months to discover the fate of all the 118 missing SOE agents. Nora was her most difficult search, as they had no word of her during the last year of the war. She gave false names to everyone who interrogated her, and even to other SOE agents she saw while in prison.

When Kieffer, the Gestapo agent in charge of the interrogations at the Avenue Foch headquarters in Paris, was an Allied prisoner awaiting trial, Vera Atkins interviewed him. He told her that Noor was one of the few agents who had never given him even one piece of information about SOE activities, actions of the Resistance groups she was working with, or about other agents. But he had no knowledge of what happened to her after she left Avenue Foch.

Vera finally received testimony from Gestapo agent Christian Ott who told her and U.S. war crimes investigators about the fate of Noor and the other three women. He described a scene where one of the other three women executed with Noor cried and asked for a priest. After refusing her request, the women held hands as they knelt, and they were shot from the back. One was shot twice as she showed signs of life.

Ott's statement was considered unreliable, but in 1958, an anonymous Dutch prisoner asserted that SS officer Wilhelm Ruppert cruelly beat Noor before shooting her from behind.

**Éliane Plewman, Yolande Beekman, Madeleine Damerment, and Noor Inayat Khan**

The three other SOE women executed with Noor were: Yolande Beekman, Madeleine Damerment, and Éliane Plewman.

The four women are believed to have been burned in the Dachau crematorium, so no burial sites exist. Plaques have been installed at the site of the Dachau concentration camp to commemorate their lives.

**Noor's memorial plaque at the Dachau Memorial Hall**

Noor has an inscription at the Air Forces Memorial at Runnymede, England, memorializing those without a known grave.

**George Cross**      **MBE**      **MiD**

The British Government posthumously awarded Noor The George Cross, Britain's highest civilian award for gallantry in the face of the enemy, on April 5, 1949. Noor was one of only three SOE female agents to receive the prestigious award. She also received the MBE, and the Mentioned in Dispatches (MiD) award for gallant or meritorious action in the face of the enemy. MiD awards were given to a member of the armed forces whose name appeared in an official report written by a superior officer and sent to the high command, in which their gallant or meritorious action in the face of the enemy is described.) Noor was one of the few SOE women who received this award.

The French Government awarded Noor the Croix de Guerre on January 16, 1946

**Croix de Guerre (CdeC)**

Noor's mother died on May 2, 1949, in Paris at the age of 56. Her death was just three weeks after her daughter received the George Cross.

In July 1967, Noor's former home in Paris was the site of a memorial ceremony attended by the Indian ambassador, the attaché of the British Embassy, and other dignitaries, including Colonel Maurice Buckmaster. At that service, Buckmaster read the following message from Brigadier Sir John Smyth, VC, the president of the Victoria Cross and George Cross Association:

*I and all members of my Association, both holders of the Victoria Cross and the George Cross, will always revere Noor Inayat Khan GC and cherish her memory as one of the most splendid and gallant women in our history. In her life – and particularly in her incredibly valiant work for the resistance – she was always utterly staunch and true to the cause of freedom and to the comrades who were working with her, and she faced her death with the same courage she had always shown in her life.*

**The Princess Royal Anne unveiling Noor's Memorial Statue**

In 2011, £100,000 was raised to pay for the construction of a bronze bust of Noor in central London, close to her former home. The unveiling of the bronze bust by the Princess Royal Anne took place on November 8, 2012, in Gordon Square Gardens, Bloomsbury, London. Noor's last word, *Liberté*, has been carved on the Memorial to remind the world that a young woman unhesitatingly sacrificed her life so the world could be free of Fascism.

In 2014, PBS made her the subject of a documentary, *Enemy of the Reich: The Noor Inayat Khan Story.*

**The memorial stamp honoring Noor**

The Royal Mail issued a stamp in her honor on March 25, 2014, as part of a set of stamps about "Remarkable Lives."

A biopic, *A Call To Spy*, released on June 21, 2019, at the Edinburgh International Film Festival, pays tribute to the work of three female British spies during the Second World War, including Noor, Vera Atkins, and Virginia Hall.

# Chapter 28

# Éliane Plewman

December 6, 1917 – September 13, 1944

Code Name: Gaby, Dean, Madame Dupont   Alias: Éliane Jacqueline Prunier

Éliane was one of four SOE women prisoners who were executed as a group at Dachau concentration camp by the Germans in September 1944. After D-Day, when the war turned against the Nazis, they stepped up their killing of prisoners in their prisons and concentration camps.

**Éliane shortly before leaving for France**

Éliane Sophie Browne-Bartroli was born to English businessman Eugene Henry Browne-Bartroli and his Spanish wife, Elisa Francesca Bartroli, in Marseille, France, on December 6, 1917. Because of her parents' mixed nationalities, she and her brothers had dual British and Spanish citizenship.

Éliane was educated in England and at the British School in Madrid, Spain. She had a gift for languages and was fluent in English, French, and Spanish and spoke some Portuguese. After finishing college, Éliane moved to Leicester, England, and worked briefly as an interpreter for a fabric and clothing import/export company's foreign customers.

In 1939, Éliane was working at the British Embassy in Madrid in the Spanish Press section. From Madrid, she transferred in 1941 to basically the same job in Lisbon, Portugal. Éliane returned to London a year later, working for the Spanish section of the Ministry of Information.

Éliane married Thomas Landford Plewman on July 28, 1942. He was an Irishman from County Kildare who had been commissioned as a lieutenant in the Royal Artillery. After their marriage, they lived in Leicester, England.

With her husband involved in the war, Éliane wanted to do also do what she could for the war effort, so she agreed to join the SOE. Her brother was already an SOE agent, and he may have recommended her. She was vetted and accepted on February 25, 1943. She was promoted to Second Lieutenant in the Auxiliary Territorial Service (ATS) at the same time. She began her SOE training in early May 1943 at Wanborough Manor in Surrey, England.

**Lt. Thomas L. Plewman (left) with O. Seman, July 1944, Normandy. At the time of this photo, unbeknownst to him, Éliane was already a prisoner. She was executed two months later. Her husband did not learn of her death for two years.**

The reports from her instructors were primarily complimentary, something unusual for the female recruits. One instructor wrote: *(She is) calm, efficient, and conscientious, and with admirable composure. A great asset to the gaiety of the party.* Another instructor wrote: *A very tough woman with unexpected charm. She was obviously most capable and acted with discretion. She was calm, and nothing rattled her. We have much esteem for her.*

After successfully completing all her training courses, Éliane parachuted into France on the night of August 13-14, 1943. To evade detection by German radar, the pilot flew at a dangerously low altitude of just 1,000 feet. The low-altitude jumps were highly risky for the agents, as there was no time to rectify any issues with the parachute. Moreover, the altitude was too low for a reserve parachute to be effective.

Due to wind currents, Éliane landed almost 20 miles from her intended drop zone, causing the SOE team to miss her arrival. She hid her gear, which included one million francs intended for payment to Resistance fighters, in some bushes. Unfortunately, she injured her ankle upon landing. She concealed herself until she could walk, then began searching for the contacts the SOE had provided. Eventually, she located a safe house where she stayed until her ankle healed. Nearly two months after her landing, she finally met with her Monk Circuit leader, Captain Charles Milne Skepper, code-named *Bernard*. However, by the time her hidden gear was recovered, the money had already disappeared.

The SOE gave Éliane the code name *Gaby*, but she was also known by *Dean* and *Madame Dupont*. The cover name she was to use with all the locals she met was *Éliane Jacqueline Prunier*. The SOE assigned her to work as a courier for Skepper. Their Circuit covered Marseille, Roquebrune, St. Raphael, and the surrounding area. Their 20-year-old radio operator was Arthur Steele, code name *Laurent*.

She usually traveled around her Circuit by bicycle but took the train or begged for a ride in an available truck when traveling long distances. Éliane served on the welcoming committee when new agents arrived in the area and helped them settle into the Circuit's work. When a parachute drop of supplies was made, she sorted them out for distribution to the Maquis groups. On more than one occasion, her driver would stop to pick up walking German soldiers, and the soldiers would happily sit on top of the tarp covering the weapons and ammunition.

One of the safe houses used by Éliane was that of Madame Chaix-Bryon. She would later marry Éliane's brother, Albert. She felt Éliane was assigned to take too many risky jobs, especially carrying explosives to future operation sites. Éliane Monk Circuit was very active blowing up train tracks and supply cars, thus disrupting rail traffic. The supply trains were the lifeblood of the occupying German military. Éliane would often help to set the explosive charges.

Albert John Browne-Bartroli, Éliane's brother, became head of the Ditcher Circuit in Bourgogne from October 1943 until September 1944. One day, while Éliane was about to board a train carrying a heavy suitcase loaded with explosives, she unexpectedly ran into her brother. After discussing her work, he expressed concern that she was being pushed too hard and feared for her safety. Éliane, however, brushed off his concerns and continued her activities.

The Maquis, working with her Circuit, blew up more than 30 trains in January 1944. They also derailed the main train line to Toulon inside a tunnel. Then they blew up the repair trains coming to fix the damage. They caused heavy damage to 30 more trains in early March 1944. In retaliation, the Germans increased the number of soldiers in the area weekly, determined to rid the area of the Maquis.

There are several differing reports about who betrayed the Monk Circuit. One theory suggests that a Circuit member was sharing a mistress with a German agent. Another attributes the betrayal to lax security, which allowed a German agent to infiltrate the Circuit. A third report claims that a man who sold food to the Circuit members shared a mistress with a Gestapo agent.

Whichever story is true, the Gestapo learned where Circuit leader Skepper often spent the night. He was captured in his apartment, along with Julien Villevieille and several other agents, on March 23, 1944. To trap additional agents, the Gestapo left soldiers in the apartment. The following day, Éliane and radio operator Arthur Steele were captured when they entered the apartment.

The Gestapo interrogated Éliane for three to four weeks at Les Baumettes prison near Marseille. They repeatedly beat her on the head and face, attempting to extract secret information about the SOE and the Maquis groups she worked with. They also used an electric shock rod between her eyes. Other prisoners reported that she became unrecognizable due to the severity of the beatings. Despite the torture, she consistently told them she was only Skepper's mistress, and the Gestapo was unable to obtain any further information from her.

The Gestapo transferred her to Fresnes Prison. After another six weeks of torture, she and seven other women prisoners were sent to Karlsruhe prison in Germany on May 12, 1944. The other SOE women were Yolande Beekman, Andrée Borrel, Madeleine Damerment, Vera Leigh, Diana Rowden, and Odette Sansom. An employee of SOE but not a trained agent, Sonia Olschanezky, was included in the same group.

On September 12, after four months at Karlsruhe, the Gestapo took Éliane, Madeleine, Yolande, and Noor and moved them by train to the Dachau concentration camp.

A description of their execution is detailed in Chapter 4 (pages 42 & 43) on Madeleine Damerment and Chapter 27 (pages 199-201) on Noor Inayat Khan. Éliane was 26 when she was killed.

**Éliane Plewman, Yolande Beekman, Madeleine Damerment, & Noor Inayat Khan**

Major General Colin Gubbins wrote of Éliane in his recommendation for an MBE on July 13, 1945: *She was dropped in the Jura and was separated from her Circuit for some time. Instead of remaining in hiding, she showed outstanding initiative and made several contacts on her own which were later of great value to her Circuit. For six months, Plewman worked as a courier, and her untiring devotion to duty and willingness to undergo any risk largely contributed to the successful establishment of her Circuit. She traveled constantly, maintaining liaison between the various groups, acting as a guide to newly arriving agents, and transporting wireless telegraphy equipment and compromising documents.*

His recommendation for Éliane to receive an MBE was denied because the award statutes did not allow it to be awarded posthumously. Instead, she was awarded the King's Commendation for Brave Conduct on August 20, 1945. She received the Croix de Guerre with bronze star from France on January 16, 1946. It is believed that her husband never remarried and lived until 2000.

The letter on the next page remains in Éliane's SOE file at the British National Archives.

Tracing the missing SOE agents after the war ended was a herculean task. The details of Éliane's Circuit leader, Skepper's final days are uncertain. In the recommendation for Skepper's MBE written by Major General Colin Gubbins on December 8, 1945, he stated: *Captain Skepper was arrested. The Gestapo severely tortured him and later transported him to Fresnes and then to Compiegne prison. There has been no news of him since. It is believed that on or after April 4, 1944, he died in Buchenwald.* The MBE award was denied for him, too, because the statutes did not allow a posthumous award.

What happened to radio operator Arthur Steele also remains vague. The SOE personnel files indicate that he was arrested, interrogated, and tortured by the Gestapo and probably sent to Germany. The citation for his posthumous Mention in Dispatches (MiD), written on August 23, 1945, by Major General Colin Gubbins, states: *he was executed at Buchenwald Concentration Camp on September 14, 1944. Other sources state that Arthur Steele was executed on September 19, 1944. It is known from German sources that between September 9 and September 19, 1944, the SS hanged several groups of captured agents held prisoner at Buchenwald.*

COPY

From: Sq/Officer V.M.Atkins,
J.A.G's Branch,
War Crimes Section,
Headquarters,
BRITISH ARMY OF THE RHINE.

25 Jun 46

J/G D.Gorrum,
M.O.1 (S.P.)
The War Office

--------------

Subject:  Mrs. E.S.Plewman F.A.N.Y.
Miss Madeleine Dammerment @ Dussautoy, F.A.N.Y.
Mrs. Y.E.M.Beekman nee Unternahrer,
S/O W.A.A.F. 9922.

--------------

     It has now been established that the above-named were executed in the camp of Dachau in the early hours of 13 Sep. 44, probably by shooting.  The full circumstances surrounding this case are not yet known but the fact that they were killed in the early hours of 13 Sep. 44 has been definitely established.  I assume that you will take the usual casualty action.

     The facts, as far as they are known, are as follows:

     Eliane Plewman was captured at Marseilles on or about 23 March 44:  it is believed that she passed through the prison of Les Beaumettes in Marseilles and was then sent to Fresnes near Paris. Ylande Unternahrer was captured near St.Quentin on or about 15 Jan 44 and she was first taken to 84 Avenue Foch, Paris and later transferred to Fesnes.  Madeleine Dammerment was captured on landing on 29 Feb 44 near Chartres.  I believe she was taken to Fresnes straight away.

     On 12 May 44, they left Fresnes Prison together with Odette Sansom, who has returned safely, and Diana Rowden, Nora Inayat-Khan, Vera Leigh and Andree Borrel, who were killed at Natzweiler on 6 Jul 44. They went straight to Karlsruhe where they were put into the civilian jail for women and they remained there until the early hours of 12 Sep 44. I have seen the following witnesses apart from Mrs.Odette Sansom in connection with their stay in Karlsruhe:-

# Chapter 29

# Yvonne Cormeau

Dec. 18, 1909 – Dec. 25, 1997

Code names; Annette, Fairy, and Sarafari

The second radio operator sent into France by the SOE was Yvonne Cormeau. Over 18 months, she sent over 400 messages back to London with crucial information about German troop movements, garrison locations, and areas that the local Resistance and fellow SOE agents were identifying as good bombing targets. She sent more messages than any other operator except for Auguste Floiras, who served in France for a more extended period.

Yvonne was an unlikely candidate for such a dangerous and stressful position. She was a widow with a young child; both situations were unusual for women recruited into the SOE.

Yvonne was born Beatrice Yvonne Biesterfeld in Shanghai, China, on December 18, 1909, to Arnold Charles Biesterfeld and Olga Daisy Smith Biesterfeld. Her father was stationed in Shanghai as a Belgian consular official; her mother was from Scotland. Yvonne was educated in Belgium and Scotland. In 1937, Yvonne married Charles Edouard Emile Cormeau, a second-generation French immigrant born and living in England, in London. They had one daughter, Yvette.

When WWII began, Yvonne's husband enlisted in the Rifle Brigade, was wounded, and sent home in 1940. Unfortunately, their home was bombed and destroyed during the Luftwaffe Blitz in 1941. She was injured, and both her husband and unborn child were killed. Her 2-year-old daughter was saved by sheltering under a bathtub.

At the beginning of WWII, the Luftwaffe was one of the most advanced air forces in the world, quickly achieving air superiority over the countries they invaded. Initially, they were highly successful in bombing London, leading the Nazis to believe that England would swiftly surrender once the city was under attack. However, they were mistaken. The relentless bombing only strengthened the resolve of the British people, prompting many Englishmen and women to respond by enlisting in the military or finding another way to support the war effort.

**Yvonne in her WAAF uniform**

After becoming a widow with no income, Yvonne needed to earn a living. In November 1941, she joined the Women's Auxiliary Air Force (WAAF) as an administrator. In early 1943, while working at the RAF Airfield Station in Lincolnshire, the SOE recruited her to become an undercover agent to serve behind German lines in France.

**Yvonne and her daughter, Yvette**

After much soul-searching regarding her fear that her daughter could be left an orphan if she were killed during the war, she agreed. She sent her daughter to a convent of Ursuline nuns in Oxfordshire, where the girl would remain until she was reunited with her mother at the war's end.

Yvonne left for training on February 15, 1943. Fellow trainees were Yolande Beekman and Noor Inayat Khan, both of whom were later executed by the Nazis. Yvonne was trained as both a radio operator and a courier with the understanding that she would primarily work as an operator.

After successfully completing her training, Yvonne parachuted into France on August 22, 1943, near Saint-Antonine-du-Queyret, east of Bordeaux. She arrived with her Circuit boss, George Starr, code-named *Hilaire*. Yvonne's communication skills proved crucial to the Resistance effort in her area. Her exceptional performance set the bar for later radio operators.

Starr set up the Wheelwright Circuit, which became the second largest in France. He eventually had 20 SOE agents working for him and thousands of Resistance fighters.

Yvonne described Starr as: *short in stature, five feet six inches in height, very nervous, a heavy cigarette smoker, and a man who took duty and responsibility seriously and would never ask a person to do anything he would not do himself.* Yvonne became his closest associate. Starr had known Yvonne's husband, and he took special care to keep her safe during her time in France. A few agents thought they might have had a romantic relationship while in France.

During the early days of his time in France, Starr complained about being required to have women working for him. He initially had Marie-Thérèse Le Chêne, Mary Katherine Herbert, and Odette Sansom assigned to his area; he called them the "three bloody women." He especially disliked and distrusted Odette, who became one of the most decorated SOE female agents. He later doubted another female agent, Denise Bloch, and even considered having her "liquidated."

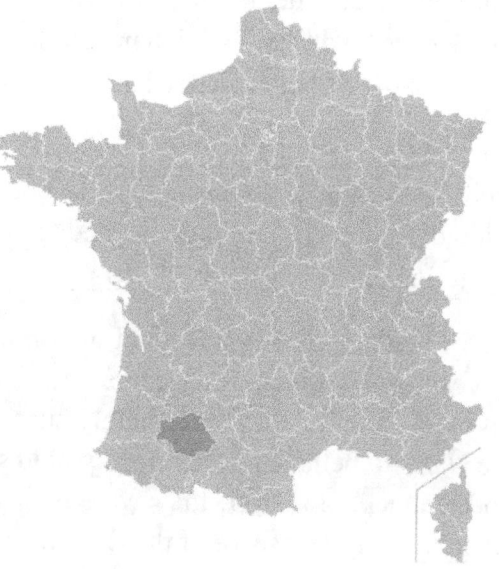

**Area of Wheelright Circuit Resistance work**

Eventually, he trusted Denise enough to send her back to England to convince the SOE to provide more support for his Circuit. However, the agent he came to rely on the most was Yvonne, and they often traveled around their area together.

Many SOE agents carried a cyanide pill when working in France, but Yvonne refused to do so. She also refused to carry the .22 revolver that had been given to her when she departed England. The SOE trainers told her that if the Germans captured her and the Germans discovered a gun or a cyanide pill, it would mean immediate execution. She wanted to return home to her daughter, so taking her own life was not an option she was willing to consider.

**George Starr, leader of the Wheelright Circuit**

Yvonne became famous within the SOE for the quantity and quality of her radio transmissions. When Yvonne first arrived in France, she was expected to code, send, and decode about three messages per week, which soon increased to sending and receiving several messages daily. Of the 400 + messages she sent, the SOE cryptographer Leo Marks said: *She never made a single mistake.* Accuracy was crucial, but so was speed. Most operators transmitted at 12 words per minute, but Yvonne did it at 18-22 words per minute in Morse code. The longer an operator took to send a message, the easier it was for the Germans to track the device, so speed was essential.

Yvonne always tried to use a battery, as she thought it was more difficult for the Germans to detect the transmissions from that power source and might keep her and the property owners hiding her safe. Many of the small villages from which she transmitted did not have electricity, so the battery was also more dependable and gave her more flexibility to move around. Later, she was provided with a lighter and more portable machine, a Type A MK III wireless weighing only 8.8 pounds.

A radio operator led a very lonely life working behind enemy lines. Their instructions from SOE were: *The ideal is for W/T operator to do nothing but W/T work, to see his/her organizer (leader) as little as possible, if at all, and to have contact with the fewest possible number of the Circuit.*

A few days after arriving in France, Yvonne passed Francis Cammaerts, a fellow SOE agent she knew from her training, on the same train traveling to Toulouse. She tried to catch his eye, but he ignored her and walked on. It was a good reminder to her never to expose another agent by acknowledging their presence. No one in the SOE ever knew if the Gestapo, the French police, or a collaborator was following them.

As the date for the Allied (D-Day) invasion of France came closer, Yvonne's work became more demanding, and she moved to the hilltop village of Castelnau-sur-l'Auvignon. Her Circuit leader, Starr, had his headquarters in the town, making his communication with London much easier when he had her close by – but it broke all the SOE rules for operators.

She remained in the village of only 300 people for six months, an unheard time for an operator to remain in one place. During all that time, a German poster with a very good likeness of her was on display throughout the area, but no one betrayed her to the Germans. Yvonne felt she could stay in the village because the Germans did not believe any Allied spy would live in a town without running water or electricity.

Yvonne worked as an operator and as a courier when necessary, taking instruction and money to Resistance groups. After D-Day, she helped cut power and telephone lines to help isolate the Wehrmacht German garrison stationed near Toulouse.

In June 1944, the Germans discovered that the Wheelwright Circuit had their headquarters in Castelnau, where about 300 Resistance fighters were based. They launched an attack on the village with 1,500 soldiers, killing many of the Resistance fighters and destroying the town. The Circuit agents fled, and during her escape, Yvonne was shot in the leg but managed to get away. The SOE group retreated to the village of Lannemaignan, some 35 miles away. However, the Germans pursued them and also destroyed that village. Ultimately, the SOE agents escaped by splitting up and hiding in the surrounding woods.

The French Forces of the Interior liberated Toulouse on August 21, 1944. It was an overarching organization of Resistance groups. Yvonne and Starr drove directly into the city with American and British flags flying on their car. Just a month before, they would have been shot on sight by the Germans.

**George Starr (in center) with Yvonne to his immediate right, and fellow SOE and military agents.**

On September 16, 1944, General Charles de Gaulle, head of the Provisional Government of the French Republic, visited Toulouse. De Gaulle had little respect for the Resistance groups, who had varying philosophies about how France should be governed after the war. On meeting Starr and some of the Resistance leaders, De Gaulle denounced them as mercenaries. He ordered Starr to leave France. Starr replied that he was in France under the authority of the Allies, and he did not recognize the authority of

De Gaulle to give him orders. De Gaulle threatened to arrest him, but Starr stood his ground, and the meeting ended with a handshake. Nine days later, on September 25, Starr and Yvonne were recalled to London.

After the war, Yvonne was awarded an MBE from England and the Legion d'Honneur, Croix de Guerre, Medaille de la Resistance, and Palmes Academiques medals from France. She was decommissioned with the rank of Flight Officer from the WAAF, but she continued to work as a translator for the SOE.

Yvonne was reunited with her daughter, Yvette, and they lived together in London until the daughter married. Yvonne's time in France had taken a toll on her, and she said in an interview: *My time in France certainly aged me considerably. I had quite a bit of white hair at thirty-three. I suppose it was the tension. It was a strain, there's no doubt about that - you couldn't help it. Still, I was pleased when I got back, and one of my codes and ciphers men said, "Mm, 402 messages, jolly good! And only one I couldn't decipher." Only one man beat my number of messages, and he was out two years.*

After the war, Yvonne became very active in the SOE "F" Section veterans' group and planned their annual Bastille Day dinner for many years. She was also one of the earliest members of the Special Forces Club and served on that Board.

The Special Forces Club (SFC) is a private members' club in Knightsbridge, London. It was established in 1945 for former SOE personnel, members of wartime resistance organizations, the Special Air Service (SAS), Special Boat Service, and First Aid Nursing Yeomanry (FANY).

The club's membership now includes those who had served or were serving in organizations and units closely associated with special operations and the intelligence community. Its founders intended the club to be a meeting place for those who had served in the SOE and members of kindred organizations. This tradition has continued, with the club maintaining a close relationship with the Office of Strategic Services (OSS) and like-minded groups in Australia, Canada, and New Zealand, along with the successors of European and other resistance organizations.

Unlike many other clubs, which were open only to men and officers, the Special Forces Club was always open to women as long as they were SOE alumni. Members had an inexpensive membership that allowed them to stay in London at a modest charge.

Yvonne was the featured guest on the BBC version of the *This is Your Life Program* in 1989. Later, she served as an advisor to the BBC TV series *Wish Me Luck*, which focused on the women who worked undercover during WWII. Yvonne was interviewed for the movie *Charlotte Gray*, and many thought that the film was based on her life.

After her daughter left home, the long-widowed Yvonne married for a second time to James Edgar Farrow in 1989. They lived in Derbyshire for eight years. He died in 1997, and she moved into the Tall Pines Nursing Home in Hampshire until her death on Christmas Day, 1997.

The governments of Great Britain and France sent representatives to her memorial service as a sign of gratitude for her service during WWII. Her story is on the Armed Forces Memorial Wall in Staffordshire, England.

Yvonne saved the bloodstained dress she was wearing when she was shot, and the radio case she had with her that day. Those items and her uniform are on permanent display at the Imperial War Museum in London.

# Chapter 30

# Yolanda Beekman

January 7, 1911 – September 13, 1944.

Code Name: Mariette

Yolanda Beekman's life was cut short by the Nazis at the infamous Dachau Concentration Camp just a few days shy of one year after she was flown behind enemy lines in France.

**Yolanda before WWII**

Yolanda Elsa Maria Unternahrer was born in Paris on January 7, 1911, to Jacob Unternahrer, a Swiss businessman of Swiss/French heritage, and his English wife. Her father moved the family to London when she was young, and she received most of her education there. As she grew older, she was sent to a Swiss finishing school. When she left school, she was fluent in English, French, and German.

At the beginning of WWII, she joined the WAAF, where she received training to become a radio operator. She worked for various Royal Air Force stations for two years until the SOE learned of her fluency in French, a skill they were in desperate need of. Her ability as a radio operator was also very important. Yolanda was recruited to join the SOE on February 15, 1943. She was in the same class as Yvonne Cormeau and Noor Inayat Khan.

In August 1943, just a month before leaving for France, she married Jaap Beekman, a sergeant in the Dutch Army and an instructor at her SOE training school. They had a short time together before she left for Tours, France, one month later, on September 18, 1943. They would never see each other again.

Yolanda was assigned to work as the radio operator for Canadian Gustave Bieler, code name *Commandant Guy*, the head of the Musician Circuit based in St. Quentin. Bieler was a large man who would stand

**Yolanda and Jaap Beekman's wedding photo**

out in any crowd. He damaged his spine in his parachute jump into France and was in constant pain for the duration of his brief life. His wife Marguerite Geymonat worked as a broadcaster to the troops in Europe on Radio Canada International. They had two children.

His personality was said to be as large as his stature, and it was difficult for the SOE to find team members to join him. Yolanda was chosen to be his radio operator because the training team thought she had a gentle disposition and could work with him without feeling overwhelmed by his strong presence. They got along without any significant problems.

**Major Gustave Bieler**

Maurice Buckmaster described Yolanda as: *having a rather typical English appearance. She was very quiet and homely – she had gained immense popularity at the Wireless school by taking over unofficially the duties of darner of socks for the men – and her unruffled cheerfulness and good humour were a great asset. She quickly developed an easy camaraderie with Bieler, which promised well for their future work. Bieler had towards all the women engaged in our work a kind of amused tolerance which some might have faintly resented. But Yolande took his attitude without offense, and her very unaffectedness and simplicity evoked his esteem and admiration.*

St. Quentin was chosen as the Circuit's headquarters because Britain thought it would become a key area for German railway and canal communications. In addition to her own Circuit, Yolanda also served as the radio operator for the adjacent Farmer Circuit because they did not have their own operator at that time. She was also responsible for the distribution of supplies when they dropped from the sky.

Although most Circuit radio operators moved frequently, Yolanda had a favorite location where she used her radio. The SOE had instructed her to use a pre-arranged schedule to send messages at specific times and frequencies three times a week. Using only one location significantly increased the danger of being detected by the Germans, and it is not known why she settled on only one place. That habit became more dangerous as her regular days and times of transmission allowed the Germans to get closer to her location.

Messages were normally sent in Morse code after being enciphered. Early radio models were heavy and bulky, but one designed in 1943 by Major John Brown, was smaller and lighter, at only 8.8 pounds.

Over Christmas, other Circuit members saw a suspicious van passing by her location, so she moved the radio to the house where she was living. She bleached her hair in case the Gestapo had a description of her. On January 12, 1944, Circuit members saw a man passing by the house who appeared to be listening to earphones – something very unusual in those days. She again moved her radio to the nearby Café Moulin Brule, as she thought it to be a safe location on the northeastern edge of the city. The following day, her boss, Bieler, arrived at the Café to discuss where they should move her next.

**Photo of suitcase radio used by most SOE agents beginning in 1943.**

Only five months after her arrival in France, both she and Bieler were arrested on January 13, 1944, when two Gestapo agents walked into the Café with pistols drawn. They had no opportunity to escape, and the Germans had the radio as proof that they were spies. Yolanda and Bieler were tortured but never gave up secret information. Yolande was beaten about the face repeatedly in the early days of her capture in an attempt to break her silence.

Bieler was taken to the Fossenburg concentration camp, where his torture continued for several months. When the Germans were convinced they could not break him, he was executed by a firing squad in May 1944.

After Yolanda's initial interrogation by the Gestapo in Paris, they transferred her to Fresnes Prison on May 13, 1944, several miles outside Paris. They continued to interrogate and torture her when she refused to give us any names or information about the Paris Resistance members. The guards seemed to especially enjoy hitting her on the face and legs.

She shared a cell with Elise Johe, who was arrested because she was a Jehovah's Witness; Clara Frank, who was jailed for slaughtering a cow on her property without permission; and Annie Hagen, who was arrested for working as a black marketeer. Another prisoner, Hedwig Muller, said that Yolanda was often confined to the cell because the injuries to her legs made walking difficult.

On September 12, 1944, Yolanda, along with seven other SOE women, Éliane Plewman, Madeleine Damerment, Odette Sansom, Diana Rowden, Vera Leigh, Andrée Borrel, and Noor Inayat Khan were sent to the Dachau concentration camp. Four of the women, including Yolanda were executed the following morning. Yolanda and Noor had been in the same training class in England only 19 months before.

A description of her execution is detailed in Chapter 4 (pages 42 & 43), Madeleine Damerment and Chapter 27 (pages 199-201), Noor Inayat Khan. Yolanda's life ended at 33 years of age.

**Éliane Plewman, Yolanda Beekman, Madeleine Damerment, and Noor Inayat Khan**

220

France awarded Yolanda a posthumous Croix de Guerre. Her name is recorded on the Runnymede Memorial in Surrey, England, and she is included in the SOE Agent Memorial in Lambeth Palace Rd, Westminster, London.

From: Sq/Officer V.M.Atkins,
J.A.G's Branch,
War Crimes Section,
Headquarters,
BRITISH ARMY OF THE RHINE.

25 Jun 46

J/G D.Gorrum,
M.O.1 (S.P.)
The War Office

----------------

Subject: Mrs. E.S.Plewman F.A.N.Y.
Miss Madeleine Dammerment @ Dussautoy, F.A.N.Y.
Mrs. Y.E.M.Beekman nee Unternahrer,
S/O W.A.A.F. 9922.

----------------

It has now been established that the above-named were executed in the camp of Dachau in the early hours of 13 Sep. 44, probably by shooting. The full circumstances surrounding this case are not yet known but the fact that they were killed in the early hours of 13 Sep. 44 has been definitely established. I assume that you will take the usual casualty action.

The facts, as far as they are known, are as follows:

Eliane Plewman was captured at Marseilles on or about 23 March 44: it is believed that she passed through the prison of Les Beaumettes in Marseilles and was then sent to Fresnes near Paris. Ylande Unternahrer was captured near St.Quentin on or about 15 Jan 44 and she was first taken to 84 Avenue Foch, Paris and later transferred to Fesnes. Madeleine Dammerment was captured on landing on 29 Feb 44 near Chartres. I believe she was taken to Fresnes straight away.

On 12 May 44, they left Fresnes Prison together with Odette Sansom, who has returned safely, and Diana Rowden, Nora Inayat-Khan, Vera Leigh and Andree Borrel, who were killed at Natzweiler on 6 Jul 44. They went straight to Karlsruhe where they were put into the civilian jail for women and they remained there until the early hours of 12 Sep 44. I have seen the following witnesses apart from Mrs.Odette Sansom in connection with their stay in Karlsruhe:-

# Chapter 31

# Nicola Trahan

? 1926 – January 18, 2024

Code Name: Teddy

A previously unknown member of the SOE female agent group is Nicola Trahan. Her identity was not known until the publication of her obituary in January 2024. Nicola may have been the youngest woman who worked directly for SOE as a field agent.

Most of the information listed below is from her obituary and from the comments of friends rather than from the author's usual sources of the National Archives and the many articles, books, and other first-hand accounts written about the SOE female agents. She is the only woman in this book who was not listed in M.R.D. Foot's *SOE in France*.

The author is still investigating Nicola's story but wanted to include her in the book to give her recognition for her work during and after the war.

Nicola Pauline Trahan was born in Pas de Calais, France, in 1926 to a French mother, Jeanne Marie Laure Bourzes, and a Scottish father, Andre Jean Emile Trahan, and she carried dual citizenship from both of her parents' home countries.

Until the age of 13, Nicola was taught at an international school in France. When Germany invaded, she and her family moved to England, where she continued her formal schooling. After hearing about the hardships in France, she wanted to help.

It is not known if the SOE recruited her or if she volunteered to join the group. Due to her young age of 16, the author assumes she may have volunteered and lied about her age. The SOE was desperate for French speakers to serve in France, and they may not have checked her age too carefully.

She claimed that the SOE taught her the necessary skills to parachute, but she has not been quoted as mentioning any other training. Nicola said that at the age of 17, she was dropped into France in 1943 (exact date unknown) by parachute from a Westland Lysander plane, which was the plane used to drop most SOE agents behind enemy lines. She would remain in France until the Allies liberated her area almost three years later.

The SOE assigned Nicola the code name *Teddy* and positioned her as a courier. According to her accounts, she undertook typical courier responsibilities, such as transporting messages between different Resistance groups and other SOE agents. The specific Circuit to which she was assigned remains unknown. Often, she was entrusted with a suitcase, which she believed contained money, though she never verified its contents.

In addition to her courier duties, Nicola performed an important role in aiding downed pilots and Jews. She helped them find refuge in safe houses and facilitated their movement from one safe location to another. On some occasions, she escorted them to the mountains, from where they began their journey to safety in Switzerland.

A friend from her church said that Nicola told her of her service at the SOE: *All of the work that was being undertaken by the networks (Circuits) in France was to disrupt the German occupation but to also disrupt their advance up to the north of the country.*

After the war, in recognition of her service, France awarded her the La Medaille de la Reconnaissance in 1948, and the Croix de Guerre in 1949.

**Nicola, on her bike**

After the war, Nicola returned to England and trained to be a nurse in Manchester, graduating in 1953. Her service to her country and the military families of England had just begun. She worked for the Soldiers', Sailors' & Airmen's Families Association (SSAFA), the Armed Forces Charity, as a uniformed member of its Nursing Service for 30 years, from 1958 – to 1988. After retiring, she became a volunteer caseworker for an additional 20 years from 1988 - 2008.

Her career led her to work in the following posts:

| | | |
|---|---|---|
| Belgium | 1958-60 | Supreme Headquarters Allied Powers, Europe (SHAPE) in Belgium |
| Germany | 1960-64 | Duesseldorf |
| | 1960-66 | Herford |
| | 1966-68 | Duesseldorf |
| | 1968-70 | Paderborn |
| | 1970-72 | Koln |
| | 1972-75 | Krefeld, Duesseldorf |
| | 1975-78 | Detmold |
| | 1978-81 | Hohne |
| Hong Kong | 1981-88 | Hong Kong |

**Nicola received the Croix de Guerre at Les Invalides in Paris on Saturday, November 5, 1949.**

In recognition of her dedication to veteran families, England awarded Nicola an MBE (Member of the Most Excellent Order of the British Empire) in 1989. During an interview following the award ceremony, she expressed her deep connection to the military, stating: *When I decided to put down roots for the remainder of my life, it had to be an Army country, after such a long relationship with the Services.*

When her official job with SSAFA ended, she returned to England and moved to Orcheston, Wiltshire, for 28 years. Service was a very important part of her life, and she volunteered to work in the Salisbury Cathedral gift shop every Friday. The shop manager said of Nicola: *She was a great character. Very dry sense of humour, a very no-nonsense, crack-on-with-it sort of person. I'm not at all surprised that she did so many great things. She was a very strong character.*

The Churchwarden said of Nicola: *(She had a ) humanity, humbleness, vast generosity, absolute toughness but also a real sense of humour for one who appeared so serious.*

**Nicola, age unknown.**

Nicola received her parachute wings very belatedly in 2018. While the SOE men who parachuted into France received their parachute wings while in the service, only a few of the SOE women received them - much later. Each woman (or their family) had to request the wings through their Council members. Many had to wait long years after their request to receive the well-earned fabric wings from the British government.

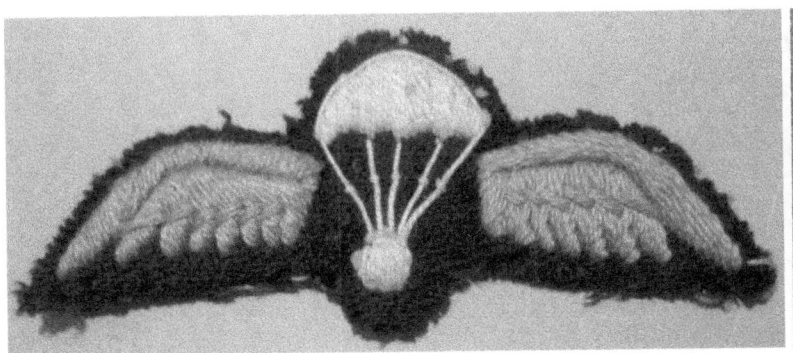
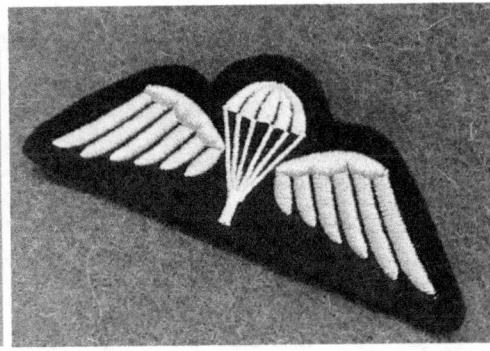

**SOE Parachute Wings Patches**

**Nicola, proudly wearing her award medals toward the end of her life**

Nicola died peacefully at her home on January 18, 2024, making her the last known of the SOE women. Her body was donated to science and then cremated at the request of her partner.

# Chapter 32

# Pearl Witherington

June 24, 1914 – February 24, 2008

Code Names: Marie, Pauline

Alias: Genevieve Touzalin, Marie Jeanne Marthe Verges

Pearl was the third woman after Virginia Hall and Liese De Baissac to officially be designated to lead an SOE Circuit and direct Maquis fighters. Her group included approximately 2000 Maquis fighters, who specialized in sabotaging telephone lines and railroads, both essential services to the German Army. M.R.D. Foot described her Circuit as being "highly successful," a rare compliment from him for a woman.

Cecile Pearl Witherington, the eldest of four daughters, was born to British ex-pats living in Paris. There had been four brothers, but they all died in infancy. Her parents were Gertrude (Hearn) Witherington and Wallace Seckham Witherington. She was raised in France, but she and the family maintained their British citizenship.

Her father came from a once well-to-do family but struggled with a drinking problem, squandering his inherited wealth, and was rarely at home. This made life difficult for the family during her childhood, and she received only minimal schooling. Her parents eventually separated, and her father died in 1932 when she was 18. Pearl learned the art of negotiating with tough men early on, trying to keep creditors at bay - a skill she would frequently rely on during WWII.

Despite her limited formal education, she served as a secretary and cipher clerk at the British Embassy in Paris. When the Germans invaded France, the embassy closed abruptly, leaving Pearl to find the doors locked upon her arrival one morning.

Her boyfriend, Henri Charles Willy Cornioley, enlisted in the British army in February 1940, and they became engaged in May of that year. They would not see each other again for three and a half years.

As the German army was approaching Paris, she, her mother, and three sisters left for England in December 1940. Their journey to the safety of London was arduous, taking until July 1941. They had to navigate a very circuitous route through German demarcation lines to Marseille and then through unoccupied countries.

Once in England, she and her sisters joined the WAAF. She later heard about the SOE and volunteered to work as a field agent. The SOE accepted her on June 8, 1943. The 29-year-old was described as: *Strong-*

*willed, cool-headed, and ferociously practical.* Meanwhile, without her knowing, her fiancé, Henri, was captured by the Germans and imprisoned.

During her seven-week training period, the weapons instructor judged her to be the "best shot" with pistols and rifles of all the trainees who had completed the SOE program, male or female. Interestingly, she never carried a gun after returning to France as a full-fledged agent. She felt that having a firearm would be dangerous if the Germans stopped and searched her.

One of her training reports noted: *(She) does not have the personality to act as a leader, nor is she temperamentally suited to work alone. She would be best employed as a subordinate under a strong leader in whom she had confidence.*

Pearl successfully completed her courses and was dropped into France by parachute from a Halifax bomber on the night of September 22, 1943. She landed near Tendu, but her parachute became tangled in a tree. Her gear, including her suitcase with personal clothing, was lost in a lake. The leader of the welcoming committee was suspicious of who she was and almost shot her. She later said that she never had adequate clothing in France and wore the same clothes repeatedly.

**Pearl, shortly after completing her SOE training**

The SOE assigned Pearl as a courier for the large Stationer Circuit, led by Maurice Southgate, code name *Hector.* The radio operator for the Circuit was Jacqueline Neane, code name *Jacqueline.* Pearl's cover story was that she was a cosmetic saleswoman, which allowed her to travel widely in her area, "selling make-up" in the local villages. Her Circuit covered a large area of central France, and she was constantly traveling, often by train, as she took messages to and from Southgate to their radio operator and the far-flung Maquis groups.

She was reported to have an air of calm even when under considerable stress. Pearl often slept on the trains or in random safe houses, as it was seldom safe to stay in hotels. Each hotel had to keep a record of the guests, which was checked daily by the local police or the Gestapo. She was frequently stopped and had to show them her fake identity papers each time. Southgate described her as "a soldier." Pearl went on several operations with the Maquis fighters and handled the explosives and weapons like the men.

From October 7, 1943, to late January 1944, Pearl took over the temporary leadership of the Circuit when Southgate returned to England for an extended time. Around Christmas, she suffered an attack of neuralgic rheumatism, which the doctors said was caused by being out in the cold weather for long periods. She was in considerable pain and was temporarily incapacitated.

Circuit leader Southgate was arrested by the Gestapo on May 1, 1944, and eventually sent to Buchenwald concentration camp. Their radio operator, Jacqueline Nearne, had been called back to London the month before, and the SOE replaced her with Sir Louis Pierre Rene "Amédée" Maingard de la Ville-ès-Offrans, code name *Samuel.* Both Pearl and Maingard were with Southgate earlier on the day he was captured but, fortunately, were not with him when he was arrested.

The SOE was very impressed with Pearl's work while Southgate was in London and agreed that Pearl and Maingard would split up the large Stationer Circuit into two new Circuits. Pearl started the new Wrestler Circuit and took on the new code name *Pauline*.

**Maurice Southgate**

Maingard received a promotion to major and took over the renamed Shipwright Circuit. During the remainder of their time in France, they worked closely together on sabotage operations. Ironically, the Queen knighted Maingard on December 31, 1981, for his work with the SOE during the war, but there was little recognition for Pearl, who successfully managed a similar-sized Circuit.

Pearl and her fiancé met up again in France for the first time in over three years after he escaped from the German prison. They still cared for each other, and she brought him in to work within the new Circuit.

**Henri Cornioley and Pearl**

The Maquis respected her, as she was often involved in the operations. Recognizing that the male egos of the Maquis would make it difficult for them to take orders directly from a woman, she found an excellent way to work around that challenge. Pearl found a willing colonel in the French army who agreed to be her stand-in to give direction to the various Maquis groups within her Circuit.

Pearl would later note that there was a level of tension between the diverse Maquis groups, some leaning toward the communist point of view, some toward the socialist, and others who were nationalistic. Those differences became more pronounced as they anticipated the Allied invasion. She did an amazing job of keeping them united on joint sabotage missions.

The Gestapo knew about Pearl, and they put a bounty on her head, dead or alive, of one million francs, the equivalent of $165,000 as this book was being written in 2023.

In June 1944, immediately after D-Day, the two Circuits caused more than 800 interruptions to railroad traffic, focusing on cutting the main line between Bordeaux and Paris. Those shutdowns seriously stalled the German army's efforts to move soldiers and supplies to the Normandy battle area. The Maquis also disrupted roads and telegraph links.

On June 11, 56 truckloads of German soldiers attacked the Circuit's headquarters at the Les Souches chateau. The Circuit had a large stockpile of weapons and money ready to disburse to the Maquis. Pearl was there with only a few men. She hid the money, and she and most of the men managed to escape into the surrounding countryside. The Germans killed 32 of the local fighters. The Germans' main goal was to destroy or take the weapons. They also took the radio, and then they moved on.

**Canisters of supplies, weapons, and ammunition dropping by parachute to waiting agents.**

Pearl's Circuit was in a crisis having lost their radio, weapons, ammunition, and supplies. Pearl bicycled to the village of Saint-Viatre, where she had Philippe de Vomécourt's radio operator contact the SOE to send new supplies and weapons. SOE sent 60 planeloads, dropping them two weeks later, on June 24, 1944

Word spread about the attack and how quickly she had managed to get resupplied from England. Her Maquis groups, which had numbered about 2000 men, suddenly grew to more than 3500. Nearly all the new men and boys were untrained and without weapons.

Pearl was very involved in teaching the recruits how to use the guns and explosives and basic guerrilla warfare practiced by the more seasoned Maquis fighters. Her respect among the Maquis grew daily, and many began calling her *Mother* or *Lieutenant Pauline*, her code name. They later complimented her for her excellent, clear-headed organization and leadership.

Pearl had been asking for a military officer to assist her since she organized the Wrestler Circuit. On July 25, 1944, Capt. Francois Perdriset from the Free French finally arrived to work with her. Pearl worked well with him and appreciated that he was experienced in warfare.

De Gaulle's networks had been flexing their muscles since D-Day, pressing to take control and credit for the Allied actions pushing the Germans out of France. In late August 1944, the SOE agreed with de Gaulle to have Pearl move her Maquis fighters to the remote Forest of Gatine to mount sabotage operations to delay or stop the German soldiers from southern France from linking up with German soldiers in northern France. Her men were guerrilla fighters and had not directly attacked large groups of German soldiers. Pearl was not happy about the orders, but London told her to comply.

The Maquis, working with her Circuit agents, engaged over 19,000 German soldiers under General Botho Elster on September 9 and 10, 1944. The Maquis fought in guerrilla fashion, and they threatened the Germans to the point where they were willing to surrender.

German General Elster was afraid of retribution from the Maquis if he surrendered to them. He knew that the Maquis did not fight within "proper" military rules and were frequently violent toward captured German soldiers. Elster requested a "regular" army to surrender to. The American Army stepped in and accepted that surrender on September 16 at Beaugency Bridge.

Pearl's Maquis fighters were not allowed to be present or participate in the surrender, and they received no recognition for the impact their sabotage operations made against the German army. Pearl and other SOE staff were furious.

**German General Elster (left) surrendered to American forces on September 16, 1944**

The American general gave the defeated Germans chocolates and oranges, luxuries that the French people and the Maquis fighters had not seen for years. Pearl was not the only one angry about how the surrender had been handled. Many local French men and women tore down American flags, threw things at the American soldiers, and wrote angry letters to the local newspapers about how the defeated Germans were treated better than the Maquis.

**Pearl, on the far right in the top picture and second from the left in the lower photo, with SOE agents and French officers**

On February 27, 1944, Major General Colin Gubbins wrote about Pearl: *Her control over the Maquis group to which she was attached, complicated by political disagreements among the French, was accomplished through her remarkable personality, her courage, steadfastness, and tack.*

```
To: D/AIR.                              From: F/REAR LINK.

                                        30 AUG 44.
─────────────────────────────────────────────────────────────────

                      S/O WITHERINGTON.

          With reference to the attached A.P.5  for the above-named.

          This Officer went into the Field in September 1943 to act as
courrier to one of our most important Organisers, and to help build
up his circuit.  Since June she has been in complete charge of this
circuit and has shown outstanding powers of leadership and organising
ability.  Her group has had several encounters with the enemy, and on
each occasion they have acquitted themselves with distinction.

          We feel that this is a most deserving case for promotion.
```

**Letter of commendation, August 30, 1944**

Pearl and her Circuit officers were told that their mission was over on September 21, 1944, and they were recalled to London. Pearl and Henri Cornioley were married on October 26, 1944, in the Kensington Register Office in London. On December 2, 1944, Pearl's pay was increased from 350 pounds to 425 pounds per year, retroactive to May 20, 1944, when she joined the SOE. The increase still did not equal what the male SOE Circuit leaders were paid.

Before leaving the SOE, Pearl turned in her expense accounts for reimbursement. She had taken copious notes on every expenditure she had made in France. The SOE accounting department told her that she was turning in the most extraordinary - and probably unique - breakdown of her expenses in the field, amounting to several million francs.

On February 27, 1945, the Wing Commander wrote the following for Pearl: *Throughout her long period in the field, Witherington showed outstanding devotion to duty and accomplished a task far greater than that which was expected of her. Her control and organization of the*

**Pearl and Henri Cornioley, it may be their wedding photo**

*different Maquis groups, despite differences in political opinion of the F.F.I. in her area, were accomplished only thanks to the exercise of her superb qualities of leadership, tactfulness, and courage. Miss Witherington was fortunate to find her fiancé in France, and he was with her throughout the fighting in the Maquis. Her story is a true romance, and our pride and esteem for this gallant girl is very great. A citation has been prepared recommending the granting of a decoration to Flight Officer Pearl Witherington.*

The Wing Commander's acknowledgment of the romance between Pearl and her fiancé is amazing, as military officers usually choose to ignore any fraternization between agents in the field. The fact that he mentions it in a very positive way indicates that he held Pearl in high regard.

She was recommended for the Military Cross but was ineligible because she was a woman. She took great exception to the fact that the men who did the same work she did qualified for the Military Cross but that women were disqualified just because they were women. When she was awarded the MBE, which she considered "puny," she sent it back with a note saying that: *She did not deserve it as she had done nothing remotely civil.* She also wrote in a note to Vera Atkins: *Our training, which we did with the men, was purely military, and as women, we were expected to replace them in the field. The work which I undertook was of a purely military nature in enemy occupied country. I personally was responsible for the training and organization of nearly 3,000 men for sabotage and guerrilla warfare.*

Many years later, Pearl accepted the award of a military MBE. In 2004, when Queen Elizabeth was visiting Paris, she upgraded Pearl's MBE to the more prestigious award of Commander of the Most Excellent Order of the British Empire (CBE). Pearl also received the Legion of Honor from France.

After the war, England sent Pearl to the United States on a propaganda tour. Unfortunately, she was a petite, reserved, uniformed woman, and the American audience was expecting someone more glamorous to represent the intelligence service, so the tour was not a great success.

Pearl and Henri moved to Paris, where she worked as a secretary for the World Bank and he as a pharmacist. She and her husband were involved in establishing the Valençay SOE Memorial in France, which was dedicated in 1991. The monument commemorated and honored the 104 SOE agents who died during the war. The couple retired near Valençay, as that town was in an area where they had both worked during their service in the SOE.

In April 2006, Pearl finally received her well-earned parachute wing patch. She considered this a greater honor than her MBE or the CBE. Pearl was only allowed three practice jumps in her training before she was sent off to parachute into France. She said when receiving the award: *The chaps (men) did four training jumps, and the fifth was operational – and you only got your wings after a total of five jumps. So, I was not entitled – and for 63 years, I have been moaning to anybody who would listen because I thought it was an injustice.*

**Queen Elizabeth awarded Pearl the prestigious Commander of the Order of the British Empire (CBE) in 2004 when the Queen visited Paris**

**Pearl when she finally received her parachute wing patch**

Pearl's husband, Henri, died in 1999. She died at a retirement home in the Loire Valley on February 24, 2008, at 93. Few around her knew of her heroic service during WWII, a fate shared by many of the SOE women.

# Chapter 33

# Anne-Marie Walters

March 16, 1923 – October 2, 1998

Code Name: Milkmaid, Colette, Paulette

Alias: Alice Davoust, Miss Fitzgerald

Anne-Marie was born in Geneva, Switzerland, on March 16, 1923, and raised within the exacting standards of the old diplomatic corps. She was the daughter of a French mother, Louise Roux-Bourgeois, and an English father, Francis Paul "Frank" Walters. Her father had been an Oxford don before joining the League of Nations and rising to the position of Deputy Secretary-General. Her childhood home was on the north side of Lake Geneva in an affluent area popular with diplomatic families.

Anne-Marie, her parents, and her younger sister, CiCi, Walters, had regular winter skiing holidays and often spent part of each summer near St. Tropez. She received her early education at the International School in Geneva, considered a finishing school for many of the children of diplomatic families. Anne-Marie was fluent in French and English and knew basic phrases in several other languages.

By May 1940, her father realized that the danger of remaining in Switzerland outweighed the negative prospects of leaving, and the family moved to London.

Anne-Marie volunteered to join the WAAF at 17, ignoring her mother's disapproval. A year later, the SOE contacted her, and she was interviewed by Capt. Selwyn Jepson, a man who interviewed many of those recruited into the SOE. She was accepted into the program and began her training. Anne-Marie joined FANY and received an honorary commission.

Anne-Marie went through the usual courses and participated in a recently added program of psychological testing with two psychiatrists and two psychologists. Her psychological report read: *A keen, very intelligent girl with a realistic practical sense. Ample courage, determination, and a sense of humour. She has marked latent possibilities but is at present immature, inexperienced, and not sufficiently in control of herself for subversive work. With maturity, she should prove a girl of exceptional qualities.*

**Anne-Marie Walters in the early 1940s**

An instructor at the Beaulieu "finishing school" for SOE agents reported: *She was very attractive and could easily influence men, which she did not hesitate to do, even during training.... She has a very strong character, is domineering, aggressive, and self-confident.... She has been badly spoilt and is always 'agin the government'... She resents discipline or any attempt to thwart her wishes. She is irritable and impatient of the mistakes of others less quick and less intelligent than herself... She has the brains and, to some extent, the character to do valuable work. Nevertheless, it is doubtful whether she should be employed. She will probably exercise an unsettling influence upon many with whom she comes into contact.* Desperate for more agents in the field, Buckmaster overrode those concerns and moved her forward to parachute training.

After completing her SOE courses, her final report read: *She is well educated, intelligent, quick, practical, and cunning. She is active-minded, curious, and has plenty of imagination. She is easily the most prolific writer amongst the party, usually to her mother.*

Anne-Marie and twenty-two SOE men were scheduled to parachute into France on December 16, 1943. The SOE had given her fake papers and a small Czech .32 caliber gun that was to be her personal weapon in France.

She would later write that Colonel Maurice Buckmaster was at the airport, kissed her goodbye, and shook the hands of all the men. She was given a gold make-up compact, and the men received gold pens – the gifts were standard practice for departing SOE agents. It was a gift, but they were told it could be sold if they should find themselves in a tough spot needing money.

Their plane took off in a very heavy fog. Once they arrived in French airspace, the pilots could not find a fog-free area to drop them off, so they returned to England. The fog was still thick, and the plane crashed on landing, shearing off the tail in a tree as they tried to land at the airport. The plane was filled with explosives intended for the Maquis, but fortunately, none exploded.

The tail gunner was injured in the crash, and Anne-Marie sustained a cut on her head. Five other agents survived, but the rest of the crew and the other agents were killed. Six other planes had crashed while trying to land in the heavy fog that same night. That crash suddenly brought home to Anne-Marie the dangers that lay ahead.

Anne-Marie would later report that the plane had landed at an airport not normally used by the SOE, and the crewman working there had not seen any SOE women going to France. She later wrote that after the crash, as she was seen climbing out of the plane: *As ground crews ran to the burning aircraft, one shouted "What the hell is this woman doing in this mess?" We decided to say we were journalists, but it was doubtful whether anyone would believe us; our jumpsuits, arms, and scattered containers would give us away.*

Finally, on January 4, 1944, she was back on a plane and headed to France. Jumping with her was fellow SOE agent Claude Arnault, code names *Hairdresser, Neron,* or *Jean-Claude.* He had been on her earlier flight and was one of the few who also survived. Their aircraft reportedly dropped them from only 700 ft. (Under normal circumstances, 1000 ft. is considered a low altitude for a parachute jump.) The two landed in the Armagnac area in southwest France. She landed in a marshy area and he landed in water up to his waist, but both were safe with no injuries. A Maquis waiting party met them and took them to a safe house.

The SOE assigned Anne-Marie and Arnault to work in the Wheelwright Circuit, led by George Starr. The radio operator for Wheelwright was Yvonne Cormeau, code name *Annette.* (It is interesting that Anne-Marie barely acknowledges Yvonne in the 250+-page book she wrote after the war, *Moondrop to*

*Gascony*.) Anne-Marie and Yvonne would have interacted during their time in France, as Anne-Marie would have repeatedly delivered and picked up messages to be sent or received on Yvonne's radio.

At only 20 years of age, Arnault was tasked with being a saboteur and weapons/explosive instructor for the Maquis, as many locals were unfamiliar with the new British weapons. Anne-Marie noted how handsome Arnault was from their first meeting in England.

During their SOE training period, Anne-Marie took Arnault to her parents' home several times for dinner. Her parents, unaware of her involvement with the SOE, assumed he was just another of her many male friends. Anne-Marie and Arnault had a brief romantic relationship while working together in France.

Starr, code names *Hilaire and Gaston*, was often called *the Patron* was one of the more successful SOE Circuit leaders. He ran an extensive network of agents and Maquis fighters. His strong personality was well known by anyone who worked with or for him. The following comment appeared in his SOE training report, dated July 1942: *He is continually making aggressive contradictions and assertions and is the worst type of know-all, namely one who is often right and can seldom be proved wrong.*

**George Starr**

Starr's cover story in France was that he was a Belgian mining engineer, which helped explain his badly accented French. By the time Anne-Marie arrived in France, the Wheelwright's Circuit stretched from Perigord to the foothills of the Pyrenees, and Starr was desperate for a courier.

Anne-Marie's cover name in France was *Alice Davoust*. Her cover story was that she was a student from Paris recuperating from pneumonia who was visiting family friends on a local farm. The fresh air would supposedly help her recover.

She lived on the Mamoulens farm for much of her time in France. During her eight months in France, Anne-Marie traveled hundreds, if not thousands, of miles by walking or riding bicycles, buses, or trains.

She later wrote of her typical days: *When I'm not in Agen, I may be in Condom, in Auch, in Toulouse, in Tarbes or Montrjeau. One day, I am sent to Auch to collect blank and stamped travel permits, then next I go to Tarbes to take some money to a man who works there. The third, I cycle to take a message to the wireless operator or someone else. Then I'm off for three days to Tarbes and Montrejeau, where I have to wait for a reply from Arnault or someone else.*

Anne-Marie, along with either Arnault or Starr (depending on different reports), was credited with arranging for fifteen (or twenty-one, depending on different reports) Maquis fighters who had escaped a French prison to go over the Pyrenees Mountains to safety.

She accompanied the men part of the way and learned that one of them was C. Sydney Hudson, the leader of the Headmaster Circuit. They climbed into the back of a truck and were driven almost 100 miles to Tarbes. Then, she found safe houses for them until they could start the hike over the mountains.

During one sabotage mission, she was tasked with taking several suitcases of explosives through a series of German roadblocks. Although she was stopped and questioned several times, the soldiers did not search her or her bike. The Maquis then used the explosives to blow up a power station.

On March 16, 1944, Anne-Marie celebrated her 21st birthday, and her SOE team and a few others gathered for a small party. Food was in short supply, but someone managed to make a cake. Rumor had it that there were even candles on the cake – something nearly impossible to come by in France. Everyone laughed when they discovered the "candles" were pieces of detonating bomb fuses – painted pink.

After the war, the ever-stylish Anne-Marie was quoted as saying: *My family might not have recognized me (during the war) had they seen me sitting in a third-class carriage with a beret tipped low over my forehead, wearing an old raincoat, and generally looking half-witted while eating a chunk of bread and sausages.*

Arnault would prove himself to be a very capable SOE agent. Many of the Marquis were farmers or village laborers, and they may have only seen old muskets or WWI weapons when they joined the fight in WWII. After each SOE drop of new weapons and ammunition, Arnault and Anne-Marie would train the new recruits on how to use and care for the guns. Arnault also carried out several very successful sabotage missions before D-Day. After the war, he received the Distinguished Service Cross from the President of the United States.

On June 21, 1944, two weeks after D-Day, the Maquis fighters were mounting operations to harass and slow down the retreat of German forces. In one engagement, the Germans turned the tables on the Maquis. Starr had a group of about 300 fighters, half French and half Spanish camping at Castelnau sur l'Auvignon. They were surrounded and attacked by some 2000 German soldiers. Anne-Marie was credited with dashing among the Maquis, distributing hand grenades and ammunition throughout the battle.

Anne-Marie quickly gathered and destroyed SOE documents and collected hidden money before the Germans overran their location. Starr ordered the fighters to evacuate the village, and all but 19 got away. After that battle, Starr and his Maquis group joined what became known as the Armagnac Battalion. It consisted of 1,900 men of a dozen different nationalities who came together to harass and slow the movement of German soldiers.

The various Maquis groups making up the battalion were running short of ammunition. Still, the SOE ignored Starr's pleas for airdrops of ammunition. Angered, he sent a wireless message to London: *I have given orders to the men under my command to manufacture bows and arrows. As soon as this is completed, we will attack and destroy these "f...." divisions.* The message had the desired effect, and ammunition began arriving.

Anne-Marie did not hold Starr in much esteem, and he felt the same way about her. Starr never liked how Anne-Marie dressed or wore her hair, and he frequently made her change her appearance. He thought she dressed too nicely and wore her hair like a city dweller rather than a country woman. Anne-Marie thought her cover story of being a city girl in the country for her health addressed those issues, but they had ongoing disagreements about her appearance.

Starr forced Anne-Marie out of his Circuit. His July 31, 1944, report explaining his actions read: *She wore high Paris fashion,* violating his principle that couriers should be inconspicuous. *Have had to send Colette (Anne-Marie) back because she is undisciplined in spite of my efforts to train her ... Most indiscreet. Very man-mad, also disobedient ... totally unsuitable. Totally unsuitable for any commission. She should not be sent back to France to work for our organization.* He did acknowledge her courage: *She possessed personal courage and never hesitated to go on any mission.* It is uncertain if Anne-Marie knew about the report Starr sent to headquarters.

Anne-Marie's report said that Starr asked her to go on a mission to Major Champion in Algiers. She hiked out over the Pyrenees on August 1, 1944. Her later report read: *Started out on August 1, lost ourselves four times: left from the Col des Arts, west of Aspet, climbed the Pic de Gard, passed near Boutx and Mollo, and arrived well east of Canejan on August 4.*

Accompanying her were: U.S. Major Fuller, Captain La Roche, a wireless operator; and Leslie Brown, a downed RAF pilot. They were arrested and jailed when they reached Spain because they had no paperwork allowing them to enter the country. They remained in jail for four days before the British Consul arranged for their release.

Anne-Marie made her way to Madrid but had to wait another four days before receiving the necessary papers to go to Algiers. While in Algiers, she was offered a job to return to France with Col. Anstey to help improve French and British relations now that the war was ending. Anne-Marie was excited by the offer, but the SOE refused to allow her to return to France and recalled her to London, apparently based on Starr's report.

When she reached London, Anne-Marie was shocked to learn that her three suitcases shipped in from France would not be returned to her. She was told the contents had been purchased with SOE funds and belonged to the SOE. Other SOE agents had been allowed to keep their belongings.

When Anne-Marie reached London, she stayed at a hotel arranged by the SOE. Two other SOE agents, Yvonne Baseden and Odette Wilen, were there, and the three women talked about their experiences in France, some of which were not positive. Their conversation bothered a male agent, and he reported it to the SOE. His report may have had an impact on how her final report was received.

The SOE debriefed her on her time in France. She was generally complementary about Starr but felt his worry and tension worsened after D-Day as the number of operations significantly increased. Anne-Marie wrote about what she considered was the mistreatment of people captured by the Maquis, and she held Starr responsible. She wrote: *A small example: he adopted a Russian as a Garde de Corps (bodyguard). That Russian, Buresie, was an ex-Foreign Legion soldier, a dangerous and blood-thirsty character, also slightly mad; he suggested and carried out absolutely horrible tortures of captured French malice* (a political paramilitary organization who were brutal to the Maquis and anyone they suspected of resisting the German occupation).

*It was also quite wrong in my opinion, to lower oneself to the standards of the Gestapo by torturing milicients and collaborators to make them reveal the whereabouts of their colleagues...some were beaten until blood spurted all over the walls, others were horribly burnt: one man's feet were held in the fire 20 minutes, and his legs were slowly burnt off to the knees; other tortures are too horrible to mention. A good number of people were also shot. Had Hilaire (Starr) not been influenced in all this (and Buresie played a great part in suggesting, encouraging, and carrying out those tortures), I am sure he would never have started it.*

Nothing came of Anne-Marie's report until Starr returned to London on November 1, 1944, and gave a talk at the Officers' mess about his experiences in France. Two days later, Colonel Stanley Woolrych, commandant of the Beaulieu training site, wrote a letter to Air Commodore Archie Boyle, head of the SOE personnel board, about Starr: *I do not think that there is much doubt that he has done a magnificent piece of work in organizing S.W. France during the last two years and has done a very excellent job personally, for which one is glad to see that he has been rewarded. At the same time, I feel that his record has been somewhat marred by a streak of sadism which it is going to be extremely hard to ignore when one comes to assess the work of his particular mission, more especially as there already exists a protest in the report of one of his junior agents (Miss A.M. Walters) of which I attach an extract.*

*There is no doubt, both from Miss Walters' report and Lt. Col. Starr's narrative on Monday, that they tortured prisoners in a fairly big way. It might be answered, of course, that this was the work of the FFI. (Free French) which Lt. Col. Starr was powerless to prevent. He recounted to us, however, with considerable relish, the episode of a capture he made personally and for which, of course, he must accept responsibility...* He gave sworn testimony about Starr's lecture: *He said that in the case of the Gestapo man, he had been hung by one foot for several hours. He also stated that a steel knitting pin had been inserted in his penis, and heat applied to the other end.* Woolrych's testimony seemed to substantiate Anne-Marie's claim.

When the SOE refused to return her to France or any other assignment, Anne-Marie resigned in late November 1944.

Starr heard about Woolrych's letter and demanded an inquiry to clear his name. A top-secret inquiry was called on January 26, 1945, and commenced on February 5. The inquiry lasted ten days, and Anne-Marie, Yvonne Cormeau (radio operator), Lt. Col. Buckmaster, and Starr all testified. Pages 18 to 172, which included Anne-Marie's testimony, are missing from that file.

Unbeknownst to Anne-Marie, Starr had put Maurice Parisot in command of the combined Maquis group on June 21, 1944.

Anne-Marie was recalled to testify again on February 15 and said under oath: *I didn't write my report with any intention of making an accusation against Hilaire (Starr.) I did not know he was not head of the Maquis, in spite of the fact that I was his personal courier. I, therefore, considered him responsible for allowing these tortures. When I said, "he would not have started it," I was referring to Hilaire, but I really meant he would not have "allowed it to be started." In the paragraphs in which these words occur, I did mean to say that Hilaire was responsible for not trying to stop the tortures. I wish to stress that I thought he was head of the Maquis...I agree that what I said may easily be construed as an accusation against Hilaire. As one of his people "de confiance," I feel I ought to have been told that Hilaire was not head of that Maquis and about administrative changes.*

The cautionary way Anne-Marie responded in her second interrogation makes one wonder if she had been encouraged to soften her language and change the focus of her report. However, due to the missing original testimony, we may never have answers to that question.

The SOE cleared Starr and condemned Anne-Marie, writing she was "excitable and romantic-minded." On February 28, 1945, the conclusion of the "rather perfunctory court of inquiry" (in the words of M.R.D. Foot – SOE historian) was that: *There is no justification whatever for any imputation against Lt. Col. Starr of inhumanity or cruel treatment to any prisoner at any time under his control or under the control or troops or resistance forces under his immediate command or control...*

Anne-Marie's report regarding Starr was quickly swept under the rug, and her claims were shrugged off as being due to emotions commonly referred to in those days as being reserved for women.

On March 5, 1945, The BBC interviewed her. The interviewer indicated that Sir Archibald Sinclair had revealed for the first time that the women in WAAF had helped Resistance groups in France, either as Liaison officers, couriers, or radio operators. They went on to ask her about her role in France. That may have been the first time that large numbers of people heard about women working behind German lines in France.

Anne-Marie was awarded the Croix de Guerre and the Medaille de la Reconnaissance Francaise soon after the war. On July 17, 1945, The *London Gazette* announced that England had awarded her an MBE.

Anne-Marie found a job as an assistant to the American Press Attache in Toulouse. She wrote and published her book, *Moondrop to Gascony,* in 1946. In December 1946, Anne-Marie married Jean-Claude Comert. He was a childhood friend in Geneva and had also attended the International School. Comert had previously been a correspondent for *Le Temps* in Vienna and Berlin. In 1940, he and a partner founded the independent Free-French paper, *France in London.* He later joined the League of Nations as the head of the information department.

He and Anne-Marie had a son, Jean-Pierre Comert, and a daughter, whose name is unknown. The family moved to New York City in 1950, where Jean-Claude served as the head of the information desk of the French Section at the UN.

The family returned to Paris in 1955, and Anne-Marie went to work as a sub-editor at *France-Soir,* where she remained until 1965. She and her husband may have separated around this time, as there was no further mention of him when she moved to Barcelona in 1968. She worked as a literary director for a Spanish publisher, Argos. She eventually founded her own literary agency, liaising between British and French authors, publishers, and their Spanish counterparts.

Anne-Marie returned to France in 1990. She developed Alzheimer's disease and moved into a nursing home, where she died on October 3, 1998.

# Chapter 34

# Marguerite Petitjean   'RF' Section

October 24, 1920 – August 1, 1999

Code Name: Binette

Marguerite was among the few SOE women from a privileged childhood. She was raised in an affluent family and, after the war, had a fairytale marriage to an American soldier from a prominent U.S. family.

Marguerite Marie Emma Petitjean was born on October 24, 1920, in Strasbourg, France, close to the German border. Her parents were Marie Emily (Biersohn) Petitjean and Georges Petitjean. Her father was a prefect magistrate and former Secretary General of the French Wards of the Nation. Prefects are tasked with upholding the law in their area, including controlling local authorities' actions to ensure adherence to national guidelines. Wards of the Nation was a French civil status for children allocated by the State to those who have a parent who was injured or killed in war, during a terrorist incident, or while carrying out certain public services. Her father's position was somewhat comparable to that of the U.S. Secretary of Veterans Affairs, except his constituents were children, not the veterans themselves.

Marguerite's father had been blinded during a battle in WWI, which may have affected his personality. He forever lamented that he did not have a son, which Marguerite found very disheartening. She grew up hearing about the exploits of the French military, and she spent hours reading patriotic books about heroic soldiers.

She spent her early years in Strasbourg, but the family moved to Nice for her mother's health when she was in high school. After graduating high school, she became interested in drawing and took courses at the Municipal Drawing School of Nice. Her interest in art would continue throughout her life.

When Germany invaded France, Marguerite enrolled in the Social Worker School, where she studied for three years. The school sent her to work as a nurse's aide at the Pasteur Complementary Hospital in Nice. While there, she became a Gaullist, and in 1941, she met another student nurse working with the Resistance movement. The nurse was distributing leaflets and the underground newspaper *Liberation*.

**Marguerite in her uniform after joining the SOE**

Marguerite agreed to help distribute the leaflets and newspaper. The French police arrested her twice, and she spent two brief stints in a local jail. Most French police departments worked closely with Nazi officials. Fortunately, her influential father was able to convince the police to release her after short periods of incarceration. She later witnessed a Nazi soldier shoot a little girl. Such cruelty inspired Marguerite to decide to do whatever she could to fight the Nazis.

In April 1942, Marguerite moved to Casablanca, Morocco, where she worked as a social worker within the French Air Force at an industrial art workshop for immigrants who fled from southern France. She met Colonel Vincent, the President of the Association of Alsatians of Lorraine. Through the Colonel, she again began taking messages to and from various Resistance groups and passed on information she gathered about German movements.

She was living with Commander Pelabon (details unknown) by August 1942 when the Germans learned that he was helping the Resistance effort. He had to flee Morocco and go to Gibraltar, which offered some safety as a British territory. From Gibraltar, he traveled to Algiers. Marguerite was questioned about his activities several times by government security forces and was beaten, resulting in head trauma, but she was not put in jail.

After the Allies landed in North Africa in November 1942, the Nazis used that as their excuse for their army to occupy southern France with large numbers of soldiers. Before that date, the German army had generally remained north of the demarcation line in France, and the southern area had continued to have considerable freedom from German oppression. That changed dramatically when the German army moved south, ending the charade that the Vichy government was in charge of the area.

Marguerite left Casablanca and traveled to Algiers, where she rejoined Pelabon. He was now head of the French Central Bureau of Intelligence and Action group (BCRA) for the American Forces Network (AFN). AFN was a government television and radio broadcast service for military personnel stationed overseas. The purpose of the network was not only to inform and boost the morale of soldiers but also to disseminate information to local people and to hopefully demoralize enemy soldiers.

Marguerite left Algiers by plane on September 27, 1943, for London. Shortly after arriving, she enlisted in the Forces Francaise Combattantes (FFCC) of the Central Bureau of Intelligence and Action of the Free French Movement (BCRA) on October 8, 1943. She was assigned to take the SOE training and return to France to work directly for the BCRA.

The SOE cooperated with de Gaulle's Free French government, trained some of its intelligence agents, and sent them to France to work in the SOE Circuits. But the SOE knew of those agents' split loyalties.

While in training, instructor reports stated that Marguerite was: *Intelligent, imaginative, hardworking, having authority, determined, having a sense of humor.* After completing the SOE courses, Marguerite, then 23, parachuted into France on February 29, 1944. With her were Yvon Morandat, Rene Obadia and Eugenie Dechelette. They were all members of the BCRA. Their parachutes drifted far afield, and it took the SOE reception group several hours to find the four of them. She was the first woman from BCRA to be dropped into France.

They landed southwest of Grenoble. Her assignment was outside the usual SOE Circuits. The SOE gave her the code name *Binette*, and she was to work as a courier/radio operator for Alexandre Parodi, a prominent figure in General de Gaulle's Free French network in Paris. He was the head of the Free French press committee and soon set up the finance committee to support the Resistance groups pledged to General de Gaulle.

Marguerite may have participated in some Resistance operations blowing up bridges and damaging power stations. After her death, there were newspaper reports that she suffered some injuries on those missions. She may have suffered a broken spine, as a spinal injury was to cause her serious pain during and after the war.

There are some vague reports that the Germans may have captured her, but she managed to escape when the soldiers fell asleep. There are no known official reports or documentation of the above missions other than newspaper articles quoting her family members after Marguerite's death. The family also said that the Gestapo put a 500,000 Franc bounty on her capture. All of the above may be correct, but the author has not been able to verify this information.

**Marguerite Petitjean with her goddaughter, Elizabeth Antébi, in Paris   Photo courtesy of the. Elizabeth Antébi collection.**

Marguerite returned to England in August 1944 by hiking over the Pyrenees Mountains into Spain and then on to England. She attained the rank of captain and was awarded the Legion d'Honneur by France. Marguarite was a five-time recipient of the Croix de Guerre, the French award for bravery. Marguerite sent all the awards to her father - perhaps to address his frequent comment of wishing he had a son. She was discharged from service in May 1946.

---

*New York Times    June 23, 1946,  PAGE NUMBER  37*

*LIEUT. H.H. BASSETT TO MARRY IN PARIS*

*AAF Officer Is Fiancé of Mlle. Marguerite Petitjean, Who Aided Resistance Groups*

*Announcement has been made here of the engagement and approaching marriage of Mlle. Marguerite Marie Petitjean, daughter of M. and Mme. Georges Alfred Petitjean of Strasbourg, France, to First Lieut. Harry Hood Bassett, AAF, son of Mrs. Edward F. Swenson of Palm Seach, Fla., and the late Harry H. Bassett.*

---

Marguerite married Harry Hood Basset at the Cathedral de Notre Dame in Paris on June 23, 1946. He was an American military officer whom she may have met when she was in Casablanca, Morocco, as they were both there at the same time. Harry was a lieutenant in the U.S. Army Air Force, and he came from a prominent and wealthy family in Palm Beach, Florida.

Before his death, Bassett's father, Harry H. Bassett, had been the President of Buick Company and a Vice President of General Motors. Bassett, an alumnus of Yale University, had been a Vice President and director of the First National Bank of Palm Beach, Florida, before enlisting in the army. The New York Times published their engagement in its Society Pages.

**Harry Bassett, June 28, 1946**

After their marriage, they moved to Palm Beach and then to Miami, where Harry soon became President of the First National Bank of Miami. Marguerite quickly moved into the city's high society. As a gift to his bride, Harry arranged for her to receive a "platinum vertebrae" to replace the damaged vertebrae that her doctor thought could paralyze her without the operation.

In 1948, they welcomed their first son, George Rodney Bassett. Harry continued establishing his excellent reputation in banking and community affairs, and Margarite moved well in his social circle. In 1950, they had two more sons, twins Harry Hood Bassett, Jr., and Patrick Glenn Bassett.

Marguerite belonged to various civic and social organizations and attended many public events with her husband and on her own. Quotes about her from the Bassett Family Foundation: *She was also passionate about the issue of desegregation. She invited black performers to her home at a time when it wasn't acceptable.*

After nine years of marriage, the couple divorced in 1955. Marguerite never remarried and devoted her life to raising their three sons. She kept a house in France, and she and her sons moved between that home and one in Miami. In 1959, Allen Dulles, then director of the CIA, invited her to a private reception that honored World War II heroes.

**Marguerite in later life, photo courtesy of Justin Davis collection**

Marguerite died in Palm Beach on August 1, 1999. Her daughter-in-law was quoted in her obituary as saying: *She was an endearing and considerate woman, who was at the same time very severe. You really saw the soldier in her.* Her goddaughter, Elizabeth Antebi, said: *I, as a goddaughter, saw more of a mother substitute in her and a very feminine, even sexy woman. In Grasse (France), where she had her house and where I often went, she had decorated her room with bear skin on the floor and swan feathers on the bed. She was magnetic, with big dark eyes and the mouth of a Hollywood star.*

Further quotes from the Bassett Family Foundation: *Yellowed newspaper clippings show that Marguerite Bassett cut a striking figure in Miami during the 1950s. Stunning was Mrs. Harry Hood Bassett, co-chairman of the grand ball, wearing a white silk brocaded sheath with a cascade of white tulle.* Reported one Miami Herald column that spotlighted her social standing: *It's just incredible how she went from her life as a war hero to become part of the social world.* Melissa Bassett said: *She was always there for the good times and bad times throughout our lives.* Her son George recalled: *She was always a supporter, and there was a complete sense of trust between her and the three of us.*

# Chapter 35

# Yvonne Baseden

January 22, 1922 -  October 28, 2017

Code Name:  Bursar, Odette    Alias: Marie Bernier

Yvonne's very existence began with an interesting adventure. Her father, Englishman Clifford Baseden, was a pilot in the British Royal Corps in WWI. His plane crash-landed close to the home of Baron de Vibraye, the Chateau de Frescines, northwest of Blois, France. The woman who would become Yvonne's mother was the volunteer ambulance driver sent to collect him from the plane wreck. The Baron invited him to have meals with the family, where he fell in love with the family's daughter, Antoinette Hurault de Vibraye. They married on July 9, 1920, in Paris, and 18 months later, they welcomed their daughter, Yvonne Jeanne Therese de Vibraye Baseden.

After leaving the military, Yvonne's father, an electrical engineer, had jobs all over Europe. She attended schools in England, France, Poland, Italy, and Spain. Between her mother's and father's heritages and her schooling in France and England, she became fluent in both French and English, as well as a smattering of other languages. In 1937, the family settled in London on a full-time basis.

Yvonne was not a good student and left her formal schooling when she was 16. In 1939, she took a job as a bilingual shorthand typist at the British Powerboat Company. Wanting to do her part when WWII began, she tried to join the Free French, but the group rejected her because she had an English father. De Gaulle's restrictive personnel policies kept many people who felt patriotic about France from working in the Free French movement.

Yvonne joined the WAAF on September 4, 1940, when she was 18 years old, as a general duties clerk. Within a year, she was commissioned and later promoted to Section Officer. She soon worked for the Royal Air Force Intelligence branch, where she helped with the interrogation of captured German airmen and submarine crew members.

Yvonne met SOE agent Pearl Witherington, who recommended her to the SOE. Her French language skills and knowledge of French customs were essential assets to the SOE, and she joined that group on May 24, 1943. Yvonne joined FANY and went through the difficult SOE training program, including radio operations, which would be her specialty once she arrived in France. The last phase of training was practicing 4-5 parachute jumps in preparation for "dropping" into France.

The SOE gave her the code name *Odette*, and her cover story was that she would be a shorthand typist and secretary named *Mademoiselle Yvonne Bernier*. Yvonne parachuted into France on the night of March 18/19, 1944, with her Circuit leader, Capt. Marie Joseph Gonzague de Saint-Genies, code name *Lucien*. He was the son of Baron Henri de Saint-Genies.

They dropped close to Mont-de-Marsan in southwestern France. They made their way separately by train to Jura in eastern France using their forged identity papers. Yvonne had her radio equipment with her in a suitcase. If discovered with a radio, it would mean immediate arrest and possible execution. It took four days to reach her destination, days she said were agonizing because the train car was filled with German soldiers.

Speaking of the trip in 2000, Yvonne said: *There was always the possibility that one would give oneself away. There were identity checks on the train, but I had my papers in order. It was difficult to relax or even fall asleep. It seemed to be a very long journey.*

**Yvonne in her WAAF uniform**

Yvonne worked with De Saint-Genies to establish the new Scholar Circuit. They discovered that the leader of the nearby Director Circuit had been arrested, and they were directed to take over the coordination of his Resistance groups and recruit new fighters. As time allowed away from her radio duties, Yvonne helped her team identify and then manage parachute drop zones to receive and distribute supplies.

As with all radio operators, she moved her transmission locations every two to three days, living in attics, basements, and other locations. She had three radios, and two of them were always hidden in case one was discovered.

After D-Day, Yvonne was deeply involved in the first daytime airdrop of weapons and supplies on June 25, 1944, code-named "Cadillac." Previously, all drops were made at night to avoid detection by the Germans. The portion of the operation in Yvonne's area was called "Zebra." She set up her radio and receiver next to the drop zone, giving the all-clear message for another drop as soon as the previous plane dropped its 400 pound containers of supplies. The parachutes on the containers were red, white, and blue, announcing to anyone viewing them that the Allies were coming.

The massive airdrop was made by 144 Boeing B-17 Flying Fortress bombers, each loaded with 400-pound parachute-equipped supply containers. About 200 Royal Air Force Spitfire fighters escorted the bombers. The bombers dropped from an altitude of only 350 ft above the marked drop zones, and the delivery accuracy was notably high.

The airdrops included personnel as well as supplies. The 3rd Bombardment Wing flew four such 'carpetbagger' missions. There was a total of 792 sorties, of which 465 were successful. They delivered 115 agents, 5,439 weapons containers, 2,707 other packages, several thousand leaflets, and 17 hampers of live messenger pigeons behind the German lines.

She later said of the airdrop and the immediate aftermath: It was extraordinary; when the planes came over, we could hear the roar of the engines. It was the middle of the morning in beautiful sunlight. We had a lot of lorries and 800 people on the ground to help move the material as quickly as possible. When we got back to headquarters, we sat down to lunch. Within half an hour, the chap at the window said, The Bosch! The Germans! We dispersed as quickly as we could to various hiding places. We heard all these cars pulling up. I had a chap hiding with me, but neither of us could talk or communicate with each other.

The Germans began an intensive search of the building, eventually finding the entire group. They captured Yvonne after killing several members of the Resistance group, including her 27-year-old Circuit leader, De Saint-Genies. According to Yvonne: *We were all found, one by one. I was one of the first. We were thrown on the ground, then taken overnight by lorry to Dijon and put into individual cells. I was interrogated, beaten up, and then dragged up the stairs past an office full of people in uniforms typing reports. I had a sense of being someone else. The only thing that kept us going was the thought that the job we'd done the day before had been a success.* The guards seemed to enjoy stomping on Yvonne's bare toes and feet, leaving them a bloody mess so she could not wear shoes for a long time.

The Germans interrogated her, but she stuck to her cover story of just being a secretary who got caught in the building. They kept her in solitary confinement with little to no food in between interrogation sessions but failed to get any useful information from her. The Germans suspected that she was a foreign agent, so she was deported to Germany as a French political prisoner. Fortunately, they never suspected she was the Circuit radio operator, or she might have been treated even worse or executed.

Yvonne was sent to the infamous Ravensbrück Prison for Women, where several other female SOE agents were held. She was given a uniform with a red triangle on the sleeve, indicating she was a political prisoner. She later said of seeing Ravensbrück for the first time: *We didn't know what was going to happen. Ravensbrück was the first time we had seen what a concentration camp really was. It was a shock. To my amazement and horror, when I was directed through one of the huts, I found friends from SOE.* For a brief time, Yvonne shared a hut for a brief time with fellow SOE agent, Odette Sansom.

Upon arrival at the concentration camp, prisoners were shown the crematorium and told that was the only way out of Ravensbrück. Yvonne and the other prisoners were subjected to the humiliating routine of frequent strip searches, random punishments, and hours of standing at attention during endless roll calls. She endured eight months of captivity, including torture. All prisoners were expected to work, and Yvonne was assigned to work as a farmhand. Weakened by the bitter winter cold with an almost starvation diet and exposure to other prisoners with infectious diseases, Yvonne contracted tuberculosis in February 1945.

She later said that the bout with TB probably saved her life. An English nurse, Mary Lindell, working in the hospital at Ravensbrück, was able to get Yvonne transferred to the hospital twice, where she could treat and help safeguard her. Yvonne spent her 23rd birthday in the hospital. Unable to escape from Ravensbrück. Mary put her nursing skills to work for both the prisoners and the Germans at the prison.

SS Officer, Dr. Percival Trieste was in charge of the prison hospital. His mother was English, and he did all he could to allow Mary to treat the British and American women prisoners. Mary kept a list of the women, and her list would later be very helpful in determining what had happened to some of the women.

Through the efforts of Swedish diplomat Count Rolke Bernadotte and the French Red Cross, an agreement was negotiated with the German government to allow what became known as the "white buses" to go into German prisons and transport women prisoners, primarily Swedish women, to safety in Sweden.

The commandant at Ravensbrück initially said that there were no British or American prisoners interred in the camp. Other prisoners credited Mary with showing her list to the German commandant, pressuring him to make the deal with the Red Cross. Commandant Fritz Suhren eventually made the deal and released 47 women to the Swedish Red Cross. The white buses entered the prison to pick up the women, and they were driven to freedom on April 25, 1945. Yvonne and nurse Mary Lindell were very fortunate to be in the group leaving the camp.

The women first went to Denmark and then on to Malmo, Sweden. Once in Malmo, the group had to be cleaned and deloused, as they were all filthy and infected with numerous bugs. Yvonne spent her first night of freedom sleeping on a mattress on the floor of the Malmo Museum of Prehistory, looking up at dinosaurs.

After arriving in England, it took Yvonne nine months at King Edward VII's Sanatorium in Midhurst to recover from TB and injuries suffered in the prison. The head of the women's section of the "F" desk at SOE, Vera Atkins, traveled to the sanatorium to interview her about what other SOE agents she had seen or heard of during her time in German custody. Vera spent years after the war tracking down each missing SOE agent and determining what had become of them. The interviews she conducted with SOE agents, German soldiers and officers, and local civilians were used as evidence during the war crime trials.

After her recovery, Yvonne was much sought after by the media, who wanted to interview her about her wartime experiences. She initially agreed to several interviews with radio and print reporters. Yvonne soon grew tired of the repetitive questions and began refusing to do interviews. She wrote a book about her wartime experiences but could not get it published. The Sunday Express Newspaper did print three excerpts from the book, but that was the end of her writing career.

Between 1946 and 1948, many guards and SS officers who had worked at Ravensbrück were tried for war crimes. Sixteen of them were found guilty of crimes against humanity and sentenced to death. The doctor who had shown some mercy to the British and American patients, SS officer Percy Treiste, was charged with war crimes. Yvonne and nurse Mary Lindell, and several other women who were treated at the hospital wrote letters in his defense. Mary and Yvonne even testified on his behalf at the trial, but the court sentenced him to death. He committed suicide in prison on April 8, 1947, almost two years from the time Yvonne, Mary, and the other 45 women were released from Ravensbrück.

Yvonne worked at WAAF and interpreted aerial photographs before being released from government employment in 1948. She had a job with the government longer than most of the SOE women, as most had been let go immediately after they returned from France. It was a common practice after the war to lay off female employees to make room for the men returning from the war to take over the job.

Little concern was given to what happened to the women who suddenly had no income. The government and societal culture assumed that the women would marry and be supported by a husband. But so many English men had been killed or seriously disabled in the war that marriage for many women never materialized.

In 1949, Yvonne married Desmond Bailey, and they moved to Rhodesia (modern Zimbabwe), where her husband worked for the Colonial Service as the French commercial attaché. They had one son, who would be Yvonne's only child. She spent the next twenty years working with her husband. In the mid-1950s, she briefly returned to England to appear as the first regular guest on the UK version of This is Your Life, hosted by the famed Irish radio and TV personality Eamonn Andrews.

Yvonne on England's

*This is Your Life* TV program

After Bailey's death, she married Anthony Burney in 1966 and relocated to Portugal. Her second husband died, and she returned home to London in 1999, where she lived quietly, doing only occasional interviews when someone remembered her work during WWII. She appeared in two documentaries, *Secret Agent* for the BBC in 2000 and a French TV program, *Robert et les Ombres*, in 2005.

England awarded her an MBE in 1946. France recognized her service in the same year with the Croix de Guerre. In 1996, she was further awarded the Chevalier of the Légion d'Honneur, the highest French order of merit, both military and civil.

Yvonne lived to be 95 years old, a very advanced age considering the conditions she endured during the war. She died on October 28, 2017.

**Yvonne in her later years**

# Chapter 36

# Maureen Patricia O'Sullivan

January 3, 1918 – March 5, 1994

Code Names: Simonet, Josette, Marie-Claire, Stenographer, and Stocking.

Alias: Micheline Marcelle Simonet

Maureen Patricia O'Sullivan, a good-looking, 26-year-old Irish redhead with a temper to match, found herself parachuting into France behind German lines. Known to everyone as 'Paddy' or 'The Irish Rebel,' she would go on to be awarded an MBE from England and the Croix de Guerre from France.

Maureen was born in Dublin, Ireland, on January 3, 1918, to Irishman John Aloysius O'Sullivan and either her German mother, Johanna Repen, **or** Englishwoman Adelaide Redmond (the records differ as to which woman was her mother). Her mother died of Spanish Flu when she was 15 months old, and her father, a journalist, raised her alone. Coming from a Catholic family, she spent much of her first years at the St. Louis Convent school in Dublin.

When she was seven, her father sent her to live with her Aunt Alice in Bruges, Belgium. Her aunt enrolled her at the Convent des Soeurs Paulines in Courtrai and the Ursuline Convent in Bruges, and then, at 15, she went to the Rathmines Commercial College back in Dublin. She finally attended the Mademoiselle de France 'finishing school' in Paris. Her diverse education, which included time in Ireland, Belgium, and France, made her fluent in English, Dutch, Flemish, and French, with a solid grasp of German. Her language skills would be very valuable in her SOE work during WWII.

In January 1939, Paddy enrolled in a two-year nursing program at Highgate Hospital in London. She was working there when WWII broke out. She joined the WAAF in July 1941 and was an acting corporal by May 1943, where she became friendly with Sonya Butt. The SOE soon recruited both young women. Told to join FANY, they acknowledged her previous WAAF service, and she was commissioned as a Second Lieutenant.

Paddy's first SOE training course was at Winterfold in Surrey, and her report stated: *She was pleasant, purposeful, independent, and able to manage people but had little mechanical or practical sense.* She had other training modules at Inverie House in Scotland and Beaulieu, England. The report from her paramilitary program in Scotland in October 1943 was less favorable: *She is stubborn and undisciplined, with an ungovernable temper and no team spirit.*

**Paddy around the time she joined SOE**

Rumors about an imminent operation about to happen (which would become known as D-Day) were rampant, and the SOE needed more radio operators to improve communication between headquarters and their Circuits in France. As a result, the SOE shortened Paddy's training, and they passed her on to the wireless course in Thame Park. They had to delay her final course because she developed pneumonia, which caused lasting damage to her lungs and resulted in chronic lung issues for the rest of her life. The SOE would have disqualified her for fieldwork in less desperate days, but they needed radio operators and passed her on.

Paddy's shortened training time irritated Major Percy "Teddy" Mayer, who would be her Fireman Circuit leader in France. He drafted a report to SOE: *Miss O'Sullivan spent six weeks in Scotland on demolition and weapon training. I suggest that this time could have been more profitably spent at a security and radio school or simply learning to ride a cycle. The requirements for a radio operator are not that she should be able to shoot straight or even shoot at all but that she should know how to use a W/T set properly. Her means of defense should be to know how to baffle the Gestapo rather than to know how to shoot them.*

After making it through her final program on parachute jumping, she flew out of Tempsford airfield and made her jump into France. She landed near Angouleme on the night of March 22/23, 1944. She later said in an interview with the *London News Chronicle*: *After I jumped, it was lovely sailing through the sky on my own.*

She carried two radios with her and, unfortunately, she landed badly and suffered a concussion. Fortunately, she also had two million francs strapped around her waist, which she said prevented her from even more serious injury. She later said that she regained consciousness when two cows licked her face.

Paddy got off to a bad start in France. The Circuit did not have a courier, so she was told she had to fill the role of radio operator and courier Her Fireman commander, Mayer, was furious that the SOE sent him a woman to be his radio operator. They eventually worked through his reluctance to work with her. Paddy's lack of mechanical ability was so serious that she couldn't even remember how to change a fuse in her radio, and then Mayer discovered that she didn't know how to ride a bicycle.

**Major Percy Mayer**

The SOE had assumed she could ride a bicycle, as she was the first agent missing that skill, so they had not provided training for it. Most Circuit officers rode bikes, walked, or took a train since cars were in short supply in France. Fellow SOE officers recounted that she practiced riding the bike near a German outpost, and the soldiers often made fun of her poor skill. She reported that she retorted by telling them they were not gentlemen, or they would help her. Her playful banter with the local German soldiers allowed her to move freely about the area.

Fortunately, Paddy soon learned to ride the bike and she could travel independently. She frequently peddled over 35 miles daily until her Circuit finally received its own dedicated courier. Her mechanical skills never improved, so she constantly asked for help with even the simplest tasks related to operating her radio.

For everyone's safety, Paddy was deliberately separated from the rest of the Circuit during the daytime. Once their Circuit courier arrived and relieved Paddy of that responsibility. Paddy eventually had seven radios hidden in various houses and sheds so she could get to one quickly when necessary.

Some Circuit members were afraid that Paddy's heavy smoking would make the Germans suspicious. Most French women did not smoke, and even if they did, few locals could afford expensive cigarettes during the war.

Paddy quickly developed into a competent operator, sending and receiving over 330 messages to/from London in her short time in the field. Her Circuit leader, Mayer, reported on her effectiveness: *Due to her patience…hard work, and willingness to learn, she improved rapidly and, after a couple of months, became a first-class W/T operator.*

She frequently sent and received messages for the nearby Warder Circuit since they had no operator of their own. Warder Circuit was led by Edmund Mayer, the brother of Paddy's leader, Percy Mayer. Multiple members of many families frequently worked in the SOE and Resistance networks.

Being resourceful, Paddy made up her own cover story. She took the alias of *Micheline Marcelle Simonet*, a woman from Belgium searching for her doctor husband. At other times, she said it was her missing lover - or her father - the stories would change depending on who she was talking to or how playful she felt.

She often stayed in farmhouses without sanitation or running water. The air in the houses was sometimes filled with hay dust, which must have been challenging for her already compromised lungs. But she didn't complain because she realized that her presence was also endangering the lives of the farm owners, who were putting her up for very little rent.

The life expectancy of radio operators working in France at that time was only six weeks. Many of her fellow SOE radio operators had already been captured and tortured, and the Germans later executed several of the women once they realized Germany was losing the war.

One encounter that Paddy related after the war was a day she was stopped at a roadblock. She had a radio strapped to her bicycle in a rucksack, and she knew that if the Germans found it, she would be arrested. Just as a guard was about to search the bag, another soldier commented that she looked like a German Fraulein. She immediately replied in German that her mother was German, but she had been killed during a bombing. The soldiers sympathized with her. She began to flirt with the officer and actually made a date with him the following day. They waved her through the roadblock without searching her bag, and she continued with her mission. She did not keep the date with the officer.

On October 4, 1944, the SOE recalled her to London, ending her service in France. Soon after, she became the subject of a series of articles in the *Daily Mail* newspaper. Paddy suddenly became known to the general public, making her one of the first SOE women to get national recognition - much to the dismay of the SOE. They were so upset by her notoriety that they posted her to Calcutta, India in June 1945 as a liaison officer for the French Force #136 deployed there. She ended her service to the SOE at the war's end.

Paddy married Walter Alvey after her release from SOE. The couple moved to Burma (Myanmar), but after the birth of their second son, they returned to England to raise the boys, John and Robin. The marriage ended in divorce. After the boys were out of school, Paddy moved to rural County Wicklow, Ireland, in the early 1970s.

Paddy and her husband, Walter Alvey . It may be their wedding photo, but the circumstances have not been verified.

Below: Paddy with her husband, Walter, on the left. Unknown man on the right. Photo courtesy Special Forces Roll of Honor

England awarded her the MBE on September 4, 1945. She also received the Croix de Guerre from France.

The "troubles" in Northern Ireland were in full fury, and the move didn't end well. She came home one day to find her house had been raided, and whoever broke in shot and killed her two pet dogs. Among the stolen items were some of her war memorabilia. The police believed the IRA was behind the robbery, but nothing was ever proven or recovered. She returned to England and never lived in Ireland again. One of her sons said she felt like a stranger in her home country after the war.

Little more is known about her later life. She moved often, and even her sons sometimes did not know where she was. Paddy died on March 5, 1994, in Ilkley, West Yorkshire, England. She was cremated, so there is no gravesite.

In 2002, long after her death, her son said: *She was a nomadic person, and she never seemed to settle down anywhere.*

# Chapter 37

# Alix d'Unienville

May 8, 1918 – November 10, 2015

Code Name: Myrtil and Marie

Alix Marnier d'Unienville was born to Helene Marrier De Lagatinerie Garcia Mansilla and Jules-Noel Marrier d'Unienville in Vacoas-Phoenix on the island of Mauritus. Residents of Mauritius hold dual French and British citizenship. Mauritius is one of the most densely populated countries in the world. Her family was wealthy and were aristocrats on the island. Her father, Jules-Noel, was a writer, and Alix would follow in his footsteps after the war.

The family moved to France when Alix was six and lived in a large chateau in the village of Vannes in Brittany. One sister, Marie-Therese d'Unienville, became a nun, and another sister, Solange d'Unienville, married a man who became an officer in the French Navy. The family was very patriotic and believed they should serve their country. Her brother, Fernand de la Tille Lolainville, joined the Free French movement when the Germans invaded France in May 1940. With their dual citizenship, the family left France and moved to England in 1940.

Alix was working on creating propaganda leaflets at the Free French headquarters at Carlton Gardens in London before being recruited to join the Free French "RF" section of the SOE. Her bi-lingual abilities and knowledge of the country would make it easy for her to blend in as an agent back in France. Following the creation of "F" Section in the summer of 1940, it became apparent that French anti-German sentiment effectively fell into two camps - those who supported de Gaulle and those who did not. To keep these camps apart, the "RF" Section (pro-Gaullists) was established in early 1941.

Like most SOE women, she joined the WAAF, and she was commissioned with the rank of Flight Lieutenant. Alix began her SOE training courses in June 1943 at the Beaulieu estate in Hampshire, England. The SOE trained their agents on various parts of the estate. The woods were excellent for covert training.

Houses on the estate were earmarked for different uses. There was a German house, a French house, and other designated setups. In these houses, agents became familiar with the customs, habits, and layouts of foreign homes so that they would immediately assimilate into any foreign home.

The SOE brought in experts from around the world to pass on expertise in specific areas. Hong Kong police experts developed a particular type of commando knife, and even King George VI's gamekeeper provided instruction on living off the land. One instructor wrote about Alix that: *she is discreet and inconspicuous – the last person to be suspected.* The final course was learning to parachute.

After the war, when asked about all the undercover skills she was taught at SOE, Alix said: *I often thought that if afterward, I had put these skills to work, my life would have been more amusing and profitable.* There were two Belgian women in her training class who intimidated her. She said they already had commando experience, and their talking about their "kills" frightened her.

The agents knew that they would be going to war behind enemy lines – and that many of them might not return. Their hard work and the awareness of the dangers ahead may have increased their desire for a bit of fun. Alix wrote later that: *We frequented the bars. We sowed seeds of scandal in the dining rooms of solemn London hotels. Clients were indignant – who had the right to frolic in war?*

After agents successfully completed their training modules, the Beaulieu Aerodrome was often used to fly them to France. A few agents departed by water on MTBs (Motor Torpedo Boats) from

**SOE training location in Beaulieu, New Forest, Hampshire, England**

the Beaulieu River. Alix dreaded the anticipation of jumping out of a plane but said that once she did, she found the experience calm and peaceful.

The SOE assigned Alix the code name *Myrtil* to be used with London and *Marie-France* to the Resistance Circuit fighters in France. She was to use the alias *Aline Bavelan* for her cover story of living in Paris as the wife of a prisoner of war. She dropped into the Loir-et-Cher area by parachute on March 31, 1944. She carried two million francs and another 40 million francs in a suitcase dangling below her legs. She gave the money to the Gaullist delegate-general to distribute to Resistance fighters.

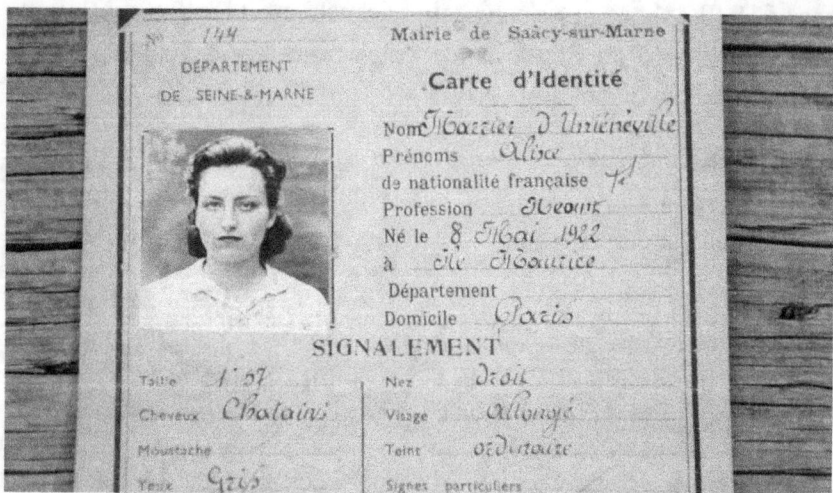

After landing, she moved on to Paris, just over 100 miles away, and settled into a grocer's shop on the Place de Passy. She was a courier for the Oronte Circuit, taking messages between various groups, including the Free French, and passing on orders from London. The threat of being caught was with her every day, and she had to be suspicious of any stranger.

**Alix d'Unienville ID card, courtesy of the Justin Davis Collection.**

Alix had been in France just over two months when Allied troops landed in Normandy on D-Day, June 6. Her delight was short-lived as she and fellow agent Pierre-Henri Teitgen, code name *Tristan*, were arrested by the Gestapo when meeting in Paris. They took Alix to Gestapo headquarters in Paris on Avenue Foch for interrogation. The SOE agents and other suspected spies were routinely tortured while undergoing interrogation in that location.

The Gestapo found her cyanide pill, which should have immediately confirmed her identity as a spy, but they didn't seem to realize what the pill was. They moved her to Fresnes prison and put her in solitary confinement. In hopes of being transferred to Saint-Anne Hospital, she pretended to be mentally ill. The Gestapo did not believe her and instead moved her to La Pitie mental prison, which had been a long-time mental hospital for women, with a terrible record of atrocities toward female patients.

**La Pitie Mental Hospital**

Alix immediately began to eat and talk again and was moved from La Pitie to Saint-Anne, but for only a brief time before the Germans sent her to Romainville prison camp. The conditions at the prison were squalid, and prisoners survived on starvation rations. As the war was turning against the Germans, they sent many of their political or high-value prisoners from France into Germany. Alix was on the last convoy to leave Romainville for Germany on August 15, 1944, possibly bound for Ravensbrück. The Germans sent many SOE women to Ravensbrück.

The convoy of prisoners had to be removed from the train because the Allies had destroyed the railroad bridge over the Marne River. When they told the prisoners to walk across the river on the roadway, Alix managed to escape. She found her way to the village of Mery-sur-Marne where a family hid her. She left the village after the guards moved on with the other prisoners and she found refuge with a woman in the countryside. She stayed there until the American army liberated the area, allowing her to return to Paris.

**Alix in a victory parade.**

Britain awarded Alix an MBE, and she received the Legion d'Honneur and the Croix de Guerre from France.

After the war ended in Europe, Alix worked for the United States as a war correspondent in Southeast Asia until the war with Japan ended. She then became one of the first female air hostesses with Air France. Her life path would continue as a writer, and she put her wide-ranging history to good use as she wrote at least twelve fiction and non-fiction books. Alix was the first woman to receive the prestigious "Albert Londres Prize" in 1950. The Albert Londres Prize is the highest French journalism award, created in 1932 in honor of journalist Albert Londres. It is the French equivalent of the U.S. Pulitzer Prize.

**Alix, photo courtesy of the Justin Davis collection**

Alix continued writing books from 1944 until 2015, with the last published after her death. Little else is known about Alix's life after 1950. Her obituary said almost nothing about her life after the war. She apparently never married or had children. She died in Paris on November 10, 2015, at 97 years of age.

**Alix in her later years**

# Chapter 38

# Violette Szabo

June 26, 1921 – c. February 5, 1945

Code name: Louise   Alias: Corinne Reine Leroy, Vicky Taylor

Violette Szabo early life was filled with difficulty, but she went on to serve Britain and the Allies with amazing courage. Her inhumane treatment and execution at the hands of the Gestapo go down as one of the more dishonorable episodes at the end of the madness of Hitler's war.

Violette Reine Elizabeth Bushell was born on June 26, 1921, in Paris, France, to a French mother, Reine Blanche Leroy, and an English father, Charles George Bushell, a lorry driver. She had four brothers and several male cousins, so she learned how to survive in their rough-and-tumble world at an early age. During the Great Depression of the early 1930s, Violette and one brother lived with their maternal aunt in Picardy, France. She became fluent in French, which was crucial for her work during WWII.

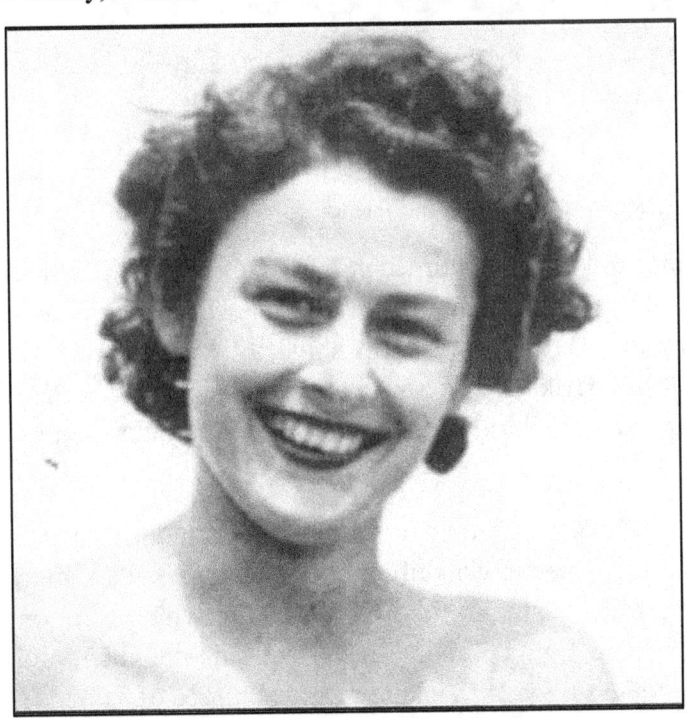

As the economy improved, the family reunited in London when she was twelve. Violette was a physically active girl who did long-distance bicycling, ice skating, and gymnastics. She was considered a tomboy, and her father taught her to shoot. She was known for being very accurate with a gun.

Violette was not known for her academics. At fourteen, she left school to go to work, which may have been because of economic hardship at home. She began working at a ladies' undergarment shop and later at Woolworths. Violette moved to the more up-scale Le Bon Marche department store in Brixton for her last retail job.

**Violette and her famous smile**

After WWII broke out in Europe, all English men and women were encouraged to help support the war effort. When she was nineteen, Violette signed up for the Auxiliary Territorial Service (ATS) or the

Women's Land Army in 1940. She was assigned to work on a farm picking strawberries in Fareham, Hampshire, a job that she found very boring. After the strawberry season ended, she transferred to work in an armaments factory in Acton. Both jobs were considered "women's work," as all able-bodied men were expected to go into the military or other government work.

Violette was enjoying the festivities of Bastille Day in London that same year when she met Etienne Szabo. He was a dashing and already decorated non-commissioned officer in the French Foreign Legion. Violette was only 19, and he was 31 years old. They had a whirlwind romance of only 42 days before marrying on August 21, 1940.

**Wedding photo of Violette and Etienne, with family and friends**

Violette and Etienne had a short one-week honeymoon, and then he returned to Africa to fight in the failed Free French attack on Dakar, Senegal. He later fought in military actions in South Africa, Eritrea, and Syria. He returned to England for a short leave in late 1941. After that trip home, Etienne returned to Africa to fight at Bir Hkeim in North Africa against the Afrika Korps 15th Panzer Division on June 10, 1942. The Afrika Korps was Germany's expeditionary force in Africa during the North African campaign of World War II.

Violette became pregnant during Etienne's last visit home, and she gave birth to their daughter, Tania Damaris Desiree Szabo, on June 8, 1942. Unfortunately, Etienne was killed on October 24, 1942, by a chest wound on the second day of the Second Battle of El Alamein, Egypt. That battle, which went on until November 11, basically ended the German threat to Egypt. Etienne never saw his daughter, and Violette was left a widow with a young child when she was only 21. Violette received notice of Etienne's death while working at the South Morden aircraft factory.

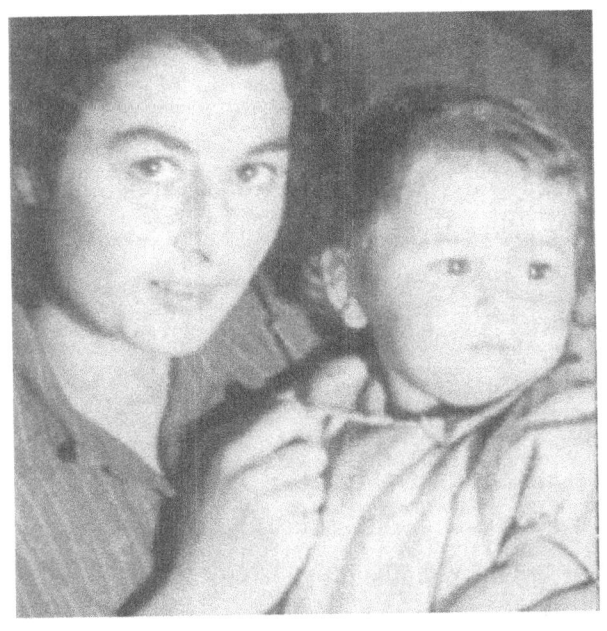

The details about when she volunteered to work for the SOE French Section are unclear, as her official record is very brief. Her qualifications included being fluent in French, a crack shot, athletic, and strong for her 5'3" height. Her interview report read: *She was persistent and a physically tough self-willed girl and not easily rattled.* The SOE hired Violette as a field agent. Violette was given a security clearance on July 1, 1943, and left for training on July 10. She left Tania in the care of her parents and officially joined FANY.

**Violette with Tania**

From August 7-27, 1943, Violette trained at Winterfold House and then moved on to Arisaig in the Scottish Highlands in September and October. She had some courses with Nancy Wake, another SOE agent, who later said that Violette "was great fun" and they became friends. Violette's reports were mediocre, but she was passed to the next phase of training. M.R.D Foot wrote that Violette: *was one of the best shots and fieriest characters in SOE.* It was an unusual description of a woman.

Violette's final instruction courses at Ringway Airport near Manchester involved parachute practice. During her first jump, she badly sprained her ankle, and she returned home to recuperate. During her time at home, she made out her will, something that all SOE agents were required to do in case they did not return home. Vera Atkins and Major Bourne Paterson of the SOE witnessed her will. She named her mother, Reine, as her executor and her daughter, Tania, as her sole beneficiary in case of her death,

After recovering, Violette retook the parachute course and passed in February 1944. Her final reports include the following statements: *She lacks ruse, stability, and the finesse which is required, and...she is too easily influenced...(but) she set an example to the whole party by her cheerfulness and eagerness to please.*

She was assigned to be the courier for Philippe Liewer's Salesman Circuit. On the night of April 5-6, 1944, she and Liewer, code names *Hamlet and*

**Violette recuperating after injuring her ankle on her first parachute jump**

*Major Charles Staunton*, flew into France and landed near the village of Azay le Rideau in the heart of the Loire Valley.

Violette's codename was *Louise*, which was also her family nickname. Her documents listed her as a commercial secretary; her alias was *Corinne Reine Leroy*, adapted from her mother's maiden name. The birthdate given on her fake documents was her actual birthdate. Violette apparently had a bad memory, so the SOE gave her cover names and information that would be easy to remember.

Violette was sent to Rouen to determine the circumstances of the capture of Claude Malraux, the second in command of the Salesman Circuit, and his SOE radio operator the month before. Violette assessed the damage that had been done to the Resistance groups in the area because of the arrests. The Circuit, which previously had 120 members, had been badly exposed. Her conclusion was that the Circuit was beyond repair and would need to be totally reorganized with new recruits. She also discovered that the Germans had found all the safe houses used by the Circuit. While in the area, Violette was picked up twice by the French police, but she convinced them that she was an innocent civilian and was released.

While she was conducting her investigation, she also gathered information about the local factories producing raw materials and weapons for the German army. After 24 days in France, Violette was sent back to England on April 30, 1944, to give her assessment in person to headquarters. Her plane to London, a Lysander, was hit by anti-aircraft fire while still over France, but they managed to make it to England without further problem.

The time in London allowed her to see her young daughter, with whom she had spent little time since her husband's death. She remained in England for over a month before returning for her second mission to France. This time, she and three colleagues parachuted onto a field near Limoges on June 8, 1944, two days after D-Day. Her fellow officers included her old leader, Liewer, Second Lieutenant Jean-Claude Guiet, and Bob Maloubier, their radio operator. Their mission was to rebuild the old Salesman Circuit into Salesman II, and to help sabotage German communications as the Allies were moving inland in pursuit of the fleeing German army.

Only two days after arriving back in France, Liewer sent her to help coordinate two Maquis groups located over 60 miles from their area. Instead of going by bicycle, as most couriers usually did, a young Maquis section leader, Jacques Dufour, code name *Anastasie*, offered to drive her, even though the Germans forbade cars in that area. They took Dufour's young friend, 26-year-old Jean Bariaud, with them.

Unfortunately, the car attracted attention as they approached a German roadblock set up by the 2nd SS Panzer Division. Before reaching the roadblock, Dufour slowed the vehicle, and Bariaud jumped out and returned to the Salesman Circuit to tell them about the situation. Knowing they couldn't get through the roadblock, Violette and Dufour fled from the car, but Violette's bad ankle slowed her escape.

There are differing accounts of what happened next. Both had weapons, and she may have had a Sten gun with eight ammunition magazines. Some reports say that Violette used a Sten gun to cover Dufour's escape and continued shooting until she ran out of ammunition. Other reports say that when trying to get over a fence, she further injured her weak ankle and could not go on, so she urged Dufour to continue without her. Regardless of what happened after they exited the car; the Germans captured her.

263

Violette was transferred to the SS Security Service in Limoges and was interrogated for four days, which usually included torture. She gave her name as *Vicky Taylor*, which was another alias SOE had given her. Getting no useful information from her, the Germans moved her north to the Fresnes Prison. They later took her to Gestapo headquarters at Avenue Foch for further interrogation, which often involved torture in the basement of the building. By then, the Germans had determined who she was and that she worked for the SOE, so the torture was more brutal than before.

As the Allies continued their push further north, the Germans decided to take their most valuable prisoners with them as they retreated to Germany. By then, Violette was with fellow SOE prisoners Denise Bloch and Lilian Rolfe, and others who were being taken to Germany by train. Violette and Denise were shackled together at their ankles. During that train ride, Violette shared her story of being captured with a fellow prisoner, SOE agent Harry Peuleve.

The group moved through Reims and Strasbourg to Saarbrucken, where they entered a camp with no hygiene facilities and only bread and water for food. The women remained there for ten days before being sent on to Ravensbrück concentration camp for women. They arrived at the camp on August 25, 1944.

Between 20,000 - 80,000 women and children died at Ravensbrück during the war. The Germans burned many records as they fled the camp at the war's end, and precise numbers are uncertain. Ravensbrück later

**Ravensbrück prisoners digging trenches**

became infamous when it became known that German doctors had subjected many women prisoners to horrific medical experiments at that facility. Fortunately, the Germans did not subject the SOE agents to that type of torture. The camp was filled with starving people, disease, and violence. Tuberculosis and dysentery were rampant in the camp.

Other prisoners credited Violette with helping them however she could, especially trying to keep everyone hopeful. During her early days at the camp, she spent time with Belgian courier Hortense Daman and American Virginia d'Albert-Lake. Virginia had been arrested because she had worked directly for the Resistance helping downed pilots and others escape France using the Comet escape line over the Pyrenees Mountains.

Both women said Violette exhibited a rebellious streak at Ravensbrück and constantly thought of possible ways to escape. She, SOE agents Denise Bloch, and Lilian Rolfe, stayed together whenever possible. Along with Virginia d'Albert-Lake, they were sent to work at the Heinkel munitions factory. All three refused to work making munitions, so the camp put them to work digging potatoes.

While moving by train between concentration work sites and concentration camps in September 1944, Violette was credited by another prisoner for her kindness: *During the early part of this journey, Violette Szabo, who was on the same train, distinguished herself by crawling around distributing water while the train car was under fire from the RAF, while the guards were hiding beside the track.*

Along with other women, the SOE agents were returned to Ravensbrück on October 6. The four women continued to be troublesome, and the Germans sent them to a punishment camp at Konigsberg, where they did hard labor cutting and hauling trees. They also had to clear boulders from a frozen field to prepare it to become an airfield.

Lilian and Denise were soon too ill from starvation and sickness to help with the work. On some days, as special punishment, the women were forced to stand outside in freezing temperatures for hours in the same summer dresses they had been wearing since their capture months before. Some women froze to death on those days. Their barracks had no heat or blankets, so the nights were almost as bad. In mid-January 1945, The Germans transferred Violette, Lilian, and Denise back to Ravensbrück again, but this would be their last transfer.

When they arrived, they were beaten and then put in solitary confinement. The women were already in terrible condition, both physically and mentally, and the final torture sessions may have pushed them to their breaking point. All three women were executed by a bullet to the back of the head.

Later, another prisoner at Ravensbrück, Mary Lindell, alleged that the three women had been hanged rather than shot. She contradicted the testimony of the Ravensbrück commandant Schwarzhuber who said that he had been trying to give some dignity to the executions when Vera Atkins interviewed him. However, Vera's report indicating the women had been shot remains the official version of their deaths. The execution of Violette, Denise, and Lilian and the trial of those responsible for killing them is described in detail in the Vera Atkins chapter 2 (Pages 16 & 17).

The SOE agent Cecile Lefort, another prisoner at Ravensbrück, was killed in the camp's gas chamber. Other well-known victims executed at Ravensbrück just before the end of the war were: Elise Rivet, a

Catholic nun; Russian Orthodox nun Sister Maria Skobtsova; Elisabeth de Rothschild, the only Rothschild family member to die during the Holocaust; French Princess Anne de Bauffremont-Courtenay; Milena Jesenska, a lover of Franz Kafka; and the wife of the Brazilian Communist leader Luis Carlos Prestes, Olga Benario.

On December 17, 1946, Violette became the second woman to be awarded the prestigious George Cross by England. Only three women from the SOE received the George Cross, the other two being Noor Inayat Khan, who had also been executed, and Odette Sansom. Odette described Violette as "the bravest of us all."

On January 28, 1947, King George VI presented the George Cross to Violette's daughter, Tania.

Violette's George Cross Award citation reads:

> *St. James's Palace, S.W.1. December 17, 1946*
>
> *The King has been graciously pleased to award the      GEORGE CROSS to Violette, Madame SZABO (deceased), Women's Transport Service (First Aid Nursing Yeomanry). Madame Szabo volunteered to undertake a particularly dangerous mission in France. She was parachuted into France in April 1944 and undertook the task with enthusiasm. In her execution of the delicate research entailed she showed great presence of mind and astuteness. She was twice arrested by the German security authorities but each time managed to get away. Eventually, however, with other members of her group, she was surrounded by the Gestapo in a house in the south-west of France. Resistance appeared hopeless but Madame Szabo, seizing a Sten-gun and as much ammunition as she could carry, barricaded herself in part of the house and, exchanging shot for shot with the enemy, killed or wounded several of them. By constant movement, she avoided being cornered and fought until she dropped exhausted. She was arrested and had to undergo solitary confinement. She was then continuously and atrociously tortured but never by word or deed gave away any of her acquaintances or told the enemy anything of any value. She was ultimately executed. Madame Szabo gave a magnificent example of courage and steadfastness.*

(The above citation differs in several details from the later testimony of several German guards and officers who testified at their trials. It is believed that the later testimony is correct because it came from several independently obtained sources, including from a few fellow prisoners.)

Violette and her husband, Etienne, were the most highly decorated couple of WWII.

The Violette Szabo Museum, founded by Violette's aunt, Rosemary Rigby, on Tump Lane in Wormelow, Herefordshire, opened in June 2000. The museum displays artifacts from people who knew Violette or served with her in WWII. The Royal College of Music offers an annual award for pianists who accompany singers called the Violette Szabo GC Memorial Prize.

On July 22, 2015, Tania, Violette's daughter, sold her parents' medals for $52,564 to Lord Michael Ashcroft, who placed Violette's George Cross medal on permanent display at the Imperial War Museum.

The movie "*Carve Her Name with Pride: The Story of Violette Szabo*" was released in 1958. It was based on the 1956 book of the same name by R.J. Minney. Many other books have been written about Violette's short life.

On a peaceful green space of the Vincennes estate in Valençay, France, a memorial was erected to honor the memory of all fallen SOE agents and Resistance fighters who worked in the Vincennes region during WWII. A house on the estate is named the Violette Szabo House.

**The SOE Memorial honors all female SOE agents.**

A likeness of Violette was used to represent all female SOE agents for the carved bust on the SOE Monument in London that is shown on the cover of this book. The sculptor was Karen Newman. Unveiled by Arthur Charles Valerian Wellesley, 9th Duke of Wellington, on October 4, 2009, the memorial is a tribute to the SOE female agents. The monument consists of a granite plinth atop a square base, with a bust of agent, Violette Szabo, atop the pedestal.

# Chapter 39

# Lilian Rolfe

April 26, 1914 – February 5, 1945

Code Names: Recluse, Nadine, Blouse    Alias: Caudie Rodier

Lilian was a twin to her sister, Helen Fedora Rolfe. They were born to a British accountant, George S.B. Rolfe, and his Russian wife, Alexandra Stern Rolfe when their father worked in Paris. Both girls were raised in France, but Lilian spent summers in England with her grandparents, which helped her improve her English language skills. Both Lilian and her sister took British citizenship through their father.

While in England one summer, she contracted rheumatic fever. After recovering, she returned to live with her family in France, but her health would never be robust. The girls were educated at the private Catholic school, the Cours Dupanloup, in the Boulogne-sur-Seine district, where she took the first part of her Baccalaureate in Sciences and Languages. Lilian studied for three years at the Conservatoire de Musique Russe in the center of Paris. She combined her music education with a two-year business secretarial course.

The family moved to Brazil in 1933 when Lilian was 19, and she finished her schooling in Rio de Janeiro. When WWII broke out, Lilian worked in the press office at the British Embassy, where her language skills were put to good use. She also helped in the department responsible for tracking German ship movements in and out of the Rio de Janeiro harbor.

Brazil declared war on Germany in August 1942. Wanting to contribute to the war effort, Lilian returned to England in February 1943 on board the S.S. Highland Brigade, a Royal Mail Line passenger ship. The boat had been chartered to take 605 volunteers to England to help with the war effort.

The ship made one stop in Bermuda and then left for the blacked-out run across the Atlantic. The situation was never clear to the passengers, but a German mine may have hit the ship. The passengers were told to muster on deck and prepare to board the lifeboats. After several hours, the passengers were allowed to return to their cabins. Later speculation was that the high seas caused some damage to the ship. The ship made a detour to New York City for repairs before Lilian finally arrived in Liverpool on April 12, 1943. The crisis on the high seas was the least of the challenges that lay ahead for Lilian.

Lilian joined the WAAF on April 16 or May 16, 1943 (records differ on the date), soon after arriving in England. She was sent to RAF Innsworth in Gloucestershire for basic training. While she was there,

**Lilian, in her FANY uniform**

she contracted chickenpox and had to be quarantined. After her recovery, the WAAF sent her for training to become a radio operator in Blackpool.

WAAF documents described her as a tall, dark-haired girl with steady dark eyes. She proudly wore a Brazilian flash on her uniform. Fellow trainees said that she was sad about a recent failed relationship but that it never affected her work.

Her ability to speak fluent French and her knowledge of the country and culture quickly brought her to the attention of the SOE. She agreed to join the organization on November 24, 1943. As was the custom for SOE female agents, she joined FANY. Lilian immediately began the SOE training program for field agents. She passed all her courses, and she received extra training to improve her existing skills as a radio operator.

Cynthia Sadler, a long-time friend, later reported that Lilian met with her in December 1943 and gave her a recent picture of herself in a FANY uniform, and letters to mail to Lilian's parents in Brazil at set intervals. She may have thought the letters would help reassure her parents that she was safe and doing well. Lilian swore her friend to secrecy and told her that she had been accepted "for special duties" without giving specifics about the SOE, which was an unknown organization to the British public.

In December 1943, her Students' Assessment Board gave her a "C" rating overall but with a high intelligence score of 8 out of 10. Very few women in the SOE received a score higher than a "C" in their final report. Based on the overall quality of their work in France, the grading may have been low simply because women were being graded by men who sometimes thought teaching women was beneath them.

Lilian completed her program, including parachute jumps at Ringway RAF base in Manchester. The following comment was written in Lilian's final report: *A highly intelligent, sensitive girl of considerable capacity and accomplishments. She is shy and reticent and needs encouragement to get the best out of her. Calm and deliberate, slow, and cautious. Very painstaking and conscientious and readily learns from her mistakes. Imbued with high ideals and very anxious to turn her training to good account. Very well suited for W/T work. She must have complete confidence in the person she is to work for, as she is a rather dependent person and needs the support of a strong and stable character.*

After finishing her SOE courses, Lilian was given an honorary commission as a Section Officer in WAAF. Before departing for France, the SOE provided her with the code name *Recluse*, and she would later also use *Nadine and Blouse*, depending on who she was dealing with. They also assigned her the alias of *Caudie Rodier* and the cover story that she was just a young woman visiting the area to escape the bombing around Paris, as her nerves were shot and she needed peace and quiet.

Only a few weeks before her 30th birthday, Lilian landed by parachute on April 5/6, 1944. André Studler, code name *Andre,* an American weapons instructor, traveled with her. Studler was a French-born agent of the American OSS (Office of Strategic Services), seconded to the "F" Section of SOE. He would be second in command of the Historian Circuit. The Circuit leader was Captain George Alfred "Teddy' Wilkinson, code name *Etienne.*

Lilian and Studler landed near Tours and went to Orleans, where the new Circuit would be based. Lilian had an 8.8-pound radio strapped to her leg during her parachute jump. Since he was away, Lilian did not meet her Circuit leader, Wilkinson, until May 9.

The Circuit was coordinating and supplying the local Maquis groups in preparation for what would become known as the D-Day landing. No one knew the exact landing site or date, but they knew it would happen soon. The primary role of the Maquis and the SOE agents in that area would be to harass and slow the German Army's retreat from France after D-Day to keep as many as possible from reaching Germany.

Lilian stayed with several families who were either working with the Maquis or being paid a rental fee by the SOE. As time allowed, she would sometimes cycle around the area looking for possible drop zones. Lilian knew a Gestapo signal-detection van was circulating in her area, and she had several close calls. Lookouts would alert her when a van was within a few blocks of her. She would move to a new location as soon as the danger passed.

The Germans almost caught her and Wilkinson when he visited her on June 5, 1944. A signal-detection van stopped right outside the house where she was staying. Both drew their guns, thinking they were about to be discovered, but the van driver moved on without entering the house.

Wilkinson and his SOE team successfully recruited and organized numerous Maquis fighting groups to work with them. The measure of their success in organizing is shown in the achievements of the Circuit on D-Day when they attacked all the railway and telecommunication targets in their area.

The Germans discovered and arrested Wilkinson on June 28, 1944. They took him to Orléans prison. In August, he was deported to Buchenwald concentration camp, where he was executed by a shot to the head on October 5, 1944.

**Gestapo radio detection van**

**George Wilkinson, head of the Historian Circuit**

Lilian continued to work with a local Maquis leader, Pierre Charie. She changed location every few days and kept extra radios stashed in different buildings in case she had to move quickly. Between her arrival in France in April and her capture on July 31, Lilian sent 67 messages to headquarters requesting air drops of supplies for the Maquis.

The Gestapo did a surprise raid on a safe house when they may have been looking for a local Maquis fighter, and they found Lilian instead. They quickly located her radio and knew they had found a "treasure," as one of their reports noted. It is uncertain if the Gestapo arrested her in a chance encounter or if she was betrayed.

Lilian was taken to the Gestapo headquarters at Avenue Foch in Paris for her first interrogation. The time with the Gestapo at Avenue Foch usually meant torture for the SOE agents. When they didn't get any useful information from her after eight days of questioning, they sent her on to Fresnes prison on August 8, 1944. Almost all the captured SOE women spent some time at Fresnes, as they had a women's wing in the facility.

By August 22, she was transferred again, this time to Ravensbrück concentration camp for women in Germany. Ravensbrück was built on the grounds of Himmler's estate, near a large lake north of Berlin. Walls and electrified fences surrounded it. S.S. guards were in elevated guard posts with machine guns trained on the prison grounds. It was a camp exclusively for women from 1939 to 1945. Britain didn't even know of its existence until the end of the war.

Lilian found the conditions worse than at Fresnes. She, Denise Bloch, and Violette Szabo were sent to one of the sub-camps, Torgau, in Saxony on September 3. The women were supposed to make ammunition, and they initially refused. After being severely beaten and put on a starvation diet, they finally gave in but tried to sabotage the bullets so they wouldn't fire. There were some reports that Lilian had a fever and was admitted to the hospital in that camp before all three were sent back to Ravensbrück in early October. They were beaten again and put in an underground bunker without any lights and with very little food or water.

**Group living conditions at Ravensbrück**

On October 29, 1944, they were taken with 200 other women to the Königsberg camp in Brandenburg, Germany, where they had to do heavy labor in the harsh winter cold. The women were forced to enlarge an airfield and build a road through the forest. Lilian again fell ill. By late January 1945, other prisoners said all three SOE women were in desperate condition, and they were sent back to Ravensbrück. Lilian could not walk, possibly because of all the beatings to her legs. Bloch was suffering from gangrene. The women probably knew that their time was coming to an end.

The execution of Denise, Violet, and Lilian and the trial of those responsible for killing them is described in detail in Vera Atkins chapter #2.

Soon after the end of the war, Lilian's twin sister had a meeting with Vera Atkins. Vera did not yet know what had happened to Lilian other than that she had been captured. The SOE would not know the details of her confinement, torture, and death until later from interviews with other prisoners and German guards and officers. Helen left the meeting feeling that Lilian was dead but uncertain about anything related to her service.

"F" Section head, Colonel Maurice Buckmaster, wrote to Lilian's family: *She volunteered for this very dangerous work with the full knowledge of its difficulties and risks. I can assure you that the work she and others like her did contribute very greatly to the rapid liberation of France.*

Pierre Charié, the man who had taken over the leadership of the Historian Circuit after Wilkinson was captured, wrote about Lilian: *My closest companion, the most precious, most daring, of my clandestine life. Her magnificent courage, her assiduous labours day and night, made possible the execution in the department of Le Loiret of excellent work that seriously upset German morale. Harried by the Gestapo, we moved together from village to village, farm to farm. We had to transport the radio set, batteries, accumulators, etc., sometimes by motorcar or motorcycle, more often by bicycle. Although frequently tired, she disregarded danger, and she never failed to make one of her radio transmissions.*

**left to right: Denise Bloch, Lilian Rolfe, Violette Szabo**

After the war, Audrey Ririe, one of the women who had worked with Lilian in the WAAF before she joined the SOE, said of Lilian: *(She was) a small, dark, pretty, little woman, earnest and serious. Later, we girls thought of her with awe at the enormity of the task she had taken on. I always shudder when I think of those vast empty fields of France and how they must have looked to a young woman dropped into enemy territory.*

Lilian received the Croix de Guerre posthumously from France, and her name is listed on many memorials to the women of the SOE.

On the Vincennes estate, West Norwood, London, England, a memorial has been erected to honor the memory of fallen Resistance Agents working in the Vincennes region of France during WWII. A house on the estate is named the Lilian Rolfe House, with a plaque remembering Lilian, the other SOE agents, and the Maquis fighters who fought and died in the war.

# Chapter 40

# Muriel Byck

June 4, 1918 – May 23, 1944

Code Name: Violette and Michele

Alias: Denise Madeline, Katrine Bernard, Danielle Wood, and Chantal Baron

Muriel Byck , another of the very brave Jewish agents, worked for the SOE in France for only two months before dying of meningitis. She knew she was taking on a dangerous assignment when she was recruited, but no one expected her life to end as it did. It was a tragic early death for a young woman who was only 26 years old.

Muriel was born to Jewish parents of Russian extraction. Her father, Jacques Itzko Byck, was born in Kyiv, Russia, and her mother, Luba Besia, nee Golinska, was born in Lviv, Russia. Both parents lived in England for a time and became British citizens. Due to her father's work, the family lived in several countries during her early years. Muriel attended grade school in Wiesbaden, Germany, from 1923 to 1926. She spent her high school years in St. Germain, France, where she attended the Lycée de Jeunes Filles school between 1926 and 1930. In 1930, the family returned to England.

Her parents divorced, and her father moved to New York City. Her mother soon remarried and moved to Torquay, Devon, England, with her new husband. Muriel attended the Lycée Francais in Kensington, London, and took her Baccalaureate in 1935, after which she attended the University of Lille in France.

She returned to England as the rumors about Hitler's ambitions in Europe became known, and she no longer felt safe in France. From 1936 – 38, she worked as a secretary in London and then became an Assistant Stage Manager at the Gate Theater.

When war was declared between England and Germany, she volunteered to work for the Red Cross. In 1941, she moved back to Torquay and worked as a government National Registration Clerk. Wanting to do more for the war effort, she joined the WAAF in December 1942 and soon became a section officer.

Within a year, the SOE noticed Muriel's French and German speaking skills, and she was recruited in September 1943. As with other recruits, she was asked if she would risk her life to spy for the Allies. She accepted that challenge.

Her initial report states: *She is a quiet, bright, attractive girl, keen, enthusiastic, and intelligent. Alert but not very practical and yet lacks foresight and thoroughness. She is, however, self-possessed, independent, persistent, and warm in her feelings for others...A girl of considerable promise who will require much training to help her overcome her lack of experience, her complete ignorance of what the work really involves, and her general guilelessness. Her temperament would appear to be suitable for work as a courier or possibly propaganda.*

After completing her courses, she received the code name *Violette*. Her first cover story was that she was a secretary from Paris on sick leave. After three weather related aborted attempts to fly from the Tempsford Airfield, she parachuted into the center of France on the night of April 8-9, 1944. With her on that flight were three male SOE agents: Captain C. Sydney Hudson, Captain Stanislaw Makowski, and Captain G.D. Jones.

**Muriel shortly after joining SOE**

Philippe Albert de Crevoisier, Baron de Vomécourt, code names *Gauthier* and *Antonine*, who had been the leader of the old Ventriloquist Circuit, chose her to be his radio operator and to work with him to rebuild the inactive Ventriloquist Circuit.

Vomécourt was said to be difficult to work with, but Muriel's cheerful personality must have won him over. M.R.D. Foot, later said that Vomécourt's book, *An Army of Amateurs,* was *a sometimes-exaggerated account of his activities.* He added that*: de Vomécourt had magnetic qualities of personality and attracted storms.* The SOE/OSS agent Virginia Hall had as little contact as possible with Vomécourt as she considered him careless about security and full of grandiose plans that she thought could create problems for his group.

**Philippe Albert de Crevoisier, Baron de Vomécourt**

Muriel's first safe house was in Salbris, where she worked in a shed behind a garage. The Germans used the garage to repair their cars and trucks. The soldiers became suspicious of her, but she moved before they searched the shed. She was fortunate to have four radios, so she had them hidden in various locations.

She moved to a blacksmith's house and began operating out of his barn. She said she was exhausted, but the work was stressful, and everyone thought that was the cause of her fatigue. A couple of days later, she lost consciousness and collapsed at the blacksmith's house. Her Circuit leader, Vomécourt, took her to a doctor who said she was seriously ill and needed to go to a hospital.

Going to a hospital was very risky for any SOE agent, but Vomécourt quickly fabricated a story that she was his niece visiting from Paris who needed urgent help. The Germans checked every admission to a hospital, but they were able to get her admitted using that story. The doctors diagnosed meningitis and gave her a lumbar puncture, but she died within a day, on May 23, 1944. Muriel was only 25 and had been in France for only two months.

They gave her a funeral and burial in Romorantin, but she had to be buried under her alias name. Vomécourt was at the burial service, but so were the Germans checking every attendee. He escaped over the cemetery wall just as they approached him to check his papers.

The local people tended to Muriel's grave for many years, but her family later had her remains moved to the Pornic War Cemetery in the Loire-Atlantique area of France. Her gravestone reads: *Here rests in peace, Muriel Tamara Byck, our only child, and beloved daughter.*

Muriel's life was cut short, but England posthumously recognized her contributions to the war effort by a Mentioned in Dispatches (MiD) for her conduct, and her name is recorded on many WWII memorials in both England and France.

# Chapter 41

# Odette Wilen

April 25, 1919 – September 22, 2015

Code Name: Sophie, Waitress

Odette was 24 when she parachuted behind German lines in France, but she had already seen heartache and loss in her life. She and her husband, Dennis H.A. Wilen, married in June 1940. He was a Finnish RAF pilot who was killed in a plane crash in October 1942. She became one of the few widows working as an SOE field agent in France.

She was born Odette Victoria Sar on April 25, 1919, to a French mother and a father from Czechoslovakia. The entire family became British citizens in 1931. Her father served as an RAF officer. Little is known

about her early life, but the SOE hired Odette as a bilingual secretary, and she later volunteered to become a field agent. At the SOE's request, Odette joined FANY in 1943.

D-Day was fast approaching (although few knew the exact date that the Allies' armies would land). Odette's training was cut short due to the need for radio operators. She trained with another female agent, Pearl Witherington, who wrote about a conversation with Odette during their training: *(she) was very, very, very feminine. Of course, she didn't know what she was letting herself in for because one fine day, we'd been blowing things up right, left, and centre, and she said, "Pearl, I must ask you for some advice. What are we supposed to be doing?" I was so surprised and said, "Don't you know?" She said, "No, I thought I was coming into this because I was recruited as a bilingual secretary"... So, I said," Well, you'd better go talk to Major Watt about this because that's not what we're doing."*

**Odette in her FANY uniform**

Odette did four practice parachute jumps from a suspended balloon before being dropped from a plane by parachute into France on the night of April 11-12, 1944. She successfully landed on a remote farm near Auvergne.

Odette was assigned to work with the Stationer Circuit, led by Maurice Southgate. Unfortunately, her lack of radio operation training soon became apparent, and he moved her to the new Labourer Circuit to work as a courier. She quickly adjusted to performing the usual courier duties.

The Labourer Circuit was led by Elisee Albert Louis Allard, a man she had trained with in England. He landed on April 5-6, 1944, just a week before Odette. The two soon became romantically involved and then engaged.

**Elisee Albert Louis Allard**

Someone they thought was a friend betrayed the Labourer Circuit, and several agents, including Allard, were captured by the Gestapo. The Gestapo arrested many agents around the same time, including Southgate and some of his agents in the Stationer Circuit. One of the men arrested was 2nd Lt. Marcel Leccia. His sister, Mimi, heard about his capture. Mimi had previously met Odette, and she quickly went to the safe house where Odette was living and took her away just before the Gestapo arrived to arrest her. Mimi hid Odette in another safe house.

Unaware of the number of prisoners, Odette and fellow agent Virginia Hall hatched a plan to get the men out of jail. However, they learned that there were eight agents, some from other Circuits, rather than the three they planned for. Their plan could not work for that many prisoners, and they were unable to help.

Allard and the other men spent 52 days in 84 Avenue Foch, headquarters of the SS counter-intelligence service, where interrogations were often brutal. On August 8, 1944, The Gestapo put Allard and the rest of the agents on a train to Germany as part of a group of 37 agents. They arrived at Buchenwald, the first and largest Nazi concentration camp within Germany's pre-WW2 borders, on August 17.

Camp records say the men were executed a few weeks later, on September 12, 1944 - hanged, with wire around their necks, from hooks in the walls of the mortuary. Their bodies were likely disposed of in one of the camp's crematoriums.

Odette tried to keep the Stationer Circuit functioning, but the Resistance fighters would not take direction from her, and she could not locate a radio operator to help her. England felt that the Gestapo had overran the area, and they did not send in another leader to reorganize it. The SOE told Odette to return to England since the Circuit would be shut down.

She finally gave up and agreed to go to Paris until the SOE could arrange for her return to London. Odette remained in the city until the guides were in place to take her across the Pyrenees Mountains. During the crossing, she had different guides for different segments of the mountain hike. One of her guides was a Spaniard, Santiago Strugo Garay. They traveled together for three days, but she obviously made an impression on him. Odette did not return to France.

Despite only knowing her for three days, her guide, Garay, traveled to London after the war and tracked Odette down. He and Odette were married in March 1946. Garay was from Spain, but he fought on the

Republican side against Franco during the Spanish Civil War. Fearing reprisal, they decided to move to Argentina. They spent the rest of their lives there, becoming pillars of Anglo-Argentinian society. Odette and her husband had two children. One was a son named Miguel Strugo Garay. The name and gender of the other child is unknown. Her husband died in Buenos Aires in 1997.

In a chance conversation with the British Air Attache in Argentina, Wing Commander Simon Dowling, Odette told him that she had never received her parachute wings from WWII. All SOE men who parachuted into France received this honorary patch, indicating they had done an official parachute jump into enemy territory. However, agents had to do a total of four practice jumps plus the jump into France to qualify. Few of the women who parachuted were allowed to do four jumps before being sent to France, so they were told they didn't qualify for the patch. After the war, a few of the SOE women received the patch – but only after they or their family made an official request for it – and it sometimes took years. Most of the SOE women never received the patch.

Odette finally received her "parachute wings" on August 9, 2007, from the British ambassador to Argentina, Dr. John Hughes. Wing Commander Simon Dowling participated by personally pinning the patch on her dress. Dowling also gave her a silver parachute wings brooch, which she wore every day for the remainder of her life.

Odette died on September 22, 2014, at the age of 96. Her obituary appeared in the *New York Times* on October 26, 2015.

**Chapter 42**

# Phyllis "Pippa" Latour

April 8, 1921 – October 7, 2023

Code Names: Genevieve, Paulette, Plus Fours, and Lampooner

Phyllis Ada Latour was born in South Africa to her father, a French doctor, and her mother, Louise (nee Bentley), a British citizen. Considerable tragedy followed her as a child. Her father died when she was only three months old. Her mother remarried a racecar driver, who later died in a racing accident. Her mother died in 1925 when Phyllis was only four years old. Phyllis was always called Pippa and is referred to by that name in the remainder of this chapter.

**Pippa as a young woman**

Late in life, Pippa talked about her early years to a reporter for New Zealand's *Army News*. In that interview, She said: *She had been born on a Belgian ship tied up in Durban, South Africa. She said her father had been killed in fighting in the Congo. My stepfather was well off and a racing driver.*

After her mother's death, her father's cousin became her guardian, and she went to live with him, his wife, and his sons in the Belgian Congo. She was quoted saying: *They were really the only parents I knew. When I was seven, my "new" mother went riding as she always did. The horse came back without her, and a lot of time elapsed before they found her, as they did not know where she had been riding. Apparently, the horse had stepped on a puff adder. She was thrown and then bitten in the face by the adder. When they found her, she was dead.*

As Pippa got older, she went first to Kenya to complete her education and then, in 1941, moved to England. She was fluent in both English and French. Wanting to do her part in the war, she joined the WAAF, where she may have been trained as an airframe mechanic.

Pippa's godmother committed suicide after being taken prisoner and probably tortured by the Nazis, and the Germans shot her godmother's father. So, Pippa had a personal vendetta and wanted to do damage to the Nazis regime. In November 1943, the SOE recruited Pippa, and she later said she was happy to join as she was looking to take revenge on the Germans. The SOE needed good French speakers to send behind German lines, and they quickly put her into their training program.

She related later in life: *They were trained by a cat burglar who had been released from jail how to get out a high window and down drainpipes, how to climb over roofs without being caught.* In addition to all the other required courses, Pippa also received special training to become a radio operator.

She successfully passed her courses, and on May 1, 1944, she parachuted into Normandy. Pippa knew that the risk to the lives of radio operators was very high, as it was considered the most dangerous position in the SOE.

There were many German patrols the night she jumped, and the aircraft had to make three passes to find a safe area for her to land. She was three fields away from the reception group, and it took them over an hour to find her. In late May, she learned that the Germans found her used parachute that had been buried and were looking for the "spy" who came from the sky.

Pippa was assigned to the Scientist Circuit, led by Claude de Baissac, code name *David*. She worked alongside Lise de Baissac, Claude's sister, who was his courier and often his right-hand woman. Lise was a great help to Pippa, who was new at the job. Claude, Lise, and Pippa lived together on the second floor of a small farmhouse with three bedrooms - no kitchen, bathroom, or water.

They had no furniture and borrowed some benches for sleeping. They also borrowed a small stove to cook on and had to forage for food in the area. An elderly woman lived on the first floor but seldom went out or interacted with them. While Claude and Lise spent much of the time at the small house, Pippa had to leave the house every day to avoid alerting the Gestapo to their whereabouts.

She was 23 at the time but looked much younger. She was given several code names, including *Genevieve, Paulette, Plus Fours,* and *Lampooner,* and a cover story of being a teenage art student who moved to the countryside, where it was considered safer during the war. When she had free time, she would travel around the Circuit looking for intel on the Germans that could be shared with the Circuit and with London. Her cover story allowed her to wander the area on her bicycle as she pretended to look for views to paint.

Pippa also used the cover of selling soap to locals and German soldiers. She later said that she drove the soldiers crazy with her constant chatter when she was stopped at their checkpoints. Traveling around gave her a great excuse to check out possible landing sites for new agents and supplies. She also noted where the Germans were gathering or if they were moving to a new location, information that she passed on to headquarters.

On one occasion, Pippa's radio broke down. She knew a radio was available in another village, so she and Lise set out to locate it. Lise carried the radio crystals and Pippa's operating codes in a belt around her waist. They had to go through several German roadblocks, and a guard even searched them, but he passed over the belt without realizing what was inside.

In advance of D-Day, the SOE sent Pippa several radios to ensure that she would always have a backup in case the Germans were too close to the hiding spot of a specific radio. She hid the radios in different houses and sheds. She was constantly on the move so she could transmit from different locations and keep ahead of the Germans looking for her. The SOE thought the Germans could pinpoint her radio within 30 minutes of her beginning her broadcast.

After the war, she explained how she kept her messages and codes safe. *I always carried knitting needles because my codes were on a piece of silk – I had about 2000 I could use. When I used a code, I would just pinprick it to indicate it had gone. I wrapped the piece of silk around a knitting needle and put it in a flat shoelace, which I used to tie my hair up. I was constantly hungry. One family I stayed with told me we were eating squirrel. I found out later it was a rat. I was half-starved, so I didn't care.*

From the time Pippa arrived in France until the liberation of her area in August 1944, she sent 135 messages to London containing information about German activities in her area, as well as the actions of the Circuit. Each message took hours to code and decode, and she was constantly worried about the possibility that the Gestapo might have a radio receiver searching for her location. Pippa was working in the Normandy area, so when the Allies began arriving on D-Day, the locale was flooded with Germans, either fighting the Allied invasion or trying to flee the area to return to Germany.

Pippa was recalled to London and decommissioned when the Allies liberated her area.

Pippa received an MBE in 1945, the French Resistance Medal, and the Croix de Guerre for her wartime service. Because she left England shortly after the end of the war, she never personally received any of the medals.

After the war, Pippa married Patrick Doyle, an Australian engineer, and they lived in Kenya, Fiji, and Australia. They had two daughters and two sons. Following her divorce in 1975, Pippa moved to Auckland, New Zealand. She never told anyone about her exploits in wartime France and did not collect her medals until her children read about her on the internet in 2000. They insisted she request receipt of her medals. She told her children: *I didn't have good memories of the war, so I didn't bother telling anyone what I did.* She shared some information and even agreed to be interviewed, after which she received considerable media and public attention for the remainder of her life. Ultimately, she collected the medals.

On November 25, 2014, at 93, she received France's highest award, the Chevallier of the Legion of Honour (Knight Class), which was presented to her by the French Ambassador Laurent Contini. He said: *What a formidable person you are, madam.*

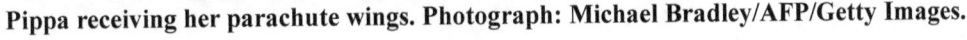

**Pippa receiving her parachute wings. Photograph: Michael Bradley/AFP/Getty Images.**     **The Légion d'Honneur.**

In 2017, she received the French Brevet Militaire de Parachutiste (French parachute wings) medal for her service at a ceremony in Auckland. At the time, Pippa – then 96 – said she was honored to receive "her wings."

Pippa lived to be 102 and died on October 7, 2023.

# Chapter 43

# Josiane and Marcelle Somers "RF" Section

(Josiane) December 17, 1925 – June 1, 2010

Josiane Code Name: Venitien,

(Marcelle) 1898 - ?

Marcelle Code Name: Albanais

Marcelle and Josiane Somers were the only mother-daughter team trained by the SOE and sent to France. Josiane was one of the youngest agents sent to France. The two women parachuted into France a few months apart. Josiane's brother, Claude Somers, was also trained by the SOE. They may have been the only mother, daughter, and son working in any capacity with the British behind German lines.

Because the three family members were initially associated with branches of the Free French movement, their service records were treated differently. Although M.R.D. Foot listed the two women as SOE female agents in his book, *SOE in France*, he gives no further information about them. Their names are rarely listed in other books referencing the SOE women, and their lives after the war do not seem to have been followed by anyone associated with the British government or interested researchers. The same applies to other women who came to the SOE from the Free French government in exile.

The author knows nothing about Marcelle's early life other than her birth year. Josiane was born in Pas-de-Calais, France, as Josiane Jeanne Elise Somers on December 17, 1925, to a British father and French

**Marcelle and Josiane,**
**photo courtesy of Justin Davis Collection**

mother, Marcelle. After the Germans invaded France, Josiane, her mother, and her brother, Claude, moved to England.

Josiane's brother joined the Royal Air Force, and in 1942, the SOE trained Claude to be a radio operator like his mother and sister, and he was also sent to France. Josiane and her mother volunteered to join the Free French movement. Her mother became a radio operator for the Central Bureau of Intelligence and Action (BCRA), a group set up by General de Gaulle in July 1940. Josiane lied about her age in order to volunteer, and it is uncertain whether she joined the Free French Air Force or the French Volunteer Corps.

Josiane was initially restricted to secretarial duties but wanted to do more. Through an agreement between Britain and the Free French, she was recruited in February 1944 and trained by the SOE to become a radio operator, as was her mother. The SOE thought that Josiane would connect with her mother in France and they would work together.

Josiane's SOE record of February 1, 1944, indicates: *She is intelligent, practical, cunning, learns quickly, and has a retentive memory. She is, however, very young and immature. She is keen and worked hard, displaying a lively imagination and plenty of initiative. For her age, she has quite a strong character, and she certainly seems to be courageous, but she is rather vain and probably inclined to be self-indulgent. She has a pleasant personality but is rather lacking in humor; she is shy and does not mix particularly well with others. Although she should do well in the job for which she had been selected, on account of her immaturity and lack of experience, she would require constant and strict supervision by a responsible superior. Codes: further practice required.*

Josiane's mother, Marcelle, was 46 years old when she parachuted into France with seven other agents on May 3, 1944. She landed near Manziat, NE of Mâcon, in the Saone and Loire area. Marcelle's unit failed soon after her arrival, and she was transferred to Paris to work in the BCRA main office. So, mother and daughter never met during their wartime service in France.

Josiane did exceptionally well in her parachute training. Her instructor said she was one of only two in the class who showed no nervousness about her practice jumps. After completing her courses, Josiane departed the Harrington Airfield and parachuted into France on the night of July 6-7, 1944, when she was 19 years old.

**Marcelle and Josiane in uniform, photo courtesy of Justin Davis Collection**

Josiane landed southeast of Blanc, halfway between Poitiers and Chateauroux. A fellow agent, Lt. Jean Sibileau, code name *Serfouette*, accompanied her. Cone Circuit leader Claude Gros, code name, *Atabaque*, met Josiane when she landed. She worked for him until the Allies liberated their area. Gros oversaw the coordination and management of Resistance groups in Landes, Charente-Maritime, Dordogne, Gironde, and Pyrenees-Atlantiques.

Josiane began sending and receiving transmissions to/from England almost immediately. Those in her Circuit were impressed with how quickly she settled in and how efficient she was despite frequently moving from safe house to safe house. Sometimes, she had to set up her small antenna in the woods to contact London.

**Josiane, photographed in 1944**

She continued working with Gros until the Allies moved in and liberated their area. Josiane was injured in a car accident in early September 1944, but she traveled to Paris on September 20 to report on her mission.

Shortly after their mission in France ended, Josiana and Gros married in London in October 1944. Unfortunately, little has been found about her or her husband after their marriage.

Josiane received the Military Cross and a letter of commendation from the SOE for her work in France. Marcelle received an MBE from England and the Croix de Guerre from France.

*de g. à d. mesdames Janine Boulanger (Hoctin), Jacqueline Raoult (Franklin), Evelyne Morlet (Fuller), Christine Levisse-Touzé, et Josiane Gros (Sommer).*

**Josiane Somers Gros, above right, in her later years.**

The author has not found additional information about Marcelle other than a statement that she survived the war. As with so many women who first worked with the Free France movement or directly with the Resistance in France and then joined the SOE, there is little further information about them.

Josiane died in Paris on May 31, 2010.

# Chapter 44

# Marguerite Knight

April 19, 1920 - ?, 2004

Code Name: Nicole    Alias: Marguerite Chauvan

Marguerite "Peggy" Diana Frances Knight was one of the few SOE women given credit for carrying on the mission of her Circuit after she lost both her leader and his lieutenant. She did that despite receiving perhaps the shortest training period of anyone in the SOE.

Peggy was born to a military family in Paris on April 19, 1920. Her Polish mother was Charlotte Beatrice Mary Ditkowski, and her English father was Capt. Alfred Rex Knight. The family stayed in France after WWI, so Peggy learned French from an early age. Peggy moved from France to England when she was sixteen, allowing her to be fluent in both French and English.

When WWII began, she joined the WAAF, but a serious bout of pneumonia damaged her lungs and caused them to release her as medically unfit in May 1943. She was living in Aylesbury, Buckinghamshire, and working as a typist in London when the SOE headquarters overheard her speaking French at a local café in April 1944. They were so impressed with her language skills that they recruited her to work at the SOE.

Peggy agreed and signed up with FANY and began her very short two-week training program at Thame Park Saltmarsh on April 11, 1944. It may have been the shortest training in the SOE. The British knew of the imminent D-Day landing, and they urgently needed more agents in France to support the Circuits working there.

The Government had taken over Thame Park as a training center very early in the war, and the owner, Sir Frank Bowden, moved out for the duration of WWII. The SOE used the house to train its agents for service in France. For a time, Thame Park was made to look like a small village in France to help prepare the agents to acclimate to the culture.

Her brief training brought her mostly excellent reviews, and one instructor wrote: *This young lady did a very good scheme and seems well suited to act as a courier. Indeed, she has the intelligence and initiative to take on even more responsible work.* Such positive comments were rare for the female agents in training, as many of the instructors had serious doubts about whether women could do the necessary work behind enemy lines.

The SOE gave Peggy the code name *Nicole* and assigned her as a courier to the Donkeyman Circuit, led by Henri Frager, code name Jean-Marie, a former French Carte member whom the SOE had commissioned. The Carte network was the brainchild of André Girard, an artist living in Antibes on the

French Riviera in 1941. Girard took the code name *Carte*, which also became the name of his mostly imaginary resistance network. It took the SOE some time to realize that the organization barely existed and was poorly organized. However, the SOE was impressed with Frager and kept him within the organization.

**Margarite Knight and unknown soldier**

Normally, all agents were required to do five practice parachute jumps from a plane before heading to France, but Peggy only had time to do one jump – and that was from a stationary balloon. Despite so little training, she made a successful parachute jump into France on May 6, 1944. Peggy was the first SOE agent dropped from an American plane. She arrived with a new radio operator, Henri Bouchard, code name *Noel*, who would also work with the Donkeyman Circuit.

They found the arrival reception group to be in a state of confusion, and a Maquis fighter named Michel assigned to Donkeyman Circuit confiscated their radio as soon as they landed. Her later report about her landing shows her frustration and confusion: *Michel was very rude, refused to give me the wireless set, and said Noel was miles away and he could not be bothered to fetch the messages. He asked me to go to a parachutage* (airplane drop of supplies) *that night – the tone of his voice was such that I thought I had better go. We did not return from the parachutage until eight o'clock the next morning – again I had missed my train.*

They were sent from place to place for several days, with no radio to report to London that they had arrived safely. Michel, instead of following the SOE rules of secrecy, told every villager they met that they had parachuted into France and people were constantly coming around to meet them. Both she and Bouchard were very concerned that their location would be shared with German soldiers or French police in the area.

Finally, Frager arrived and got them settled on the outskirts of Paris. He immediately asked her to travel to another area to obtain a radio for them to use.

Peggy quickly settled into the frantic routine of Circuit life and was responsible for the usual responsibilities of a courier, ensuring good communication between her Circuit and the Maquis groups in their area. She used a bicycle to travel through German lines almost daily. Being a woman allowed her to get through the roadblocks with less suspicion than a man. She located safe areas where British planes could drop in new agents and supplies. She sorted the supplies and helped to distribute them to Maquis groups.

In addition to her courier work, Peggy began conducting reconnaissance on German troop movements, supply depots, and transportation routes that could be sabotaged. When needed, Peggy took her turn as a sentry and volunteered to go on missions with the men. One night, she marched over 20 miles with a sabotage party.

Donkeyman Circuit leadership determined that there were two traitors in their group, the first being Michel, the Maquis leader who had been troublesome to Peggy when she arrived. The second was a man called Landsell. Peggy learned they were traitors when Frager and others in the Circuit had long discussions that ended with them executing Michel. No further information has been found on the fate of Landsell.

On June 5, 1944, the night before the D-Day Landing, word came to Donkeyman that the invasion was about to happen. London directed them to sabotage the railway line at Cezy, which was over 18 miles from the area where their fighters were camped. They knew the roads had extra German security patrols. The SOE agents, including Peggy and the Maquis fighters, walked, carrying explosives, on smaller roads to get to the railroad. They set the charges and retreated to safe houses.

Early the next morning, Peggy bicycled back and forth from the safe house to the railroad, giving ever-changing messages about the timing to set off the explosives. The explosives were not set off for three days as they waited for word that German soldiers fleeing from the D-Day invasion area would be using trains to leave the area. The explosives blew up the tracks and derailed train engines, killing many German soldiers.

The Germans moved quickly to try to repair the tracks, and as soon as they were unguarded, the Maquis would set more charges and blow them up again. Between the various Circuits operating in France, there were 960 sabotage strikes on French railroads immediately following the D-Day landing.

In late June 1944, Peggy and a group of Maquis fighters got into a gun battle with a troop of German soldiers but managed to escape before being captured. Peggy used her Sten gun in that fight, one of the few instances where an SOE woman actually used their firearms in France.

Peggy was frustrated with what she considered the haphazard way things were run in Donkeyman. Frager was usually in Paris, leaving Peggy and Bouchard to run the Circuit as best they could. The Maquis leadership was often disrespectful to both of them, and they didn't seem to maintain security within their ranks. After several requests for a meeting with Frager were ignored, she demanded a meeting, and he came to their area.

She and Bouchard also voiced their concerns that they didn't trust some of the Maquis leaders, and had serious doubts about Roger Bardet, an SOE agent. Frager finally paid attention to them and tightened up the Circuit organization. But it was too little, too late.

It turned out their doubts were well founded, as the second in command, Bardet, was a double agent helping the Germans. Unbeknownst to the SOE, Bardet had previously betrayed the Inventor Circuit, leading to the arrests in October/November 1943 of its organizer Sidney Jones, wireless operator Marcel Clech, and courier Vera Leigh, resulting in the collapse of the Inventor Circuit. All three were later executed,

Bardet betrayed Frager, who was arrested in July 1944. After his initial interrogation, Frager was deported to Buchenwald concentration camp, where the Germans executed him on October 5, 1944. Bardet was responsible for the arrest and execution of several additional SOE agents, and he also betrayed the Prunus Circuit in Toulouse, leading to the arrest of leader Maurice Pertschuk, Jewish radio operator Marcus Bloom; and several of their key colleagues, resulting in the collapse of that Circuit. Pertschuk and Bloom were later executed by the Nazis.

The Allies captured Bardet after the war and turned him over to the French military police. He was tried and found guilty of treason and condemned to death by a French court. Despite causing the death of so many SOE agents and Maquis fighters, he was reprieved and released from prison in 1955.

M.R.D Foot later wrote the following about Peggy: *She was naïve, modest, efficient, and self-effacing; her French was good; everyone liked her, and no one noticed her. She was quite out of her depth in the personal and political intrigues that riddled Donkeyman; though she was shrewd enough to observe that Bardet 'looked to me like a hunted man very often, he never smiled, had big lines under his eyes and always looked as if he had something on his mind.'*

On August 15, 1944, a three-man American team landed to work with the Donkeyman Circuit. They were surprised to find almost 500 organized and armed Maquis already working in the area. The Americans were able to call in more firepower from the sky, and they had direct communications with the incoming Allied troops. Peggy continued to ride her bicycle through German lines and would report back about where there were heavy concentrations of German soldiers. She felt she was making a real difference as the war was coming to a close.

Once the American Army moved into her area in large numbers, Peggy was recalled to England. She hitchhiked to Paris, where she boarded a plane for London on September 13, 1944. She left the SOE in November.

For her service, she was awarded the Croix de Guerre by France, and a Member of The Most Excellent Order of the British Empire (MBE.) The U.S. awarded her the Presidential Medal of Freedom for her assistance to the American troops when they arrived in her Circuit area.

**Croix de Guerre**          **MBE**          **Presidential Medal of Freedom**

The Presidential Medal of Freedom is the highest civilian award of the United States, along with the Congressional Gold Medal. It is an award bestowed by the President to recognize people who have made "an especially meritorious contribution to the security or national interests of the United States, world peace, cultural or other significant public or private endeavors." The award was established in 1945 by President Harry S. Truman to honor civilian service during World War II.

One month after her service to the SOE ended, Peggy married Sub-Lieutenant Eric C. Smith of the Royal Navy. At the war's end, Eric returned to his prior job as a River Lea police inspector. The couple lived in Waltham Cross, Hertfordshire County, England. After her life of adventure and danger in the SOE, Peggy settled into a life as a wife and mother and raised their two children.

**Peggy with her children after the war.**

In 1947, the *Sunday Express* published an article titled 'Mrs. Smith' with the photo (left): *You would not expect that the prim little woman who comes out of the newly built house, 61 Eastfield Road, Waltham Cross, Essex, wheeling her 16-month-old and four-month-old in a second-hand tram with shopping basket on the handrail, is our trusted and well-beloved Marguerite Diana Frances Smith who once blazed away with a Sten gun at Germans hunting her down as a secret agent in France.*

Peggy died in 2004. Her death was recorded in Truro, England.

# Chapter 45

# Sonya Butt D'Artois

May 14, 1924 - December 21, 2014

Code Name: Blanche    Alias: Suzanne Bonvie

Sonya Esmée Florence Butt was one of the youngest SOE agents sent to France. Her time in France was brief, as she parachuted in only nine days before D-Day, but she served with bravery and did what needed to be done in her SOE Circuit. After the war, she also had one of the most "normal" lives of any of the SOE women agents.

She was born in Eastchurch Isle of Sheppey in Kent, England, on May 14, 1924, to Charles Butt, an RAF officer, and his French wife, Ada Cordon Butt. Her parents split up shortly after their daughter's birth, and her mother returned to her family's home in southern France, taking Sonya with her. Sonya spent much of her youth in France growing up with the country's language, customs, and traditions, knowledge that would be very important during WWII.

When the war began, she and her mother returned to England. Sonya was only 15 but wanted to follow her father into the military. She tried to enlist in the WAAF, but their minimum age was 17 ½, so she waited and signed up at that exact age on November 14, 1941. She served in the administrative branch. Women were banned from front-line service at that time, but in April 1942, the government dropped that restriction.

While working at WAAF, she met and became friendly with Maureen O'Sullivan (no kin to the actress.) They both became SOE agents and trained together at the SOE training program.

One of the first organizations to take advantage of women being allowed to serve in combat zones was the SOE, which began recruiting soon after England declared war on Germany. They did not advertise their openings but relied on word of mouth and personal referrals. Sonia applied to the SOE to work as an interpreter, but things turned out differently. Learning of her French language skills and knowledge of the culture of France, the SOE recruited Sonya for fieldwork in France. She joined when she was only 19, on December 11, 1943. She was promoted to WAAF Assistant Section Officer.

Sonya was reported to be very proficient in preparing and using explosives, and her instructors thought she could easily train Resistance members in their use. She trained alongside Maureen O'Sullivan, and a man who would become her husband, French-Canadian Captain Lionel Guy D'Artois, who went by Guy.

During her training, she earned the respect of her fellow trainees and her instructors.

She was given the code name *Blanche*, and her cover story was that she was *Suzanne Bonvie*, an employee of a Paris fashion house sent to the country to recuperate from a serious illness. Words that showed up in her reports mentioned her being spirited, confident, determined, etc., traits that would be very important in her work behind German lines.

After getting to know each other, she and Guy decided at the last minute to get married during a weekend's leave, just the day before departing for France.

**Sonia with husband Guy D'Artois on their wedding day**

The SOE had planned for her to be dropped into the Saône-et-Loire district of eastern France to be the courier and explosive expert for the Ditcher Circuit, which would be organized by her new husband, Guy D'Artois. However, Maurice Buckmaster changed the plans, fearing their marriage might leave them more vulnerable should either of them be captured and tortured for information.

So, Guy was sent to Saône-et-Loire with a different explosive expert, and Sonya was sent to the Headmaster Circuit in the cathedral city of Le Mans under Major Sydney "Soapy" Hudson.

On the night of May 28, 1944, only nine days before D-day, she landed at La Cropte, west of Le Mans, and less than 100 miles south of the Normandy beaches. The location was perfectly placed to sabotage the German troops and disrupt reinforcements moving up from the south.

Unfortunately, she landed badly, and the injury would bother her for years and eventually require two surgeries. Upon landing, she could not find the container holding the designer clothes that were part of her cover story. The Germans later found the wardrobe trunk, which alerted the Gestapo to the arrival of a female agent.

As directed by the SOE, Sonya began frequenting the restaurants used by German officers and flirting with them to gain their confidence. The intent was to establish her false credentials as genuine and to begin gathering intelligence that drinking soldiers might let slip. She was only nineteen, but she was five feet seven inches and attractive, and she deliberately attracted attention.

The Maquis groups had expanded in the months before D-day, and the SOE sent in a man to train the new recruits in using British weapons and explosives. Sonya took over that role when that man was killed in an ambush. She was said to have a natural gift for creating explosives.

Most days, Sonya traveled to the various Maquis groups, passing on cash and supplies. While with the group, she trained new recruits in using and caring for the weapons. By night, she helped to coordinate sabotage operations.

After D-day, she and the Circuit leader, C. Sydney Hudson, were constantly on the move. They often had to sleep in barns or haystacks. One day, she was stopped at a roadblock and questioned because the German soldiers were suspicious of her papers. She was carrying forged documents, but she kept to her cover story. Her confidence and fluency in colloquial French eventually persuaded them she was genuine, and they let her pass.

Sonya later said: *You just react to the moment and think, I'll get by alright with a nice smile. I just sort of smiled and waved to them. All the time… no matter what you had hidden in your handbag or your bicycle bag, if you had a nice smile, you know, just give them a little wink.* No doubt, Sonya's beauty helped as she traveled through German checkpoints.

One day in late June 1944, the dreaded thing happened, and she was again stopped by the Gestapo and questioned. They were not happy with her responses and took her to jail. She was interrogated several times in small dark cells. Fortunately, she kept her head and convinced them that she was an innocent resident and they released her.

She and Hudson were always just a step ahead of the German search parties who desperately wanted to capture foreign agents who were supplying the Maquis. A Maquis fighter betrayed the Circuit when the Gestapo was torturing him, and they lost several men and some supplies when the Germans raided their location. Nevertheless, the Maquis the Circuit was working with managed to blow up railway lines, supply dumps, and, crucially, the important Le Mans telephone exchange. The destruction of the phone lines forced German commanders south of Normandy to use radio rather than telephone communications. The SOE agents could intercept their communications, just as the Gestapo could intercept the SOE radio signals.

Much later, when talking about her time in France, Sonya said that a fellow male recruit: *He made me lead all the time. I'd be the first of the group of five when we were going on a mission or doing whatever. His theory was if I did it, they'd have to even if they found it tough. They'd have to keep up with a girl.*

The Americans finally liberated the Le Mans area, and the locals celebrated the defeat of the German army. Sonya had a very scary experience when local French men "arrested" and beat her because they believed she was a collaborator who had worked with the Germans because she shared meals with German officers, as she had been directed to do by the SOE. The men were preparing to shave her head and tie her to a lamppost when a group of the Maquis who knew her real identity rescued her.

Sonya and Circuit leader Hudson remained in France for several weeks after their area was liberated. The Americans asked them to share their knowledge of the area and its people. They traveled through areas still occupied by the Germans to gather intelligence and shared it with the Americans. By the war's end, Sonya had lost 40 pounds.

She and her husband finally had a reunion in Paris before she returned to England in October 1944, only five months after arriving in France. At 20, she became pregnant with the first of their six children.

Shortly after the war ended, she received the Mention in Dispatches (MiD) medal for her bravery in France, and she was awarded an MBE. The MBE recognizes the efforts of civilians and service members in non-combat roles.

Her husband was awarded the Distinguished Service Order (DSO) from England and the Croix de Guerre from France.

After the war, Sonya and her husband moved to Canada and lived in Montreal, where she was known as Sonia or Toni D'Artois. Sonya quietly disappeared from public view to become a wife and mother.

Sonya raised a family of three boys and three girls. Her husband remained in the military and was away much of the time. Though not unique by any means, this must have been one of the most decorated couples of the war.

In 1947, her husband received the George Medal from England for his rescue of a severely injured missionary from a remote district in the far north of Canada. The mission took seven weeks to reach the man and return him for medical care. While still in the military, he served in Japan and later in the Korean War.

Guy died in March 1999, and Sonya died in Montreal on December 21, 2014, at 90 years of age. She was survived by their three sons and three daughters and by her companion for the last seven years of her life, John Tozer.

**Sonia, in July 2011, at her grandson's wedding**

# Chapter 46

# Ginette Jullian

December 8, 1917 – August 4, 1952

Code Name: Adele

Ginette was one of the few SOE radio operators never captured by the Gestapo for even a brief time. During her short time in France, she managed to elude the Germans and keep one step ahead of their roving radio wave detection equipment. It is interesting to note that Vera Atkins later said she had never heard of Ginette despite the fact that M.R.D. Foot included her in his list of agents.

Jinette Marie Helene Jullian was born in Montpellier, France, but lived in Algeria during her youth. She married at 16, had a child, and then divorced before ever coming to the attention of the SOE. She lived in France before WWII but moved to England when the Germans invaded. She wanted to be of help during the war and applied to become a pilot in the British Air Transport Auxiliary (ATA), the group that ferried empty planes to locations where they were needed. Unfortunately, she failed her pilot license exam in 1943.

Ginette

The SOE recruited her for her French language skills and knowledge of French culture. Ginette joined FANY with the rank of lieutenant and proceeded to an abbreviated SOE training program for radio operators. After she completed her courses, she was given the code name *Adele* and matched with the man who would be her Circuit leader, Gerard Dedieu, code name *Jerome*.

Dedieu had been working with the Maquis since 1942. He had been captured and imprisoned by the Germans, but he and 20 other prisoners escaped in a daring breakout from the Eysses prison in early 1944. He made it safely back to England and was returning for a second assignment in France.

Ginette and Dedieu parachuted into France, along with Yvan Galliard and Henri Fucs, on June 7, 1944, the day after the D-Day landing. Ginette and Dedieu composed the only SOE team that spoke only French.

Upon landing, an SOE agent met them, but one of his Maquis leaders confiscated Ginette's radio, leaving her and Dedieu with no way to communicate with London.

Ginette and Dedieu stayed at a safe house for one night and then got on a train for Paris. From there, they moved into the country, looking for the addresses of houses that were supposed to be safe, but each house had been compromised, so they kept moving. They were traveling by bicycle in their search for a safe place to stay. When they arrived in one town, Beauvais, they found the Germans had taken over the entire town, so they decided to return to Paris, where they could easily blend into the population.

Ginette and Dedieu found France in chaos. Thousands of people were evacuating ahead of the oncoming Allied army, afraid of being caught in fighting between the Allies and the fleeing German army. Frenchmen suddenly understood that the Allies would win the war. Those who had been on the sidelines or collaborated with the Germans suddenly signed up to serve with the Resistance so they could be seen as being on the winning side.

Dedieu was worried about his father-in-law in all the chaos, and he went off searching for him, leaving Ginette to try to find a radio so she could contact London. She asked to use a radio held by a pro-Gaullist group, but they refused. Ginette finally was allowed to use a radio from an American group she connected with in the Seine-et-Marne area. She contacted London, updated them on the situation, and requested a new radio. The SOE had feared that she and Dedieu had been arrested or killed by the fleeing Germans.

The SOE parachuted in a new radio, and she and Dedieu began to do the work assigned to them. Several SOE Circuits had been betrayed to the Germans, and many SOE agents and Maquis fighters had been arrested or killed. Knowing which Circuits to trust was difficult, so Dedieu reestablished the Permit Circuit in the Chartres area.

They contacted and coordinated the efforts of 13 different Maquis groups who had been left with no contact with England when other Circuits were compromised. Ginette requested supplies and weapons, which resulted in 450 containers being dropped by parachute in July 1944. Ginette distributed the supplies to over 2000 Maquis fighters.

Some Maquis groups that previously worked together with only one purpose - to fight the Germans - began fighting among themselves over the political results they wanted to see after the war. Many hoped for communism or socialism. Some strongly supported General de Gaulle. Others wanted to stop his efforts to become head of post-war France.

Dedieu was arrested on August 8 but escaped a few days later and rejoined Ginette. The Allies soon arrived in the area, and the brief mission for the Permit Circuit ended. Dedieu found himself snubbed by General de Gaulle's officers, and he left for England on August 20. General de Gaulle ordered all SOE agents to leave France so he and his Free French movement could take the sole credit for "liberating" France.

Ginette remained in France for another month because an American officer asked if she could stay and help with radio communications as his soldiers continued their efforts to capture the remaining German soldiers around Dijon. By September 22, 1944, the Americans no longer needed her assistance, and the SOE recalled her to England after only three months in the field.

After the war, Dedieu described Ginette in his reports as: *My radio operator always gave me excellent work, even on the most demanding of days. She was very brave and never lost her nerve, even when the SS arrived to search the house from which she was transmitting.* Buckmaster, head of the "F" Section, described Ginette as exceptionally courageous and recommended her for the OBE.

In August 1945, Ginette married Philippe de Scitivaux, a French naval officer. Together, they raised her son from her previous marriage.

**Ginette and her husband, Philippe de Scitivaux**

Philippe's military career took them around the world. From 1945 to 1946, Philippe took command of the French naval aviation troops that were training in the United States. Back in France, he oversaw a variety of naval stations before being promoted to rear admiral. He was commander-in-chief for the Pacific from 1962 to 1964.

Ginette died in a scuba diving accident in Tahiti on August 4, 1962.

# Chapter 47

## Additional "RF Section Agents

The author believes that the following women were sent to France through an agreement between Britain and General de Gaulle that the SOE would train some of De Gaulle's Free French intelligence agents. The SOE trained and sent several of these women into France after D-Day, but Vera Atkins never considered them to be "real" SOE agents.

Many SOE records were disposed of when the organization was disbanded at the end of the war. The records of the Free French women were probably not considered important when the organization was shut down.

# Aimee Raymonde Corge "RF" Section

Born January 11, 1920, <u>OR</u> March 11, 1922, <u>OR</u> March 14, 1922 – Died ?

Code name: Hellene

Aimee was the last SOE female agent sent into France, and she disappeared from history after making her parachute jump. Did she die during the jump, was she captured and possibly executed, or did she slip back into life as a civilian in France at the end of the war? When the author queried the National Archives in London about Aimee and the other RF women, she discovered that Aimee's file was still classified. The National Archives did agree to declassify her records, but the record only covers her training period – nothing after she parachuted into France. Aimee remains a mystery.

The results of the brief records from the National Archives are shown below:

The different birth dates shown in the title are all listed on her SOE files in the National Archives in London. Based on the dates listed in her file for school attendance, the 1920 date would seem more appropriate.

She was born in Tunis, Tunisia, to Raymond Corge and Maria Dumont. The official records conflict, as one page says: *Daughter of Raymond, (who) died in 1937 from war wounds and is buried at Marseille; and of Maria Dumont, (who) died in 1942 at Bourg en Bresse, where she is buried.* A different record page said her parents: *Are living in Syria.*

Aimee went to grade school in Marseille, France, from 1925 – 1932. She attended high school in Bourg en Bresse, France, from 1932 – 1937. After high school, her guardian, M. Tissot, employed her to do secretarial work. The record states: *In the absence of the parents, M Tissot Alexandre, agricultural engineer 39, Avenue de Macon in Bourg, took an interest in the family and was appointed as legal guardian.*

When she was recruited by the SOE, two brothers were in Syria, and one sister lived in Algeria.

On her recruitment history sheet, it reads that she was: *Member of French Volontairest, her hobby was reading, she had some military experience of three months with French Signal Coy at Tunis and five months with French Sig Coy at Algiers in which she did wireless work. Required as W/T Operator.* She may have been doing wireless work during the fighting between the Allies and the Axis forces in Tunisia before joining the SOE.

A page written in French is in the files asking the SOE to approve her security: *Be honored to ask you to pass the security formalities of who is going on mission. See some information which may be useful to you. Aimee Raymonde - currently in Moncorvo - male T-31, born March 14, 1922, in Tunis - arrived in*

*England on March 26, 1944 (Bristol) coming from Allgee.* The French report identified her as a male! Based on another page giving her detailed measurements, that comment seems to be in error.

Aimee was 5'3" and 119 pounds. The application also listed her various measurements, presumably to fit a uniform. It says she landed at Bristol from Algiers on March 26, 1944, and was to be trained as an "agent in the field commencing June 2, 1944."

The recruitment sheet goes on to report: *Intelligence: 9 (superior intelligence), Morse (code): Good, Mechanical: Good, An unobtrusive, mouse-like girl, timid rather than nervous, but with no fundamental weakness of personality; on the contrary, a good deal of quiet determination and independence. The latter, however, needs developing through a larger experience of the world. She is a level-headed, sensible, unaffected person already fully trained as a W/T Operator and who is likely to prove conscientious both in training and in the field. Her retiring manner and unremarkable appearance suggest that she could profitably be used in some centre of population where her chance of detection would be slight.*

June 8, 1944: *It is understood that this student is ready to proceed to 52 (next training segment.) She should be tested and proceed directly to 52 as soon as possible. A wireless student. A very quiet girl, efficient and keen and also discreet, a trifle shy but by no means physically nervous, taking a great delight in weapon training.*

Aimee's shyness was remarked on again on June 16: *This student appears to be a very quiet and unobtrusive person. She mixes well with the others in a quiet way, does not seem attracted by the other sex, and has very sober habits. Her character seems to be stable and straightforward. Her reaction to the initial security talk was satisfactory.* By July 15, there appears to be an increased appreciation for her quiet character: *A very calm and quiet girl, the exact opposite of (FFC.AA.20.), with whom she is very good friends. She never speaks unless spoken to and is then only as brief as possible. She is, however, intelligent and possesses a stable character. Her habits are very moderate indeed. Her security is good, and she is the type of person who will always think things over well before committing herself.*

On August 8, 1944: *This student still keeps very much to herself and remains quiet and inconspicuous. She takes her work very seriously and is very keen. She mixes well with the others but does not go out at all, and usually spends her time on the grounds by herself. Her security is good, and she realizes its importance.*

Towards the end of her training, the instructors had refined their opinion of her, and felt that she would be a good agent. The last phase for most SOE agents was parachuting. Aimee initially had difficulty but did pass with the following report: *Was slow in picking up the main essentials of parachuting but tried hard all the time during ground training. Her performance was marred by her temporary condition of ill-health. All her descents were completed satisfactorily, and she is quite capable of making a descent whenever called upon to do so.* She did three parachute jumps before leaving for France.

The following write-up cleared her for duty: *A quiet but very intelligent and painstaking student. Her sending and operating (Morse code) are first class, and any weakness in receiving that still remains will be cleared up with more experience. She made careless errors in coding in her last scheme – she seems to have lost interest since events in France have progressed so rapidly that she fears she will not be used in the field.*

Aimee signed her Declaration of Secrecy on August 21, 1944.

Aimee parachuted into France on September 11, 1944, and no further record of her has been found in the National Archives in London or elsewhere. MRD Foot lists her as an SOE agent but does not show her working in a Circuit. She is the only female agent that does not have a Circuit listed. She may have worked directly with the Free French in France, rather than with an SOE Circuit. Col. Maurice Buckmaster does not mention her in his book *They Fought Alone – The True Story of SOE's Agents in Wartime France*.

The SOE work that may have been done by Aimee and any information about her after the war – including when she may have died - remains a mystery.

There are no known photos of Aimee.

**Secrecy Declaration for Aimee Corge**

# Cécile De Marcilly

Code Name: Altesse  Alias: **Cécile Levasseur**

The following information is included in M.R.D Foot's book *SOE in France*. The author has not been able to find other reference to Cécile De Marcilly nee Prichard in England's National Archives, or in any other documentation or books dealing with the SOE or World War II:

She belonged to the French Corps Auxilaire Feminin, which was the equivalent of the British Auxiliary Territorial Service (ATS), the women's branch of the British Army during the Second World War.

Cécile parachuted into France on Aug. 11/12, 1944.

# Marguerite Françoise Gianello  " RF" Section

March 19, 1923 - ?

Nothing is known about Marguerite other than her birthdate and when she parachuted into France on the night of September 1-2, 1944. M.R.D. Foot lists her as an SOE agent, but the listing seems uncertain about which Circuit she was to be assigned to in France. He had no organization listed that she was affiliated with other than the Resistance in France.

Her name does not show up in other records to indicate what position she was to hold when she arrived in France. She previously worked for the Resistance in France, and the SOE sent her back after training her in spycraft. She may have worked for a brief time in the Peritone Circuit, but information about that Circuit is also scanty. Her tour ended when the Allied Army arrived at her area.

There are no known photos of Marguerite.

# Eugenie Gruner   "RF" Section

Birth and Death Dates Unknown

Code Name: Bulgare

Eugenie parachuted into France on the night of August 10-11, 1944, and was to be assigned to the Rectangle Circuit. The author believes that Eugenie first worked with the Free France movement. She may have been trained by the SOE and sent to France to work with other agents. She went to France the same night as several other women who had worked for Free France. The SOE records on all those women are almost non-existent.

The author can find no other record of her except for her listing as an SOE agent by M.R.D. Foot. There is a note that her later married name was Le Berre.

There are no known photos of Eugenie.

# A. Germaine Heim "RF" Section

Birth and Death Dates Unknown

Code Name:  Danubien

Germaine was attached to the French Corps Auxiliaire Feminine, the female auxiliary of the Free French Army. She parachuted into France from an SOE plane on July 5-6, 1944, and was assigned to the Perimetre Circuit.

As with several other women affiliated with the Free French movement, their only record is in M.R.D. Foot's book *SOE In France*.

There are no known photos of Germaine.

# Epilogue

The female agents of the SOE contributed to the war effort through their work to gather intelligence regarding German activities; they ensured good communications between the Circuit agents and Resistance groups and assisted with sabotage to disrupt and delay the German war machine that occupied France. Their bravery cannot be denied, as they worked under constant threat of discovery and capture by the French police, German soldiers, and the Gestapo. Many were captured and tortured, and too many were executed or died from the conditions of their confinement.

Their sacrifice should be acknowledged and remembered.

# Agent Longevity

**Fifty-two women are listed in this book; thirteen of them were either executed or died in German concentration camps due to their conditions. Names of the 13, plus one woman thought to be SOE by the Gestapo**

- Yolande Elsa Maria Beekman – executed at Dachau

- Denise Madeleine Bloch – executed at executed at Ravensbrück

- Andrée Raymonde Borrel - executed at Natzweiler-Struthof

- Muriel Tamara Byck – died of Meningitis

- Madeleine Zoe Damerment – executed at Dachau

- Noor Inayat Khan – executed at Dachau

- Cecile Margot Lefort – sent to the gas chamber at Uekermark,

- Vera Eugenie Leigh - – executed at Natzweiler-Struthof

- Sonia Olschanezky - executed at Natzweiler-Struthof (considered SOE by the Gestapo)

- Éliane Sophie Plewman – executed at Dachau

- Lilian Vera Rolfe – executed at Ravensbrück

- Diana Hope Rowden – executed at Natzweiler-Struthof

- Yvonne Claire Rudellat – died of Typhus

- Violette Reine Elizabeth Bushell Szabo – executed at Ravensbrück

Those who survived the war lived long lives. Several of the surviving women never married, and very few had children.

Ages at the death of the female SOE field agents who survived the war:

1 lived to be 102

7 lived into their 90's, plus Vera Atkins, their "Spy Master" who lived until she was 92

9 lived into their 80's

5 lived into their 70's

2 lived into their 60's

2 lived into their 40's

2 lived into their 30's – One died in a scuba diving accident, and one died from an embolism (blood clot)

# Code and Alias Names by Agent First Names

**A. Germaine Heim**        Code Name: Danubien

**Aimee Raymonde Corge**    Code name: Hellene

**Alix d'Unienville**       Code Name: Myrtil and Marie

**Andrée Borrel**           Code Names: Denice and Monique   Alias: Denise Urbain

**Anne-Marie Walters**      Code Name: Milkmaid, Colette, Paulette
Alias: Alice Davoust, Miss Fitzgerald

**Blanche Charlet**         Code Name: Christiane  Alias: Madame Sabine Lecomte

**Cécile De Marcilly**      Code Name: Altesse

**Cecile Lefort**           Code Name: Alice and Teacher   Alias: Cecile Marguerite Legrand

**Christine Granville Also known as: Krystyna Skarbek, Maria Skarbek , Krystyna Gettlich, and Karystyna Gizycka**        Code Name: Madame Marchand
Alias: Madame Pauline, Jacqueline Armand

**Danielle Reddé**          Code Name: Marocain or Morroccin, Camille Fournier
Alias: Maria Kermarec, Edith Daniel

**Denise Bloch**            Code Name: Ambroise

**Diana Rowden**            Code Name: Chaplin, Marcelle, Paulette
Alias: Juliette Therese Rondeau

**Eileen Nearne**           Code name: Rose
Alias: Mademoiselle du Tort, Jacqueline de Tertre

**Éliane Plewman**          Code Name: Gaby, Dean, Madame Dupont
Alias: Éliane Jacqueline Prunier

**Elizabeth Devereux-Rochester** Code Name: Typist, Elizabeth  Alias: Elizabeth Le Grande

**Eugenie Gruner**          Code Name: Bulgare

**Françoise Agazarian**     Code Name: Marguerite

**Giliana (Gillian, Gigliana) Balmaceda Gerson**   No known code name or alias

**Ginette Jullian**         Code Name: Adele

| | |
|---|---|
| **Jacqueline Nearne** | Code name: Jacqueline   Alias: Josette Norville |
| **Josiane Somers** | Code Name: Venitien, |
| **Julienne Aisner** | Code Name:  Claire |
| **Lilian Rolfe** | Code Names:  Recluse, Nadine, Blouse     Alias: Caudie Rodier |
| **Lise de Baissac** | Code Name:  Odile, Irene, Marguerite, & Adele.  Alias: Madame Irene Brisse, Madame Janette Bouville |
| **Madeleine Damerment** | Code Name: Solange, Alias: Martine Dussautoy |
| **Madeleine Lavigne** | Code Name: Leveller, Isabelle  Alias: Marianne Latour, Marianne Henriette Delormes |
| **Marguerite Gianello** | No known code names or aliases |
| **Marguerite Knight** | Code Name: Nicole, Alias: Marguerite Chauvan |
| **Marguerite Petitjean** | Code Name: Binette |
| **Marcelle Somers** | Code Name: Albanais |
| **Marie-Thérèse Le Chêne** | Code Name: Adele   Alias: Madame Marie-Thérèse Ragot |
| **Mary Herbert** | Code Name: Claudine, Maureen    Alias Marie Louise Vernier |
| **Maureen O'Sullivan** | Code Names: Simonet, Josette, Marie-Claire, Stenographer, and Stocking.  Alias: Micheline Marcelle Simonet |
| **Muriel Byck** | Code Name:  Violette and Michele  Alias: Denise Madeline, Katrine Bernard, Danielle Wood, Chantal Baron |
| **Nancy Wake** | Code Name: Helene  Alias: Madame Andree Joubert |
| **Noor Inayat Khan** | Code name:  Madeleine, Alias: Jeanne-Marie Renier |
| **Odette Sansom** | Code Name: Celine, Lise   Alias: Madame Odette Metayer |
| **Odette Wilen** | Code Name: Sophie, Waitress |
| **Pearl Witherington** | Code Names: Marie, Pauline  Alias: Genevieve Touzalin, Marie Jeanne Marthe Verges |
| **Phyllis Latour** | Code Names: Genevieve, Paulette, Plus Fours, and Lampooner |
| **Sonia Olschanezky** | Code Name: Tania, Alias: Suzanne Ouvrard |
| **Sonya Butt D'Artois** | Code Name:  Blanche    Alias: Suzanne Bonvie |
| **Vera Leigh** | Code Names: Simone, Almoner  Alias: Suzanne Chavanne |
| **Violette Szabo** | Code name:  Louise    Alias: Corinne Reine Leroy, Vicky Taylor |
| **Virginia Hall** | Code Names:  Marie Monin, Diane, Camille, Philomene,  Alias: Mlle. Marcelle Montagne |

| | |
|---|---|
| **Yolanda Beekman** | Code Name:  Mariette |
| Yvonne Baseden | Code Name:  Bursar, Odette    Alias: Marie Bernier |
| **Yvonne Cormeau** | Code names; Annette, Fairy, and Sarafari |
| **Yvonne Fontaine** | Code Name: Nenette and Mimi |
| **Yvonne Rudellat** | Code Names: Soaptree, Jacqueline, Suzanne, Christiane<br>Alias: Jacqueline Viallet, Jacqueline Gautier, Jacqueline Leclaire |

# Bibliography by Publication Date

**National Archives of England -** The National Archives is the official archive and publisher for the UK government and for England and Wales.

**Moondrop to Gascony** by Anne-Marie Walters, published by Macmillan & Co., 1946

**Hide and Seek: The Story of a Wartime Agent** by Xan Fielding, London, Secker & Warburg, 1954

**Carve Her Name With Pride** by R.J. Minney, published by George Newnes, 1956

**Nancy Wake, World War Two's Most Rebellious Spy**, by Russell Braddon, published by Cassell, 1956

**They Fought Alone – The True Story of SOE's Agents in Wartime France** by Maurice Buckmaster, published by Oldhams Press Ltd., 1958

**Inside SOE** by E.H. Cookridge, Published by Odhams Press Ltd., 1966

**Ravensbrück** by Germaine Tillion, published by Anchor Press, 1975

**Heroines of World War II** by Robert Jackson, published by Arthur Barker Limited, London, 1976

**Full Moon to France** by Elizabeth Devereux-Rochester, published by Harper & Roe, 1977

**Nancy Wake, The White Mouse, Autobiography of Australia's Wartime Legend**, by Nancy Wake, published by Pan McMillan Australia, 1985

**A Quiet Courage: Women Agents in the French Resistance** by Liane Jones, published by Transworld Publishers Ltd, 1990.

**Mission Improbable: A Salute to the RAF Women of SOE in Wartime France** by Beryl E. Escott, published by Patrick Stevens Limited, 1991

**SOE in France** by M.R.D. Foot, published by HMSO, 1996

**Sisterhood of Spies – Women of the OSS** by Elizabeth P. McIntosh, published by Naval Institute Press, 1998

**The Special Operations Executive 1940–1946** by M.R.D. Foot, published by Pimlico, 1999

**Nancy Wake**, by Peter Fitzsimons, published by Harper Collins, 2001

**The Women Who Lived for Danger: The Women Agents of SOE in the Second World War** by Marcus Binney, published by Hodder and Stoughton, 2002

**Operatives, Spies, and Saboteurs, The Unknown Story of the Men and Women of WWII,** published by Free Press, 2004

**OSS** by Patrick K. O'Donnell, published by Free Press, 2004

**A Life in Secrets – Vera Atkins and the Missing Agents of WWII** by Sarah Helm, published by Anchor Books, a division of Random House, 2005

**Christine: A Search for Christine Granville, G.M., O.B.E., Croix de Guerre** by Madeleine Masson, published by Virago, 2005

**Spymistress: The Life of Vera Atkins, the Greatest Female Secret Agent of World War II** by William Stevenson, published by Arcade Publishing New York City, 2006

**Spy Princess: The Life of Noor Inayat Khan** by Shrabari Basu, published by Roli Books, 2006

**French Resistance Fighter: France's Secret Army** by Terry Crowdy, published by Osprey Publishing, Oxford, UK. 2007

**Wolves at the Door** by Judith Pearson, published by Lyons Press, 2008

**Wanborough Manor: School for Secret Agents** by Patrick Yarnold, published by Hopfield Publications. 2009

**Pippa's War** New Zealand *Army News,* by Martin, Judith, 2009 www.nzdf.mil.nz/army/magazine/

**The Heroines of SOE** by Beryl E. Escott, published by The History Press, 2010

**Churchill's Angels** by Bernard O'Connor, published by Amberley Publishing, 2012

**Unearthing Churchill's Secret Army: The Official List of SOE Casualties and Their Stories** by Andrew Field and John Grehan, published by Casemate Publishers, 2012

**Sisters, Secret, and Sacrifice** by Susan Ottoway, published by Harper Element, 2013

**They Fought Alone: The True Story of SOE's Agents in Wartime France** by Maurice Buckmaster, published by Biteback Publishing, 2014

**The French Resistance** by Raymond Aubrac, published by Hazan Editor, 2014

**Setting France Ablaze: The SOE in France During WWII,** by Peter Jacobs, published by Pen and Sword, 2015

**The Women Who Spied for Britain**: Female Secret Agents of the Second World War by Robyn Walker, published by Amberley Publishing, 2015

**French Circuits** by Robert Bourne-Patterson, published by Barnsley, UK Frontline Books. 2016

**SOE Heroines** by Bernard O'Connor, published by Amberley, 2016

**They Fought Alone** by Charles Glass, published by Penguin Press, 2018

**D-Day Girls** by Sarah Rose, published by Random House – Penguin Books, 2019

**A Woman of No Importanc**e: The Untold Story of the American Spy Who Helped Win World War II, by Sonia Purnell, published by Viking, an imprint of Penguin Random House, 2019

**Mission France: The True History of the Women of SOE** by Kate Vigurs, published by Yale University Press, 2021

**Salisbury Journal**, February 3, 2024

# INDEX

326